Sex before Sex

Sex before Sex

FIGURING THE ACT IN EARLY MODERN ENGLAND

James M. Bromley and Will Stockton, Editors

Afterword by Valerie Traub

University of Minnesota Press
Minneapolis · London

Published by the University of Minnesota Press
111 Third Avenue South, Suite 290
Minneapolis, MN 55401-2520
http://www.upress.umn.edu

A Cataloging-in-Publication record is available from the Library of Congress.

ISBN 978-0-8166-8076-4 (hc)
ISBN 978-0-8166-8077-1 (pb)

Printed in the United States of America on acid-free paper

20 19 18 17 16 15 14 13   10 9 8 7 6 5 4 3 2 1

Contents

Acknowledgments

This book came together through a series of conversations about the need to think a bit harder about what we mean by "sex" in the Renaissance. As editors, we would therefore like to thank all our wonderful contributors, whose participation in these conversations has produced, if certainly not consensus on each point, a stimulating, pleasurably frictional set of essays.

We would also like to thank our editor, Richard Morrison, for his expert guidance and support of this project. The readers for the University of Minnesota Press, Melissa E. Sanchez and Ian Frederick Moulton, provided generous, helpful reports to which we hope we have done justice in revision. Erin Warholm, Anne K. Wrenn, Holly Monteith, Denise Carlson, and David Fideler provided expert production assistance. Ross Watson graciously supplied the cover art.

Introduction: Figuring Early Modern Sex

WILL STOCKTON AND JAMES M. BROMLEY

We open on an apparent misunderstanding. When Hermia and Lysander get lost in the woods in the second act of Shakespeare's *A Midsummer Night's Dream,* Lysander suggests that they stop and rest for the night. Hermia tells him that they should sleep apart, yet Lysander has a different idea: "One turf shall serve as pillow for us both; / One heart, one bed; two bosoms, and one troth" (2.2.47–48).[1] The knowing tone of Hermia's response—"Nay, good Lysander; for my sake, my dear, / Lie further off yet; do not lie so near" (2.2.49–50)—prompts Lysander to protest that she has misunderstood him:

> O, take the sense, sweet, of my innocence!
> Love takes the meaning in love's conference—
> I mean that my heart unto yours is knit,
> So that but one heart we can make of it.
> Two bosoms interchainèd with an oath;
> So, then, two bosoms and a single troth.
> Then by your side no bed-room me deny;
> For lying so, Hermia, I do not lie. (2.2.51–58)

Hermia heard something other than what he meant, or so he claims. He meant they would be joined in *meta*-physical union. Picking up on Lysander's quibble on "lie," Hermia replies that she, too, has been misunderstood: "Lysander riddles very prettily. / Now much beshrew my manners and my pride / If Hermia meant to say Lysander lied" (2.2.59–61). Lysander likewise heard something other than what she meant, or so she claims. She never meant to imply that he was trying to deceive her when he suggested they share the turf. She knew what he meant all along.

But what was that exactly? When she repeats her request for Lysander to lie apart, she explains, “such a separation as may well be said / Becomes a virtuous bachelor and a maid” (2.2.64–65), but her appeal to “love and courtesy” (2.2.62) does not clarify what she thinks his intentions were. Does she mean “courtesy” as proper behavior, and thus she pled for distance to avoid appearing unchaste (as perhaps happens when Theseus and the hunting party discover the sleeping couples in Act 4, scene 1) or even being tempted to do something unchaste? Or does she mean that he should be courteous to her and respectful of her chastity because his less than innocent intentions were plain to her even when wrapped in metaphor? Where is the concupiscence? In Lysander’s suggestion? In Hermia’s interpretation of it? In the temptations to which an innocent intent can lead? In those who might see them innocently napping in the forest and jump to the wrong conclusion? Furthermore, considering that Hermia and Lysander “upon faint primrose beds were wont to lie” (1.1.215) in the very same forest, why should this time be more vexed and more sexed than previous times? Why was his virtue her privilege then, but not now?

The sense of the suggestion to which Lysander perhaps too earnestly objects now goes by the name “sexual.” This sexual sense is certainly the one that most readily presents itself to any ear attuned to the rhetorical tricks people use to get one another “in bed.” In the Renaissance, such tricks include men promising marriage to gain sexual access to women and then denying the existence of the *de futuro* trothplight.[2] *All’s Well That Ends Well* and *Measure for Measure* both pivot around such lies. Yet Lysander is not like Bertram or Angelo; he is not lying about, or he gives us no reason to suspect, his intention to marry Hermia when he asks her to sleep with or near him. As the questions we have raised about their exchange nonetheless suggest, his “honest” intentions, and her interpretation of them, warrant scrutiny at the level of the act to which this sexual sense refers—the level at which sex itself is defined. This volume seeks to destabilize scenes like this one in early modern English literature by pressuring the definition of sex that one might presume in construing Lysander's meaning. Definitions of sex, we argue, are just as shifting and variable, shaped by contexts and assumptions, ideologies and idiosyncrasies, as Lysander's intentions are in this exchange.

The question at the core of this volume—what is sex?—seems a simple one. The answer is anything but. As Valerie Traub, the author of this volume's afterword, has written in a previous essay that also pursues this question, "the *content* of sex has been strangely presumable, apparently interpretable through . . . ready-to-hand transhistorical rubrics."[3] A work like *A Midsummer Night's Dream* tells us much about our presumptions as well as our ignorance in this regard. We may begin by asking what Hermia and Lysander might do when lying together. Does the act have to be penile–vaginal intercourse? What about fondling? Mutual masturbation? Anal sex? Oral sex? Why would such alternative possibilities even occur to us? To what extent might any of these acts actually be compatible with lying bound by heart and troth? Does any act other than penile–vaginal intercourse even count as sex? Would such an act be one that the law recognized as translating their betrothal into marriage? Does an act have to be recognized by legal or some other discourse for it to count as sex? With respect to *Measure for Measure* and *All's Well,* we assume we know what acts take place in the bedtricks, especially Helena's because it results in pregnancy, but we cannot be sure what else might happen. Sex is even more obscure in *A Midsummer Night's Dream* because Lysander's request does not turn into action.

These questions about acts arise in part because there is no single, transhistorical definition of sex. Most people today at least define penile–vaginal intercourse as sex, but even this definition is complicated. A recent study by the Kinsey Institute of almost five hundred Indiana residents aged eighteen to ninety-six (204 men and 282 women) reveals that 95 percent of respondents defined penile–vaginal intercourse as sex.[4] If intercourse did not end in ejaculation, agreement dropped to 89 percent. Around 70 percent of respondents defined oral–genital contact as sex. (President Bill Clinton's 1998 impeachment turned on this issue.) On the question of whether anal–genital contact is sex, 81 percent said yes, although the answer varied by age, with men aged sixty-five and older less likely to agree. Manual stimulation also proved controversial, with slightly fewer than half saying yes and people aged eighteen to twenty-nine quite likely saying no. This study has its temporal, geographic, and interrogative limits, to be sure. One wonders to what extent its findings are particular to Hoosiers and to people in the first part of the twenty-first century. One wonders whether the ejaculation on which an act's sexual status sometimes depends has to take place inside the vagina, anus, or mouth. (And if it does, does the "money shot" prevalent in so much pornography mean that pornography does not actually show people having sex?) One also wonders how strongly those who answered no to a given proposition actually disagreed. In particular, did the 5 percent of respondents who did not consider penile–vaginal intercourse to be sex strongly maintain that position, or, as seems more likely, was their answer dependent on an unmeasured context and qualification (how deeply the penis penetrates, how long it stays in the vagina, among others)? Even without asking respondents about acts with oblique or no genital involvement, such as BDSM play, the study itself reveals considerable variance among present definitions of sex, and pursuit of these and other questions would presumably reveal far more. What is more, the study, along with the unmeasured (and likely unmeasurable by a survey) contexts for its answers, gestures toward the epistemological recalcitrance of sex and the complexities of sexual signification.

As both *Midsummer* and the Kinsey study demonstrate, sex is a non-self-identical concept, subject to different constructions, and thus to playing different roles, within narratives of sexuality, love, intimacy, relationality, pleasure, criminality, and reproduction. Asking both what sex is and how we construct knowledge about sex, this volume contributes to ongoing inquiries into the early modern and modern forms of these narratives. These questions themselves are not entirely new ones, as the Traub essay we cited earlier indicates. Mario DiGangi has also observed that we "cannot always be entirely confident that we know which bodily acts count as 'sexual.' When is kissing an expression of sexual desire, of affection, or of a social bond? Under what circumstances might our ability even to distinguish these realms be frustrated?"[5] DiGangi's notion of "the indeterminacy of 'the sexual'" proves especially useful as a way of framing our efforts against the backdrop of the numerous explorations of the epistemological contours of sex and sexuality in early modern England that contribute directly and indirectly to this volume's specific interest in the sex act's definitional and temporal flexibility.[6] This indeterminacy both results from and gives rise to questions about the relationship between the sexual, the affective, the social, and other categories. It requires us to reflect on the theories we use both to locate acts within these categories and to monitor relationships between these categories. Crisscrossing the vexed terrain in which literary criticism engages the facts of the past and the construction of these facts through early modern and modern epistemologies, this volume dwells at the limits of sex and sexuality's legibility and, in doing so, contributes to the ongoing effort to theorize and historicize both.

The indeterminacy of the sexual persists even around adjudications of acts that we are otherwise hard-pressed to describe in any other terms. In the Kinsey study, 5 percent of respondents, again for unknown reasons, declined the name of "sex" to what otherwise seems the sine qua non of sex: penile–vaginal intercourse with ejaculation. How, then, to classify this act? Is it a sexual act but not sex? What would this distinction mean? The assenting 95 percent evince the now dominant cultural narrative of sex that positions this act at the apex of sexual experience, but this narrative was subject to contestation in the early modern period and still is now.[7] In this narrative, this act is the one toward which all other acts, usually defined as foreplay, lead and against which the distinction between the sexual and nonsexual is forged. Gestures, language, and images that allude to this act, to foreplay, or to the genitals in turn readily signify as sexual, although not always without ambiguity. Ejaculation matters most in one early modern form of this narrative: what might be called the early modern economy of sex placed a high premium on the expenditure of sperm into productive (vaginal) rather than unproductive (oral and anal) orifices or no orifices at all. In this economy, most famously explored in Shakespeare's sonnets, the location of ejaculation distinguished between licit and illicit forms of sex, if the latter forms even qualified as sex at all.[8] At the same time, penetration, rather than simply ejaculation, also proved determinative of sex crimes. As that master of English jurisprudence Edward Coke explains, "The emission of semen maketh it not Buggery, but is an evidence in case of buggery of penetration; and so in Rape . . . there must be penetration, and emission of semen without penetration maketh no Rape."[9] If buggery and rape are sex, does sex itself, as an act abstracted from these particulars, therefore depend on ejaculation, as the economic model implies, or penetration, as the criminal model implies? Moreover, why should legal or economic discourses be privileged in the definition of sex? To the extent that we assume that economic, legal, and other discourses draw a line between sex and its others, rather than drawing a line between illicit and licit forms of sex, we risk foreclosing possible resistances to dominant understandings of the licit. We also risk failing to notice acts that are unremarkable within those discourses' criteria but that might be otherwise useful to call "sex."

Traub reminds us that "because of the opacity of sexuality, the relation between the material and the metaphoric, reality and representation, will remain both inextricable and shifting, subject to temporary stasis only through the discursive framing we impose upon it."[10] The essays in this collection are therefore not limited in their scope to recovering alternative sexual acts as recorded in the early modern literary archive. Although some essays do perform this archival work, this volume also reflects on the methodologies through which we think we know what sex means in the early modern past and the modern present. It rematerializes sex in representation and investigates the hermeneutic complexity of sexual signification. Consider, with respect to these objectives, the potentially pornographic significance in *A Midsummer Night's Dream* of the juice from "love-in-idleness," generated when Cupid's arrow "fell upon a little western flower— / Before, milk-white; now, purple with love's wound" (2.1.166–67). If a reading of the flower's juice as female ejaculate proves controversial, it does so in part because the sexual is a nebulous category in which the genitals are not always metaphorized as arrows and flowers. This argument may also prove controversial because of the persistent desire of some critics to police the boundary between "reading" and "reading into"—a boundary perhaps nowhere more contested than around sex.

In the chapter devoted to readings of *Midsummer* in *Looking for Sex in Shakespeare,* for instance, Stanley Wells takes to task critics whose "sexual interpretations proceed from what once would have been considered the 'dirty minds' of the interpreters rather than from the imagination of the dramatist and of his early audiences."[11] Refusing to equate the lewd interpreter with the misinterpreter, the contributors to this volume do not assume that we can know for certain that the imaginations of early modern authors, audiences, or readers were free of the sexual, nor do they adjudicate sexual interpretation solely on the basis of authorial intent or historical reception. The misunderstanding between Hermia and Lysander with which we began this introduction pivots around this difficulty of locating the origins and specifying the content of sexual meanings and intentions. Viewing this difficulty as an opportunity, the contributors believe that much work remains to be done in terms of understanding both how texts created and circulated sexual knowledge in the early modern period and how these texts shape the contours of what currently constitutes the sexual. Furthermore, as several of the contributors make clear, the sexual interpretations that Wells would impute to a critic's dirty mind are actually the result of a complex, unpredictable mixture of the ideology, imagination, and experiences that a critic brings to a text. A number of questions that Wells would foreclose the essays in this collection thus raise and complicate. What authorizes resolving ambiguity in favor of the sexual? To what extent does sexual meaning need to be shared between an early modern and a modern audience? Why presume that only modern critics—and not, as Wells's sentence implies, early modern ones—have "dirty minds"?

The circulation of representations outside both the culture that originally produced them and the audience (never itself an absolutely homogenous group) that originally received them provides further opportunities to broaden what qualifies as sex. The meaning of a play like *Midsummer* can change with each new performance and adaptation, as the play itself, as a play about (mis)playing, is well aware. His desire to distinguish right from wrong sexual interpretations notwithstanding, Wells himself acknowledges that works "exist finally only in the minds of those who experience them."[12] We maintain that admitting the element of indeterminacy within sex overcomes this impasse between readings oriented toward reception and those oriented toward intention. It also reorients the discussion about intentionality and definition by recasting sex as something *spoken* rather than merely spoken *about*. Linda Williams explains the crucial distinction in her book on sex in modern film: "Speaking *about* sex presumes a stable object of investigation;

speaking sex implies that the very speaking forms part of sex's discursive construction."[13] In its relationship to the material realities of bodies, sex only comes to be through speech, which is also to say through language, and this language includes that of the texts under investigation as well as that used by the critic. Put another way, language does not simply make sex mean; it more simply makes sex.

This claim builds on the Foucauldian notion that sex is a product of discourse, specifically the discourse of sexuality—that nineteenth-century term knitting together desires, acts, and identities. As Foucault insists before issuing his famous rallying cry for a turn away from sex and toward "bodies and pleasures," "we must not refer a history of sexuality to the agency of sex; but rather show how 'sex' is historically subordinate to sexuality."[14] The field of early modern studies has for decades been in the process of internalizing Foucault's corollary arguments that sex is both discursive and subordinate to sexuality. Even Wells, who does not cite Foucault, can himself be read as wrestling with the Foucauldian idea that sex is not "really" there apart from specific discursive "deployments of sexuality." The wealth of extant work on early modern sexuality and sex often accordingly begins not with "the agency of sex" but rather with discourses, such as sodomy, homoeroticism, lesbianism, friendship, and intimacy, that speak sex in ways that roughly anticipate, as the period's moniker implies, more modern forms. We make no argument here against historically subordinating sex to sexuality in this way, and we certainly do not mean to imply that all work in early modern sexuality studies simply assumes a teleological model of sexual development. The essays here nonetheless suggest that this subordination simultaneously contributes to the field's relative inattention to acts that have no immediate connection to the most prevalent, politicized, identitarian discourses of sexuality in the present. These discourses of gay, lesbian, and heterosexual identity have often implicitly and explicitly guided analyses of sex and the sexual in early modern texts. One essay in this volume does address the relationship between early modern sex and modern sexual identity, in this case gay male identity. Other essays explore sex acts, such as chin chucking, anilingus, drinking, and sex with trees and animals, that have no immediate connection to these identitarian discourses. This volume thus contributes to a history of sexuality that both includes and exceeds a history of sexual identity. It does so through the construction of histories that reshape, expose the limits of, and challenge the dominance of current discourses of sexuality.

These histories are sometimes queer. The term might trope our collective recognition that heteronormative assumptions about gender, as well as imperatives to reproduce—assumptions that queerness notoriously flouts—shape the teleological narrative of sex that ends in penile–vaginal intercourse. Although queer theory also certainly has as one of its raisons d'être complicating definitions of sex and sexuality, we stop short of characterizing this volume as another effort to queer the Renaissance because not all the contributors take a stake in the term. Traditionally, to queer the Renaissance has meant to expose the ways that heterosexuality and heteronormativity shape critical perspectives on the Renaissance past as well as to recover expressions of homoerotic desire and evidence of homoerotic relationships before the advent of homosexual identity.[15] Jonathan Goldberg and Madhavi Menon take stock of some of these efforts in their 2005 essay "Queering History," which takes the additional step of opposing queerness to supposedly dominant practices of historicism.[16] Goldberg and Menon maintain that "history as it is hegemonically understood today," in its difference from but also teleological anticipation of the present, "is inadequate to housing the project of queerness," with its own connotations of sameness and developmental disturbance.[17] While "Queering History" usefully challenges scholars to theorize the relationship between historical difference and sexual difference, we suggest that the relationship that most historically oriented sexuality scholars already have to the past does not reduce to one of mere difference or development. By bringing together queer, historicist, and queer–historicist essays, this volume yields a more nuanced map of the convergences and divergences of queer and historicist critique. We embrace the messy relationship between queerness and historicism by allowing the contributors who see their work as queer to define and utilize the term as they see fit and also by recognizing that not everyone who works on sexuality necessarily sees her work, or all aspects of it, as queer—a term whose political efficacy is diluted through its universalization. The strict equation of sex with penile–vaginal intercourse is vulnerable, for instance, not only to a queer critique that conjures up images of gay sex but also to a more generic critique of erotic banality and overdetermination. Lysander and/or Hermia may have something other than coitus in mind during their playful exchange, just as any flirting lovers might, but this point is not necessarily a queer one. What exactly Titania and the suggestively named Bottom do in Titania's bower is likewise never specified, and one does not have to be a queer scholar to point out that it may well encompass a variety of acts, including, as Gail Kern Paster has memorably argued, laxative purgation.[18] Defaulting all sex to penile–vaginal intercourse, and relegating all other acts to the category of the queer, reveals an erotic imagination with a narrow sense of the sex acts practiced both then and now.

In terms of our qualified contribution to queer studies, we nonetheless do focus on sex acts by way of insisting that the field has unfinished business. A 2007 issue of *South Atlantic Quarterly* titled "After Sex? On Writing since Queer Theory" queries whether queer criticism might be "over," "beyond," or "past" sex. Queer theory has now arguably "moved on" to topics like affect, shame, justice, globalization, and publics and counterpublics—topics that are hardly asexual but that, as the editors note, are "not explicitly 'about' sexuality."[19] The essays here begin instead from the proposition that the sex act itself actually remains an undertheorized and underhistoricized concept. While we would question whether moving beyond sex should be a goal of queer criticism, just as several contributors to *After Sex?* do, our primary concern lies in exploring acts of sex in their historical, theoretical, and textual specificity and complexity. This concern places these essays "after sex" in ways that do not imply abandonment or lack of interest. These essays are situated temporally and methodologically after what Foucault notes is sex's use in the deployment of sexuality, and they do not pretend their analyses are hermetically sealed from the ideological effects of such a deployment, even as some push back on those effects. These essays also are unabashedly after sex in the sense of reflecting on the hermeneutics of looking for sex in a text. Acknowledging that readers, at least in part, approach the interpretation of texts after their own real or imagined sexual experiences and desires, these essays seek not to police such influences but to understand interpretation as an embodied, sometimes even erotic (a term that may or may not be synonymous with sexual), act. As Lara Farina has argued in an essay on erotically reading medieval texts, "erotic response . . . [is a] learned practice, dependent on individual and cultural memory and therefore variable."[20] The meaning and legibility of sex depends on the characteristics, such as age, sex, personal history, cultural location, etc., of those performing the sex as well as those performing the reading. The essays that follow reveal an early modern sexual landscape organized in multiple, often contradictory ways and a modern critical landscape guided by assumptions that have rendered illegible acts we might variably understand as sexual in the period. They make no effort to catalog the many different ways of reading every particular sex act; rather, with a sometimes queer awareness of sex's simultaneous definitional capaciousness and resistance, the essays pivot instead around the challenge of determining what counts as sex in the early modern past.

Several factors combine to make this challenge a particularly difficult one, not least of which is the philological fact that "sex" did not describe acts in the early modern period. It instead denoted sexual difference. According to the *Oxford English Dictionary (OED),* the use of the word *sex* to mean "physical contact between individuals involving sexual stimulation; sexual activity or behavior" dates only from the dawn of the twentieth century. This definition is currently "the most common general sense," and it presumptively means "heterosexual intercourse" (hence the tendency to specify gay sex, oral sex, or phone sex; hence, too, varying definitions of virginity). Before this definition, however, the word *sexual* could describe something other than sexual difference. *Sexual acts,* defined as acts "relating to, tending towards, or invoking sexual intercourse, or other forms of intimate physical contact," dates from the eighteenth century, as do *sexual intercourse* itself and *sexual organs.* What, sex historians might ask, prompts the shorthand reduction of *sexual acts* and *sexual intercourse* to *sex*? What forms of erotic experience get lost in the process? The nineteenth century gives rise to the concepts of sexual conduct, sexual virtue, sexual selection, sexual assault, sexual excitement, sexual experience, sexual offense and offender, sexual partner, sexual pervert and perversion, and sexual repression. Sexual politics is a twentieth-century invention, and with it come concepts of sexual harassment and sexual revolution. In the *OED*'s history of sex, these concepts are technically absent in the early modern period, or they are present under different names that may nonetheless present problems of translation.

Paradoxically, this volume explores what counts as sex in the early modern period before the term actually comes into existence. Implied in phrasing our objective this way is our near-collective belief that relinquishing the term to seek out alternative vocabularies is not historiographically mandatory. Early modern scholars are well aware that terms like *homosexual, heterosexual, gay, lesbian,* and even *homoerotic* are anachronistic—and are often, as Alan Bray said of *homosexuality,* "ruinously misleading"—but these terms are nonetheless the ones that orient even the most historicist of relations to the past.[21] The continuing reference to and utilization of these terms is predicated not only on the fact that they are ultimately inescapable as analytical reference points but also on the fact that there is no single definition of them. There are many different ways of being sexual or being gay, for instance. We seek here to exploit the current incoherence of sex by analyzing acts that seem, more but also less obviously, to warrant the term. A history of sex that simply refuses the term may deafen one to these resonances in much the same way that a heteronormative notion of sex may obscure the range of sexual acts that do not end in vaginal penetration and ejaculation.

Methodologically relinquishing the term *sex* would also risk letting the most common general sense of sex as heterosexual coitus calcify as *the* definition. Such calcification renders the practices, cultures, identities, and intimacies organized around alternative acts illegible, invisible, or subject only to a disciplinary, corrective scrutiny. These alternative acts are often unrecognizable to those who might find pleasure in them and to those who might be in a position to protect the rights of the participants in such acts. As various essays demonstrate, a calcified definition of sex also presents an additional obstacle to historicizing concepts that lay behind certain determinants of the sexual—concepts including chastity and the human, both subjects of multiple essays here. The contradictory title of this book, *Sex before Sex,* signals our dual perspective on this lexical problem.[22] We are interested, on one hand, in demarcating the early modern period as a period before the invention of sex, with all its attendant narratives of intimacy and relationality. On the other hand, we recognize, along with most premodern and early modern sexuality scholars, that such before-and-after histories—what Eve Kosofsky Sedgwick calls "supersessionist histories" and Goldberg and Menon call "heterohistories"—are always oversimplified, that temporal markers keep moving depending on the specific concepts, cultures, texts, and persons under discussion.[23] Whereas the charge of anachronism or belatedness may seek to straighten out the multiple temporalities of the critic's relation to sex, the essays collected here instead embrace the possibilities of the critic's simultaneous anteriority and posteriority. They recognize that there is no way now for a critic to stand before sex in early modern texts without locating herself after it.

To reject supersessionist models of history is not necessarily to discount the sheer temporal distance between an early modern text and a modern reader. This distance contributes to the difficulty of determining what did count or might have counted as sex in the early modern period. How can we know what signifies as sexual in a culture from which we are separated by hundreds of years? What barriers of language and sensibility do we confront? Literature and other forms of art often present the additional difficulty of exploiting their cultures' own incoherencies, contradictions, and confusions about sex and eroticism. Such exploitation is certainly the aim of *A Midsummer Night's Dream.* We can offer no single answer to the questions we have raised about this play: what Lysander means when he proposes to sleep with Hermia, what the love juice signifies, and what Titania and Bottom do together. "What happened" is not merely a question that Bottom and the lovers ask. We as audience members, readers, and critics ask it too. That there is no definitive answer to this question is also not a textual or critical lack but instead an opportunity. Our historical distance from the text's production and first reception prompts us to consider how many different ways early modern audiences could have responded to the play. Shakespeare's efforts throughout *Midsummer* to make an epistemological mess of the relationship between reality and the imagination muddy and multiply the possible responses. The confused relationship between reality and imagination in the play and in the theater generally reflects the process by which, to craft an answer, past audiences drew and present audiences draw on pleasures from their own experiences and the new pleasures the play prompts them to imagine. In the circulation of sexual knowledge, old pleasures are confirmed, and new ones are invented.

The indeterminacy of the sexual extends beyond any textual representation. It ultimately troubles the topical and temporal boundaries of sexuality studies itself, opening the field to work on gender, affect, race, politics, religion, class, textuality, aesthetics, and other areas of investigation. While we have placed artificial boundaries of Englishness, early modernity, and the literary on our inquiry into this indeterminacy here, several essays gesture beyond these boundaries: Melissa J. Jones's toward modern porn studies, Will Fisher's toward art history, James M. Bromley's toward the continental history of an obscene gesture, and Will Stockton's toward the indeterminacy of the sexual within psychoanalysis. We further hope that our organizing question about what counts as sex, as well as many of the more specific claims of the essays themselves—claims about reading strategies, the history of sexual violence, the boundaries of the human, constructions of chastity, and techniques of reproduction—will prove provocative and useful to scholars in other fields.[24]

Further still, we hope that our framing focus on literature, itself a notoriously fraught, often anachronistic term, proves intellectually generative rather than limiting. Literature here includes textuality, but we distinguish it, although not completely, from legal, medical, and other nonfiction texts because of its distinct capacity to facilitate imaginative, cross-temporal connections while reflecting on and responding to fault lines in cultural concepts of desire, the body, and relationality.[25] Several essays in this collection explicitly explore how sex indexes the fault lines within past and present discourses of friendship, pornography, chastity, and rape. These essays do not relinquish the Foucauldian premise that sex is a product of discourse, but they emphasize that these discourses are not static. These discourses grapple with the meaning of acts, and they speak sex in changing, often conflicting and internally incoherent ways. We frame all these essays in terms of the figuration of sex acts on the grounds that the act itself is a discursive construct and a site of contestation—a contestation not necessarily less acute in the early modern period than in the current one. To represent sex, or to make a claim for its representation, is to define it, or to critique another definition.

The first two essays in this collection center on different aspects of the construction of sexual knowledge. In "'Invisible Sex!': What Looks Like the Act in Early Modern Drama?" Christine Varnado picks up on our introductory thoughts and examines the imaginative possibilities and erotic identifications that structure modern readings of early modern texts. Varnado argues that present assumptions about what sex looks like condition a critic's recognition of sex in literary representations. She juxtaposes the morning-after scene in Shakespeare's *Romeo and Juliet* with scenes from Thomas Middleton and William Rowley's *The Changeling* and Middleton and Thomas Dekker's *The Roaring Girl* to reveal the asymmetries that structure critical recognition of what she calls "invisible sex," in which plays gesture toward but do not stage sex acts. At issue in the reception of these plays are the deeply subjective, emotional, embodied, and erotic responses that inform even the most historicist responses to sexual representation. Often veiling these responses is a pose of disembodied, rational empiricism that renders heteroerotic practices self-evident, while laying the burden of proof for other practices on queer reading.

Another form of retrospective interpretation, that of reputation, is the subject of Kathryn Schwarz's "Death and Theory: Or, the Problem of Counterfactual Sex." The Lucretia figure, among others, points to the shaky foundation of patrilineal reproductive futurity in ravished and conveniently dead women. Men attempt to construct the reputation of these women as chaste, yet they do so in the absence of their bodies, which resist yielding such knowledge. While figurations of sex thus lie at the core of social contracts, sex acts and the bodies involved in these acts also prove to be figural fugitives. In the various texts Schwarz discusses, the female body's sexual particularity returns to destabilize the disembodied icon that men build out of the disposal of that body. The other possible sexual histories of that body provide the counterfactual sex of Schwarz's title—the sex occluded in the forward march of history. Schwarz thus implicitly calls on modern readers to re-"member" the bodies and acts that do not contribute raw materials to such retrospective reinterpretations.

The next two essays similarly rethink sexual history and its relevance for the present by focusing on gender identity as abstracted from representations of sex. In "Spectacular Impotence: Or, Things That Hardly Ever Happen in the Critical History of Pornography," Melissa J. Jones takes up the recurring representation of impotency as both humiliating and titillating in early modern erotica, specifically Thomas Nashe's "Choice of Valentines" and John Marston's *Metamorphosis of Pigmalion's Image*. While the category of sex and histories of pornography typically exclude sexual failure, Jones demonstrates that "spectacular impotence" is nonetheless a minor trend in modern erotica produced for women. This trend bucks the popular assumption that the audience for pornography is male. It also challenges the phallic masculinity constructed in traditional porn as well as the active and passive roles of spectator and participant on which theorists of pornography have relied in their analyses. Evincing the intimate connection between the two definitions of sex as a difference and an act, Jones's essay summarily demonstrates that the inclusion of sexual failure in the category of sex may depend on the gender position of those doing the work of categorization.

A different but still dissident masculinity emerges from expressions of homoerotic desire in two plays by John Ford, according to Nicholas F. Radel's "'Unmanly Passion': Sodomitical Self-Fashioning in John Ford's *The Lover's Melancholy* and *Perkin Warbeck*." Analyzing the intersection of homoerotic desire and practices with social markers such as class, Radel argues that Ford points to the sodomitical potential of all early modern male homosocial relations. Utilizing, as Schwarz and Jones do as well, feminist and queer theory in his effort to historicize sex as a practice indexed by speech, Radel further claims that status-based prohibitions on expressions of desire between men helped to arrange and distinguish between authorized and unauthorized homoeroticism in the period. While maintaining that there is no sex before sex, or no sex before that perceived by a necessarily anachronistic gaze, Radel argues that Ford glimpses a modern, minoritizing discourse of sexual identity in figures who seek to wrest definitional control of these unauthorized expressions of their own sexual desires.

Will Fisher's "The Erotics of Chin Chucking in Seventeenth-Century England" and James M. Bromley's "Rimming the Renaissance" zero in on histories of specific sexual practices. In doing so, they resist the abstraction of sexual identity from sexual activity. In his essay on chin chucking, or the erotic stroke or pinch of a person's chin, Fisher assembles an impressive archive of texts that represent this overlooked amorous action. Mobile within narratives of sexual activity, chin chucking subverts the temporal organization of sex into foreplay and consummation. Furthermore, chin chucking alternately constructs and destabilizes the active and passive rubrics used in the early modern period to parse sexuality according to participants' gender, age, and status. Bromley similarly demonstrates that anal–oral contact, or anilingus, throws active and passive roles into disarray by uncoupling them from penetration. Bromley challenges critics to think of sex as more than penetration and to think of nonnormative sex as more than transgressive: etymologically, transgression implies a boundary crossing and is thus linked to penetration, which only a subset of sexual acts necessitate. As glimpsed in a number of early modern plays, anilingus collapses the difference between penetrative and nonpenetrative practices by bringing together two surfaces that are also holes. Bromley further argues that rimming brings bodies together in ways that prove indifferent to the construction of selfhood through the usual indices, such as the face and the genitalia. Rimming consequently exemplifies an erotic practice resistant to being abstracted into a sexual identity.

References to anilingus both sustain and dissolve several boundaries that structure early modern culture, including the boundary between the human and the nonhuman. This boundary, and its role in categorizing, historicizing, and mapping sexual practice more generally, is the subject of Stephen Guy-Bray's "Animal, Vegetable, Sexual: Metaphor in John Donne's 'Sappho to Philaenis' and Andrew Marvell's 'The Garden'" and Holly Dugan's "Aping Rape: Animal Ravishment and Sexual Knowledge in Early Modern England." Guy-Bray examines attempts by Thomas Browne, John Donne, and Andrew Marvell to conceptualize human sexuality with reference to animal and plant reproduction. These authors not only register a troubling resemblance between these human and nonhuman forms of sex but also express, through interspecies desire, a sense of human inadequacy vis-à-vis nonhuman reproductive methods. Looking also at Donne as well as at Shakespeare's *Comedy of Errors,* Holly Dugan argues that highly improbable yet recurring early modern narratives of human rape by simians contributed to the construction of early modern male sexual dominance. Working this largely ignored fantasy of sexual violence into the history of rape, Dugan argues that it establishes, through interspecies projection and analogy, a gendered and heteronormative role for men as the impenetrable penetrators of women.

In "The Seduction of Milton's Lady: Rape, Psychoanalysis, and the Erotics of Consumption in *Comus,*" Will Stockton also examines rape in the context of fantasy, specifically by reading Milton's *Comus* as a rape fantasy. According to the reading, which draws on Freudian seduction theory, drinking itself becomes legible as a sexual act, not simply as a metaphor for sex, as many critics have claimed when discussing Comus's cup. Psychoanalysis both provides Stockton with a way of attending to the epistemological resistance of sex and allows him to create a theoretical space for the strategic use of sex as an anachronism in the retrospective reconstruction and broadening of sex as a historical category. Focusing likewise on Milton, Thomas H. Luxon's "'How Human Life Began': Sexual Reproduction in Book 8 of *Paradise Lost*" translates the before of sex into Milton's account of prelapsarian existence. Before sex comes "conversation," such as that between Adam and God and Adam and Raphael. In a Lucretian meditation on mixed modes of generation, or the mixing of "seeds," Luxon argues that the first human sexual reproduction occurs between God and Adam in an act that overwhelms Adam and produces Eve as a new sexual partner for man. Luxon's displacement of the first sex act makes a materialist and philosophical contribution to the discussion of Milton's construction of paradise as a place notoriously resistant to but tempted by anachronistic and "fallen" forms of categorization.

The contributors to this volume responded to our prompting question—what is sex?—with essays whose lines of flight we did not predict. As Valerie Traub points out in her afterword, these essays converge and diverge around questions of epistemology and historical alterity. They lay no claim to accessing the real history of early modern sex; instead, they reflect on the mediating role of representation, language, and fantasy in figuring sex. While often distinct, their methodologies produce the past not as irreducibly Other or a mirror image of the present but as a space in which temporal sameness and difference present complicated entanglements. Taken together, these essays perhaps most simply suggest that we as critics do not always mean the same thing when we talk about sex. Rather than trying to make sex knowable as some monolithic category, the authors here tarry with the unknowable, ignored, alternative forms of sex and with the way these dimensions of sex ramify in other cultural sites. The deliberate anachronism of "sex before sex" allows these essays to remap the early modern sexual landscape while reframing modern criticism as an embodied, erotic practice situated within cultural definitions of sex that the essays simultaneously seek to trouble. This collection positions itself before sex in its commitment to a future that recognizes the definitional capaciousness of the term. It envisions a future critical practice that does not presume to know in advance what sex is and has been. It tries, in short, to imagine how representations of sex in early modern literature might open up new avenues into sexuality's past, present, and future.

Notes

1 All quotations from *A Midsummer Night's Dream* are drawn from *The Norton Shakespeare,* 2nd ed., ed. Stephen Greenblatt, Walter Cohen, Jean E. Howard, and Katharine Eisaman Maus, 805–64 (New York: W. W. Norton, 2008).

2 See Martin Ingram, *Church Courts, Sex, and Marriage in England, 1570–1640* (Cambridge: Cambridge University Press, 1987), 199.

3 Valerie Traub, "Making Sexual Knowledge," *Early Modern Women: An Interdisciplinary Journal* 5 (2010): 254.

4 Stephanie A. Sanders, Brandon J. Hill, William L. Yarber, Cynthia A. Graham, Richard A. Crosby, and Robin R. Milhausen, "Misclassification Bias: Diversity in Conceptualisations about Having 'Had Sex,'" *Sexual Health* 7, no. 1: 31–34.

5 Mario DiGangi, *The Homoerotics of Early Modern Drama* (Cambridge: Cambridge University Press, 1997), 11.

6 A necessarily incomplete list of relevant monographs includes Rebecca Ann Bach, *Shakespeare and Renaissance Literature before Heterosexuality* (New York: Palgrave Macmillan, 2007); Mary Bly, *Queer Virgins and Virgin Queans on the Early Modern Stage* (Oxford: Oxford University Press, 2000); Alan Bray, *Homosexuality in Renaissance England* (1982; repr. New York: Columbia University Press, 1995) and *The Friend*

(Chicago: University of Chicago Press, 2003); Gregory Bredbeck, *Sodomy and Interpretation: Marlowe to Milton* (Ithaca, N.Y.: Cornell University Press, 1991); Mario DiGangi, *The Homoerotics of Early Modern Drama* (Cambridge: Cambridge University Press, 1997) and *Sexual Types: Embodiment, Agency, and Dramatic Character from Shakespeare to Shirley* (Philadelphia: University of Pennsylvania Press, 2011); Jonathan Dollimore, *Sexual Dissidence: Augustine to Freud, Wilde to Foucault* (Oxford: Oxford University Press, 1991); Will Fisher, *Materializing Gender in Early Modern English Literature and Culture* (Cambridge: Cambridge University Press, 2006); Carla Freccero, *Queer/Early/Modern* (Durham, N.C.: Duke University Press, 2005); Richard Halpern, *Shakespeare's Perfume: Sodomy and Sublimity in the Sonnets, Wilde, Freud, and Lacan* (Philadelphia: University of Pennsylvania Press, 2002); Graham Hammill, *Sexuality and Form: Caravaggio, Marlowe, and Bacon* (Chicago: University of Chicago Press, 2000); Jonathan Goldberg, *Sodometries: Renaissance Texts, Modern Sexualities* (Stanford, Calif.: Stanford University Press, 1992) and *The Seeds of Things: Theorizing Sexuality and Materiality in Renaissance Representations* (New York: Fordham University Press, 2009); Stephen Guy-Bray, *Homoerotic Space: The Poetics of Loss in Renaissance Literature* (Toronto, Ont.: University of Toronto Press, 2002), *Loving in Verse: Poetic Influence as Erotic* (Toronto, Ont.: University of Toronto Press, 2006), and *Against Reproduction: Where Renaissance Texts Come From* (Toronto, Ont.: University of Toronto Press, 2009); Cynthia Herrup, *A House in Gross Disorder: Sex, Law, and the 2nd Earl of Castlehaven* (Oxford: Oxford University Press, 1999); Theodora A. Jankowski, *Pure Resistance: Queer Virginity in Early Modern English Drama* (Philadelphia: University of Pennsylvania Press, 2000); Arthur L. Little Jr., *Shakespeare Jungle Fever: National–Imperial Re-visions of Race, Rape, and Sacrifice* (Stanford, Calif.: Stanford University Press, 2000); Jeffrey Masten, *Textual Intercourse: Collaboration, Authorship, and Sexualities in Renaissance Drama* (Cambridge: Cambridge University Press, 1997); Madhavi Menon, *Wanton Words: Rhetoric and Sexuality in English Renaissance Drama* (Toronto, Ont.: University of Toronto Press, 2004) and *Unhistorical Shakespeare: Queer Theory in Shakespearean Literature and Film* (New York: Palgrave Macmillan, 2008); Ian Fredrick Moulton, *Before Pornography: Erotic Writing in Early Modern England* (Oxford: Oxford University Press, 2000); Stephen Orgel, *Impersonations: The Performance of Gender in Shakespeare's England* (Cambridge: Cambridge University

Press, 1996); Richard Rambuss, *Closet Devotions* (Durham, N.C.: Duke University Press, 1998); Melissa Sanchez, *Erotic Subjects: The Sexuality of Politics in Early Modern English Literature* (Oxford: Oxford University Press, 2011); Kathryn Schwarz, *Tough Love: Amazon Encounters in the English Renaissance* (Durham, N.C.: Duke University Press, 2000) and *What You Will: Gender, Contract, and Shakespearean Social Space* (Philadelphia: University of Pennsylvania Press, 2011); Laurie Shannon, *Sovereign Amity: Figures of Friendship in Shakespearean Contexts* (Chicago: University of Chicago Press, 2002); Alan Sinfield, *Shakespeare, Authority, Sexuality: Unfinished Business in Cultural Materialism* (New York: Routledge, 2006); Bruce Smith, *Homosexual Desire in Shakespeare's England: A Cultural Poetics* (Chicago: University of Chicago Press, 1995); Alan Stewart, *Close Readers: Humanism and Sodomy in Early Modern England* (Princeton, N.J.: Princeton University Press, 1997); Dorothy Stephens, *The Limits of Eroticism in Post-Petrarchan Narrative: Conditional Pleasure from Spenser to Marvell* (Cambridge: Cambridge University Press, 1998); Bette Talavacchia, *Taking Positions: On the Erotic in Renaissance Culture* (Princeton, N.J.: Princeton University Press, 2001); Sarah Toulalan, *Imagining Sex: Pornography and Bodies in Seventeenth-Century England* (Oxford: Oxford University Press, 2007); and Valerie Traub, *Desire and Anxiety: Circulations of Sexuality in Shakespearean Drama* (New York: Routledge, 1992) and *The Renaissance of Lesbianism in Early Modern England* (Cambridge: Cambridge University Press, 2002).

7 On early modern resistance to penetration and ejaculation as the culmination of sexual activity, see James M. Bromley, "'Let It Suffise': Sexual Acts and Narrative Structure in *Hero and Leander*," in *Queer Renaissance Historiography: Backward Gaze*, ed. Stephen Guy-Bray, Vin Nardizzi, and Will Stockton, 67–84 (Burlington, Vt.: Ashgate, 2009).

8 On this economy of sex in Shakespeare's sonnets, see Halpern, *Shakespeare's Perfume*, 11–31.

9 Quoted in Kenneth Borris, ed., *Same-Desire in the English Renaissance: A Sourcebook of Texts, 1470–1650* (New York: Routledge, 2002), 98.

10 Traub, "Making Sexual Knowledge," 255.

11 Stanley Wells, *Looking for Sex in Shakespeare* (Cambridge: Cambridge University Press, 2004), 2.

12 Ibid., 3.

13 Linda Williams, *Screening Sex* (Durham, N.C.: Duke University Press, 2008), 10.

14 Michel Foucault, *The History of Sexuality, Volume I: An Introduction,* trans. Robert Hurley (New York: Random House, 1990), 157.

15 For volumes that do seek to queer the Renaissance, see Jonathan Goldberg, ed. *Queering the Renaissance* (Durham, N.C.: Duke University Press, 1993); Vin Nardizzi, Stephen Guy-Bray, and Will Stockton, eds., *Queer Renaissance Historiography* (Burlington, Vt.: Ashgate, 2009); and Madhavi Menon, ed., *Shakesqueer: A Queer Companion to Shakespeare* (Durham, N.C.: Duke University Press, 2011).

16 Jonathan Goldberg and Madhavi Menon, "Queering History," *PMLA* 120, no. 5 (2005): 1610.

17 Ibid., 1609. On heterosexual sex and temporality, see also Lee Edelman, *No Future: Queer Theory and the Death Drive* (Durham, N.C.: Duke University Press, 2004), and Judith Halberstam, *In a Queer Time and Place: Transgender Bodies, Subcultural Lives* (New York: New York University Press, 2005).

18 Gail Kern Paster, *The Body Embarrassed: Drama and the Disciplines of Shame in Early Modern England* (Ithaca, N.Y.: Cornell University Press, 1993), 125–43.

19 Janet Halley and Andrew Parker, "Introduction," *South Atlantic Quarterly* 106, no. 3 (2007): 422. An expanded version of this issue was subsequently published as Janet Hallet and Andrew Parker, eds., *After Sex? On Writing since Queer Theory* (Durham, N.C.: Duke University Press, 2011).

20 Lara Farina, "Lesbian History and Erotic Reading," in *The Lesbian Premodern,* ed. Noreen Giffney, Michelle M. Sauer, and Diane Watt (New York: Palgrave Macmillan, 2011), 51.

21 Bray, *Homosexuality in Renaissance England,* 16.

22 As we discovered late in the production process, our title also echoes the title of a recent book and journal issue. Kim M. Phillips and Barry Reay's *Sex before Sexuality: A Premodern History* (Cambridge: Polity, 2011) more vigorously polices ananchronistic parsings of early modern sexuality, even as it leaves the definition of sex itself relatively untroubled. On the basis of a 2009 conference at Rutgers University titled "Before Sex," the journal *Signs* 37, no. 4 (2012) contains a forum of essays collected under the same name. Weighted more toward the Restoration and the eighteenth century, the essays in "Before Sex" are primarily interested in the history of sexual difference.

23 Eve Kosofsky Sedgwick, *Epistemology of the Closet* (Berkeley: University

of California Press, 1991), 44–48; Goldberg and Menon, "Queering History," 1609ff. See also Menon, *Unhistorical Shakespeare.*

24 For a volume that addresses sex acts in Renaissance Italy, including its history, art, and literature, but without theorizing the concept of the sex act itself, see Alison Levy, ed., *Sex Acts in Early Modern Italy: Practice, Performance, Perversion, Punishment* (Burlington, Vt.: Ashgate, 2010).

25 We owe the idea that literature explores discursive and ideological fault lines to Alan Sinfield's work, particularly *Faultlines: Cultural Materialism and the Politics of Dissident Reading* (Berkeley: University of California Press, 1992).

1

"Invisible Sex!": What Looks Like the Act in Early Modern Drama?

CHRISTINE VARNADO

In one of the sublimely curious Internet-spawned subcultural phenomena of the past few years—the widely recognized language and iconography known as the "LOLCats" fad or "meme"—photographs of cats in absurd, anthropomorphic poses are captioned with tag lines meant to be imagined as their speech. These utterances follow a specific grammar and syntax (a hybrid of the early Internet gaming code-dialect "133t" or "leetspeak" and the stereotype languages of "Ebonics" and Japanese "Bad Engrish") and a stock set of idiomatic formulations. One particularly versatile LOLCat phrase is used for cats who appear to be miming a recognizable human activity: the caption "Invisible ________!" is filled in with whatever the cat can be imagined to be doing (e.g., "Invisible Bike!" for a cat who appears to be pedaling a bicycle). On the more risqué edge of the trend, cats who appear to be caught in the act of humping the air—or being humped—have been captioned "Invisible Secks!" or, for more salacious specificity, "Invisible Buttsecks!!!"

I want to be clear that in approaching the question of sex in early modern literature through this meme, I am *not* equating early modern subjects with cats whose chance postures can be imagined by humans to simulate sexuality or the period's drama with candid photos of oblivious animals. To the contrary, I think that the past three decades of increasing critical emphasis on historical alterity, or the "otherness of the past," have primed us to think too readily in terms deemphasizing the humanness—the constitutive capacity for complex, irreducible, unpredictable tides of erotic feeling that (I presume) we share—of early modern subjects.[1] Starting from Stephen Greenblatt's adoption of Clifford Geertz's anthropological methodology to analyze early modern English culture through an ethnographic framework that avoids the assumption of correspondence between the subjectivity of the "other" and one's own, the New Historicist strain of literary criticism has come to insist (more absolutely than Geertz himself did) that attempts to account for the forces of power, conflict, desire, need, and beyond that animate culturally specific social structures are misguided because "the processes of definition and abstraction that enable us to establish such unchanging inner necessities often do away with exactly what would constitute the interest, both theoretical and practical, of the intertextual connection."[2] For Greenblatt and his critical descendants, "the meaning and function of the texts that concern both literary critics and anthropologists are established only in historically specific relation to other circumambient texts."[3] This methodology, with its preference for historical difference and its rigorous requirements for contemporary evidence, creates a problem for the study of sex, erotic desire, and other affective states. In my view, limiting what we can say about early modern sex to the specific meanings we can reconstruct from the period's extant discourses leaves out a great deal of possible sex, and even more possible eroticism, which was not explicitly named *as* sexual in the period—much of it nebulously queer eroticism unconnected to any specific social discourse of sex. But the alteritist, empiricist approach also leaves out the many other forms of insight readers can have about a text by too quickly dismissing what may *look* erotically recognizable as coincidence, as inconsequential, or, in the absence of corroborated cultural context, as behavior from a world so inaccessible that it cannot meaningfully be called erotic at all.

I am using the "Invisible Sex!" LOLCats, instead, to situate myself firmly athwart the theoretical rift between the contingency of any one cultural moment's ideas about sex and the recurrent, transhistorical quality of our reactions and responses to it, pointing to these images as an extreme limit case for the question that concerns me in this essay: what do we think *looks like sex,* and why?[4] This is, crucially, a different question from a corollary one—what does sex look like?—broached by other essays in this volume. In both the "Invisible Sex!" LOLCats and in certain scenes from Shakespeare, Middleton, Dekker, and Rowley (to be puzzled out in what follows), what comes first is not a discursive concept of "sex" but a gesture, a simulacrum, a compromising pose or posture that may evoke something that can be given that name. I want, in this essay, to unpack what I will argue are the complex and ambivalent acts of imagination, recognition, and affective hailing required to read or watch a play—especially an early modern play, where the direct staging of sexual contact is impossible and all erotic relations must be communicated through suggestion and double entendre—and to think "sex!" about what we see there.

These LOLCats serve as an apt metaphor for that act of interpretation because whatever impulse spurs a denizen of the Internet to caption an image "Invisible Buttsecks!" is so indisputably a function of the creator's time, place, and milieu. In fact, the gestures of cats (or dogs or people, including, in at least one instance, George W. Bush) that merit the pointed anatomical specificity of the "Invisible Buttsecks!!!/Buttsex!" caption fall into two nonoverlapping categories of pose: paws or hands that appear to be grasping another body and holding it in place near the groin, for violent hip thrusting into the "invisible bottom," or an immobilized, hunched-over, or prostrated body with a face looking out in apparent chagrin, shock, terror, or pain, as though being anally penetrated by an "invisible top." The "Invisible Buttsex!" LOLCats, then, contain a host of current culture-bound assumptions about what looks like or is reminiscent of "buttsex," including a very specific set of ideologies about how power, gender, shame, violence, identity roles, pleasure, and pain are experienced in the act of anal intercourse. These LOLCats provide an example of Foucault's claim that sex itself—as a goal-oriented process and delimited set of acts—is not a self-evident starting point but rather a "complex idea that was formed inside the deployment of sexuality."[5] That the LOLCats anthropomorphically graft sex (*invisible* sex no less) onto images of animals makes them an even more extreme example of how "sex" can be "recognized" *purely* in the eye of the beholder—in this example, an eye conditioned by a masculinist, heteronormative-homophobic regime of sexuality, with all its categorical definitions and assigned values. If a fad for dirty captions on pictures of cats on the Internet can hold that much content about what *looks like sex* to a certain sector of contemporary culture, how much more insight stands to be gained by stepping back and analyzing the assumptions folded into our practices of reading, naming, and classifying the invisible sex we see in early modern texts? I want to shed light on how these critical practices work by bringing the same kind of close reading to bear on a few well-known early modern English plays, focusing specifically on the criteria by which different kinds of invisible sex acts are and are not noticeable.

My agenda in doing this may differ a bit from some of the other contributions to this volume. I aim to analyze the presentist baggage attached to any effort to read for representations of sex in early modern literature *not* so as to reconstruct how sex was "really" thought about in the period. In fact, rather than seeking to remedy the definitional anachronism of Renaissance "sex" by historicizing it, my interest lies in exploring how sex acts in literature resist historicization, where this resistance comes from, and what can be learned from it. I submit that sex—paradoxically, in light of its inherent inexpressibility to others—functions as the linchpin of critical identification. I hold the insights of reader-response theory to be useful here in thinking about both reading a play and watching a performance, namely, the contention that there is no reading or interpretation without a dynamic process of imagination, propelled by identification and lack and originating with the receiver.[6] Reading for sex acts, then, is a complex and self-contradictory endeavor, shaped by a paradox at the heart of how we theorize eros itself: subjective erotic experience is inherently solitary and ineffable, incommunicable and inaccessible to another—even within the same culture, time, and place and even, indeed, to a coparticipant in the same specific sex act.[7] Yet at the same time, that experience can only be represented or communicated *as erotic* by asking a reader—or an audience member—to identify with it, to compare it with their remembered experiences of different sexual acts and feelings. The category of "sex" can only be invoked by soliciting a reader's or hearer's recognition of a certain similarity or comparability of feeling across vastly disparate subjective experiences—experiences that vary, as Eve Kosofsky Sedgwick explained eloquently and often, along infinite axes, far beyond genital configuration or gender, even within one historical moment.[8] Thus representations of sex are, in effect, both impossible to access by identification and *only* understandable via empathetic identification with some sensed, ineffable quality marking what is "erotic." I argue, then, that sex (the act) has resisted historicization because, as an object of inquiry, it necessarily solicits readers' affective and erotic identification with the text—triggering a kind of engagement that conventional academic discourse downplays in favor of a disembodied, rationally engaged reader whose ideas about sex in literature proceed only from the higher mind.[9] Historicist forms of criticism in particular have regarded such critical reactions as at best insignificant, at worst narcissistic and misleading, rather than as a form of reader response and a potential source of insight.[10] How critical identification with literary sex acts occurs depends, in this analysis, on two seemingly countervalent claims about the force of eros in history.

The first premise, the one illustrated by the LOLCats example, is that what "looks like" erotic activity—what we recognize as sex (or at least sex-*y*) when we see it—is historically conditioned, arbitrary, and deeply specific to each culture, place, and time. As Valerie Traub emphasizes in her study of lesbian sex acts, mining the queer eroticism of other time periods is not about asking whether a certain figuration "was" erotic but about stepping back and asking "how do we know what is erotic?" in the art or literature of the period in the first place.[11] Attending to the rubrics for perceiving sexual practices as much as to the practices themselves allows eroticism to be analyzed "less as a self-evident category of behavior or identity than as a heuristic tool. Like gender, eroticism becomes *a category of analysis* rather than a self-contained object."[12]

This brings me to the second premise: that eroticism exists as an objective phenomenon, that eroticism is there, afloat in the archive of early modern texts and artifacts and in our relations with and to them. What I mean by eroticism can be conceived as an invisible force—a form of energy much like heat or electricity—connecting bodies to material objects, aesthetic forms, and other bodies. These two claims are by no means mutually exclusive or new: they are Freud's claims, the paradox underpinning the psychoanalytic conception of eros. I see "eroticism" as a constitutive force on the same order as "language" and "culture"—as the same kind of thoroughly constructed yet totally fundamental and pervasive structure through which the rest of existence is experienced: neither outside or prior to language and culture, nor merely a contingent ideological effect of language and culture, but a coeval element of the human. Sex—like language—can be at once originary, constitutive, powerful, and everywhere at once and, at the same time, only ever experienced through arbitrary, consensual regimes of classification and discipline. Sex—like culture—can be entirely determinative *and* entirely without a single causal origin.

Positions like the one I am outlining have been called for in some of the recent, psychoanalytically inflected queer scholarship that critiques New Historicism's emphasis on the alterity of early modern subjects and desires, seeking to revivify transhistorical recognition and identification based on affect and desire as important, productive forces in criticism. Building on the influence of texts like Carolyn Dinshaw's *Getting Medieval* and L. O. Aranye Fradenburg and Carla Freccero's edited collection *Premodern Sexualities*—as well as on newer interventions such as Freccero's *Queer/Early/Modern,* Madhavi Menon's *Unhistorical Shakespeare,* and Jonathan Goldberg and Menon's essay on method in *PMLA,* "Queering History"—I would assert that a fuller understanding of early modern sex needs to include, in addition to historicizing early modern sexual practices and the social relations that produced them, an exploration of where early modern eroticism might, in a certain participatory, experiential sense, be less unrecognizably foreign than we modern critics have been trained to expect.[13]

By looking for where a frisson of erotic energy and interest—in its myriad forms, including prurient pleasure, shock, humor, self-recognition, suspicion, and offense—leaps out and hails our libidinal participation in a text as readers or audience members, we can actually harness and use the power of erotically and affectively invested critical identification as a new, queer form of knowledge production that can uncover new sites, new forms, and new valences of "sex" within the vastly different social and discursive contexts of the early modern world. This openness to being surprised by what Carolyn Dinshaw calls the "touch" of the past demands new methodological paradigms for articulating and directing erotic critical investment and recognition in nuanced and sophisticated ways that do not depend on imposing inappropriate identity categories or making sweeping historical claims. It is in the service of this demand that I would like to perform what I call a "close reading experiment," scrutinizing how sex is represented and how we recognize, or do not recognize, it in three early modern plays: Shakespeare's *Romeo and Juliet* (1595), Middleton and Dekker's *The Roaring Girl* (1611), and Middleton and Rowley's *The Changeling* (1621). I want to get as close as possible to the scene of first encounter with these well-known, much-studied texts—to the imaginative leap that has to happen for the modern reader to envision an invisible, offstage or unspecified sex act and to be hailed, across a vast temporal span, into fantasmatic participation in it. In fact, I argue, the literary critic's suddenly being seized with the intuitive idea that an unrepresented or almost-represented act of sex may be occurring, just out of sight, in the fictive world of a text from a bygone era can be considered as a primal scene of critical—indeed, of *readerly*—identification.[14]

First, I will read a moment of almost universally agreed on "straight" invisible sex: the morning-after bedroom scene between the secretly married Romeo (a boy) and Juliet (a girl played by a boy actor), who are presumed to have consummated their marriage before the scene. Act 3, scene 5 opens with the stage directions "*Enter* Romeo *and* Juliet *aloft*":[15]

> JULIET. Wilt thou be gone? It is not yet near day.
> It was the nightingale, and not the lark,
> That pierced the fearful hollow of thine ear.
> Nightly she sings on yonder pomegranate tree.
> Believe me, love, it was the nightingale.
> ROMEO. It was the lark, the herald of the morn;
> No nightingale. Look, love, what envious streaks
> Do lace the severing clouds in yonder east.
> Night's candles are burnt out, and jocund day
> Stands tiptoe on the misty mountaintops.
> I must be gone and live, or stay and die.
> JULIET. Yon light is not daylight, I know it, I.
> It is some meteor that the sun exhales
> To be to thee this night a torchbearer
> And light thee on thy way to Mantua.
> Therefore stay yet; thou need'st not be gone. (3.5.1–16)[16]

The entire history of performance, reading, and reception of this scene has, virtually speaking, captioned this stage moment "Invisible Secks!!!"

of the legally significant, penis-in-vagina variety. And to be sure, this aubade-duet, the pivot point of the entire play, is saturated before, behind, and all through with erotic suggestion. But, given the interest of this volume in supplying the sexual specificity of early modern representations and nonrepresentations of sex, exactly *what sex acts* are figured here if we don't assume that we already know? Can a queer reading perceive other possibilities—other possible acts and nonacts and partial acts—in place of the penetrative, goal-directed heterosexual intercourse with which it has been culturally "captioned"? My reading of this scene will function as a foil to my readings of other, less-accepted scenes of possible sex to point out that in fact, *nothing* would have to be different in the text of the play to imagine the invisible sex act before this dialogue as something else: some nonpenetrative erotic act of a more diffuse and mutual *jouissance* or some suspended dilation of pleasure that gets cruelly interrupted by the lark. Nor would anything have to be different, for that matter, if the unseen act were an unclimactic fumble, a premature climax, an impossible penetration, or a dysfunctional episode. Nor would anything have to change if Romeo did the same thing (any of the things) with Juliet that he would do with a boy. In fact, there is no textual reason to assume that this offstage act of "sex" (whatever it is) follows the strict phallocentric plot telos that furnishes the patriarchal definition of sex. It takes a certain perverse reader or audience member to think such things, of course—who would question that Romeo and Juliet spent a night of passion after their secret marriage and that it included the kind of sex act that constituted "marriage" as a physical state? A queer reader—a reader seeking out the possible other sides to heterosexuality and attracted to the negativity and excess of erotic energy that exists beside and behind the normalized sexual narrative—would.

This queer reader may observe that while a "fearful hollow" has been "pierced," that hollow was Romeo's; as he is on his way out the window, Juliet swears it was the feminine bird of night that pierced it. The scene opens not with a gesture toward Juliet's being pierced, stained, marked, taken, or any other allusion to heterosexual penetration but with an image of erotic role reversal: Romeo fleeing from this aural piercing, which Juliet insists was seduction and not violence. Romeo's next line figures the "envious streaks" across the "severing clouds," and the "jocund day," which "stands tiptoe on the misty mountaintops," as towering, phallic powers which have burned out the brief "candles" of his one (part of a) night of sexual agency with Juliet. She insists, out of an overpowering desire for it to be so, that the light they see is not the bright, predictable sunlight of the stirring patriarchal social order but a queer, nighttime astronomical singularity of incandescent gas, animistic in cause: "some meteor that the sun exhales / To be to thee this night a torchbearer."

The tonality of the invisible sex act for which this scene stands in is marked above all by conflict and struggle between the lovers over the gendered and epistemological ramifications of what they have just done (or are doing). Romeo insists repeatedly that he is emasculated by the necessity of leaving prematurely, that he is cock blocked by the law of the Father—in both the familial and legal senses—which impinges on him even in the act of sexual consummation with his socially impossible wife. Juliet seems bent on denying Romeo's subjection or on claiming some delusional agency for herself and for the feminine powers of night and eros as the force mastering him. His next lines can be chilling if we read them as an earnest response, embracing perjury and death as the consequences of Juliet's reading of the moment: "Let me be ta'en, let me be put to death. / I am content, so thou wilt have it so" (3.5.17–18). Juliet immediately switches to Romeo's former position, ordering him out over the intensifying noise of the lark:

> It is, it is! Hie hence, be gone, away!
> It is the lark that sings so out of tune,
> Straining harsh discords and unpleasing sharps.
> Some say the lark makes sweet division;
> This doth not so, for she divideth us. (3.5.26–30)

The "straining harsh discords" here are between the lovers, who remain "out of tune" in the urgent, unreadable, divisive aftermath of whatever has just transpired between them. What I find paradoxical, and potentially destabilizing to how we perceive and consider offstage sex acts here, is that this iconic scene of heterosexual invisible sex in early modern drama is figured *not* as Romeo's phallic possession or penetration of Juliet but as emasculation and conflict—to the extent that the text figures any sex act at all, which is not much.[17] Romeo's language of penetration, mockery, peril, and suicidal erotic abandon and Juliet's desperate wish for a queer utopian alternate universe of perpetual night and seduction figure a social context for this sex act that makes it far less "straight," privileged, legitimate, or heteronormative than it is generally perceived to be.[18]

Many modern stagings of this scene attempt to trace a much closer outline around the invisible sex envisioned in it than was possible in Elizabethan performance, perhaps none closer than Franco Zeffirelli in his 1968 film. This scene opens inside Juliet's bedroom, with a shot of the two lovers asleep in a bed of tangled white sheets—not intertwined, but each lying solitary side by side, Juliet on her back covered by the sheets and Romeo prone, his beautiful backside uncovered to the camera. In a concerted effort to verge as close as possible to a representation of the absent heterosexual sex act, Zeffirelli gives us breasts (Juliet's) and buttocks (Romeo's) over the course of the five speeches cited earlier. But even here, any act of heterosexual sex remains invisible—the body parts we see allude to erotic contacts that are infantile (breasts) and sodomitical (buttocks).[19] There is a sense in which, much like many queer sex acts in the early modern period (and today as well), this unseen, unspecified act between a man and a woman lacks *any* discursive existence *as an act,* either legitimating or transgressive. This act drives Juliet and Romeo to kill themselves, but only the Friar and the Nurse have any knowledge of it. Even in his ultimate confession, the Friar mentions only the legal-sacramental fact of their marriage and in fact could be read as implying that because "their stol'n marriage day / Was Tybalt's doomsday" (5.3.233–34), the marriage was unconsummated. In another resonance with queer relationships, Romeo and Juliet's love is suppressed to the point of suicide during their lifetimes and is not only condoned but extravagantly memorialized by their parents once they are no longer alive to pursue it.

My contention is that in the absence of any significant textual figuration or dramatic efficacy for heterosexual intercourse in *Romeo and Juliet,* generations of readers and interpreters of the play have imagined that act taking place offstage, right before the aubade scene, *because they wanted to*—because that is what *they* would do, what they imagine a generalized "one" or "anyone" would do. This projection is the stubborn anachronism inherent in representations of sex acts, especially the "invisible," indirectly figured sex acts in early modern plays. The very notion of "sex" can only be conjured in the audience's or reader's mind via erotic identification—or disidentification—with the acts being suggested, and that fantasmatic act of identification is inevitably structured by the reader's or viewer's desire. If sex's epistemological slipperiness and textual invisibility can therefore illuminate queer valences to what is always read as "straight" sex in *Romeo and Juliet,* where else in early modern drama can reading through a queer, erotically invested and identificatory critical lens reveal other nonnormative erotics lurking in the silences and negations of the text? Why not imagine acts of offstage or unarticulated sex in other, less-expected contexts and configurations? How can returning to Valerie Traub's question—"how do we know what is erotic?"—help us to tease out previously unnoticed possibilities of queer sex within what does not at first look like sex at all?

I want to compare the invisible sex in *Romeo and Juliet* to two moments in other plays that are not so widely captioned "Invisible Secks!!!"—two possible erotic transactions that might or might not be classifiable as "sex" but are unabashedly *queer*: De Flores's murder–buggery–finger amputation of Alonzo in *The Changeling* and the three-way kissing–viol-playing scene in *The Roaring Girl.* These queer test scenes provide a valuable counterweight to the centrality of *Romeo and Juliet*'s imagined offstage sex in that there is a high degree of ambiguity as to what kind of representational relationship they bear to unstaged erotic acts. They can be read as hinting at offstage sex, which may have just taken place or is about to take place—but they can also be considered as metaphorical enactments of unrepresentable sex acts, where dialogue and stage action stand in for the erotic congress itself. What ties these potential instances of sex to *Romeo and Juliet*'s widely assumed one is that they do not have any explicit dramatic efficacy as literal acts of sex within the action of the respective plays, just as the straight sex in *Romeo and Juliet* does not effect the dramatic consequences that might have been its heterosexual birthright. Instead, these even-more-invisible queer erotic contacts signify only indirectly. In fact, all three of these scenes dubiously, unevenly, represent sex, requiring varying degrees and kinds of erotic identification from audiences and readers to recognize its possible presence. The difference in *The Changeling* and *The Roaring Girl,* however, is that the expectation of seeing sex of the penetrative, heterosexual kind has been removed. In its place, the following tableaux flout all kinds of normative parameters for what looks like sex—not only in terms of the participants' sexes or genders but also in their number and relational dynamic (as in *The Roaring Girl*) or in the affect and purpose of the encounter (as in *The Changeling*). Reading them as instances of queer invisible sex is my attempt to circumvent heteronormative bias with an affectively invested, creative reading practice more immediately attuned to desire and pleasure. My aim is to expand the range of questions we can ask about moments that "look like sex" beyond how they register in contemporary discourses—what other kinds of archives, quite apart from the codification of certain sexual acts within the social order, might furnish material to flesh out our picture of sexuality in early modern literature?

Sex acts are inextricably linked to violence in Middleton and Rowley's 1623 revenge tragedy *The Changeling,* in which the scheming antiheroine Beatrice-Joanna suborns the murder of the man her father wants her to marry, commissioning the lecherous De Flores to "take him to thy fury," to which De Flores replies, "I thirst for him" (2.2.133).[20] De Flores plays on a masculine homoerotics of service to offer his target, Alonzo, a tour of the castle's narrow halls, gloating that "he's safely thrust upon me beyond hopes" (2.2.165). In the interval between Acts 2 and 3, the stage directions state that De Flores "hides a naked rapier" somewhere in the set; this extradramatic, interstitial touch makes the rapier a remnant that sticks in the audience's memory, a hidden reminder of the threat of penetrative sexual violence to come. He solicitously removes both their swords, the better to penetrate deeper into small passageways, and promises to show Alonzo "A place you little dream on" (3.2.2). Finally, De Flores "places" Alonzo at a little window through which he can see the castle's battery of weapons, inviting him to "spend your eye awhile upon that object" (3.2.6–8). The tableau in which the two men are seen here is replete with *resemblances* to anal sex: the one looking through an underground aperture in a hallway too narrow for swords and the other standing behind him, agreeing with his every word. (The narrowness of the anus is a conventional trope in the period.) But this scene of "invisible buttsex" is saturated not only with the dramatic irony of the audience's knowledge that Alonzo is about to be killed but with the particular eroticized threat of violence De Flores embodies. When he cajoles Alonzo to "keep your eye straight, my lord" and to "dwell awhile" on a small sconce, as he takes up the rapier from its hiding place and moves in behind, his actions are congruent with seduction, or at least homoerotic flirtation. In fact, it is easy to imagine a staging of this scene in which, when Alonzo assents, "I am upon't," he expects—and perhaps even receives—the caress of a sexual advance accompanying De Flores's pun, "And so am I" (3.2.12–14).[21] But at the same instant, De Flores stabs him with the rapier, violating him at close range in an attack that may also include a literal rape as well as the symbolic penetration of stabbing:

> ALONZO. De Flores! O De Flores,
> Whose malice hast thou put on?
> DE FLORES. Do you question
> A work of secrecy? I must silence you.
> ALONZO. Oh, oh, oh!
> DE FLORES. I must silence you. (3.2.15–18)

These lines can be read as De Flores sexually assaulting Alonzo: either buggering him while stabbing him repeatedly or sodomizing him *with* the rapier. What happens afterward also points to a reading of invisible sex taking place in this scene. De Flores wants Alonzo's ring to confirm the murder, but the ring won't come off—De Flores jokes that the dead man will not part with it—so he takes the ring, "finger and all" (3.2.25). The word "ring" is *anus* in Latin; Alonzo's ring is the trophy De Flores must possess. More than just a pun, this image pointedly materializes the unstageable act of anal defloration: Alonzo is symbolically castrated in having his ring taken from his body. The finger and the hidden "naked rapier" can both be seen as metonymic substitutes for the phallus in a homoerotically charged act of violence. But a finger through a ring—a finger that is then amputated because it has entered a ring, by the taker of that man's ring, who at the same time draws out his involuntary "Oh, oh, oh!" and silences them with rapier thrusts—indicates a kind of penetration that is specifically sodomitical. De Flores claims and keeps

Alonzo's manhood as well as his "ring," regendering his victim's body and in fact replacing Alonzo's member with his own in future sexual congress with Beatrice.

The sodomitical reading I am offering here is perverse, and it takes a perverse critical imagination to formulate it. Recognizing sex at this moment in the text requires not only imagining invisible sex in homosocial scenes between men but also being alert to nonconsensual sex acts based in violence rather than affection. Once recognized, however, this moment of invisible sex also prompts a reconsideration of the play's gender politics, for it dilutes the misogyny that is usually read as the play's predominant theme. If De Flores has erotic designs on Alonzo, and especially if he rapes him, he shares more agency in the crime than if he acts solely at Beatrice's request. Beatrice's sexual corruption is also complicated and decentered if De Flores takes sexual gratification in the murder for its own sake rather than strictly as a means to possessing her: the sex De Flores extorts from Beatrice at the end of Act 3 becomes one of the predations of an indiscriminate rapist rather than the attained goal of heterosexually driven, rationally self-interested violence.

The invisible sex in early modern drama does not always involve two participants. Middleton and Dekker's *The Roaring Girl* features the real-life transvestite and cutpurse Mary Frith (or "Moll Cutpurse"), who agrees to perform as a monstrous decoy fiancée—and a sexual go-between—for her gentleman friend Sebastian Wengrave, whose father has forbidden his marriage to a poorer woman. At the climax of Moll's unabashedly androgynous erotic agency in the play, Moll brings Sebastian's fiancée, Mary, to a secret meeting with him in his father's study, with Mary disguised in men's clothes from Moll's own tailor. Moll not only facilitates their erotic interaction but participates in it, winkingly commenting on their onstage kiss, "How strange this shows, one man to kiss another" (4.1.47).[22] Sebastian jokes with Moll, while kissing Mary, that the kiss's doubled masculinity makes it doubly pleasurable: "I'd kiss such men to choose, Moll; / Methinks a woman's lip tastes well in a doublet ... As some have a conceit their drink tastes better / In an outlandish cup than in our own, / So methinks every kiss she gives me now / In this strange form is worth a pair of two" (4.1.48–58). Moll's instrumental role in the triad is made literal when Sebastian offers her his father's viol to play for them. She assents: "I'll play my part as well as I can; it shall ne'er be said I came into a gentleman's chamber and let his instrument hang by the walls . . . I ne'er came into that chamber yet where I took down the instrument myself" (4.1.89–95). The long song Moll then plays and sings—a bawdy ballad of female economic and sexual agency, about a mistress, her money, her lovers, and her sisters—serves in the scene as a dramatic substitution, or an accompaniment, for a three-person sex act centered on Moll. Her singing is constructed as an intimate and socially transgressive activity, one that Moll does better than her critics: "Pish, let 'em prate abroad; th' art here where thou art known and lov'd. There be a thousand close dames that will call the viol an unmannerly instrument for a woman and therefore talk broadly of thee, when you shall have them sit wider to a worse quality" (4.1.96–99). The three refer to the song as a "dream" (4.1.103)—a dream Moll orchestrates with her legs spread apart, playing on the (borrowed) instrument between them. After one verse, Sebastian and Mary want her to "dream again" (4.1.113). The ostensibly heterosexual couple are satisfied with the erotic connection Moll has effected for them in the assignation:

> SEBASTIAN. This is the roaring wench must do us good.
> MARY. No poison, sir, but serves us for some use,
> Which is confirm'd in her. (4.1.150–52)

The three-person, doubly cross-dressed invisible sex implied in this scene is substantially less invisible—less dramatically repressed in the text, and more socially consequential—than the heterosexual coupling in *Romeo and Juliet.* The three participants comment on what they are doing and what it means, "captioning" the cross-dressing, the clandestine meeting, the location, the kissing, and the viol playing as highly secret, sexually transgressive, and potentially incriminating. The array of garments and props decorating the bodies onstage—Moll's breeches, ruff, doublet, and hose; Mary's breeches, doublet, and hose; the rapier Moll carries; and the father's viol—become erotic prostheses that can be put on, borrowed, and used for the playing of different sexual "parts" among the three. It may even be that the audience would understand the scene itself, the kiss, and Moll's song on the father's borrowed viol as a three-person sex act that cannot be staged, hiding in plain sight for those able to imagine it. As in the scene from *The Changeling,* different stagings of this scene could augment its queer erotic valences, for instance, through keeping the three bodies entwined together and collectively tensed in excitement during the rendezvous and the song; playing up the mutually transitive, tridirectional quality of the compliments and gestures of affection exchanged among the three; or emphasizing Moll's instrumental facilitating role. However, the text contains all of the material of this three-way queer eroticism in the dialogue and stage directions. Far from only being brought out by suggestive staging, it is immediately legible in the mind's eye of a watcher, or even a reader, attuned to and interested in such things.

And, perhaps not coincidentally, the play provides an intensely erotically invested watcher, standing just outside this moment of perfectly triangulated reverie: the father, Sir Alex, is lying in wait, hoping to catch his son and Moll "in conjunction . . . both with standing collars!"—that is, in sexual congress as both are dressed in men's clothing. The father enters unseen during Moll's song and lurks where he can hear it but perhaps not see it. Overhearing his son's enthusiastic interjections—"That's a free mistress, faith"—he curses Moll under his breath, in a series of progressively more furious asides: "Ay, ay, ay, like her that sings it, one of thine own choosing" (4.1.111–12). At the end of the song, Moll comments that they must reassemble their bodies and minds into socially acceptable states: "Hang up the viol now, sir: all this while I was in a dream; one shall lie rudely then, but being awake, I keep my legs together" (4.1.128–31). (Sir Alex: "Now, now she's trapp'd" [4.1.132].) Sir Alex cannot see what the audience can: that Moll is playing on his viol, that Mary is there too in men's clothes, or that they have been kissing. He hears enough, though, to take it as verification of his own crazed fantasies about queer sex between Moll and his son—essentially standing outside the scene as an interpreter, performing an act of readerly identification informed by his own desires and anxieties. His paranoid gloss of the situation layers onto what the audience has seen and points up the explicitly sexual transgressiveness of the meeting. The father's reaction, in fact, might serve to insert a reading of the chamber rendezvous as an invisible sex scene into a reader's or audience member's mind, if the thought had not already occurred.

Throughout the play, Moll's instrumental function in facilitating Sebastian's forbidden marriage turns on the homophobic rage and Oedipal anxiety she incites in his father—and although the pleasure of the comedy is in watching her torment and trick him by means of his own gender panic, in a structural sense, Sir Alex is right about Moll's sexual implication with his son and the virtuosic, versatile potency of her prosthetic masculine body that makes her such an erotically suspect (and alluring) figure. He fixates on her flamboyant men's garments and the sodomitical eroticism that they construct for her, lamenting that "I have brought up my son to marry a Dutch slop and a French doublet, a codpiece-daughter!" (2.2.78–79). Yet, earlier in this scene, as he decks his chamber with all his most valuable things—his watch, chains, and diamond-studded ruffs—as bait in hopes of framing Moll for stealing it, he dithers obsessively over which of his accessories she will like and how best to arrange them so as to attract her. When Sir Alex surprises the threesome by revealing himself, Moll instantly assumes the ruse of a male musician, with a silent Mary as "his" page, to cover up what they had been doing. Sebastian (out of a sense of irony or in a state of erotic transport?) cannot resist punning on her erotic prowess: "a gentleman, a musician, sir, one of excellent fing'ring" (Sir Alex: "Ay, I think so; I wonder how they scap'd her"), who "has the most delicate stroke, sir" (4.1.169–74). (Sir Alex: "A stroke indeed; I feel it at my heart.") These doubled ironies and double entendres continue to swirl around what has just happened: "You teach to sing too? . . . I think you'll find an apt scholar of my son, / Especially for prick-song" (4.1.190–93). The pun, coupled with Moll's reply—"I have much hope in him" (4.1.194)—"captions" the song as a scene of sexual pedagogy, directly insinuating the possibility of a threesome facilitated by Moll just before, after, or invisible underneath this scene.

The Roaring Girl furnishes an example of how possible sex in an early modern play might not be registered under the assumption that a sex act definitionally involves two people. Configurations like this one could only be perceived as sex, and thus analyzed, by a queer act of imagination on the part of a reader or audience member who happens to recognize a grouping of three characters onstage as possible parties to a sex act. We would also miss this possible sex scene if we were to read only for indicators of sex in a patriarchal, heteronormative mode, involving an active, agentive "top" and a passive, receptive "bottom." This scene requires the ability to think early modern sex as a category that includes acts not structured by a binary of dominance and submission but by more multiple and mutual pleasures such as cross-dressing and role-playing, pimping and procuring, secrecy and trespassing in forbidden space, borrowing others' clothes and accessories, and using and being used.

Reading these unorthodox representations of sex alongside the unseen sex act in *Romeo and Juliet,* what is remarkable to me is how little absolute difference there is between these textual figurations of tenuous, only faintly suggested queer sex acts and the sex act of the famous heterosexual consummation. The examples of invisible sex, straight and otherwise, that I've juxtaposed here arguably push the outer limits of sex. My intention is to use their liminality strategically, to put pressure on what constitutes an early modern representation of a sex act and to complicate what it means to recognize the presence of eroticism in literary representation. I suggest that what we take to be a representation of an erotic act in early modern drama is inherently, and almost entirely, dependent on what kinds of erotic acts are available to be conjured by the play in a reader's or watcher's imagination.[23] In fact, physical, genital sex acts between a man and a woman are *no more or less* directly represented than a moment of nonconsensual sex between men or a three-way act involving men and women and transvestites. A critical leap of identification—not necessarily a desired or pleasurable one—must happen in both instances, and the willingness or ability to see the queer possibilities requires a particularly strong investment of prurient, participatory imagination.

Gathering knowledge of sexual practices in the period is one possible angle of inquiry; such work can shed light on what exactly the contemporary audiences who first consumed these plays might have been doing and hence identifying with in lived experience. But within the world of a work of literature, the fabric of sexual practices is one of the subtexts that must be filled in by imagination. No matter how exhaustive one's knowledge about cultural discourses of sex as an act in 1595, 1611, or 1621, these works of dramatic fiction still require each reader to supply invisible sex acts that are fictive and hence spring out of identification. The recognition we grant, the acts we imagine, and the mental images we attach to sex therefore belong inescapably to us, the modern readers and critics of early modern plays—with both problematic and productive consequences for the study of early modern sexuality.

It seems evident that the undertheorization of sex in early modern studies that is the raison d'être for this volume has manifested, in part, as an enormous discrepancy in our critical tendency to notice and discuss offstage, invisible heterosexual sex, as opposed to moments of nonheterosexual, nondyadic, and other nonnormative eroticism. Relatively few sex acts are in any way made visible, even indirectly, on the early modern stage—and those acts, unsurprisingly, tend to be the procreative or potentially procreative acts of heterosexual intercourse that have some effect on the patriarchal social order. Shakespeare's problem comedies, for example, rely extensively on the post facto revelation of heterosexual intercourse to induce patriarchal consequences, as in Mariana's assumption of her rightful place as Angelo's wife in *Measure for Measure* and Helena's doing likewise to Bertram in *All's Well That Ends Well.* But what is interesting to me, and what is seldom remarked on, about these nonimaginary straight sex acts is that they are still very much invisible—not just dramatically but even, crucially, to the male participant in the unrepresented scene as he carries out the act with a woman other than the one he thought was there. The usual reading of the bedtrick emphasizes its dependence on misogyny, in the view of women's bodies as indistinguishable and sexually interchangeable. But what other aspects of the embodied *practice* of heterosexual intercourse could emerge if we think about the bedtrick queerly, imagining a queer perspective for the unwilling, unwitting husband? What if, rather than women's identities, it is heterosexual sex itself that is in some sense essentially imperceptible, or at least totally unremarkable, and devoid of any real erotic specificity on the part of the man? And what about the possibility, rarely raised with regard to straight acts of invisible sex in early modern drama, that the act of penetration was not successfully completed or did not take place at all? The usual critical assumption is that a sex act occurred in the heteronormative way, but in fact, the putative pregnancies resulting from these alleged acts—the technical potentiality of which is all that allows the sex to have social existence, as Romeo and Juliet's sex never does—do not come to any visible fruition, remaining in the early stages of unseeable and unknowable social fiction as the plays end.

Straight sex in *The Changeling* is somewhat more visible than homosexual rape—yet at the same time, it recedes even more inexorably into lies, slander, and annihilation. The play dramatizes a few almost visible acts of heterosexual intercourse as intrinsic components of its tragic climax: De Flores's apparent extortion of sex from Beatrice causes her to send her waiting woman Diaphanta to her husband, Alsemero, on their wedding night, but the originary, sinful act between Beatrice and De Flores actually remains invisible. A conversation in the garden that is not shown in the play, immediately before act 5, scene 3, is taken by Beatrice's husband to stand in as proof of their impropriety. The play's climactic sex act, however, derives much of its horror from how near it comes to being visible. Alsemero puts De Flores in the closet, where he is holding Beatrice prisoner for the murder of Alonzo, telling him above her protestations and cries to have his way with her:

> I'll be your pander now; rehearse again
> Your scene of lust, that you may be perfect
> When you shall come to act it to the black audience
> Where howls and gnashings shall be music to you.
> Clip your adulteress freely; 'tis the pilot
> Will guide you to the Mare Mortuum,
> Where you shall sink to fathoms bottomless. (5.3.114–20)

Beatrice's voice later interrupts the scene from "within," repeatedly crying, "Oh, oh, oh!" and De Flores is heard responding, "Nay, I'll along for company" (5.3.139–40). He refers to himself as part of the "recompense" demanded by Alonzo's brother, but this line can also easily mean that "he"—his penis—will come (the word *come* is emphasized in its absence) "along" with his knife "for company" in penetrating Beatrice's body.

This combination act of rape-and-stabbing then mirrors the earlier potential buggery-and-stabbing encounter between De Flores and Alonzo in another small, enclosed space of the castle. While this heterosexual act is violently public, with a voyeuristic audience standing around damning both perpetrator and victim, the earlier homosexual act went completely undetected by anyone but the dead man. Alonzo's body is subsumed into the bowels of the castle, and his disappearance is interpreted as an inexplicable flight. The only lingering trace of him is his nine-fingered ghost, which appears only to his rapist–murderer.[24] This structural contrast echoes the social significance of the two different sex acts: the heterosexual one defiles and invalidates patriarchal marriage, whereas the homosexual one does not. But it also underscores the heteronormative assumptions through which we have tended to read *The Changeling* for representations of sex. Alonzo and Beatrice both cry out "Oh, oh, oh!" to De Flores as he stabs them. There is a critical consensus that Beatrice's cries "could be" cries of sexual violation—that a double meaning is at least insinuated, even if the possibility is then disavowed.[25] Of the enormous body of criticism published on *The Changeling,* it has been noted only obliquely, and only by a handful of critics, that straight sex in the main plot is never properly consensual or marital and that the play's language consistently conflates marriage and rape.[26] Celia Daileader, touching on Middleton's bent toward sodomitical imagery, comes closest to characterizing the sexual congress between De Flores and Beatrice as figuratively sodomitical in its secrecy and transgressiveness.[27] However, despite the play's rejection of heterosexual reproductivity, which resonates with the figure of the "changeling" as a queer fantasy–origin myth, I have found no evidence of any previous critic reading Alonzo's murder as a homosexual rape.

This disconnect between how straight sex acts and other kinds of sex acts are read and discussed is a symptom of how differently the reader's or critic's (or teacher's or student's) leap of erotic identification is valued, intellectually and socially, in a heterosexual versus a queer context. In the heteronormative world we inhabit (especially if we take into account the accumulated readings of this period's drama over the past four rather exceedingly heteronormative centuries), the basic cognitive and affective responses that make up how readers read for sex—those impulses of transhistorical identification by which one can imagine the sex taking place just out of sight in a text as the same act, in a basic ontological sense, as the sex that one might have in one's own life—have resulted, on balance, in a modern heteronormative "common-sense" about sex.[28] *The Changeling* makes a particularly stark example here because it would seem to take desire, or at least pleasure, out of the equation: I am comparing two instances of potential rape and murder. The heterosexual one is widely discussed as a textual figure and a possibility; the homosexual one is as submerged in the criticism as Alonzo's deflowered corpse in the bowels of the castle.

I would contend that, contra the discourse of sex's escape from historicization, sex in early modern literature has been historicized—only immaterially, implicitly, and invisibly so—as surely as the "Invisible Buttsecks!!!" LOLCats contain implicit, historically contingent ideologies about what "Buttsecks!!!" is like: in critical assumptions that all too easily confirm as true the identifications and investments of a hetero-oriented reader, thereby inadvertently constructing a hetero-oriented early modern subject and culture. For the past fifteen or twenty years, queer historicist scholarship on early modern sexuality has defined queerness in the period as a matter of "acts, not identities," after a reading of Foucault, which emphasizes a strict "before" to the existence of "homosexuality" as a discrete social discourse and a fairly absolute disjunction between what existed then and our present subjective experience of sexuality.[29] One issue I have with this position is that it makes representations of bodily sex acts in the early modern archive, and whatever contemporaneous social meanings can be historically linked to them, the privileged locus of content about what queernesses, or sexualities, or desires, might have been. In light of the persistent presentism that I have shown informing what gets read as a representation of a sex act and what does not, I maintain that limiting our focus to sex acts that are explicitly represented and remarked on as such carries with it a high risk of missing much—maybe most—of the possible queer sex in literature.

The way to turn this quandary into an opportunity for innovation is to rehabilitate and retheorize the centrality of the critic's identification to how sex is defined as an act, and to do so in a way that denaturalizes a heteronormative set of expectations for what early modern eroticism will be. As José Esteban Muñoz observes about the intellectual labor of contesting heteronormativity in the practice of queer history,

> queerness is rarely complemented by evidence, or at least by traditional understandings of the term. The key to queering evidence, and by that I mean the ways in which we prove queerness and read queerness, is by suturing it to the concept of ephemera. Think of ephemera as a trace, the remains, the things that are left, hanging in the air like a rumor. . . . Ephemeral evidence is rarely obvious because it is needed to stand against the harsh lights of mainstream visibility and the potential tyranny of the fact. (Not that all facts are harmful, but the discourse of the fact has often cast antinormative desire as the bad object.)[30]

In the interest of taking up this challenge, I am advocating a critical practice that can strategically deploy the epistemological slipperiness as well as the anachronism inherent in defining sex—as I have tried to do with my readings of invisible sex scenes of various kinds. One received assumption of historicism is that the relative obscurity and invisibility of queer eroticism in the archive and its lack of a fixed social signification are obstacles to studying it. In fact, it is central to my agenda to work at the margins of perceptible sex, constantly re-remembering that not all erotic yearnings are articulated to the desire to do a particular sex act, not all desires to act are acted on, not all acts are detected, and not all detected acts are met with the prescribed social consequences—then or now. This is, after all, what makes literature interesting, what makes it more than a source of historical data. But heteronormativity has made it more difficult to remember this—that sex might be legible, if we look for it, precisely where its effects or its social significance is uncertain—about queer sex than about heterosexual intercourse.

In embracing this stance and this practice of reading for marginal eroticism, I am locating myself in a long line of prurient readers and critics who have rifled through the corpus of early modern drama finding instances of sex in ever more unlikely places and nonnormative configurations; however, I am also attempting to change the terms of the search. I would argue that beyond proving the historical basis of each discovery of possible sex (which can veer too easily into the fallacy of treating the text as if there were a right answer, as if we could know, or as if these were not works of fiction), we need to interrogate our own flashes of transhistorical erotic identification as readers. We must begin to pay attention to subtle, even subconscious capacities of critical recognition—or critical arousal. These perceptions are almost sensory, manifesting as a hunch, a tickle, a blush, a daydream, a fantasy, a trauma, a Freudian slip; they constitute a queer way of knowing and bear investigating. In Muñoz's terms, I see them as nothing less than "the trace, the remains, the things that are left hanging in the air, like a rumor" of four hundred-year-old queer desires. As such, we can use these critical feelings to unsettle what we think we know about periodized models of sex and sexuality and about the affective contours of historical time. What I am arguing for, in conclusion, is a perverse, perverted, and queer critical attitude toward the figuration of sex, visible and invisible, in early modern cultural artifacts: an unseemly seeming affective investment in reading for queer desires and queer acts against—or better, outside of—conventional erotic plots but also a mutable identification with textual ephemera, traces, or figurations of eros that is anti-identitarian, that cathects and projects in ways not organized by bounded categories, historical or genital.

Notes

1 Greenblatt, for example, defines the subjectivity of early modern people as "peripheral," as "the *product* of the relations, material objects, and judgments" of their particular historical contexts, "rather than the producer of these relations, objects, and judgments." Selves are "brought into being by . . . institutional processes," and the focus is on the person not as subject but as object, "a placeholder in a complex system of possessions, kinship bonds, contractual relationships, customary rights, and ethical obligations." "Psychoanalysis and Renaissance Culture," in *Literary Theory/Renaissance Texts,* ed. Patricia Parker and David Quint (Baltimore: The Johns Hopkins University Press, 1986), 216. This phrase "otherness of the past" is from Mary Beth Rose, "Where Are the Mothers in Shakespeare? Options for Gender Representation in the English Renaissance," *Shakespeare Quarterly* 42, no. 3 (1991), 291.

2 Stephen Greenblatt, "The Eating of the Soul," *Representations* 48 (Autumn 1994): 99.

3 Ibid.

4 According to the *Oxford English Dictionary, athwart,* which means "across or transversely to the length, direction, or course of anything," "usually, but not necessarily, in an oblique direction," is derived from the Old Norse word *Þvert,* meaning "across" or "transverse." "The word *queer* itself means *across*: it comes from the Indo-European root *twerkw,* which also yields the German *quer* (transverse), Latin *toquere* (to twist), English *athwart.*" See also Eve Kosofsky Sedgwick, *Tendencies* (Durham, N.C.: Duke University Press, 1993), xii.

5 Michel Foucault, *The History of Sexuality, Volume 1: An Introduction,* trans. Robert Hurley (New York: Vintage Books, 1990), 152.

6 My account of how readers fill in unseen early modern sex is based in this central contention of Wolfgang Iser's reader-response theory; see "Interaction between Text and Reader," in *Prospecting: From Reader Response to Literary Anthropology* (Baltimore: The Johns Hopkins University Press, 1989), 31–41; *The Act of Reading: A Theory of Aesthetic Response* (Baltimore: The Johns Hopkins University Press, 1978); and "The Reading Process: A Phenomenological Approach," *New Literary History* 3, no. 2 (1972): 279–99.

7 This idea originates in a Lacanian notion of erotic desire as something that cannot be directly expressed in language. Leo Bersani further elaborates on the solipsistic quality of subjective sexual experience in his queer and deconstructive reading of psychoanalytic theories of sexual development, chiefly his deprivileging of the partner relation and reclamation of the queer potential of primal, antirelational narcissism in "Is the Rectum a Grave?" in *AIDS: Cultural Analysis/Cultural Activism,* ed. Douglas Crimp, 197–222 (Cambridge, Mass.: MIT Press, 1988).

8 Eve Kosofsky Sedgwick, *Epistemology of the Closet* (Berkeley: University of California Press, 1990), 25–26.

9 Theorists offering queer critiques of this privileged fantasy of a perfectly disinterested and Cartesian critical subject include Carla Freccero, who invokes "identification and one of its common effects, anachronism, as two intimately related and hallowed temporal processes that make up—like and along with desire—queer time." See Freccero, *Queer/Early/Modern* (Durham, N.C.: Duke University Press, 2006), 5. See also Freccero, "Queer Times," *South Atlantic Quarterly* 106, no. 3 (2007): 485–94; Carolyn Dinshaw, *Getting Medieval: Sexualities and Communities, Pre- and Post-Modern* (Durham, N.C.: Duke University Press, 1999); and Louise

Fradenburg and Carla Freccero, eds., *Premodern Sexualities* (New York: Routledge, 1996).

10 David Scott Kastan expresses the historicist longing for history to function "as some apotropaic fetish to ward off our narcissism, or at least to prevent the premature imposition of present-day interests and values." See Kastan, *Shakespeare after Theory* (New York: Routledge, 1999), 12. He says this by way of differentiating his historical practice from New Historicism, however, which he accuses of "exactly the narcissism that history should counter" (13).

11 Valerie Traub, *The Renaissance of Lesbianism in Early Modern England* (Cambridge: Cambridge University Press, 2002), 11.

12 Ibid., 21; emphasis original. Traub goes on to emphasize eroticism's historical dependency on other areas of analysis: "preeminently a form of negotiation between desire and the gendered body, eroticism also informs, and is informed by race, age, status hierarchies, and nationality. Like a kaleidoscope, it accrues different meanings with each shift in the angle of vision" (21–22).

13 See Madhavi Menon, *Unhistorical Shakespeare: Queer Theory in Shakespearean Literature and Film* (New York: Palgrave Macmillan, 2008); Jonathan Goldberg and Madhavi Menon, "Queering History," *PMLA* 120, no. 5. (2005): 1608–17; and note 8.

14 By "readerly," I mean not only the reading that literary scholars, students, and teachers do but also the "reading" that an audience member performs of a performance. In performance, however, directors' and actors' choices in staging take on a decisive role in inviting an audience to recognize possible sex or in effacing that possibility (except, of course, for those audience members who will think of it on their own).

15 This is the stage direction in the Second Quarto, commonly used as a copytext for modern editions; see William Shakespeare, *The most excellent and lamentable tragedie, of Romeo and Iuliet* (London, 1599), H2v. The First Quarto has "*Enter Romeo and Juliet at the window*"; see *An excellent conceited tragedie of Romeo and Iulie*t ([London: Printed by John Danter (and Edward Allde?)], 1597), G3r.

16 Text citations from *Romeo and Juliet* are from *The Pelican Shakespeare,* ed. Peter Holland (New York: Penguin Books, 2000).

17 In *Wanton Words: Rhetoric and Sexuality in English Renaissance Drama* (Toronto, Ont.: University of Toronto Press, 2004), Madhavi Menon argues that this act of invisible sex, which is "actively represented in the form

of dramatic repression," has the rhetorical function of a metalepsis—a figural link between two terms, where the link must obscure itself, rendering its rhetorical function invisible—between Romeo and Juliet's love and their never-to-be-lived marriage (77). Menon locates the tragedy of the play in this aubade's symmetrical indeterminacy, where, she says, sex metaleptically fails to function as performative proof to the world of their legal marital bond. Her comparison of this absent sex act with the patriarchal spectacle of displaying sheets bloodied with hymenal blood the morning after a wedding is a reminder of "how insignificant sex can be"—and, for my purposes, is also a reminder of how utterly dependent sex is on figuration, on the constraints of aesthetic representation, and on the merciless social order around which it orbits, for any discursive existence at all.

18 Jonathan Goldberg has touched on the ways in which the iconic heterosexual couple is instrumentalized within a complex of social—and specifically *homosocial*—ends, and objected to the stridently heterosexualizing history of this scene's reception, in "*Romeo and Juliet*'s Open R's," in *Queering the Renaissance,* ed. Jonathan Goldberg, 218–35 (Durham, N.C.: Duke University Press, 1994). Goldberg's interest is less in the specificity of the imagined invisible sex, however, than in queering the social and gendered meanings of the play by making Romeo and Juliet's pairing "available for forbidden desires that really do call patriarchal arrangements into question" (227).

19 Not only still invisible, in fact, but still—at the cinematic as well as the textual level—illicit: Zeffirelli had to circumvent legal restrictions to show Olivia Hussey's breasts, and, the apocryphal story goes, she was legally barred from watching the premier of the film because it included a nude shot of herself. Hussey appears neither to confirm nor deny the rumor in an interview with *Groucho Reviews* on January 10, 2008 (http://www.grouchoreviews.com/interviews/229).

20 Citations from *The Changeling* are from *The Revels Student Edition,* ed. N. W. Bawcutt (Manchester, U.K.: Manchester University Press, 1998).

21 This act is also a reversal of the normative masculine social order, enabled by De Flores's sneaky manipulation of its homosocial affective structures: a nobleman is charmed, invited, disarmed, fooled, flattered, distracted, surprised, penetrated, silenced, killed, robbed, and emasculated by a servant of his host (at the behest of the woman offered to him in marriage).

22 Citations from *The Roaring Girl* are from *The Revels Plays Edition,* ed. Paul Mulholland (Manchester, U.K.: Manchester University Press, 1999).

23 Experiential evidence for this claim is easy enough to come by. Watch a reasonably physical, non-Bowdlerized production of a Shakespeare play with a diverse group of attendees (including people unlikely to read this book). After the play, share with the group the least heteronormative erotic dynamic (homosexuality, an orgy, incest, sexual torture) that you *legitimately*—no cheating—saw convincingly suggested in the production. Every time I have this experience, I am amazed anew at the determinative force of sexual identification—and I mean not identity but identifiability, flexibility, or openness to identificatory hailing—on the faculties of perception.

24 Ironically, it is the heterosexual rape–stabbing that is concealed from view in a closet, while the homosexual rape–stabbing in the castle hall takes place onstage, in at least partial view of the audience. This discrepancy is consistent with the all-male transvestite theater's taboo on staging explicit heterosexual erotic contact and the comparative social acceptability of suggesting—although still not staging—male–male buggery.

25 N. W. Bawcutt, introduction to *The Changeling,* 19.

26 See Judith Haber, "'I(t) Could Not Choose but Follow': Erotic Logic in *The Changeling,*" *Representations* 81 (Winter 2003): 79–98, and Michael Neill, "'Hidden Malady': Death, Discovery, and Indistinction in *The Changeling,*" in *Issues of Death: Mortality and Identity in English Renaissance Tragedy* (Oxford: Clarendon Press, 1997), 168–200.

27 Celia R. Daileader, "Back Door Sex: Renaissance Gynosodomy, Aretino, and the Exotic," in *Straight Writ Queer: Non-normative Expressions of Heterosexuality in Literature,* ed. Richard Fantina, 25–45 (Jefferson, N.C.: McFarland, 2006).

28 In Gramsci's sense of the term, a culturally hegemonic "common sense" without single cause or origin—a consensus-effect, so to speak, which is nonetheless always already multiple and potentially fluid. See *Selections from the Prison Notebooks of Antonio Gramsci,* ed. and trans. Q. Hoare and G. Nowell Smith (London: Lawrence and Wishart, 1971).

29 See, chiefly, David Halperin, *How to Do the History of Homosexuality* (Chicago: University of Chicago Press, 2002), and Alan Bray, *Homosexuality in Renaissance England* (New York: Columbia University Press, 1995).

30 José Esteban Muñoz, *Cruising Utopia: The Then and There of Queer Futurity* (New York: New York University Press, 2009), 65.

2

Death and Theory: Or, the Problem of Counterfactual Sex

KATHRYN SCHWARZ

The bond between sex and death is so familiar as to offer a chilly sort of comfort. Through figural reciprocity, each might palliate the graver dangers of the other: death is an auxesis that overstates the dissolution of sex; sex is a meiosis that undermines the finality of death. But these abstract mitigations are not secure, and a tic of notional literalism—as in Helena's "I'll follow thee and make a heaven of hell, / To die upon the hand I love so well" (2.1.243–44)—fuses linguistic convention to bodily risk.[1] The slippage between emblematic and corporeal modes is less an accident than a drive. It informs a scheme, rooted in preoccupations with chastity, in which the demand for figures that signify fixed sexual states generates the need for persons who are dead. *The Lawes Resolutions of Womens Rights* describes the ingrained violence that connects those who would destroy virtue to those who would protect it:

> But to what purpose is it for women to make vowes, when men have so many millions of wayes to make them break them? And when sweet words, faire promises, tempting, flattering, swearing, lying will not serve to beguile the poore soule: then with rough handling, violence, and plaine strength of armes, they are, or have beene heretofore, rather made prisoners to lusts theeves, than wives and companions to faithfull honest lovers.[2]

At the risk of a certain cynicism, I would note that this indignant account of brutality appears in the service of a social contract, which disciplines persons to protect shared meanings. Such contracts have an instrumental brutality of their own, and in this sense, the conflict might be more aptly populated by those who seek to demonstrate something about virtue and those who, obstinately if not intentionally, withhold the grounds of proof. Important scholarship has traced the incoherence of chastising ideologies; as a social requisite that impersonates a physical fact, chastity raises the question of whether sexual virtue can either derive from or refer to an embodied condition.[3] The repercussions extend beyond the idea that sex can elude knowledge, to foreclose a *way* of knowing. In his disquisition on virginity, Juan Luis Vives writes,

> As for a woman hathe no charge to se to, but hir honestee and chastitee. . . . Wherfore theyr wyckednesse is the more cursed and detestable, that go about to perisshe that one treasure of women: as though a man had but one eye, and an other wolde go about to put it out.[4]

This analogy to an act of abuse that leaves clear signs implicates a wider field of displacements, which shift the inaccessible distinction between virtue and its absence to the legible difference between bodies that do damage and those to which damage is done.

The virginal body is one of early modernity's great escape artists, receding ever farther from proof as the technologies of verification advance.[5] Dissection fires a debate about the significance and even the existence of the hymen; chastity tests inspire tales about the ease of faking them.[6] Kathleen Coyne Kelly offers a provocative summary of the problem when she describes virginity as "an abstract idea residing in an anatomical metonym."[7] A metonymic interrelation between the local and the conceptual takes one part for a whole constellation of thoughts and deeds, but metonymy can no more be reduced to synecdoche than an engine can be reduced to a carburetor. Metonymic figuration conjoins incongruent parts; as Dudley Fenner writes,

> It is double,
> • When the cause is put for the thing caused, and contrariwise.
> • When the thing to which any thing is adjoyned, is put for the thing adjoyned, and contrariwise.[8]

John Barton comments emphatically on the mystifying effect of doubleness: "whereas I have made Metonymie twofold, Perfect and Elliptick, I say boldly, that nothing in all Rhetorick doth more puzzle scholars, then not being made acquainted with this difference of Metonymicall examples."[9] In applying this figure to virginity, Kelly encapsulates the sense in which both operations of metonymy—substitution and association—create substantial problems for any system of reference. Influenced by their classical predecessors, such rhetorical theorists as George Puttenham and Richard Sherry offer illustrations of "*Metonimia,* or the Misnamer" that drastically confuse relationships among internal and external, object and agent: "When the place, or that that conteineth, is put for the thyng that is in it"; "When that that is conteyned is put for that that doth conteine"; "When the doer is put for that that is done"; "When that is done is put for the doer."[10] And the fickle logic of contiguity forms attachments only to discard them, leading Jacques Lacan to define metonymy as "being caught in the rails—eternally stretching forth towards the *desire for something else.*"[11] As an "anatomical metonym," then, virginity makes inner truths interchangeable with public performances, confounds the actor with the target of action, and threatens to escape along an illimitable progression of desire.[12] The struggle to pin down an inalienable truth seems lost before it has begun.

Violence forces sex to accrue meaning by abstracting the body from its potential vicissitudes, stopping it cold in a particular state. Lauren Berlant theorizes such reifications in her account of dead citizenship, which she links to dead metaphors: "A metaphor is dead when, by repetition, the unlikeness risked in the analogy the metaphor makes becomes so conventionalized as to no longer seem figural, no longer open to history." This moribund reduction, she argues, shapes idealized forms of social viability: "In the fantasy world of national culture, citizens aspire to dead identities—constitutional personhood in its public-sphere abstraction and supra-historicity, reproductive heterosexuality in the zone of privacy. Identities not live, or in play, but dead, frozen, fixed, or at rest."[13] Throughout this chapter, I will suggest that early modern subjects aspire to the dead identities of others and derive guarantors of "citizenship"—that meeting point of self-possession and assimilation—from bodies on which those precious shared meanings can be etched. Embodiment becomes not an isolation of unreadable data but a focal point for communal belief, a fleshly supplement to the social artifact of reputation. Mediated through that intangible commodity, sex migrates toward something we might recognize as sexuality, with the implications of circulation and annexation attendant on that term. Yet as violence collapses the sexual and the social, it conjures certainties it cannot secure. The process through which a collision of bodies becomes a revision of names begs more questions than it answers: what acts precipitate or substantiate judgment, in what register do they occur, and in what sense does their connection to social edicts define them as sexual acts or fix their agents and objects in some relation to sexual identities? Nor is flesh, however frozen, damaged, or dead, so easily transformed into currency. The arrested body has its own stubborn capacities, which project histories and futurities ungoverned by exigent demands.[14] A link between social and sexual transactions informs the narratives I take up, but if that link produces social or sexual subjects, it does so through engagements that breach rhetorical codes and explode corporeal limits in simultaneously ruthless and speculative ways.

Sovereignty, Authorization

I focus this discussion on stories, at once exemplary and eccentric, that tell awkward truths about the relationship between experience and belief. These stories map the processes that transform intractable questions into contracts of faith and that publish the dubious equation of answer and corpse. They narrate the double move of reputation, which shelters the vagaries of personhood under the aegis of common sense but binds social subjects to their sacrificial dead. I follow these stories as they expose the knot of performance, interpretation, violence, and doubt that masquerades as iconic virtue, and as they link that mythic production to the strategies of everyday life. But I begin with a Shakespearean prologue and preface it in turn with a story of my own—slight, comic, ephemeral, yet theoretically dense in its distillation of rhetorical conjuring acts. When a friend of mine first taught Shakespeare, her students asked how Renaissance history plays got the horses onstage. Beset by this sudden historicism, she gestured somewhat wildly and declaimed, "Yonder is my horse!"

She was, of course, quite right. "O for a Muse of fire, that would ascend / The brightest heaven of invention! / A kingdom for a stage, princes to act, / And monarchs to behold the swelling scene!" the Chorus of *Henry V* famously begins, only to abandon this abstract meditation to get the horses onstage (1.1.1–4). "Think, when we talk of horses, that you see them / Printing their proud hoofs i' th' receiving earth; / For 'tis your thoughts that now must deck our kings" (1.1.26–28). In the course of this prologue, one mode of invocation displaces another: the idealism that calls on full presence yields to the pragmatism of participatory illusion. The wistful "if we could transform a stage into a kingdom" imagines a world of self-sufficient and self-evident materiality; the propositonal "if you would transform what we say into what you know" offers a world in which conviction produces rather than follows from evidence, and in which rhetorical formulations, through a shared act of will, supersede ocular proof. Summoned as that which will already have been recalled, an agreed-on past forecasts a desired future, which reciprocal acquiescence might instantiate as the next phase of actuality. Horses are shorthand for an epistemological contract.

What do horses have to do with sex? At the start of an essay which has at most an asymptotic relation to historicism, I would say that these horses I have brought so oddly to the fore are figural bodies that perform vital functions without staking any nontransactional claim on truth. And I would follow this with the assertion that sex, with its power to make and unmake social subjects, is neither more nor less present in early modern culture than horses are on the early modern stage. Both materialize acts of faith, which shape rather than sever ties to the real. *Henry V*'s prologue iterates the circumstances under which qualitative identities attach to bodies, circumstances defined less by correspondence than by concurrence. In her account of consent theory, Elaine Scarry writes, "The body is, then, the thing protected. But the body is also the lever across which sovereignty is gained, authorization achieved."[15] The Chorus evokes a rather different connection between embodiment and consent, a set of practices through which the disposable bodies of others confer an aggregate sense of self. History proceeds through a motivated calculus that not only counts the dead but accounts for them, using their disconnection from the living to construct relational criteria of worth: value is confirmed in the gap between persons who perish and subjects who endure. To accept the Chorus's invitation is to trade knowledge for power; as we witness spectacular violence through an already-focused lens, we use the dead to decide what lives are worth living, not to "them" but to a consensually manufactured "us."

In such a way, sovereignty is gained, authorization achieved. When Bruce Smith interrogates the constancy of pronouns in Shakespeare's *Sonnets,* he concludes with a trenchant caution: "If the 'I' in these poems is so difficult to locate, then how wary you and I—or you, I, and *they*—should be in presuming to say 'we.'"[16] The seduction of death lies in its assurance that you and I need not be wary of "we" at all. "We" is the pronoun of survivors. Whether it articulates a royal prerogative ("France being ours, we'll bend it to our awe" [*Henry V,* 1.2.224]) or a collective one ("We few, we happy few, we band of brothers" [4.3.60]), its sovereign authority is preserved by the rights and obligations of social contract: by patrilineal inheritance, heroic renown, exemplary legend, or poetic tribute, forms of immortality conferred by a common investment in reputation. Reputation creates a system in which durable value reflects consensus, a system that dispenses with bodies to safeguard names. Anyone not so protected is no longer one of "us," and self-loss is always someone else's problem. History plays usefully condense the idea that death might fix a particular condition of worth; whether necrophilic or necrophobic, history digests its victims in the service of its authors. "While both cannibalism and haunting are relationships to the past, to ancestors, and to the future, to descendants, they are fundamentally different," Carla Freccero writes. "Cannibalism is an act of erotic aggression, however ambivalent, that effaces alterity."[17] Alterity disappears when others cease to matter, and death is an evaluative tool that exploits the divide between bodies and subjects, between disposable persons and the social accommodations by and for which those persons are consumed. This follows the familiar pattern of abjection, which consolidates the center by exacting its price from the margins; it echoes the still more familiar maxim that history is written by the victors.

But history plays also reveal that death stands in for the insufficiencies of sex. These plays stage massacres to confirm the right of succession and thereby undercut the patrilineal axiom on which they rely: sex makes history, which means only that history derives a form of stability from summative opinions about the terms on which bodies are made, named, and vested with significance.[18] When those bodies are routinely exposed to violent revisions—from sovereign to usurper, from loyalist to rebel, from heir to bastard, from ally to traitor—ties of blood are submerged in the gore. The veracity of that "muse of fire" cedes place to verisimilitude, and an interested assent animates a just continuity. Survival imparts legitimacy through its differential relation to loss, yet it also draws attention to the other, equally plausible lines along which the narrative might progress. The comparative logic of triumph means that no tenure can be unqualified or entirely free of its attendant ghosts. If, as Freccero contends, "all movements take up the dead and carry them into battle like a banner," this baggage has the weight of other stories that might have been.[19] As reputation buries mutable persons in the foundations of social contract, it discloses the limits of that contract: "we" cannot know but can only agree, and those agreements hover above bodies that absorb and transmit unstable, enigmatic meanings. Death yields not facts but counterfactuals, conditional trajectories structured by a speculative "what if" and glossed, in the *Oxford English Dictionary,* by two provocative examples: "counter-factuals constitute an irreducible form of statement" and "the analysis of counterfactuals should parallel that of 'fugitive propositions.'"[20] Those opaque and crucial terms, "irreducible form of statement" and "fugitive proposition," provide a terse vocabulary for the sacrificial body—"incapable of being resolved into elements, or of being brought under any recognized law or principle"—which cannot be confined to strictly instrumental use.[21]

The idea that reputation, as a ratified form of social knowledge, can be anchored by persons who are not agents bears within it an awareness that the anchor may not hold. Attempts to fix a particular condition of worth collide with the polyvalence of that counterfactual "what if." The survivor's last word asserts that the dead lend a monologic ascendancy to those who rewrite them, but as Michel de Certeau notes, such dominion is always under siege: "Any autonomous order is founded upon what it eliminates; it produces a 'residue' condemned to be forgotten. But what was excluded re-infiltrates the place of its origin."[22] The critical point for my purpose is that we—"we"—cannot know what language the unforgotten will speak. Jonathan Goldberg invokes "the multiples of history" as he disjoins historical eventualities from a providential heterosexuality: "Any number of voices, now, could find themselves in the open space of implicit rejoinder."[23] A rejoinder—in legal terms, "a defendant's answer to a claimant's reply"—in more general contexts, "an answer to a reply"—proliferates contentions around an original premise that has been submerged beneath layers of nonidentical response.[24] It counters that which is already at odds and speaks to the process through which counterfactuals draw dominant lines into conditional webs. This process, with its recalcitrant plurality, absorbs the reified certainties of sex and transmutes them into insubstantial strands of retrojection and prolepsis. While I would hesitate to identify a source of this phenomenon, I suggest that it finds one dense and powerful myth of origin in the story of Lucretia.[25]

Classical accounts of Lucretia record a violence that forfeits body to name. Livy pinpoints the shift within Tarquin's threat: "When he found her obdurate and not to be moved even by fear of death, he went farther and threatened her with disgrace."[26] A simile that slips toward equation stresses the heft of dishonor—"At this dreadful prospect her resolute modesty was overcome, as if with force"—and implies that Lucretia's projected fate leaves her with neither choice nor guilt. When her audience arrives, she herself takes this line: "Yet my body only has been violated; my heart is guiltless, as death shall be my witness." Death bears witness to innocence—but what knowledge can it impart? Verification has a peculiar irrelevance, for Livy tells us that Lucretia's interlocutors accept her innocence as absolute: "They tell her it is the mind that sins, not the body; and that where purpose has been wanting there is no guilt." Lucretia did not intend to transgress; by what logic, then, and for whose purpose, does she intend her death? Still more obscurely, death reanimates the specter of fault, but fault floats free of cause. From Ovid: "Her husband and her sire pardoned the deed enforced. She said, 'The pardon that you give, I do refuse myself.'"[27] From Livy: "for my own part, though I acquit myself of the sin, I do not absolve myself from punishment; nor in time to come shall ever unchaste woman live through the example of Lucretia." Such claims make corporeal meanings indecipherable. Does she refuse pardon because it is unmerited or because it is misdirected? What correlation, if any, does she impose between sin and punishment?

If living would permit a corrupt exemplarity, does dying secure a chastised one? Lucretia's death stands in both a belated and an anticipatory relationship to reputation—the reputation she has preserved by choosing life, the reputation she will safeguard by choosing death—which excises the moment of embodiment, even as that moment provides the evidence on which reputation stakes its claims. According to Ovid, an other-directed imperative shapes not only the idea of self-sacrifice but the act: "Without delay, she stabbed her breast with the steel she had hidden, and weltering in her blood fell at her father's feet. Even then in dying she took care to sink down decently: that was her thought even as she fell." What can we possibly know about this body, overlaid with the protocols of decorum as it bleeds on the floor?

Augustine cannot leave the problem alone. He begins his chapter on Lucretia with a clear premise: "We maintain that when a woman is violated while her soul admits no consent to the iniquity, but remains inviolably chaste, the sin is not hers, but his who violates her."[28] After a potted history of Lucretia's travails, he asks, "What shall we call her? An adulteress, or chaste?" only to add, "There is no question which she was." Yet the chapter is a litany of questions, directed less to the issue of innocence (although that has its place) than to the linked production of justice and iconicity. "But how is it, that she who was no partner to the crime bears the heavier punishment of the two?" he demands, and he confronts his reader with a conundrum: "This crime was committed by Lucretia; that Lucretia so celebrated and lauded slew the innocent, chaste, outraged Lucretia. Pronounce sentence." The command provokes a further question—"Or perhaps she is not there, because she slew herself conscious of guilt, not of innocence?"—and another challenge:

> But this case of Lucretia is in such a dilemma, that if you extenuate the homicide, you confirm the adultery: if you acquit her of adultery, you make the charge of homicide heavier; and there is no way out of the dilemma, when one asks, If she was adulterous, why praise her? if chaste, why slay her?

Augustine promises to demonstrate both the logical fallacy and the moral frailty of suicide. But his argument demonstrates something else as well: it excavates the irreducible bodily statement that underlies the edifice of name. The scene in which a celebrated Lucretia slays a chaste Lucretia might recapitulate the cannibalistic drive of history, or it might forge prophylactic armor against the caprice of opinion, or it might—and, I think, it does—enact the paradox of reputation. Built on bodies it cannot use and cannot afford to need, character is a finished product that eclipses its raw materials, but that evocative, constitutive matter is shrouded rather than erased. In his analysis of the "citizen as social corpse," Russ Castronovo writes,

> Such a postpolitical category takes reactive shape against an alarming recognition that social corpses, ghosts, passive citizens, and other moribund bodies can also exert an excessively vibrant and ungovernable materiality that resists spiritualization or stasis. The corpse may be dead, but it is nonetheless a body, one that recalls a life of social and political engagement.[29]

Augustine's last, oddly anticlimactic claim can only stifle this resurgent individuation under the weight of collective belief: "It is enough that in the instance of this noble Roman matron it was said in her praise, 'There were two, but the adultery was the crime of only one.' For Lucretia was confidently believed to be superior to the contamination of any consenting thought to the adultery." If reputation appears fully vested in a public voice—"it was said"—that common ground is enough, and though "enough" may seem a hollow term, it echoes with the righteous partiality of social necessity.

Lucretia's reputation survives in many forms: as personal choice and public service, as chastity and empire, as the altar of sacrifice and the touchstone of consent. It survives precisely because her body does not, because corporeal dissolution leaves an empty space within the carapace of public certainties. Yet the idea of that body retains vitality, an intricate, obscure power of touch that might collapse the structures built in its name. Shakespeare reifies its perilous ambiguity in two extraordinary lines—"Some of her blood still pure and red remain'd, / And some look'd black, and that false Tarquin stain'd" (1742–43)—but it may be Augustine's notorious waffle on violence and consent that cleaves to the heart of the problem. "She herself alone knows her reason," he writes, and this returns us to the question of what anyone can know of a body that speaks from the mystified space between chaste life and chastising death. Lucretia mobilizes the counterfactual fission that resists reduction to one. When she refers, in Shakespeare's poem, to "my good name, that senseless reputation" (820), her cross-coupled phrases project a future in which renown evacuates self-possession, in which an "I" who might claim to know has vanished among the "we" who are moved to conjure, in which the name that bears too much meaning can hold no single sense. Every attempt to fix reputation in perpetuity accelerates its fluctuations across time. And time is itself a false comfort, its suspect distinctions between history and futurity recalling Theseus's smug fallacy: "Never excuse; for when the players are all dead, there need none to be blam'd" (*A Midsummer Night's Dream,* 5.1.356–57).[30] When the players are all dead, praise and blame become infinitely fungible in a limitless expansion of judgment's synchronic moment. Reputation endlessly summons and dislocates the persons it puts to use, exploiting changeable relations among bodies, occasions, and effects. In his extraordinary study of matter and temporality, Jonathan Gil Harris poses a series of questions about itinerant objects:

> How might things chafe against the sovereignty of the moment-state? What do we do with things that cross temporal borders—things that are illegal immigrants, double agents, or holders of multiple passports? How might such border crossings change our understanding of temporality? What, in short, is the time of the thing?[31]

Where persons become things in the service of names, I would add questions of my own: what do we witness, what do we recognize, what do we choose to ratify (the "we" who preserve ourselves by the sanctity of our agreement) from the copia of here and now?

Senseless Reputation

"Lucretia" is an encrypted reputation, both code and tomb, which bears within it not the transparency of virtue but the proximities of corpse and sign, idiosyncrasy and community, enigma and guarantee. The stakes of these convergences appear clearly in early modern texts that represent chastity as a fulcrum for the shifting weight of bodily truths. Here I consider three narratives that revolve around the impasse of motivated belief.[32] Each emphasizes the urgency of that problem when the author suspends his inventory of iconic figures and turns instead to a story of quotidian experience. Each of these stories, as it entangles the risks of social performance with the requisites of social survival, at once highlights and mystifies the evidentiary value of death.

In his encyclopedic *Gynaikeion,* in the book "Of Women Incestuous, Adulteresses, and such as have come by strange deaths," Thomas Heywood breaks off his catalog of familiar exempla—classical and biblical, historical and mythological—to quote "seaven short questions asked of the seaven wise men of Greece, and by them as briefely answered."[33] Two of the questions concern chastity and reputation: "*Womans chiefe beautie what? Chast life is such. / Who's chast? She onely whom no fame dares tuch*" (193).[34] Heywood comments, "They that can containe themselves within these few prescriptions, may undoubtedly store up a good name to themselves, and honour to their posteritie," and illustrates the point with "a moderne Historie lately happening, and in mine owne knowledge" (193). An old man, "as well growne in reputation, as yeares," marries a beautiful young woman; when they have no children, he befriends a young man who will inherit part of his property. Heir and wife develop "an honest, yet a kind of suspected familiaritie," and because honesty matters less than suspicion, the friendship "grew to a calumnie, till passing from one man to another, it arived at length to the eares of the young mans father, who sorted opportunitie to talke with his sonne, demaunding of him how that fire was kindled from whence this smoke grew" (193). Rumor molds the voice that grants or withholds good names, and the young man agrees to cease his visits. Heywood posits an opposition between fact and opinion, yet reveals that supposed guilt has a basis in conditional betrayal: the young man and woman have vowed to marry if the old man dies. It may well be unfair to call this infidelity, and Heywood remains silent about the relative import of a counterfactual future and an experiential present. He does, however, declare that other futures have been foreclosed: "as shee had bound her selfe by one oath, she imposed upon him another, namely, that till that time of her widdowhood, he should neither associate him privately, converse nor contract matrimonie with any woman whatsoever" (194). The story suspends readers among judgments, poising a public misapprehension of now against a private expectation of then, an unconditional verdict based on falsehood against a provisional duplicity grounded in intent.

We can imagine various paths: the lovers—conditional to themselves, conjectural to others—might anticipate events by committing adultery, or alter circumstances by committing murder, or turn theory into practice by running away. Heywood instead holds his characters between the declarative and the subjunctive. The young man talks with a chambermaid, who tells him his beloved "onely bore him faire outwardly and in shew, when another injoyed both her heart and body inwarldly [*sic*] and in act, and that upon her owne knowledge" (194). As another authority enters the fray, the young man pins his faith to manifest truths: "he began againe to itterate and call to mind, with what an outward integritie shee had still borne her selfe towards him, and with a puritie by no womans art to be dissembled" (194). "Outward integrity" and "suspected familiaritie"—those touches of fame the wise men condemn—are the only reference points. Where reputation is communal property, formed by the transactional dynamics of assessment and persuasion, individuated interiority becomes food for general consumption.[35] This becomes still clearer when the young man's patron questions him about his absence:

> Hee answered, that notwithstanding his owne innocence, and his wives approoved Temperance, yet bad tongues had beene busie to their reproach, measuring them by their owne corrupt intents, and therefore to avoyde all imputation whatsoever, his study was by taking away the cause to prevent the effect: his reason was approoved, and the old man satisfied concerning both their integrities. (195)

The connotation of "approved" shifts in this brief passage, from "verified" to "accepted," and that second meaning trumps the first.

In a further turn, the suspected adulterer becomes a witness to the deed he has himself committed in a projected, chastised future: he eavesdrops on his beloved and the man the chambermaid has accused, "where hee might evidently understand more than protestations passe betwixt them, namely the mechall sinne it selfe" (195).[36] The situation demands both revenge and proof: "hee remembred him of his sword in his chamber, whether hee went instantly with intent to returne, and breaking open the doore to transpierce them both in the adulterate act" (195). Transpierced, the illicit lovers would supply apotropaic evidence, caught forever, if not for good, in a fusion of sex and death that confines betrayal to bodies that cannot dispute the charge. But the young man is trapped in double vision: "withall remembring her beautie, their often meetings, kisses, and imbraces; his heart became too tender to destroy that goodly frame, in which nature had shewed her best of art, though the divell his worst of envy" (195–96). Strangely, he considers himself bound by his oath:

> beeing not onely debarred from marriage, but as it were banished from the societie of women; that shee onely reserved him as a stale or shadow, whilest another carryed away the substance; that shee kept her selfe to bee his wife, and anothers whore; and that from all these no safe evasion could bee devised to come off towards her like a gentleman. (196)

The endurance of contractual obligation seems inexplicable, as if when a tree fell in the forest, the person who heard it could neither report the phenomenon nor get out of the way. The young man imagines marriage as a social frame disconnected from sexual exclusivity, within which children can be produced with, but not by, a legal father who will transmit his property and his name. The social pact that defines a gentleman disengages from the sexual guarantee that builds a patriline. Common sense notwithstanding, this position is neither as antisocial nor as absurd as it might appear; in fact, the end of the story suggests that "common sense" may be exactly what is at stake.

When the young man decides to leave, the woman weeps, "beseeching him to have a care of his safetie, but especially of his vow and promise; all which proceeded from such a counterfeit passion, as hee almost began to question, what in his owne notion hee knew to bee infallible" (196). This moment, with its simultaneous certainty and doubt, sums up the problem of the body as data. Socially appropriate performance does not simply cover for sexually improper acts; two layers of impersonation weave a fabric that individual judgment fails to unstitch. The young man resolves his dilemma with a text and a death:

> But in stead of reply hee delivered her a letter . . . wherin was layd open every passage concerning her lust, what hee himselfe personally had heard and knowne, the place where, the time when, the very words whispered, with every undeniable circumstance, and these exprest with such passionate efficacie, in which hee laboured to make knowne his injuries, and her treacheries (the sole occasions of his voluntarie exile;) all these (I say) were so feelingly set downe, that they strooke her to the heart, insomuch that shee fell into a present frenzie, and dispairingly soone after dyed. (196)

Written and delivered, read and recognized, passionate efficacy crafts an artifact that kills. "The sender, we tell you, receives from the receiver his own message in reverse form," Jacques Lacan writes in his seminar on "The Purloined Letter," and he adds his famous conclusion: "a letter always arrives at its destination."[37] While this particular communiqué seems certified by its effect, I am more interested in the first point: in what sense does the sender receive his message back again "in reverse form"? I think we must take reversal to mean something more complex than opposition; the letter, in Heywood's story, answers the need to shift from proof to accord. The woman's adultery is a concealed act; her death is a spectacle, which makes her character available to those who observe. A private claim to know, subject to the variables of motive, error, and doubt, becomes a public validation of opinion—becomes, in short, common sense. I lay such stress on this story in part because its investment in plot conspicuously exceeds the requirements of exemplarity. Peter Brooks, who links the desire for plot to the death drive, writes, "All narrative may be in essence obituary in that . . . the retrospective knowledge that it seeks, the knowledge that comes after, stands on the far side of the end, in human terms on the far side of death."[38] In the morality tales of social self-preservation, "the knowledge that comes after" emerges on the far side of someone else's death and consolidates the "we" who survive to know. Obituary, like the entombment described by de Certeau, reifies a privilege that allows the living to make what they will of the dead.

In this case, they make something peculiar. The ostensible purpose of discovering an adulterous wife, of burying her ambiguous body beneath the clear-cut verdicts of social condemnation, is to broadcast the restored integrity of bloodlines. Heinrich Bullinger draws on this truism when he indicts adultery as a threat to inheritance and concludes with a damning nod to history: "This dyd the auncient and noble men of olde, pondre and consydre, and therfore ryghteously and of just occasyons appoynted they the punyshment of death for aduouterers."[39] Chastisement is not meant for errant women. It is a luxury reserved for those who retain social value, as the spectacular display of a dead adulteress consolidates a unit that identifies its constituents through their decontaminated, reintegrated links to one another. In the clichés of well-ordered continuity, a credible patriline funnels connections between men through sanitized women and bases homosocial parthenogenesis on female bodies rendered at once fecund and sterile. But if Heywood's tale concludes in triumph, it is not this triumph. When the young man hears of the woman's death, "hee understood himselfe to be quite released of all his intricate oathes and promises: whose noble disposition the old gentleman understanding, instated him in a great part of his land, which he injoyes to this day" (196). Rather than restore two men to the prospect of paternal certainty, the excision of adultery translates birthright into a contract of opinion. The old man perceives the young man's virtue; the young man receives the old man's land. Inheritance is mediated through a woman, but not through her capacity to produce children who exhibit their correspondence to the patronymic they assume. Instead, property passes across the calcified reputation of a body rendered dead because it answers, in the negative, an always debatable question of guarantee. With a perversity that exposes the groundwork of connection—groundwork laid not in flesh but in construal—the obviousness of negation substitutes for the enigma of knowledge and more efficiently supports a system of bonds. Testator and inheritor share not blood but belief in the relative value of the woman who dies and the men who outlive her. Here, as for Augustine, common ground must be enough, and the narrator's final words on the young man's fortune endorse its logic as sufficient rather than absolute: "and in my opinion, not altogether undeservedly" (196).

If Heywood's "history" exemplifies anything, it is the recognition that birthright is *always* a contract of opinion; the narrative detaches lineage from proof and records the adequacy of consensus.[40]

Heywood's conclusion models a true-enough answer, a bare sufficiency that conserves belief but not blood through a consensual approximation of death to proof. For a patrilineal culture, this reeks of pyrrhic victory. And if it is difficult to make good sense of a body that is literally dead—if even that silent, motionless, undefended commodity cannot be turned to its proper ends—how much harder might it be to carve out useable things with the more abstract weapon of social erasure? Judith Butler's analysis of melancholic aggression leads to what could be a rhetorical question: "And can the sense of 'triumph' be won precisely through a practice of social differentiation in which one achieves and maintains 'social existence' only by the production and maintenance of those socially dead?"[41] But this is an open question, which leaves space for a paradoxically simultaneous yes and no. Rather than safeguard a narrow space of legitimacy, practices of excision might create porous borders traversed by ambiguous subjects. In his chapter "*Estimation, a Gentlewomans* highest prize," Richard Brathwait declares his intention to build a fence, "to shew you how this *Estimation,* which is your *highest prize,* may be discerned to be *reall*; which is not gathered by the first appearance, but a serious and constant triall" (105).[42] To this end, he surveys a long list of illustrious virgins, many of whom violently avenge threats to their honor. Then, like Heywood, he calls on the here and now, "to draw nearer home, and instance this Maiden-constancy in one of our owne" (126). "I have heard of a notable spirited Girle, within the walls of this City," he begins; the young woman is virtuous, "albeit she frequented places of publike Concourse boldly, discoursed freely, expressed her selfe in all assayes forwardly." Determined to chastise a would-be seducer, she agrees to a clandestine meeting, only to engage him in a duel: "Draw he must, or she will disgrace him; in which combat, instead of a more amorous Conflict, shee disarm'd him, and with a kicke, wish'd him ever after to be more wary how he attempted a Maidens honour" (126). Violence, even in this muted and near-comic form, proves an effective arbiter of reputation, disgracing the debaucher as it elevates his conqueror. The marginal note reads, "An English Amazon."

As if a single stratagem cannot suffice, an anecdote that appears two pages earlier preiterates this efficient discretion. The exemplary prequel also invokes the present place and moment; it participates, too, in the project that differentiates virtue from vice. "One of this ranke have I ofttimes observed tracing the streets of this flourishing City; who, as one weary of her sexe, forbore not to unwoman her selfe, by assuming not onely a *virile* habit, but a *virago's* heart," Brathwait writes, but this mirror image reverses the criteria of value. "Nothing desir'd she more then to give affronts in publike places, which she did with that contempt, as the disgrace she aspers'd on others, was her sole content" (123–24). The catalog of acts—public appearances, uninhibited articulations, belligerent conflicts—leads to a stern judgment:

> Now could these courses any way choose but cause that to be *irreparably lost,* which by any modest woman should be incomparably lov'd? Tell me, were not his spirit armour of proofe, who durst encounter with so couragious an *Amazon?* or enter nuptiall lists with such a feminine *Myrmidon?* Surely, these, as they labour to purchase them opinion of *esteeme,* by their unwomanly expressions of valour, so they eclypse their owne fame, and by these irregular affronts, detract highly from their essentialst honour. Such may gaine them *observance,* but never *esteeme.* (124)

As readers, we confront the same spectacle twice and watch its significance turn around a constant axis. An amazonian woman stalks "our" streets, imposing disgrace on those who threaten her self-worth. Both parables construct a chiastic intimacy between the violation of heterosocial codes and the eruption of heterosocial violence. Yet where the virago squanders her "essentialst honour," the maiden, who is the virago again from an altered line of sight, earns renown. The stories converge as they bind aggression to reputation, but disparate conclusions render the nature of that bond opaque. This is Brathwait's near-simultaneous yes and no: social existence is preserved by a subject's zealous force, which recoils on an identical subject (her avatar? her demon? her twin?) to impose social death. "None can preserve what he loves, by mixing it with the society of that he loathes," Brathwait warns, immediately before he embarks on these doubled and divergent tales. "If you be companions to *Ostridges,* you shall savour of the wildernesse" (122). If, in the small space of two pages, female violence both destroys and confirms virtuous reputation, Brathwait himself seems to have loosed the ostriches among his more domestic birds.[43]

Brathwait notes that lineal history depends on the difference between purity and corruption, the unbridgeable divide between social value and social waste.[44] Yet from his first premise—"Estimation is a good opinion drawne from some probable grounds" (101)—he recurs to the attenuated link between truth and show. He advocates perfect correlation—"Thus by seeming what you are, and *really* expressing what you seeme, you shall purchase that *esteeme* with God and good men, which is *reall*" (117)—yet admits that it may be no defense. "Take heede then, lest publique rumour brand you. Scandall is more apt to disperse what is ill; then Opinion is to retaine what is good" (124). The easy triumphs of perception haunt his indictment of false appearances: whose insight could distinguish between the "vizards and semblances" of the deceivers and the "*inward beauty*" of those who are as they seem, between "*reall Estimation*" and "*Superficiall Esteeme*" (105, 114)? Brathwait, whose discourse on reputation sets out to do just that, admits that the task may be beyond human capability: "I will not say, but the bleered eye of humane reason may bee taken with these; and conceive them *reall,* which are onely *Superficiall*" (116–17). More ominously, he suggests that women themselves may not know the difference: "These that walke in the Clouds, though they deceive others much, yet they deceive themselves most" (106). At one point he seems to throw up his hands and conclude that only divine intervention can sort out the mess: "But the *All-seeing eye* cannot be deceived; hee sees not as man seeth. Neither distance of place, nor resemblance of that Object, whereon his eye is fixt, can cause him to mistake" (117).[45] God will arbitrate difference and assign value, a promise that carries the arc of public judgment to its vanishing point: God, after all, is the ultimate survivor.

My last story, from the 1599 translation of *A Womans Woorth,* still more tightly interweaves public judgment, public action, the precariousness of character, and the slipperiness of proof. This doggedly protofeminist text argues that women, by nature, hold a spiritual ascendancy that men can only beat down by force. The reader is advised to

> looke then on detestable and ungratefull *Theseus,* on *Paris* the lyer and perjurde wretch, on inconstant *Hercules,* and disloyall *Jason,* who all most falselye deceived their friends, after they had triumphed by their meanes and credit, I will not say on their honors: for these men (none woorse that ever were) could not any way wound the happie and laudable reputation, of these their faire fosterers. (fol. 43–43v)[46]

This faith in the transcendence of virtuous reputation falters somewhat in the next lines—"these Ladyes, whose vertues may perhaps bee toucht with some slaunder, but their innocent natures stand free from injurie, and their good cariage from all base suspition"—leaving the reader unsure how to differentiate slander from injury or suspicion. And injury is much on the author's mind; in language that anticipates *The Lawes Resolutions,* he describes the fundamental danger men pose to women:

> Yet let us consider heerewithall, that a woman can have no greater enemy then a man, who is like unto a ravenous Lyon continuallye seeking to devoure new spoyle. Oh sexe abhominable, thou art too much affected to thy selfe, to knowe rightly indeede howe to use women kinde especially in these days. (fol. 43v–44)

The particular degeneracy of "these days" is illustrated by a "Gascoigne Gentleman," who, having failed to beguile a virtuous woman, spreads rumors that he has seduced her. The narrator records her revenge:

> She having no other supporte for her innocencie, then the true witnesse of her soule, unattainted and free from so vile an infamie; raisde up her spirits with such rightfull disdaine, against the unjust ravisher of her reputation, as she spared not to kill him in the middest of a verye honourable assembly, where she waited long for the effecting of such a woorthy enterprise. (fol. 44v)

The "ravisher of her reputation" assaults the woman's name, and she responds by attacking his body; for the narrator at least, this "woorthy enterprise," purposefully consummated in public space, incites no sense of disproportion. Instead, his verdict suggests that the scales have been balanced: "which (under correction of better judgement) in my minde deserved rather pardon and recompence, then any ill reproche, scandale or punishment" (fol. 44v). He supports this conclusion with a poem, which refers the entire sequence of causes and effects to the issue of nominal integrity: "*Pacience importun'de dooth convert to hate, / And who so quitteth not an offered blame: / Waites but a second blemish of his name*" (fol. 44v).

The parable suggests that legible answers might appear not in the compromised bodies of women but in the devastated bodies of men, whose deaths prove something about sex. But if men speak sexual acts onto women, and if women destroy the bodies that populate those spoken acts, in what sense can we understand a term such as "sexuality"? The entanglement of linguistic and bodily intercourse, their inextricable reciprocity as modes of assault and as forms of evidence, unfixes both ideological abstractions and material points of reference. The ravishing of reputation generates a counterfactual discourse (what if she did? what if he didn't?), so that killing men relegates sex to the register of conceptual plurality. Killing women only shifts the problem, as explanatory structures multiply around an evocative corpse. Deployed as an affirmation of knowledge, violence—indistinguishably rhetorical and corporeal—fractures that knowledge into imaginative possibilities and obscures the social meanings of sex. The narrator concludes with a flourish that escalates the confusion he seeks to resolve. The woman is condemned to death, but her sentence is commuted: "shee was confyned unto perpetuall prison, wherout I would very willinglie deliver her, if I could convert my selfe into a shower of golde, as sometime did the Sonne of *Saturne*" (fol. 45). The virtuous, murderous hero becomes another Danae, the narrator another Zeus, their encounter another ravishment that would release her body from prison and sacrifice her name to myth.

There are many more stories. Virgins who kill themselves and their ravishers populate chapters on honest conduct; constant and faithless viragoes illustrate exemplary catalogs; and, as Frances E. Dolan has shown, the deadly animosity between husbands and wives fuels a narrative industry. Dolan reminds us, too, that these stories may tell more about what is important than about what is true:

> In so succinctly articulating deep and complexly linked fears of disorder, these stories become a cultural resource for evoking and

> manipulating anxieties about that intersection of culturally determined boundaries and individual agency that is both the location of the subject and, in accounts of petty treason, a collision, a site of violence.[47]

I have chosen my own texts for their particular ways of staging collisions: between private claims and public consensus; between essential ties and manufactured attachments; between calcified certainties and reversible propositions; between, most of all, the narrow drive of social contract and the counterfactual spread of individuals who persist as alternative directional signs. They will not go away, those unassimilated persons, not even when they are dead; they animate the shadow lives of an amalgamated subjectivity that may deny their consequence, but cannot evade their touch. Even those persons who masquerade as subjects do not break the shared bond of death. Jean-Luc Nancy writes of the body, "it is the truth of the intersection and co-penetration of monads in their totality," and this intimacy bleeds through the screens of judgment and disavowal.[48] Battles waged over reputation reveal, however inadvertently and obscurely, that every impulse to kill is a temptation to die, not only as a viable social entity, but as a self who inhabits a small tract of flesh. In *The Care of the Self,* Michel Foucault deeply complicates the conventional relationship between willful bodies and reasonable souls. Reason, he argues, must impose a regimen that conforms to the body itself, "but it will be able to assign this regimen correctly only provided it has done a good deal of work on itself: eliminated the errors, reduced the imaginings, mastered the desires, that cause it to misconstrue the sober law of the body" (133).[49] A counterfactual maze deflects the trajectory of order—"only provided" is surely another version of "what if"—but these fugitive propositions emanate from the compromised objectives of order itself. The body follows its own immanent law.

Foucault's study does not focus on early modernity, nor does it imagine radical escapes. But his inclination to take seriously both the body and the self, and his willingness to interrogate the coincidence of embodied self and social subject, speak to the crises of univocality with which I am concerned. "From the viewpoint of the relation to the self, the social and political identifications do not function as authentic marks of a mode of being; they are extrinsic, artificial, and unfounded signs," he writes (93). This is not to say that such identifications do not matter, any more than the rational soul is irrelevant to the body's work. But they reflect the intersections of orthodox doctrine and idiosyncratic choice; concurrence is not a basis but a derivation. "The task," he writes, "of testing oneself, examining oneself, monitoring oneself in a series of clearly defined exercises, makes the question of truth—the truth concerning what one is, what one does, and what one is capable of doing—central to the formation of the ethical subject" (68). For early modern social subjects, the truths of the self must emerge from the evidence of others. In the desert of that stark necessity, patrilines work best as gentleman's agreements; women give and draw blood to prove nothing at all; and the only cure for a ravished reputation is the pharmakon that must ravish it all over again. Or so, at least, conventional narratives would attempt to affirm. That "would" is misleading; it is far from clear whose will, if any, conveys the message, which is perhaps the point of those letters that so ruthlessly arrive at their destinations. The anonymous author, conceived as ideology or hierarchy or common sense or God, may speak to all subjects, but the stories I have discussed imply that such an author does not speak for all persons, and subjects may tend toward personhood in the interstices of a collective will.

It is suggestive that Foucault's meditations on the self revolve around sex, not as the ground on which "behavior will have to submit to the universal form of law" (68) but as a negotiation that turns discipline and damage inward:

> Sexual pleasure as an ethical substance continues to be governed by relations of force—the force against which one must struggle and over which the subject is expected to establish his domination. But in this game of violence, excess, rebellion, and combat, the accent is placed more and more readily on the weakness of the individual, on his frailty, on his need to flee, to escape, to protect and shelter himself. (67)

That phrase—"this game of violence, excess, rebellion, and combat"—condenses the dynamics I have traced in these pages. Foucault's contemplation of reproductive imperatives, like the anecdotal ruminations of early modern social theorists, shows that the game must be played by volatile bodies, even when the stakes are those of social survival. "The *logos* that builds the natural order is in a situation rather similar to that of the founder of a city," Foucault observes. "The latter may very well bring men together to form a community; however, the city will disappear, will fall into oblivion, if one does not discover how to make it endure beyond the death of its first citizens. A means is necessary to surmount this fundamental difficulty" (105). The means is sex, but this poses a problem of carts and horses: sex is required to forge the communities that determine whether sex does anything to secure identities, futurities, or a sense of common cause.

Coda. Don't Tell

For the early modern stories I consider, the "fundamental difficulty" of communal self-perpetuation is tied to the strategic endorsement of community itself: reputation circulates as the currency of inclusive identity, but the scheme that fixes dangerous names to disposable bodies fails to insulate social subjects. Chastity, which affords the sole security for legitimate bonds, magnifies the problem; as Laura Gowing writes, "the potential consequences of women's unchastity undermine the very basis of a society structured—practically and conceptually—in familial terms."[50] In *Wits Theater of the little World*, Robert Allott cites a pithy bit of advice: "Thucidides was of opinion, that those wemen were most honest, of whose commendation and disprayse there is least speech used."[51] Attempts to adjudicate public forms of feminine virtue enmesh themselves in contradiction, as in William Baldwin's aphoristic chapter on women: "The withdrawing and keping weomen close, is a bridle to the tongues of all men: and the woman that doth otherwise, putteth her good name in daunger"; "A woman of good lyfe feareth no man with an evill tong"; "It were better for a woman never to be borne then to be defamed"; "It were great wickednes of men to say that all women shoulde be evyll that be evill spoken of."[52] Even this limited set of examples reveals the scope of the dilemma. Are women judged by the lives they live or by the identities prefabricated for their habitation? Is reputation the articulate mode of identity or an assumption that circulates until it sticks?

Throughout the 1598 translation of *The Arte of Love,* the female speaker refers truth to the flux of misreading: "Figures are fallacies, and shewes no substances; love more privately, than may be noted apparantly."[53] Such precepts suggest that there can be no knowledge uncompromised by preconception, situational exigency, or doubt. Brathwait sums up that deficit in his epilogue on estimation: "Her desire is to *be,* rather than *seeme,* lest *seeming* to *be* what she *is not,* shee gull the world, but her selfe most, by playing the counterfeit."[54] If "playing the counterfeit" connects the deception of others to an alienation of self, what ground of proof—whether body or subject, person or corpse—can bear the weight of social need?

No one has answers, but people will talk. And so we arrive back at Lucretia's vexed intimations of futurity, a counterfactual space from which to glance at three Shakespearean characters who bind sex to death only to disaggregate reputation. What might we make of Lavinia, who survives bodily devastation to participate in the ruin of her destroyers? And what does it mean that Titus cites the story of Virginius when he kills his own daughter, invoking a muddled precedent of fossilized chastity that locates Lavinia's survival in nonlinear time?[55] What should we do with Cleopatra, who counters Caesar's iconic future with "Rather a ditch in Egypt / Be gentle grave unto me!" (5.2.57–58), who refutes the symbolic body for the body as flesh yet predicts her own unbearable survival: "I shall see / Some squeaking Cleopatra boy my greatness / I' th' posture of a whore" (5.2.219–21)? As we watch this play, do we see the Cleopatra who declares, "I am fire and air; my other elements / I give to baser life" (5.2.289–90) or the Cleopatra who postures and squeaks her ceaseless infamy? And finally, what can we say of Desdemona? She dies for a crime she scarcely seems to apprehend, and when—another figure who is in all senses out of time—she returns to explain her fate, she says, "A guiltless death I die," then names her murderer: "Nobody; I myself" (5.2.122, 124). Such puzzles underscore the uncanny familiarity of the pattern I have traced. Irreducible statements and fugitive propositions constellate around early modern sex; as contingent subjects live and die in the name of what they may or may not be, they do not produce a taxonomic sexuality for our edification, and it seems entirely imaginable that they do not possess one for their own.

In the context of the argument I have pursued, there is something markedly and deliberately problematic about "our" and "their," collective pronouns that recur to the "we" who make such profligate use of "them." In this way, I turn to a final, troubling, and not at all rhetorical set of questions. What of the "we" gathered here, the "I" who exhumes these stories and the "you" who consume them? Are we the cannibals of shared knowledge, the belated, necrophilic architects of name? Or do we accept Judith Halberstam's proposition about history and accountability: "to tell a ghost story means being willing to be haunted"?[56] Do we participate in the differential calculus Madhavi Menon indicts as "compulsory heterotemporality," or do we engage in the principled labor Freccero links to pain? "Insofar as queer historicism registers the affective investments of the present in the past," Freccero writes, "it harbors within itself not only pleasure, but also pain, a traumatic pain whose ethical insistence is to 'live to tell' through complex and circuitous processes of working through."[57] And if we make use, any use, of the privilege that draws on past lives, is there something specious about the notion of choice, about the conceit (in both senses) that "or" is available to us at all? As we stake our reputations on the quality of our knowledge and the ethics of our methods, does even our conscientious pain require the sacrifice of someone not known, not here, not *us*—the sacrifice of someone else?

Notes

1 All quotations of Shakespeare's works follow *The Riverside Shakespeare,* 2nd ed., ed. G. Blakemore Evans (Boston: Houghton Mifflin, 1997). Bracketed passages in this edition are silently retained.

2 [Thomas Edgar], *The Lawes Resolutions of Womens Rights: or, The Lawes Provision for Woemen* (London: John More for John Grove, 1632), 377. In citing early modern texts, I have retained their spellings; however, I have modernized typography in several ways. Consonantal *u* and *i* have been revised to *v* and *j,* and vocalic *v* has been revised to *u*; long *s* has been revised to *s*; ligatures of *æ* and *œ* have been expanded; *&* and *ye* have been altered to *and* and *the*; and where a macron indicates the suspension of *m* or *n,* I have supplied the letter.

3 Many scholars have also challenged the idea that chastity can only objectify women; their analyses recover the potential for chaste agency and trace its implications in a range of compelling ways. For accounts of sexual self-possession as a challenge to heterosocial hierarchy—as an alternative, an escape, a weapon, a mystification, or a screen—see, e.g., Philippa Berry, *Of Chastity and Power: Elizabethan Literature and the Unmarried Queen* (London: Routledge, 1994), 1–37 passim; Laurie Shannon, *Sovereign Amity: Figures of Friendship in Shakespearean Contexts* (Chicago: University of Chicago Press, 2002), 54–89; Constance Jordan, *Renaissance Feminism: Literary Texts and Political Models* (Ithaca, N.Y.: Cornell University Press, 1990), 29–30, 82–83; Amy Greenstadt, *Rape and the Rise of the Author* (Farnham, U.K.: Ashgate, 2009); John Rogers, "The Enclosure of Virginity: The Poetics of Sexual Abstinence in the English Revolution," in *Enclosure Acts: Sexuality, Property, and Culture in Early Modern England,* ed. Richard Burt and John Michael Archer, 229–50 (Ithaca, N.Y.: Cornell University Press, 1994); Valerie Traub, "The Perversion of 'Lesbian' Desire," *History Workshop Journal* 41 (1996): 19–51; Theodora Jankowski, *Pure Resistance: Queer Virginity in Early Modern English Drama* (Philadelphia: University of Pennsylvania Press, 2000); Nancy Weitz, "Romantic Fiction, Moral Anxiety, and Social Capital in Cavendish's 'Assaulted and Pursued Chastity,'" in *Authorial Conquests: Essays on Genre in the Writings of Margaret Cavendish,* ed. Line Cottegnies and Nancy Weitz, 145–60 (Madison, N.J.: Fairleigh Dickinson University Press, 2003); Kathleen Coyne Kelly and Marina Leslie, eds., *Menacing Virgins: Representing Virginity in the Middle Ages and Renaissance* (Newark: University of Delaware Press, 1999); and Richard Halpern, "Puritanism and Maenadism in *A Mask,*" in *Rewriting the Renaissance: The Discourses of Sexual Difference in Early Modern Europe,* ed. Margaret W. Ferguson, Maureen Quilligan, and Nancy J. Vickers, 88–105 (Chicago: University of Chicago Press, 1986). This list is necessarily suggestive rather than exhaustive.

4 Juan Luis Vives, *A Very Fruteful and Pleasant Boke Called the Instruction of a christen woman,* trans. Rycharde Hyrde (Londini: in [a]edibus Thom[a]e Berth[eleti], 1547), sig. A3. For an insightful reading of Vives's figurative treatment of chastity, see Nancy Weitz Miller, "Metaphor and the Mystification of Chastity in Vives's *Instruction of a Christen Woman,*" in Kelly and Leslie, *Menacing Virgins,* 132–45.

5 For detailed historical accounts of uncertainties surrounding the virginal

body, see Kathleen Coyne Kelly, *Performing Virginity and Testing Chastity in the Middle Ages* (New York: Routledge, 2000), 1–39, and Marie H. Loughlin, *Hymeneutics: Interpreting Virginity on the Early Modern Stage* (Lewisburg, Pa.: Bucknell University Press, 1997), 13–52.

6 Beatrice-Joanna's manipulation of the chastity test in *The Changeling* offers one obvious example. For readings of the complex dynamics of custom, performance, deception, and revelation in this play, see, e.g., Sara Eaton, "Beatrice-Joanna and the Rhetoric of Love: *The Changeling* (1622)," in *Staging the Renaissance: Reinterpretations of Elizabethan and Jacobean Drama,* ed. David Scott Kastan and Peter Stallybrass, 275–89 (New York: Routledge, 1991), and Marjorie Garber, "The Insincerity of Women," in *Subject and Object in Renaissance Culture,* ed. Margreta de Grazia, Maureen Quilligan, and Peter Stallybrass, 349–68 (Cambridge: Cambridge University Press, 1996).

7 Kelly, *Performing Virginity and Testing Chastity,* 7.

8 Dudley Fenner, *The Artes of Logike and Rethorike, plainelie set foorth in the Englishe tounge* (Middelburg, Zeeland: R. Schilders, 1584), sig. D2. Fenner bases his text on works by Petrus Ramus and Omar Talon.

9 John Barton, *The Art of Rhetorick Concisely and Compleatly Handled, Exemplified out of holy Writ* (London: Printed for Nicolas Alsop, 1634), sig. A4. Barton's sense of opacity is shared by modern theorists; so Roman Jakobson argues that metaphor presents an explicable pattern, while metonymy eludes the interpreter's grasp. "Similarity connects a metaphoric term with the term for which it is substituted. Consequently, when constructing a metalanguage to interpret tropes, the researcher possesses more homogeneous means to handle metaphor, whereas metonymy, based on a different principle, easily defies interpretation." Jakobson, "Two Aspects of Language and Two Types of Aphasic Disturbances," in *On Language,* ed. Linda R. Waugh and Monique Monville-Burston (Cambridge, Mass.: Harvard University Press, 1990), 132. See also Paul de Man, who, in his scrutiny of the apparent preeminence of metaphor, refers to "the contingency of a metonymy based only on the casual encounter of two entities that could very well exist in each other's absence." De Man, *Allegories of Reading: Figural Language in Rousseau, Nietzsche, Rilke and Proust* (New Haven, Conn.: Yale University Press, 1979), 63.

10 George Puttenham, *The Arte of English Poesie* (London: Richard Field, 1589), 150–51; Richard Sherry, *A treatise of Schemes and Tropes very*

profytable for the better understanding of good authors, gathered out of the best Grammarians & Oratours (London: John Day, 1550), sig. C5v.

11 Jacques Lacan, "The Agency of the Letter in the Unconscious," in *Écrits: A Selection*, trans. Alan Sheridan (New York: W. W. Norton, 1977), 167; emphasis original. I discuss these metonymic processes at length in *What You Will: Gender, Contract, and Shakespearean Social Space* (Philadelphia: University of Pennsylvania Press, 2011); see esp. chapter 2.

12 In a reading of Augustine's connection between corrupted will and uncontrolled sexual response, Amy Greenstadt makes an intriguing point about female bodies and inscrutable desires: "Lacking the visible outward sign of erectile movement, the female body keeps its sexual secrets. . . . In evading the punishment for the Fall in which carnal disobedience manifested as a visible sign, it seems the female sex also escaped the regime of postlapsarian sexuality in which willful intention could never fully be distinguished from carnal desire and pleasure." Greenstadt, *Rape and the Rise of the Author*, 18.

13 Lauren Berlant, *The Queen of America Goes to Washington City: Essays on Sex and Citizenship* (Durham, N.C.: Duke University Press, 1997), 60. See also Russ Castronovo: "Despite significant differences in rhetoric and epistemology, a range of figures . . . all converged in linking questions of social death, the hauntings of memory, and disembodied citizens to the political forms of U.S. democracy. Citizenship is paramount among these forms, naturalizing the transformation of persons into official political entities as well as social corpses." Castronovo, *Necro Citizenship: Death, Eroticism, and the Public Sphere in the Nineteenth-Century United States* (Durham, N.C.: Duke University Press, 2001), xiii.

14 This resonates with scholarship on early modern anatomies, which explicates the highly ambiguous status of the corpse. See, e.g., Katharine Park, "The Criminal and the Saintly Body: Autopsy and Dissection in Renaissance Italy," *Renaissance Quarterly* 47, no. 1 (1994): 1–33, and "The Life of the Corpse: Division and Dissection in Late Medieval Europe," *Journal of the History of Medicine and Allied Sciences* 50, no. 1 (1995): 111–32; Katherine Rowe, *Dead Hands: Fictions of Agency, Renaissance to Modern* (Stanford, Calif.: Stanford University Press, 1999), 24–51; Jonathan Sawday, *The Body Emblazoned: Dissection and the Human Body in Renaissance Culture* (New York: Routledge, 1995), and "The Fate of Marsyas: Dissecting the Renaissance Body," in *Renaissance Bodies: The Human Figure in English Culture c. 1540–1660*, ed. Lucy Gent and Nigel

Llewellyn, 111–35 (London: Reaktion Books, 1990); Valerie Traub, "Gendering Mortality in Early Modern Anatomies," in *Feminist Readings of Early Modern Culture: Emerging Subjects,* ed. Valerie Traub, M. Lindsay Kaplan, and Dympna Callaghan, 44–92 (Cambridge: Cambridge University Press, 1996); and Luke Wilson, "William Harvey's *Prelectiones*: The Performance of the Body in the Renaissance Theater of Anatomy," *Representations* 17 (Winter 1987): 62–95.

15 Elaine Scarry, "Consent and the Body: Injury, Departure, and Desire," *New Literary History* 21 , no. 4 (1990): 871.

16 Bruce R. Smith, "I, You, He, She, and We: On the Sexual Politics of Shakespeare's Sonnets," in *Shakespeare's Sonnets: Critical Essays,* ed. James Schiffer (New York: Garland, 1999), 427; emphasis original.

17 Carla Freccero, *Queer/Early/Modern* (Durham, N.C.: Duke University Press, 2006), 90–91.

18 For accounts of the conflicts between masculine and feminine knowledge in the production of patrilineal history, see, e.g., Coppélia Kahn, *Man's Estate: Masculine Identity in Shakespeare* (Berkeley: University of California Press, 1981); Phyllis Rackin, "Anti-Historians: Women's Roles in Shakespeare's Histories," *Theatre Journal* 37 (1985): 329–44; Carole Levin, "'I Trust I May Not Trust Thee': Women's Visions of the World in Shakespeare's *King John,*" in *Ambiguous Realities: Women in the Middle Ages and Renaissance,* ed. Carole Levin and Jeanie Watson, 219–34 (Detroit, Mich.: Wayne State University Press, 1987); Virginia M. Vaughan, "*King John*: A Study in Subversion and Containment," in *King John: New Perspectives,* ed. Deborah T. Curren-Aquino, 62–75 (Newark: University of Delaware Press, 1989); Jeanne Addison Roberts, "Birth Traumas in Shakespeare," *Renaissance Papers* (1990): 55–66; Mary Beth Rose, "Where Are the Mothers in Shakespeare? Options for Gender Representation in the English Renaissance," *Shakespeare Quarterly* 42, no. 3 (1991): 291–314; and Jean E. Howard and Phyllis Rackin, *Engendering a Nation: A Feminist Account of Shakespeare's English Histories* (New York: Routledge, 1997).

19 Freccero, *Queer/Early/Modern,* 72.

20 *Oxford English Dictionary,* s.v. "counterfactual" (n).

21 Ibid., s.v. "irreducible" (adj), 1b.

22 Michel de Certeau, *Heterologies: Discourse on the Other,* trans. Brian Massumi (Minneapolis: University of Minnesota Press, 1986), 4. See Freccero's incisive analysis of de Certeau's comments on historiography

in *Queer/Early/Modern,* 70–72. Freccero writes, "This melancholic model is also a response to trauma—the trauma of historicity—yet it is a response that will not acknowledge the trauma or the loss and seeks instead to hush the voices or to 'understand' or master them with meaning and discourse" (71).

23 Jonathan Goldberg, "The History That Will Be," in *Premodern Sexualities,* ed. Louise Fradenburg and Carla Freccero (New York: Routledge, 1996), 4.

24 *Oxford English Dictionary,* s.v. "rejoinder" (n), 1, 2; both meanings were current in sixteenth- and seventeenth-century usage.

25 In discussions of sexual violence and its implications for sexual and social agency, the story of Lucrece is a crux. Catherine Belsey argues that self-sacrifice can challenge social formations: "[Lucrece] reaffirms her own sovereignty in an action that is deliberately and independently chosen. The effect is a change of regime to one based on consent: *propriety* will no longer be synonymous with *property.*" Belsey, "Tarquin Dispossessed: Expropriation and Consent in *The Rape of Lucrece,*" *Shakespeare Quarterly* 52, no. 3 (2001): 333; emphasis original. See also Laura G. Bromley, "Lucrece's Re-creation," *Shakespeare Quarterly* 34, no. 2 (1983): 200–211; Joel Fineman, "Shakespeare's *Will*: The Temporality of Rape," in *The Subjectivity Effect in Western Literary Tradition: Essays toward the Release of Shakespeare's Will* (Cambridge, Mass.: MIT Press, 1991), 165–221; Amy Greenstadt, "'Read It in Me': The Author's Will in *Lucrece,*" *Shakespeare Quarterly* 57, no. 1 (2006): 45–70; Coppélia Kahn, "The Rape in Shakespeare's *Lucrece,*" *Shakespeare Studies* 9 (1976): 45–72; Arthur L. Little, *Shakespeare Jungle Fever: National-Imperial Re-visions of Race, Rape, and Sacrifice* (Stanford, Calif.: Stanford University Press, 2000), 25–48; Katharine Eisaman Maus, "Taking Tropes Seriously: Language and Violence in Shakespeare's *Rape of Lucrece,*" *Shakespeare Quarterly* 37, no. 1 (1986): 66–82; and Jane O. Newman, "'And Let Mild Women to Him Lose Their Mildness': Philomela, Female Violence, and Shakespeare's *The Rape of Lucrece,*" *Shakespeare Quarterly* 45, no. 3 (1994): 304–36.

26 Livy, *History of Rome,* vol. 1 (Loeb Classical Library), trans. B. O. Foster (London: William Heinemann, 1919), section 58.

27 Ovid, *Fasti,* Book II (Loeb Classical Library, 2nd ed.), trans. James G. Frazer, rev. G. P. Goold (London: W. Heinemann, 1996), VI. Kal. 24th, 111–17.

28 Augustine, *The City of God* (Modern Library Edition), ed. Thomas Merton, trans. Marcus Dods (New York: Modern Library, 1993), 23–25.

29 Castronovo, *Necro Citizenship,* xiii.

30 For important challenges to linear history and teleological historiography, see de Certeau, *Heterologies*; Louise Fradenburg and Carla Freccero, "Introduction: Caxton, Foucault, and the Pleasures of History," in *Premodern Sexualities,* ed. Louise Fradenburg and Carla Freccero, xiii–xxiv (New York: Routledge, 1996); Goldberg, "The History That Will Be"; Lee Edelman, *No Future: Queer Theory and the Death Drive* (Durham, N.C.: Duke University Press, 2004); Judith Halberstam, *In a Queer Time and Place: Transgender Bodies, Subcultural Lives* (New York: New York University Press, 2005); Jonathan Goldberg and Madhavi Menon, "Queering History," *PMLA* 120, no. 5 (2005): 1608–17; Freccero, *Queer/Early/Modern*; Madhavi Menon, *Unhistorical Shakespeare: Queer Theory in Shakespearean Literature and Film* (New York: Palgrave Macmillan, 2008); and Jonathan Gil Harris, *Untimely Matter in the Time of Shakespeare* (Philadelphia: University of Pennsylvania Press, 2009).

31 Harris, *Untimely Matter,* 2.

32 I have cited two of these stories elsewhere to illustrate problems posed by militant virginity, female masculinity, and heterosocial contract; here I engage their complex portrayals of reputation and consider their dynamics and implications in considerably more detail. See Kathryn Schwarz, *Tough Love: Amazon Encounters in the English Renaissance* (Durham, N.C.: Duke University Press, 2000), 16; "Chastity, Militant and Married: Cavendish's Romance, Milton's Masque," *PMLA* 118, no. 2 (2003): 271; and *What You Will,* 13, 166.

33 Thomas Heywood, *Gynaikeion: or, Nine Bookes of Various History Concerninge Women* (London: Adam Islip, 1624), 193. All page citations appear parenthetically in the text; all emphasis is in the original.

34 This complete ban on "fame," or public reputation, has at best a vexed relationship to Thomas Tuke's much-cited dictate on being and seeming: "It is not enough to be good, but she that is good, must seeme good: she that is chast, must seeme chast: shee that is humble, must seeme humble: shee that is modest, must seeme to bee so. . . . It is not enough for Christian chastitie that it be, but that it be also seene." Tuke, *A Discourse against Painting and Tincturing of Women. Wherein the abominable sinnes of Murther and Poysoning, Pride and Ambition, Adultery and Witchcraft are set foorth and discovered* (London: Edward Marchant, 1616), 10. For

a reading of this passage in terms of "a double-bind of either being pure but not seeming so or seeming so but not according to male conventions," see Eaton, "Beatrice-Joanna and the Rhetoric of Love," 275.

35 In her study of inwardness, Katharine Eisaman Maus compellingly links the mystified body to the opacity of intent: "In sixteenth- and early seventeenth-century England the bodily interior is still mysterious in a way perhaps hard to recapture in an age of medical sophistication, and in a way quite precisely analogous to the mysteriousness of human motives and desires." Maus, *Inwardness and Theater in the English Renaissance* (Chicago: University of Chicago Press, 1995), 196. See also Lorna Hutson's cogent argument that forensic transactions, informed by the reciprocal intentions of persuasion and verification, construct an idea of character on the early modern stage: "[The] judicial pedagogy of narrative fostered an awareness of the 'facts' as having been generated by the order and coherence of their telling. In other words, it fostered a tendency to represent dramatis personae as, on the one hand, forensically engaged in persuading one another of the truth of highly disputable 'facts,' and, on the other, as suspiciously testing and trying out the grounds for belief in one another. In this way, the diffusion of judicial rhetoric through the education system facilitated the kind of writing which produces the illusion that behind speech headings and speeches are the consciousnesses of 'characters.'" Hutson, *The Invention of Suspicion: Law and Mimesis in Shakespeare and Renaissance Drama* (Oxford: Oxford University Press, 2007), 7.

36 The *Oxford English Dictionary* defines *mechall* (also spelled "mechal," "michall," and "michol") as "adulterous" and traces its derivation to the postclassical Latin *mechalis* and the classical Latin *moechus*. Intriguingly, the *Oxford English Dictionary* adds that the English word is "only recorded in the works of Thomas Heywood." *Oxford English Dictionary*, s.v. "mechal" (adj).

37 Jacques Lacan, "Seminar on 'The Purloined Letter,'" trans. Jeffrey Mehlman, in *The Purloined Poe: Lacan, Derrida, and Psychoanalytic Reading*, ed. John P. Muller and William J. Richardson (Baltimore: Johns Hopkins University Press, 1988), 52–53.

38 Peter Brooks, *Reading for the Plot: Design and Intention in Narrative* (Cambridge, Mass.: Harvard University Press, 1992), 95. For Brooks's explication of the relationship between the death drive and the pleasure principle, see esp. chapter 2, "Narrative Desire," 37–61, and chapter 4, "Freud's Masterplot," 90–112.

39 Heinrich Bullinger, *The Christen State of Matrimony,* trans. Miles Coverdale (London: John Mayler for John Gough, 1546), fol. 34v. Bullinger's denunciation is utterly conventional: "It servethe to our purpose, that thorowe aduoutry, great enheritaunces are altered, and the ryght heyres dysherited. For oft tymes it fortuneth, that an aduoutresse hath children by an aduoutrer, and then muste the sayd chyldren enherite all the substaunce of theyr pretenced fathers, as laufull chyldren, which yet are unlawful, wherby the father leseth his honoure, hys kynred, hys body and goodes" (fol. 34).

40 While the story has clear parallels to the plot of Heywood's play *A Woman Killed with Kindness,* several differences are particularly worthy of note. In *Gynaikeion,* Heywood locates his tale in an explicitly exemplary context, which begs the questions of what advice might be extracted from it and how, in an environment of quotidian social experience, that advice might be followed. Through the presence of the elderly husband, the tale also introduces the strangely plausible concept of subjunctive adultery, which, with the passage of time, might become legitimate marriage. By giving the wife two lovers, it opens a crucial but unfathomable gap between conditional betrayal—which might or might not resolve itself into betrayal at all—and literal infidelity. Its conclusion preserves an inheritance transmitted between men, but does so by dispensing entirely with the patrilineal connection of blood.

41 Judith Butler, *The Psychic Life of Power: Theories in Subjection* (Stanford, Calif.: Stanford University Press, 1997), 27.

42 Richard Brathwait, *The English Gentlewoman, drawne out to the full Body: Expressing, What Habilliments doe best attire her, What Ornaments doe best adorne her, What Complements doe best accomplish her* (London: B. Alsop and T. Fawcet for Michaell Sparke, 1631). All page citations appear parenthetically in the text; all emphasis is in the original.

43 A hint of this confusion appears early in Brathwait's chapter when he writes of virtuous women, "These, so cautelous are they of suspition, as they will not ingage their *good names* to purchase affection" (102). *Cautelous,* in the sixteenth and seventeenth centuries, held meanings that appear to conflict: the first, "full of cautels; deceitful, crafty, artful, wily," seems directly at odds with the second—"cautious, wary, heedful, circumspect"—on which Brathwait draws. Yet their common source in the noun cautel suggests that these two meanings have a more reciprocally causal relationship; a *cautel* is (in order of appearance) "a crafty device,

artifice, stratagem; a trick, sleight, deceit"; "cunning, craftiness, wiliness, trickery"; "caution, wariness, heedfulness"; "a precaution; in *Law,* etc., an exception, restriction, or reservation made for precaution's sake"; "*Eccl.* A caution or direction for the proper administration of the sacraments." *Oxford English Dictionary,* s.v. "cautelous" (adj), 1, 2; s.v. "cautel" (n), 1, 2, 3, 4, 4b. The potential for deceit engenders the need for precautions, which is Brathwait's repressed, reluctant, but recurrent point.

44 Brathwait describes a visible trail of bad blood: "You observe what staines have laid, and do yet lie upon many ancient families by means of attainders in their Progenitors. Their bloods (say we) were corrupted, whereby their estates became confiscated, their houses from their lineall successours estranged, and they to lasting infamy exposed" (102–3).

45 "In *Philosophy,* a man begins with experience, and then with beleefe; but in *Divinity,* wee must first beginne in faith, and then proceed to knowledge," Brathwait writes (105); the very attempt to secure virtue by attaching it to divine authority relegates knowledge to a leap of faith.

46 [Alexandre de Pontaymeri], *A Womans Woorth, defended against all the men in the world. Prooving them to be more perfect, excellent and absolute in all vertuous actions, then any man of what qualitie soever,* ed. Anthony Gibson (London: John Wolfe, 1599). All page citations appear parenthetically in the text; all emphasis is in the original.

47 Frances E. Dolan, *Dangerous Familiars: Representations of Domestic Crime in England, 1550–1700* (Ithaca, N.Y.: Cornell University Press, 1994), 58. See her caveat on evidentiary status: "The proliferation of texts about petty treason does not demonstrate that wives and servants suddenly began killing their husbands and masters in record numbers" (25).

48 Jean-Luc Nancy, *Corpus,* trans. Richard A. Rand (New York: Fordham University Press, 2008), 27.

49 Michel Foucault, *The Care of the Self,* vol. 3 of *The History of Sexuality,* trans. Robert Hurley (New York: Vintage Books, 1988). All page citations appear parenthetically in the text.

50 Laura Gowing, *Domestic Dangers: Women, Words, and Sex in Early Modern London* (Oxford: Clarendon Press, 1996), 4.

51 Robert Allott, *Wits Theater of the little World* (London: J[ames] R[oberts] for N[icholas] L[ing], 1599), 102. Allott himself does not take this advice; his chapter "Of Wemen" consists entirely of brief exemplary anecdotes, which invoke a wide range of female accomplishments and transgressions without imposing either taxonomy or judgment (see fol. 101v–104).

52 William Baldwin, *A treatyce of Moral philosophy containing the sayinges of the wise* (London: Rycharde Tottill, 1564), fol. 133v–134.

53 Leon Battista Alberti, *Hecatonphila. The Arte of Love. Or, Love discovered in an hundred severall kindes* (London: P.S. for William Leake, 1598), fol. 19v.

54 Brathwait, *English Gentlewoman,* sig. Gg2v.

55 The footnote in *The Riverside Shakespeare* is quite fabulously stern on this point: "Virginius. This Roman centurion killed his daughter to *prevent* her rape. Either the dramatist has got the story wrong or he is failing to convey the idea that Titus has a better case for killing Lavinia than Virginius had for killing his daughter." *The Riverside Shakespeare,* 1095n36; emphasis original.

56 Halberstam, *In a Queer Time and Place,* 60.

57 Menon, *Unhistorical Shakespeare,* 1–4; Freccero, *Queer/Early/Modern,* 79.

3

Spectacular Impotence: Or, Things That Hardly Ever Happen in the Critical History of Pornography

MELISSA J. JONES

The history of English pornography is relatively straightforward—or at least that is how it is written. In his groundbreaking *The Secret Museum: Pornography in Modern Culture,* Walter Kendrick notes the Victorian coinage of the term *pornography* and explores the generic consolidation that inheres in this naming.[1] Kendrick's influential cultural history proposes that the mode we now recognize as pornographic emerged most clearly in the nineteenth century as a backlash against an increasingly polite and increasingly discursive society. For him, it is a regulatory category defined—then *and* now—as an argument against decorum rather than by any textual particularity. Scholars of the early modern period have pushed this timeline back three hundred years or so in claiming Pietro Aretino's exploitation of an emergent print culture as the forerunner of the Anglo-American triple-X, but emphasis on the categorically transgressive nature of pornography still closely follows Kendrick's lead.[2] Such vanguard scholarship emerged out of the controversial "sex wars" of the 1980s and 1990s, pushing against the deterministic claim that all forms of graphic sex represented violence against women and establishing pornography not only as a legitimate site of historical inquiry but also as one with the power to upset conventions of sex and text.[3]

However, there is a risk in this defensive posture. By repeatedly pinching pornographic expression into narrow categories of "subversive" and "hegemonic," we chance limiting the affective range of response to such spectacles to an equally reduced dialectic of pleasure and unpleasure.

With this kind of "gradual evacuation of substance," Eve Sedgwick warns, comes the erasure of all the "middle ranges of agency" where individuals might assume gender and sexual specificity as active pleasure seekers rather than just abstract power players in a timeless cultural war.[4] The erotics of impotency, for instance, is downplayed in the history of pornography precisely because erectile dysfunction—among other failures of gender—encodes a kind of shame that stumps the phallic order of modern sex and derails ideological critique that, following its logic, depends on a metaphorics of "sticking it" to the establishment.[5] Yet the libidinal charge of much erotica from the past is sparked by images of an exposed, embarrassed penis—either in a spectator's masturbatory hand or in a protagonist's dramatic erectile miscues. By spotlighting the interplay of impotency, humiliation, and titillation in two poems noted in the late sixteenth century for sexual explicitness, Thomas Nashe's "Choise of Valentines" (1592) and John Marston's *Metamorphosis of Pigmalion's Image* (1598), I uncover tableaux of "sex before sex" that vex the very binary of *before* and *after* implied in such a recovery project. Reimagining the rigid lines of pornography's history in this way opens up critical space not only to expand thinking about how early moderns might have named and ordered their sexual action but also to consider the long-standing but often invisible place of such pleasures in today's own erotica market.

Nashe's "Choise of Valentines" (also called "Nashe's Dildo") solidified the author's reputation in his own time as a pornographer, or "English Aretine," by inscribing graphically sexual content alongside aggressively matter-of-fact depictions of erectile dysfunction and female masturbation.[6] Recounting a country boy's Valentine search for his buxom lass and his discovery of her in a city brothel, "Choise" overturns the typical pastoral narrative and its implicit reproductive imperative when—overcome by excitement—the lover prematurely ejaculates before the moment of penetration. *Then* he's unable to achieve erection. *Then* he disappoints his partner by failing to sustain the intercourse he does finally manage. In a scene of protracted mortification, the heroine castigates his pathetic genitalia (derided elsewhere as a "sillie worme" [33]), and he looks on with jealousy as she pleasures herself with a reliable "little dilldo" (239) in his stead. Stylistically, the poem is as all over the place as is its sexual trajectory, collapsing forms (including Ovidian, Petrarchan, pastoral, and satirical) in a way that is only slightly less disorienting than the occasional confusion of male, female, authorial, and fictional voices. Critics tend to read this stylistic excess and the looming spectacle of impotency together as evidence of a historical crisis in masculinity or as a token of Nashe's playful, persistent challenge to logocentrism.[7] Yet the erotic potential of the "sillie worme" itself is seldom talked about in conversations about Nashe or in histories of pornography. Perhaps this is because, as Lynda Boose insists, the poem is "too jocular and invests too much self-mocking humor in exposing the comedies of male impotence ever to reach the dark depths and psychic defenses that underlie the pornographic."[8] But erectile dysfunction in a text celebrated in its time not just for what it *says* but for what it *does* might be more than just an allegory of—or comical digression from—the heat of a "real thing." It might just be the thing itself.

On first seeing his Francis seductively posed in bed, Nashe's hero, Tomalin, cries, "Oh, who is able to abstaine so long? / I com, I com" (98–99).[9] Yet the spectacle of his deflation is quickly overwritten by—even as it underwrites—his bawdy Petrarchan glance at Francis's body:

> Softlie my fingers, up theis curtaine, heaue,
> And make me happie stealing by degreese.
> First bare hir leggs, then creepe up to hir kneese.
> From thence ascend unto hir mannely thigh. / . . . /
> A prettie rysing wombe without a weame, / . . . /
> A loftie buttock barred with azure veine's. (100–15)

The oscillation between aroused looking, pornographic description, and sexual dysfunction intensifies with Tomalin's immediate moan against "Ouid's cursed hemlock" and "limm's" that "spend their strength in *thought* of hir delight," hinting at the writer's "unarm'd" (123) pen in the lover's impotent penis and raising this sexual mishap to the level of ontological crisis: "What shall I doe to shewe myself a man?" (125–28; emphasis added). A moment like this explores the effect of pornographic imagery on male authors and consumers, both of whom Tomalin manages to represent when he loses control of the issue of his imagination.

This anxious elision of textual and sexual authority also serves to locate the poem neatly within a tradition of impotency poetry that begins at Ovid's frustrations in *Amores* and reaches (anti)climax in English literary culture with John Wilmot, the Earl of Rochester's, "Imperfect Enjoyment" (1680). But, as Bruce Boehrer notes, Nashe parts from this literary tradition when he puts gender itself into question, thereby disrupting the normative sexual narrative that underwrites both Ovid's earlier and Rochester's later disappointments.[10]

We glimpse this gender destabilization on several occasions: in Tomalin's perception of Francis's thighs as "mannely," for instance, or in his description of his phallic replacement as a "Eunuke dilldo" (263). But Tomalin's fantasy of gender transivity is most notable at poem's end, when he swaps the poem's male audience for a female one and then undermines even this conceit with a claim for autotelism intended to excuse both the text's failure to touch its readership and the narrator's failure to please his mistress (a letdown curiously figured as breast-feeding). "Regarde not Dames, what Cupids Poete writes," Tomalin insists:

> I pennd this storie onelie for myself,
> Who giuing suck unto a childish Elfe,
> And quitte discourag'd in my nurserie
> Since all my store seemes to hir, penurie. (296–300)

Nashe's authorial postscript indulges this queer sexual–textual fantasy further, beginning with a deployment of the familiar "pen" pun pointed at an unmarked, perhaps even self-referential, "friend"—"Thus hath my penne presum'd to please my friend"—and concluding by imagining the pen's ejaculate as feminine superfluity: "Forgiue me if I speake as I was taught, / A lyke to women, utter all I knowe / As longing to unlade so bad a fraught" (Epilogue 6–8). Authorship constitutes both the site of self-assertion for a "mannely" man and a masturbatory, feminizing, and ultimately penurious process—a "storie" that never ends, a self never re-stored.

This hermaphroditic fantasy of the seductions and dangers of erotic imagery to a masculine self is not entirely unique to Nashe, however, nor does it necessarily spell the kind of gender trouble that would substantively rewrite systems of sexual chauvinism. In a study of shame in late Elizabethan literary culture, Georgia Brown reads for ways in which male authors, including Nashe, John Marston, and Shakespeare, embraced just such feminized degradation in their writing "to construct a hermaphroditic model of literary prowess" that is not altogether unpleasurable.[11] The misogyny of Renaissance print culture is, as Brown implies, tempered by such fantasy role-playing, yet the consistent alignment of shame with the feminine seems at the same time to uphold the very binary logic that sustains gender inequality. It might be useful, therefore, to expand this conversation about the performative dimensions of sexual fantasy to distinguish men's pleasure and disgrace at hermaphroditic identification and/or effeminization from the other fantasy roles that such tableaux of sexual shame might invite. This is not to suggest that Nashe's poem does not feminize Tomalin for his failure to prove himself a man in his inability to control his verbal and physical ejaculate and in his general incompetence at securing Francis's sexual pleasure and directing the poem to a generic end. But limiting the range of imaginative response to spectacles of impotency to effeminization *alone* discounts the possibility of seeing Tomalin's penis—in its detumescence—as an erotic scene in its own right. The poem itself suggests a place for the shame of impotence in realms that are, if not entirely outside gender ideology, then certainly located in more perverse relations to it than the popular gender-bending tropes of male transvestitism or hermaphroditism alone allow.

Of course, seeing Tomalin's spectacularly embarrassed penis as a stand-in for the male spectator's own erection (subtly called out in all the punning on pens and [self-]pleasing friends) makes it easy to grasp Boose's previously noted incredulity that any man could derive typical pornographic pleasure from the poem. But this is perhaps the point: Tomalin represents a site of failed mastery on so many levels as to be illegible to discourses looking through—or for—the penetrative lens of a "male gaze." At the same time, Nashe's closing bid to pleasure, alongside the overall discomfort the poem inspires in detractors like Gabriel Harvey, suggests that male readers might *somehow* use the pages of "Nashe's dildo" as erotic stimulus in the same way that Francis does her own dildo, which moves like paper itself, "as light as leaues by winde; / . . . / And doeth my tickling swage with manie a sighe" (240–44). Perhaps we need to ask the question of pleasure again, then, in a different lexicon, such as that of S/M, where the play of power and submission suggests the delectable performativity of all sexual action. Amalia Ziv's critical reading of queer S/M pornography offers useful language to parse the "intrasubjective" experience of shame, involving an "external negative judgment against oneself," from the sort of erotic humiliation taken on in S/M scenarios, which seem to respond to the same linguistic cues as shame but can be "strictly situational . . . involv[ing] not only purposive action but also a certain ceremonial dimension."[12] This differentiation allows the shame of identification with socially despised sexual acts and desires, along with the failure to accede to norms of pleasure and person, to be transfigured into the sort of self-shattering *jouissance* Georges Bataille describes as the end of a most sacred eroticism.[13] Even just allowing a *certain* performative dimension to Tomalin's self-abuse—"She lyeth breathless, I am taken doune" (312)—helps to reimagine his spectacular embarrassment and the derision of his lover as instances of male pleasure at odds with a representational economy that would equate sex with power, power with pleasure, and (so-called) failed sex with (so-called) unpleasurable disempowerment. Tomalin's adjourning disclaimer, "Iudge gentlemen if I deserue not thanks, / . . . / For loe, our threed is spunne, our plaie is donne" (314–16), might be seen in this light to reframe the male reader's complicated appreciation of the preceding narrative as in line with Tomalin's own deliberative erotic play.

My search for affective possibilities here along lines of connectedness rather than drawn according to the logic of symbolic filiation gestures toward what Sedgwick defines as a *beside* critical reading position, which she imagines in Deleuzian terms as "offer[ing] some useful resistance to the ease with which *beneath* and *beyond* turn from spatial descriptors into implicit narratives of, respectively, origin and telos."[14] In addition to allowing us to see impotency as viable pornographic subject matter, such perspective enables me to claim impotency—and the failure of closure it suggests—as a metaphor for my own critical method, which seeks to open up possible readings without foreclosing others. I would therefore also like to consider how differently a desiring female reader might respond to "Choise['s]" unique concatenation of male shame, female aggression, and autoeroticism, to push this question of impotency's erotic and social dimensions further still. In doing this, I do not mean to insist on an essentialist difference between male and female response to pornographic stimulus, which would inevitably reinforce precisely the oppressive regulatory ideals I seek to disarm, nor do I intend to deny the relative stranglehold of patriarchal symbolic order on women's real and imaginative lives in the early modern period, which drastically limited women's access to erotic texts and tableaux. But I believe that it is important to make a conscious effort to avoid talking *only* about men's desires when speculating about the uses to which readers put pornography, to avoid reproducing the very sort of masculinist logic that would mire inventive thinking on the topic of sexual representation by holding women—implicitly or explicitly—to the line of normative sex, while men get to have all the fun.

An example of the way this bias slips into even feminist and progressive analyses of pornography can be found in one of the most exciting archival studies of Nashe's poem in recent years, Ian Moulton's *Before Pornography.* Despite his keen reading of the poem's sensitivity to the fluidity of gender, Moulton's interpretation ultimately defines erotic pleasure as culminating in penetrative sex qua male accomplishment. His reading of the poem's different manuscript editions thus vacillates between discovering "male sexual anxiety" in versions that emphasize Tomalin's phallic mishaps and identifying "a narrative of successful male sexual performance and conquest" in texts that downplay this arc.[15] The most conventionally pornographic text, in Moulton's reckoning, is one "firmly centered on the graphic description of the sex act itself . . . to bring it closer to a fantasy intended to arouse its (male) readers."[16] In the single manuscript known to have been owned by a woman, Margaret Bellasys, the absence of the dildo episode signals "female sexual frustration more than male anxiety."[17] But can we find—or are we not at least obligated to seek—female pleasure, as well as pornographic pleasure, that does not always reproduce the dominant paradigm of sexuality, with enjoyment spelled once more by self-satisfied patriarchal subjectification?

Tomalin's address to an audience of "Dames" at poem's end suggests that this question is at least in *his* purview. And the poetic narrative itself envisions Francis's focus on Tomalin's underwhelming body part to be mocking *and* excited, removed *and* complicit, but always integral and active. Even Francis's chiding at Tomalin's inadequate performance, "Oh not so fast" (179), comes together with Tomalin's description of her looking at his penis. "On him," he writes of it, "hir eyes continually were fixt" (155). Her gaze suggestively "melts" and "reguilds" his erection, as its undoing and its redoing:

> With hir eye-beames his melting looke's were mixt
> Which lyke the Sunne, that twixt tuo glasses plaies
> From one to th' other cast's rebounding rayes.
> He lyke a starre, that to reguild his beames
> Sucks-in the influence of Phebus streames. (156–60)

Not only is this abuse of simile funny, reveling in the semantic pleasure of meaning that fails just slightly, like Tomalin, to hit its target head-on, but the interplay itself positions Tomalin's penis, in its erection and flaccidity, as the explicit, titillating object of a desiring female eye.

Today's hard-core sites aimed at women, like Hot Porn for Women,[18] Google's second listing for "women's porn" in April 2011, suggest a critical model for reading this dynamic in accord with a distinctly female pornographic gaze. The site lists eight categories of professional and amateur video and stills, including "Handsome Hunks," "Couple's Erotica," "Cunnilingus," and "CFNM" (clothed female, naked male). Men in this latter category tend to be found naked, disempowered, and sometimes humiliated at the center of a group of female voyeurs. Coded most often as strippers, "lucky fellas," or "poor slobs," the men, when they are authorized to speak at all, only talk to the women according to the strict protocol of the pornographic performance ("oh, yeah," etc.). By contrast, women in the vignettes generally laugh and talk conversationally with one another. Even scenes that feature a single woman regarding a lone man hint at a collaborative female perspective with verbal asides and textual tags addressed to fellow women. In addition to reversing the usual visual and narrative dynamics of pornographic cinema, which arguably only reproduces its binary logic, this genre imagines women's desire as collaborative, public, and not necessarily organized around the icon of the erect penis or its triumphal procession.

CFNM links to sites with titles such as My Tiny Dick[19] and Little Dick

Humiliation[20] suggest the logical extension of these fantasies to be images of men with small and/or flaccid penises that are eroticized in even more elaborate rituals of public shaming. My Tiny Dick, for example, features sequences of color photos that focus on the escapades of a single small penis belonging to "Jack" (whose full body is never seen) and his "wife" and/or one of her friends. The wife's marginal comments describe and interpret the sexual action, while the exaggerated facial expressions and pantomimic gestures of the women in the scenes with Jack complete the picture. In one aside, the wife writes, "Teddi is one of my friend who i thought would have a really fun time with jack, although she wasn't too happy when she saw what little he was working with, she ended up having fun with it. She laughed at him and made fun of his little pee-pee." On one level, this statement claims the penis as an object of sexual "fun" despite—or perhaps because of—its shortcomings, as in "having fun with." Yet this sexual pleasure also seems to be augmented by Jack's shaming, as in "making fun of." The oscillation of affect, from titillated to tickled, seems designed to evade the critical impulse to separate out pornographic forms and functions from satirical and comical ones, delighting in pleasures that resist generic and normative categorization.

The complexity of both the fictional and spectatorial responses to this "underperforming" penis can be gleaned in the 5,949 member postings to the site that chronicle how viewers first consume the spectacle of the embarrassed, embarrassing "small penis" and, then, how they imagine that spectacle within the realm of a female cybercommunity. It turns out that even though the site is aimed at women, its visitors claim to be both male and female, and they share feelings that range from titillation to celebration and even revulsion, frequently engaging one another in commiseration, community building, and information sharing along the way. Sedgwick's insight into shame's performative dimension, as "more than just [shame's] result or a way of warding it off," offers one way to think about this dissident sexual community, brought together by the recognition of a shared failure to accede to fantasies of the male sexual ideal. For Sedgwick,

> the forms taken by shame are not distinct "toxic" parts of a group or individual identity than can be excised; they are instead integral to and residual in the processes by which identity itself is formed. They

> are available for the work of metamorphosis, reframing, refiguration, *trans*figuration, affective and symbolic loading and deformation, but perhaps all too potent for the work of purgation and deontological closure.[21]

My Tiny Dick's communal identity is cathected by the shame of personal identification with the humiliated male, by participating in a woman's shame at consuming pornography in the wake of feminist diatribe, and by experiencing the imaginative pleasures peculiar to S/M fantasy. Yet this shame is also metamorphosed by the excitement of shared sexual enjoyment. The solitary masturbatory experience of pornography is thus swapped for the frisson of community brought together by an array of penile disappointments.

To insist on "Choise['s]" early place in this particular niche not only denaturalizes the phallic logic of pornography's critical history but also debunks the ideological underpinnings of mainstream straight and gay porn, both of which would train male and female desire along equally oppressive lines by suggesting that sexual action—like masculinity itself—must be defined by pushy, penetrative "pricks" (to borrow Tomalin's own term).[22] It is worth pointing out, though, that Nashe's poem seems to waver in this assertion in its final lines, threatening to betray such a radical sexual vision with an abrupt genre "fix" that promises to swap profane language and subject matter for a sacred lexicon "purg'd of such lasciuious witt, / With purified word's, and hallowed verse" (Epilogue 9–10). The overall spirit of the poem makes it impossible to see such a conversion as ever fully serious, however. Far from affirming an absolute distinction, the barely audible pun on "hallowed" hints that the pleasures of the sacred itself might not feel or look much different from those of the phallic "hollows" on which the poem's thrills depend.

Taking up this question of the relationship between pornographic and devotional feeling more explicitly, John Marston's *Metamorphosis of Pigmalion's Image* (1598) repeatedly compares the masturbatory pleasures of male authorship to multiple experiences of religious shame and female spectatorship. Based loosely on Ovid's tale of a sculptor who falls in love with his creation, whom Venus animates in answer to his prayers, Marston's poem, like Nashe's, invokes the familiar metaphor of the artist's pen and his penis to depict the "loue-hating" (1) Pigmalion as an artist-cum-poet whose clichéd infatuation with "his owne workmanships perfection" (14) turns out to be rigidly self-regarding: "thus enamour'd, [he] dotes on his owne Art / Which he did work, to work his pleasing smart" (71–72).[23] As Lynn Enterline's virtuoso reading of the poem points out, Marston's slightly awkward but persistent reference to the statue as an "image" recalls the verbally drawn images of the day's courtier poets, making clear that Marston's close-range target is "the verbal fetishism" of Petrarchism.[24] Even the sort of bawdy emphasis on female nakedness common to early modern erotica—like the stanza that begins "naked as it stood before his eyes" (19) and ends "All beautie in her nakedness remaines" (24)—serves ultimately to pun on Pigmalion's sexual discovery, his "descrying," as also an act of erotic describing: "O what alluring beauties he descries" (21). Marston reflects on his own verbal play, too, as a form of sexual incontinence when asking the reader, "pardon if I doe trip, / Or if some loose lines from my pen doe slip" (227–28), and confessing shame that his "lines are froth" and "stanzaes saplesse be" ("The Authour in prayse of his *precedent Poem*" [43]).

A contrast between Pigmalion's masturbatory energy and the poet's own emerges at the narrative's closing, however, when the character manages to incorporate his excitement into an act of procreation—the statue eventually comes to life and, "Mid'st all there pleasing . . . / *Paphus* was got" (231–32)—yet the poet finds himself unable to get *his* Petrarchan mistress "In such a wished state / As was afforded to *Pigmalion*" (189–90). Stephen Guy-Bray's *Against Reproduction* convincingly reads this final bid to impotency as revealing writing itself to be no more than "pointless" tumescence, akin to an "idle erection."[25] Rather than serving as a site of self-confirmation for the male poet, it dead-ends in a failure to become teleological that sharply contradicts the textual logic and subjective mandates of reproductive heterosexuality. Yet, in seeing female sexual agency as no more than a structuring absence to the male poet's narcissism and/or abjection, and in reiterating the trope of women as nothing but statues and wombs, Guy-Bray risks affirming the very rules of gender difference that gird Pigmalion's loins and undergird the sexual norm. To press this salvo against normative sexual practice even further, then, I would like to turn a more attentive eye toward how such spectacles of impotency might matter in terms of *her* pleasure. Marston himself pushes a reductive vision of female sexuality to the point of ironic inversion when he posits the most iconic "statue/womb" in Western culture—Mary, the mother of Christ—at the intersection of sacred and profane gazing. Indeed, in animating religious traditions that link female voyeurism, spectacles of impotency, and salvific shame over the course of the poem, Marston effectively dissolves the conventional "Pyg-male gaze" into variants of the sort of erotic undoing that Carolyn Walker Bynum attributes to female mystics and male devotional writers, who employ "female images to attribute an inferiority that would—exactly because it was inferior—be made superior by God."[26] But unlike in Bynum's formula, Marston's degraded, laughable concatenation of base and transcendent eroticism resists a sanitizing distinction of sexual and spiritual experience, taking pleasure in thwarting any—and every—anagogical impulse.

Marston first establishes pornography's typical parameters in a humorous take on the familiar "peep-show," which features the sculptor initially keeping his gaze to the Petrarchan poet's usual sites of interest (lips, cheeks, hair, etc.); but the erotic pull of his creation soon leads him downward, "Vntill his eye discended so far downe / That it descried Loues pauillion, . . . / There would he winke, & winking looke againe" (49–53). Despite the momentary pain of visual privation, given that "Both eies & thoughts would gladly there remaine" (54), Pigmalion's winking seems only to enhance his thrill at the sight of his statue's genitalia by according him an additional measure of control over his pleasure. This game of occultation resonates with Freud's theory of the subject-forming *Fort! Da!* in which, Lacan explains,

> the subject is not simply mastering his privation by assuming it, . . . he is raising his desire to a second power. For his action destroys the object that it causes to appear and disappear in the anticipating *provocation* of its absence and its presence. His action thus negatives the field of forces of desire in order to become its own object to itself.[27]

That this rule of objectification and self-actualization applies to the reader's own pornographic enjoyment is suggested in the reader's implicit identification with Pigmalion's authoritative male gaze.

The very next stanza confirms this analogous relationship by reproducing the dynamic of a pleasurable absence on the narrative level. Turning away from the scene of sexual action, the narrator asks,

> Who euer saw the subtile Citty-dame
> In sacred church whe[n] her pure thoughts shold pray,
> Piere through her fingers, so to hide her shame,
> When that her eye her mind would faine bewray.
> So would he view, and winke, and view againe[.] (55–59)

The reader's voyeurism, like Pigmalion's, is materialized in retrospect against pleasure's privation (and in the contradictory pleasure *of* privation). But unlike Pigmalion's deliberative mastering of his desire, the reader's earlier enjoyment stands in sharp, unwilling relief not only against the passage's dryness but also against such a striking dissonance that it feels, instead, like a moment of acute readerly disciplining. The subtle shift of registers (Pigmalion winks for fun, the city-dame for shame) transforms the affirming pleasure of identification with power into the murkier, masochistic pleasure of a city-dame's public humiliation. This is now not voyeurism at all but the corrosive internalization of social regulations. At the same time, such shame seems to reach beyond the confines of the social when felt in the context of "sacred church," suggesting the sort of "perverse eroticism" Leo Bersani finds at the heart of religious modes of "self-abasement" and "masochism [in which] the self is exuberantly discarded."[28] Such ecstatic pleasures forcibly disrupt the kinds of identity-based "fantasies of bodily power and subordination" that would compel a city-dame to feel shame at her sexuality in the first place.[29]

The second icon of religious devotion that gives context to Pigmalion's "doting" (73) and "dally[ing]" (74) seems to part from this image of penitent female gazing. "Looke how the peeuish Papists crouch, and kneele / To some dum Idoll with their offering, / As if a senceles carued stone could feele," Marston writes, "So fond he was, and earnest in his sute / To his remorsles Image, dum and mute" (79–81; 83–84). However, the city-dame's mixed feelings of desire and shame can be seen to forecast the reader's structural recognition of her own peeking pleasure, as graphic images of "lip[s]" and "Iuory breasts" (73–74) are once again dangled forth only to be abruptly snatched away. The imaginative shift to the scorned Papists' contemplative devotion builds on this recognition, clarifying and enacting the ritual aspects of humility. Marston's self-flagellation in the author's postscript over his own "penning" part extends this comparison further, culminating in a vow to "vse Popelings discipline / . . . [to] Censure my selfe" ("The Authour" 37) that reimagines the depths of religious subjection as a performance of self-abuse and abusive cynicism. He concludes, "Thus hauing rail'd against my selfe a while, / Ile snarle at those, which doe the world beguile" ("The Authour" 43–44).[30] Although Marston's satirical edge invites an easy reading of this shameful—and shaming—spectacle of male masturbation and impotence as a culminating indictment of erotica, such a conclusion would be premature. Significantly, Marston's pornographic scenarios also uncover new possibilities for sexual action and feeling when they incorporate their complex and resonant rituals of self-exposure and prostration into traditions of authorized male and female gazing.

The poem's most charged sexual moment, when the statue herself rouses to life at Pigmalion's urging, brings this into focus, taking shape against and in concert with the most profound religious allusion yet: the mother Mary's visual and emotional experience looking on Christ's inert, then rising, form. Describing Pigmalion's excitement, "when his hands her faire form'd limbs had felt" (169), Marston proceeds to ask his reader,

> Doe but conceiue a Mother's passing gladnes,
> (After that death her onely sonne hath seazed
> And ouerwhelm'd her soule with endless sadnes)
> When that she sees him gin for to be raised
> From out his deadly swoune to life again[.] (175–79)

"Such ioy," we are told, in a play on erection and resurrection, "*Pigmalion* feels in *euery* vaine" (180; emphasis added). The protagonist's arousal appears possible only as the *afterimage* of another man's "deadly swoun," and the reader's own pornographic gaze must first pass through the eyes of a woman looking on a spectacle of absolute male impotence to imagine conventional sexual action. Within such an affective frame, *Pigmalion*'s distinctive pornographic pleasure emerges as the painful and exciting negotiation between patriarchal forms of viewing, like those lampooned in the poem, and a sacred visual experience that abandons just such symbolic order.[31] Yet here we do not quite find the sort of "salvific transgressivity" that Richard Rambuss uncovers in the "devotional eroticism" of Tudor–Stuart poets like John Donne, George Herbert, and Richard Crashaw, whose religious expression Rambuss identifies with a masochistic homoeroticism and "radical gender *undecidability*."[32] Even though a poem such as Donne's "Holy Sonnet 14"—"Batter my heart, three-person God / . . . / That I may rise, and stand, o'erthrow me, and bend / Your force, to break, blow, burn, and make me new" (1, 3–4)—highlights the "complementarity" of sacred and illicit eroticism, Donne ultimately plumbs the depths of devotional sensation to "rise" to religious and social duty.[33] Marston's pornographic enactments of shame, by contrast, seem at pains to debase this ideal of erection.[34]

The reader's own body finds place in this intricate imaginative skein in images of both male and female—and homo and hetero—sex "parts," alternately hailed as "Mistres," "Ladies," "him," and "he" and described as "some wanton itching eare" (193), "gaping eares that swallow vp my lines" (224), and "tickle[d] up," "leud Priapians" ("The Authour," 6). Although cross-gender referencing like this might just partake in the popular trend of male poets invoking an imaginary female audience to impress a strictly homosocial cohort, it is just as reasonable to read the poet's audience as the sort of women Renaissance writers obsessed over when they imagined a female readership for popular romances or Ovidian narratives.[35] Such heterogeneity enables a wider range of readings and reading positions, exemplified in a passage addressing a party of "Ladies" with advice on sex and seduction—"thinke that they nere loue you, / Who doe not vnto more then kissing moue you" (119–20)—which momentarily establishes sympathy with women, only to undercut it a few stanzas later, when the poet turns to a male coterie with mocking commentary on just such women. Rather than find in this Marston's underlying misogyny, I follow critics like Brown who read it as enacting the same dialectic of power and disempowerment that, throughout the poem, defines pleasure as the destabilization of gendered and sexual selfhood. Moreover, in harnessing the affective legacy of religious shame to pornographic modes of speculation, Marston activates a spectrum of feelings that resist normative models of sexuality, licensing women to "look" and "feel" even in response to literature in which they are typically looked at and, as it were, felt up.

Mainstream conversations about pornography in recent years have followed Marston's and Nashe's move away from the focus on women's victimization associated with the MacKinnon–Dworkin set, yet new emphasis on men's victimization only serves to replay the same old tired parts, with the online porn "addict" now taking center stage as a man "Lyke one with Ouids cursed hemlock charm'd" ("Choice" 124). And no one in today's mass media seems to be laughing or even thinking seriously about the range of meanings that might attach to these public spectacles of impotency. For example, Pamela Paul's *Pornified,* with its subtitle *How Pornography Is Damaging Our Lives, Our Relationships, and Our Families,* focuses on the way men's increasing use of Internet pornography is harming their "real" sex lives. Paul quotes Mark Schwartz, the clinical director of the Masters and Johnson Clinic in St. Louis, who complains, "You may be making love to your wife, but you're picturing someone else. That's not fair to the woman, and it's miserable for the man."[36] Paul's numerous case studies find echo in Robert Jensen's *Getting Off: Pornography and the End of Masculinity* as well as in Michael Leahy's *Porn Nation,* to name just a few voices in the growing cacophony of men who confess "shame"—after pornography usage, in sexual encounters with "real women," and in life in general.[37] This exclusively negative and overtly simplistic focus on masculine shame and humiliation, emblematized in the impotent penis, leads to the thesis that "pornography not only objectifies women . . . it eventually becomes self-objectifying [for men]."[38] Clinical assessments of cybersex similarly bemoan the connection between compulsive porn surfing and men's sexual dysfunction.[39] Even feminist icons seem to be taking patriarchal prerogatives—tumescence, ejaculation, insemination—quite seriously, complaining, as Naomi Wolf does, that "the onslaught of porn is responsible for deadening the male libido in relation to real women."[40]

In their efforts to return sexuality to an original, "natural," and intimate state, this uniform reinscription of heterosexual values and patriarchal ideals disallows the possibility that alternative modes of erotic understanding and pleasure might be at play here, both at the level of consumption and in the discourse that emerges out of these spectacles of "addiction" and detumescence. My aim in drawing attention to these early modern exempla as well as to the conversation today on the subject of male impotency is not only to revalue (devalue) penetrative narratives of hetero- and homoeroticism in pornography but also to activate the shifting lens of a female pornographic gaze to glance askance at reigning histories of pornographic representation. Indeed, despite all the attention paid to men, now as porn's addicts rather than its goons, a 2003 Nielsen/NetRatings survey reveals female viewers to account for 30 percent of all Internet traffic on adult content sites.[41] Star producers like Candida Royale, Annie Sprinkle, and Nina Hartley have begun to target this new consumer base with vigorous experimental films that are alert to women's visual pleasure, and the burgeoning market in self-imagined and self-directed "amateur" pornography perhaps most dramatically fleshes out the feminist and demotic potential of the graphic sex trade. To admit the viability of women's pornographic spectatorship would seem to do more than just overturn assumptions about whose desires are "soft" (narrative, romantic) and whose are "hard" (visual, explicit): it would force the doomsday rhetoric regarding the survival of the species to be a bit more honest about the difference between exploring pleasure and guarding privilege.

Notes

1 Walter Kendrick, *The Secret Museum: Pornography in Modern Culture* (1987; repr., Berkeley: University of California Press, 1997).

2 See Ian Fredrick Moulton, *Before Pornography: Erotic Writing in Early Modern England* (Oxford: Oxford University Press, 2000), and David O. Franz, *Festum Voluptatis: A Study of Renaissance Erotica* (Columbus: Ohio State University Press, 1989).

3 See Feona Attwood's thorough study of scholarly trends in pornography research, particularly her focus on the historicizing works produced in the decades following the divisive pornography debates of the 1980s, which are intent on "shifting attention away from the pornographic 'things' that have been placed centre stage of the porn debate and on to the cultural

anxieties surrounding pornographic consumption by particular groups." Attwood, "Reading Porn: The Paradigm Shift in Pornography Research," *Sexualities* 5, no. 1 (2002): 95.

4 Eve Kosofsky Sedgwick, *Touching Feeling: Affect, Pedagogy, Performativity* (Durham, N.C.: Duke University Press, 2003), 12. Sedgwick's introduction offers an insightful and lyrical exploration of the limits of the prohibition/repression model of criticism, arguing that the "pseudo-dichotomy between repression and liberation has led, in many cases, to its conceptual reimposition in the even more abstractly reified form of the hegemonic and the subversive," with the former standing in for the status quo and the latter posed in "a purely negative relation to that" (12). This binary formulation in and of itself, she argues, tends to erode the vital in-between spaces where "effectual creativity and change" (13) might take root. My inspection of pornography's lost history is guided by Sedgwick's critique of "suspicious," or ideological, reading practices and by her exploration of a theory of affect—particularly shame—that would sidestep the poles reified by this reigning critical method.

5 This is not to suggest that impotency as subject matter entirely escapes critical notice, only that critics tend to abstract its meaning as a *sign of* gender, class, or sex politics rather than to confront it as sexually arousing in and of itself. A notable exception is Constance Penley's "Crackers and Whackers: The White Trashing of Porn," in *Pornography: Film and Culture*, ed. Peter Lehman, 99–117 (New Brunswick, N.J.: Rutgers University Press, 2006). Penley points out that much of pornography's film history, right up until the so-called golden age of the 1970s, was deeply invested in pranks on male impotence and sexual folly; but Penley reads these pranks and follies more often as tickling the popular funny bone by underwriting "attacks" on religion and class than as deliberately courting an affect of shame. Literary histories of impotence such as Roger Kuin and Anne Lake Prescott's "The Wrath of Priapus: Remy Belleau's 'Jean qui ne peult' and its Traditions," *Comparative Literature Studies* 17, no. 1 (2000): 1–17, and Hannah Lavery's "Exchange and Reciprocation in Nashe's 'Choice of Valentines,'" *Appositions: Studies in Renaissance/Early Modern Literature and Culture* 1 (2008), http://appositions.blogspot.com, offer equally insightful readings that nonetheless follow a similar pattern of ideological critique.

6 Moulton's *Before Pornography* ably explores the role of Italy's Pietro Aretino in structuring the English pornographic imagination in the

sixteenth and seventeenth centuries, and Paula Findlen's excellent essay "Humanism, Politics, and Pornography in Renaissance Italy," in *The Invention of Pornography: Obscenity and the Origins of Modernity, 1500–1800*, ed. Lynn Hunt, 49–108 (New York: Zone Books, 1993), notes the ways in which Aretino's legendary prostitute dialogues, *Ragionamenti* (1534, 1536), and his graphic sonnet and image pairings, *Sonetti lussuriosi* (1526), enriched the early modern pornographic imagination and, with it, the world of social and international politics. For additional context, see Franz's seminal *Festum Voluptatis* and Bette Talvacchia's insightful *Taking Positions: On the Erotic in Renaissance Culture* (Princeton, N.J.: Princeton University Press, 1999).

7 For the former reading, see Moulton, *Before Pornography*, 158–93. For the latter, see Jonathan Crewe, *Unredeemed Rhetoric: Thomas Nashe and the Scandal of Authorship* (Baltimore: The Johns Hopkins University Press, 1982), 48–54.

8 Lynda E. Boose, "The 1599 Bishop's Ban, Elizabethan Pornography, and the Sexualization of the Jacobean State," in *Enclosure Acts: Sexuality, Property, and Culture in Early Modern England*, ed. Richard Burt and John Michael Archer (Ithaca, N.Y.: Cornell University Press, 1994), 192.

9 All in-text line citations from "The choise of valentines" are drawn from *The Works of Thomas Nashe*, vol. 3, ed. Ronald B. McKerrow (New York: Barnes and Noble, 1966).

10 Bruce Thomas Boehrer, "Behn's 'Disappointment' and Nashe's 'Choise of Valentines': Pornographic Poetry and the Influence of Anxiety," *Essays in Literature* 16, no. 2 (1989): 172–87.

11 Georgia Brown, *Redefining Elizabethan Literature* (Cambridge: Cambridge University Press, 2004), 108.

12 Amalia Ziv, "Shameful Fantasies: Cross-Gender Queer Sex in Lesbian Erotic Fiction," in *Gay Shame*, ed. David M. Halperin and Valerie Traub (Chicago: University of Chicago Press, 2009), 170.

13 Georges Bataille, *Erotism: Death and Sensuality*, trans. Mary Dalwood (San Francisco: City Lights, 1986).

14 Sedgwick, *Touching Feeling*, 8.

15 Moulton, *Before Pornography*, 190.

16 Ibid., 189.

17 Ibid., 192.

18 http://www.hotpornforwomen.com/.

19 http://www.mytinydick.com/.

20 http://www.heylittledick.com/.

21 Sedgwick, *Touching Feeling,* 63.

22 In his study of user-generated Internet sites such as RedClouds and Voyeurweb, Peter Lehman tracks the amateur images of flaccid or small penises that he claims challenge the hegemonic ideal of masculinity by taking the phallus and penetration out of its central position, "assault[ing] the controlled, orderly photographic and filmic history of the sexual representation of the male body." "You and Voyeurweb: Illustrating the Shifting Representation of the Penis on the Internet with User-Generated Content," *Cinema Journal* 46, no. 4 (2007): 114. Tomalin's aggressive description of his own sexual action reveals in its violence what is at stake in reimagining this phallic ideal: "He rubd', and prict, and pierst hir to the bones" (145).

23 All in-text line citations from Marston's poem are drawn from John Marston, *The Metamorphosis of Pigmalions Image. And Certaine Satyres* (London: Printed for Edmond Matts, 1598).

24 Lynn Enterline, *The Rhetoric of the Body from Ovid to Shakespeare* (Cambridge: Cambridge University Press, 2000), 125–51.

25 Stephen Guy-Bray, *Against Reproduction: Where Renaissance Texts Come From* (Toronto, Ont.: Toronto University Press, 2009), 135.

26 Carolyn Walker Bynum, "The Body of Christ in the Late Middle Ages: A Reply to Leo Steinberg," *Renaissance Quarterly* 39, no. 3 (1986): 436.

27 Jacques Lacan, "Function and Field of Speech and Language," in *Écrits: A Selection,* trans. Alan Sheridan (New York: W. W. Norton, 1977), 103.

28 Leo Bersani, "Is the Rectum a Grave?" *October* 42 (1987): 217, 218.

29 Ibid., 217.

30 Douglas Bruster's "The Structural Transformation of Print in Late Elizabethan England," in *Print, Manuscript and Performance,* ed. Arthur F Marotti and Michael D. Bristol, 49–89 (Columbus: Ohio State University Press, 2000), provides insight into the way that early modern satirical forms got mixed into (and up with) erotica; he argues that the abusive pamphlets of the Marprelate era accustomed readers both to "sadistic" literary treatments of the body and to looking for "real" bodies behind characters and authors, resulting in a form of "embodied writing" that brought readers into the sort of close imaginative proximity to literary texts that is necessary for porn to touch its readers most intimately.

31 Sarah Stanbury's study of Middle English lyrics of the Passion reveals such identification with Mary's transgressive and eroticized female gaze

to be a powerful vehicle for devotion in medieval Catholicism. In these texts, the reader is invited to look "not only at Christ's suffering and mutilated body but also at the Virgin gazing on that body, a spectacle that is further mediated by the poet, often in the persona of an actual watcher at the scene." Stanbury, "The Virgin's Gaze: Spectacle and Transgression in Middle English Lyrics of the Passion," *PMLA* 106, no. 5 (1991): 1086.

32 Richard Rambuss, *Closet Devotions* (Durham, N.C.: Duke University Press, 1998), 58, 37.

33 John Donne, *The Complete English Poems,* ed. A. J. Smith (New York: Penguin, 1986).

34 In a "Reactio" poem included among the *Certaine Satyres* that follow the 1598 text of *Pigmalion's Image,* Marston launches a brief defense of Robert Southwell against "swinish" (31) detractors who would "scent and grunt" (32) "Gainst Peter's tears and Mary's moving moan" (37), suggesting the play of gazes and powerful lines of maternal loss from Southwell's "The Virgin Mary to Christ on the Cross" (1595) as a possible backdrop for Marston's image here. We must take Marston's religious allusion as grasping at something more profound than mere cynicism if we hear in it traces of Southwell's earnest pathos: "Iesus my loue, my sonne, my God, / behold thy mother washt in teares" (3).

35 Richard Halpern's "'Pining their Maws': Female Readers and the Erotic Ontology of the Text in Shakespeare's *Venus and Adonis,*" in *Venus and Adonis: Critical Essays,* ed. Philip P. Kolin, 377–89 (New York: Garland, 1997), examines the circulation of Shakespeare's 1593 epyllion as a sign of women's erotic reading habits (and men's sexual anxieties). Sasha Roberts's *Reading Shakespeare's Poems in Early Modern England* (New York: Palgrave Macmillan, 2003) chases this discursive affiliation even further, reading it against the poem's actual place and usage in the libraries of women in the seventeenth century. See also Sarah Toulalan, *Imaging Sex: Pornography and Bodies in Seventeenth-Century England* (Oxford: Oxford University Press, 2007), and Helen Hackett, *Women and Romance Fiction in the English Renaissance* (Cambridge: Cambridge University Press, 2000).

36 Quoted in Pamela Paul, *Pornified: How Pornography Is Damaging Our Lives, Our Families, and Our Relationships* (New York: Holt, 2006), 105.

37 Robert Jensen, *Getting Off: Pornography and the End of Masculinity* (Cambridge, Mass.: South End Press, 2007); Michael Leahy, *Porn Nation: America's #1 Addiction* (Chicago: Northfield, 2008).

38 Paul, *Pornified,* 105.

39 See Jennifer P. Schneider, "The New 'Elephant in the Living Room': Effects of Compulsive Cybersex Behaviors on the Spouse," in *Sex & the Internet: A Guidebook for Clinicians,* ed. Al Cooper, 169–86 (New York: Brunner-Routledge, 2002).

40 Naomi Wolf, "The Porn Myth," *New York Magazine,* October 20, 2003, http://nymag.com/nymetro/news/trends/n_9437/.

41 Gretchen Gallen, "More Women into Porn," http://www.xbiz.com/news/1161.

4

"Unmanly Passion": Sodomitical Self-Fashioning in John Ford's *The Lover's Melancholy* and *Perkin Warbeck*

NICHOLAS F. RADEL

The title of this collection notwithstanding, there may be no such thing as sex before sex, and—as I should make clear up front considering the subject of my particular essay—no such thing as homosexuality before its emergence in the modern period. This is true even (especially) in the most literal sense. Only in the late nineteenth or early twentieth century did *sex* acquire its present common usage as sexual intercourse. Before that, it tended to refer to the two main categories that distinguished people according to their relation to reproduction: male or female. As for homosexuality, the word did not exist, as is by now well known, until the late nineteenth century, and, as Foucault wrote—famously igniting a controversy in which this essay takes small part—it was only in the nineteenth century that the "homosexual became a personage—a past, a case history, a childhood, a character, a form of life; also a morphology, with an indiscreet anatomy and possibly mysterious physiology."[1] When one inquires after sex or homosexuality in premodern Europe, and especially in the English Renaissance with which these essays are concerned, one has to inquire into those defining discourses and material practices that accrue around desire and the body that are often—but not always—different from those we take for granted. Looking for sex before sex is an always already queered enterprise because it involves exploring erotic behavior or practice with an eye to its strangeness, the ways it reveals itself in terms different from our own normative and heteronormative ones.

This idea—now more or less widely accepted—is one I will illustrate by looking at two works by John Ford, his early tragicomedy, *The Lover's Melancholy* (circa 1628) and his only history play, *Perkin Warbeck* (circa 1632), for Ford's plays are an especially revealing location for discerning the ways erotic activities and practices were embodied in Renaissance England. Although they have long been noted for their sensitive elaboration of the social regulation of women and women's bodies that precipitates female psychic disorder, they have not, oddly enough, been systematically investigated for their insights into masculinity and male erotic practices. My primary purpose in this essay will be to show not only how historically specific discourses of male desire were dispersed through normative homosocial bonds in the two plays I examine but, more significantly, how these discourses were regulated and defined more restrictively in relation to the instantiation of types of masculine perversion in the works.

In making such a historical argument, I also want to make clear that I take it as a given that while there is no such thing as sex before sex—in the sense that Renaissance bodily practices differ so much from ours as to be seemingly different species of behavior—there is also no way to access an understanding of bodies in aesthetic texts that is not inflected by and does not revise the present in which we write. "Sexualities of the past, especially queer sexualities," Graham L. Hammill explains, "demand modes of cultural memory in our present and their future (the two are not the same) that attend to temporality."[2] There is no sex before sex precisely because we cannot speak about the arrangements of bodies and desires in earlier ages without at least referencing our own normalizing constructions and thereby participating in a process of reading both backward to the past and forward into our present. I qualify my historical argument in this way in part as a form of disclosure: my reading of the dialectic between perverse embodiments of masculinity and normative homosociality in Ford's plays is obviously conditioned by my own minority homosexual experience and engagement with critical minority studies. More to the point, however, I want to evoke a past in which some—if not these particular—minoritizing understandings of same-sex sexuality did obtain in order to highlight its resemblance to a present in which our minority understandings are not exhaustive.

I take to heart recent arguments challenging "the historicist investment in a progressive chronology according to which the stable present becomes the point from which to map an unstable past," but I want to resist their understanding that such readings are always chronological or proceed necessarily from a present always conceived as stable.[3] Writing from the perspective of a homosexuality that did not exist in the past may tend to universalize the present—in the sense in which Eve Kosofsky Sedgwick evokes that term to describe a "universalizing" as opposed to "minoritizing" view of "homo/heterosexual definition" as "an issue of continuing, determinative importance in the lives of people across the spectrum of sexualities."[4] That is, it may remind us that other ways of prioritizing the relations between "minoritizing" and "universalizing" views of sexuality remain implicit in our own.[5]

If, as current orthodoxy insists, there was no homosexuality in the English Renaissance, Ford's plays suggest that there were prohibitions on speaking male–male desire that link modern and early modern constructions of masculinity and sexuality (including homosexuality). The perverse articulations of male desire I examine in Ford's plays are not modern homosexuality, and they do not constitute the origins of that historically specific instantiation of sexuality. But their prohibition, and their appearance in a structure of prohibition that enabled other male bonds to be read as nonthreatening or even nonsexual, is not unlike the structure of prohibitions in modern thinking that enforces preternatural distinctions between male erotic desires and so-called sexual activities or behaviors. The plays reveal something about the prohibitions on male–male desire that were imagined in terms of dominant masculinity and issues of privilege in the defining and articulating of the social hierarchies of manhood. In so doing, they demonstrate a link between the two periods—not around sexual identity but around the transhistorical play of minoritizing and universalizing constructions of masculine identities.[6] Thus Ford's plays might be read as part of a genealogy of modern homosexuality, which, as a category, Sedgwick argues, is important not "from its regulatory relation to a nascent or already-constituted minority of homosexual people or desires, but from its potential to give whoever wields it a structuring definitional leverage over the whole range of male bonds that shape the social constitution."[7]

In Renaissance England, an era before sex, normative masculine desire was a carefully regulated discourse that, when allowed, could be effectively silenced in its potential to represent disruptive sexual activity by being absorbed into various other cultural institutions enabled by it, institutions such as friendship, service, or political loyalty. The language of passionate, normative male bonding resonates in Ford's plays, as it does throughout the Renaissance drama. But some men in these works seem more empowered than others to represent themselves as maintaining bodily and social control that removes their desires (and indeed perhaps their erotic acts) from the realm of explicit disclosure.[8] They are so empowered precisely because they can be distinguished from other, abject voices of masculine desire that are represented as noisy, effusive, socially transgressive, or lacking control, prohibited voices that provide the true dramatic interest of Ford's fascinating works.[9] Status quo, hierarchical, authorized masculinity is reflected in one's ability to silence desire that exceeds social norms. Masculinity and masculine desire in Ford's plays, then, are not always and never necessarily sexual in precisely the ways we might understand them (penetrative, phallic, or primarily heteronormative, for instance), and the playwright's exploration of perversely embodied versions of both tends to draw boundaries around normative homosocial bonds that restrict their meanings to the social and not the sexual.[10]

As a historical argument, this chapter suggests that Ford's plays bring to the fore and attempt to reconcile the tensions in distinguishing a category such as friendship from sodomy, tensions that Alan Bray long ago argued troubled male relations in Elizabethan England.[11] They do so by giving specific, embodied shape to troublesome or perverse expressions of male desire. Although these perversions were subject to and never far from the generalizing prohibitions on sodomy in Renaissance England, their appearance in Ford's plays also suggests that sodomy itself was becoming domesticated as perversion, incorporated into everyday understandings of masculine behavior in ways that reveal how masculine eroticism was not so much about particular sexual acts as about the contest to control who defined the meaning of these acts and how they were or were not to be put into discourse. Such masculine perversions as we find in the plays help define and delimit some men's access to power, self-description, and sexual agency, and what is especially compelling about a play such as *Perkin Warbeck* is that Ford comes very close to valorizing the perverse agency of his eponymous hero.

Similar ideas have seemed obvious to feminists studying the representation in the Renaissance of women, whose varied possibilities for social agency were (often ineffectively, it must be conceded) policed by sexual categories such as whore, maid, or wife. Whereas women's silence was (misogynistically) presumed to embody assent to their particular place in the sex–gender structures of the period, and their speech a mark of social resistance that was policed through other sexual embodiments, the same might be usefully argued about particular men who were not otherwise empowered to speak either their social or sexual desires with regard to more powerful men.[12] As I hope to show through my reading of Ford, men's silence about their desires (social and sexual) could be understood as a productive discourse of assent to their privileging within heteronormative, homosocial, and homoerotic structures that bound them; and, more important, their active speaking could be construed as an individualizing and dangerous assertion that demarcates the normative elsewhere. Indeed, Carla Freccero has argued with regard to women that when gender is factored back into the equation for understanding early modern sexualities, we find something of the kinds of perverse embodiments that Foucault, in the first volume of the *History of Sexuality,* argued appeared only in the nineteenth century. The same thing seems to hold true for men as well: when we consider early modern masculinity not as a monolithic entity over and against female subjectivity but as a variegated category inflected by class, social position, and age, among other factors, we discover a "tendency in premodernity—as in modernity," to use Freccero's words, "to produce particular normalized embodied subjects through a discursive implantation of perversions."[13] It is precisely this tendency I want to demonstrate in the plays of John Ford, undoing in the process something of the history of sodomy as a supposedly unnameable concept.

Early in his career as a solo dramatist, in what may be his first singly authored play, *The Lover's Melancholy,* Ford manifests discomfort with masculine desire that seems (perhaps only deceptively) like those discomforts revealed in the prohibitory structures of modern homophobia. We find in the play evidence of how normative modes of masculine desire, otherwise unmarked and unremarked as sexual, get enfolded into perverse structures that announce themselves—noisily—as potentially homoerotic desire or even sex. Clearly written in the tradition of political commentary that underlay Beaumont and Fletcher's tragicomedies, the play's romance plot reflects, in Mario DiGangi's reading, not only Ford's interest in psychology but the political issues of a disordered state. "Excessive passion," including same-sex disorder, points toward the political dysfunctions of Prince Palador's reign subsequent to the attempt of the prince's father, Agenor, to seduce or rape his son's betrothed, Eroclea.[14] When the play opens, Eroclea has fled the state, and Palador has lapsed into a melancholy that leads him to neglect his civic and political duties. It is the cure of this melancholy, and the return of Eroclea, that provides the substance of the plot as well as the play's tragicomic closure.

As Brian Opie argues about two of Ford's other plays, *Loues Sacrifice* and *The Ladies Triall,* a characteristic strategy for Ford is to construct his particular (and in Opie's reading unique) vision of affective love by contrast with older, material ones:

> Ford's selective emphasis upon young people of marriageable age, lacking parental oversight or involvement, reveals a new generation attempting, on the basis of "free affects" and the harmonizing of gender differences through moral virtues and self discipline, to institute a model of social being in which intrinsic qualities ("love") rather than extrinsic rules ("law") and kinship networks are determinative.[15]

Indeed, Opie's argument anticipates and is reinforced by one Mario DiGangi makes. Whereas Opie argues that much of the moral virtue and self-discipline that lead to love are exemplarily embodied in male friendship, DiGangi writes that "intimate male friendship provides a model for conjugal harmony because both relationships depend on an 'equal love' between two souls. . . . Eroclea and Palador must achieve the harmonious union already enjoyed by Menaphon and Amethus before the play can end happily."[16]

Yet, while the equal affections of Menaphon and Amethus certainly help reinforce the necessary attributes of love that are implied by Ford's tragicomic ending, when Palador reunites with Eroclea, and Thamasta with her erstwhile-spurned lover Menaphon, the friend of her brother, it is not only older people who represent the opposite of affective, equal love (Opie's reading), and it is not simply valorized homosocial bonds that provide the model for such relationships (Opie's and DiGangi's readings). Something else written into the structure of the play serves as an antithesis that helps define these love relationships: an abiding association of homoerotic attraction—especially that between Palador and the supposed boy, Parthenophill—with the troubling and "tragic" aspects of this drama of mixed genre.

Disorderly, same-sex desire figures into this dysfunctional state in at least three ways. First, it appears in the seemingly sexually threatening appearance in Palador's court of Parthenophill, who reminds the prince of Eroclea and who, thus, becomes the obsessive focus of his interest. Parthenophill, as any number of Fletcherian tragicomedies will have reminded the audience, is, of course, the disguised Eroclea, and the complications engendered by her disguise lead to the second seemingly same-sex provocation, when the haughty Thamasta falls in love with Parthenophill and yet persists in her devotion even after she is assured that "he" is Eroclea: "It will be / A hard task for my reason to relinquish / The affection which was once devoted thine" (3.2.176–78).[17] Finally, Ford seems to parody both these provocations in his subplot, in which the absurd courtier Cuculus attempts to introduce to the court a new fashion for female pages. His absurdities occasion the sexual jokes one might imagine, but these jokes are made double-edged by the fact that his page, Grilla, is, unbeknownst to Cuculus, actually a boy. Although as Alan Sinfield puts it, "same-gender relations were relatively unimportant in the sex/gender system" of Renaissance England, and the potential sexual availability of the boy Ganymede figure was widely recognized, the figure could also manifest "signs of humour, disapproval and envy, alongside opportunities for unorthodox sexual feelings."[18] Ford taps into this complex of negative feeling to help characterize those same-sex desires that in other, more normative contexts may well have passed unremarked.

That these same-sex desires slide almost imperceptibly toward a specific sexual formulation might initially be discerned by examining the play in its dramatic contexts. When, at the beginning of *The Lover's Melancholy,* Eroclea, disguised as Parthenophill, returns to Cyprus unbeknownst to Palador (and initially to the audience), Palador becomes fascinated with "him." The prince's desire cannot be wholly explained by the fact that Parthenophill is really a woman, for Ford provides credible evidence that Palador believes him to be a boy. Even in the final scenes, when Eroclea appears on stage in women's garments to reveal herself to Palador, the prince continues to respond to her as if she were still Parthenophill. Ford's characterization is subtle and psychologically complex as it represents Palador's initial inability to recognize what he has lost, except in the image of what has been found.

Yet, despite its historically specific and genre-linked assumption that Palador is capable of an eroticized interest in boys as well as girls, Ford's handling of this cross-dressing plot combines the sexual possibilities of such cross-dressing motifs to be found in Shakespeare with the prurience and paranoia more typical of Fletcher's tragicomedies.[19] Although Palador's urgent desire to connect with Parthenophill and his fear that the boy has betrayed him recalls the relationship of Orsino and Caesario in *Twelfth Night,* Ford is somewhat coy about dramatizing the connection. He tends to report rather than dramatize Palador and Parthenophill's interactions and so brings them into being almost under erasure. He also names his character in a way that explicitly undercuts his homoerotic potential (reversing Shakespeare's use of names in *Twelfth Night* or *As You Like It*). Parthenophill is the lover of virginity, and early on, Ford provides strong hints to the audience (if not to the disordered and disorderly Palador) that "he" is really a she.

It is almost as if, in recognizing the utility of the cross-dressing plot to develop his theme of the cure of melancholy and the revival of the state, Ford also recognizes and abjures the potential homoerotic possibilities the genre occasioned. So, as part of the cure for his melancholia, Palador's response to the supposed Parthenophill is dramatized as that which is exchanged for the normalizing (in terms of the social and political plot) relationship to Eroclea. Although Palador's reunion scene with the now clearly identified woman, Eroclea, remains charged with sodomitical imagery in which "Parthenophill" is accused of dressing as a woman to bewitch the prince and perhaps assassinate him, such sodomitical fears gradually give way to a redemptive discourse in which heteronormative love embodies effective political functioning:

> Hymen shall now
> Set all his torches burning to give light
> Throughout this land, new-settled in thy welcome. (4.3.141–43)

Against a long unraveling of the confusions of Eroclea's identity and explanation of her absence, and against his own introspective analysis of his mental confusion and openness to political threat, Palador settles on the only seemingly mixed metaphor of marriage in a "new-settled" land to image a restitution both of his personal and political person. Heteronormative love and marriage effect a restoration of Palador's formerly disordered S/state that is represented in the prince's giving over misperceptions that had been homoerotically embodied. Same-sex desire in the play seems to be rendered in a disorderly space, a space in which it is paradoxically not to be spoken.

Nevertheless, the play has in fact spoken it rather explicitly, so Palador's articulation of homoerotic desire gets encoded as social and sexual dissonance in relation to the normative settlements of the play's tragicomic ending. As is true of many of Fletcher's tragicomedies, the ending of *The Lover's Melancholy* cannot easily erase the tragic aspects of the drama it has carefully constructed. Rather than simply bring its prince back into the heteronormative society imagined at its conclusion, the play reveals—indeed, Ford seems deliberately to exploit—tensions implicit in its Fletcherian structure.[20] In particular, the play dramatizes those possibilities for masculine and same-sex desire that had been explored by earlier playwrights through transvestite comedies, but in doing so, it literally reveals the masculine relations of Palador and Parthenophill as a love not usually spoken, indeed perhaps one not to be named. It is a love that exists on the threatening side of a dividing line between political instability and state order, sickness and health, the unnatural and the natural, the ruined and restored. Thus *The Lover's Melancholy* produces competing structures of homosocial and homoerotic affiliation that hint at aspects of masculine and/or homoerotic perversions in relation to more normative structures of valorized male bonding. Masculine homoeroticism is never simply or fully subsumed into the laudable homosocial bonding represented by Menaphon and Amethus or the heteronormative conclusion. It remains in excess of the play's social settlements to suggest that there are right and wrong ways to perform masculinity and same-sex desire, and it links these varieties of masculine performance to the play's assumptions about who maintains political and social sway.[21]

The clue to this phobic structuring of the play's sexual and political tensions—and further evidence that these tensions evoke perverse masculine, even same-sex desire—might be discerned in Ford's subplot. Although Ford's subplots have traditionally been maligned as gratuitous and excessive in their sexual innuendo and immoral actions, DiGangi argues that Cuculus's absurd failure to recognize the male sex of his "female" page serves to chastise Thamasta's arrogance and pretension in rejecting Menaphon in deference to the "female" Parthenophill.[22] The subplot points as well toward masculine sexual disorders in parodying the sexually stigmatized dysfunction of men who do not assent to their subordinate place in the scheme of male homosocial relations—a dysfunction given a distinctly sexual and sodomitical coloring. Cuculus and Grilla become the objects of bawdy jokes about Cuculus's failure to recognize sexual difference and Grilla's perverse cross-dressing. They are associated with unnatural animal phenomena, as when Rhetias titillates Cuculus with news of a "sow-pig [that] hath sucked a brach" (1.2.76–77). They are vilified by Rhetias, the railing figure that recalls any number of Jacobean malcontents who isolate and reveal corruption in the court. In this instance, he reflects no one so much as *Troilus and Cressida*'s Thersites, who, Gregory W. Bredbeck points out, almost single-handedly imports sodomy into the play through his scurrilous construction of Patroclus.[23] (Rhetias's name seems to be a near-anagram of that Shakespearean character's.) Cuculus is, of course, represented as desiring women—indeed, his courting women above his station makes him the object of other men's invective. But his skill in that endeavor is represented as being so useless that Rhetias imagines him and Grilla within discourses of the monstrous gender and sexuality of the sodomite in Elizabethan–Jacobean satire: "My Lady Periwinkle here [Grilla] never sucked; suck thy master, and bring forth moon-calves, fop, do" (1.2.92–93). When it is first used, *suck* probably means *suckle,* and hence references the fact that the "Lady Periwinkle" is not the product of biological conception or nurturing mothering. But equivocation on the second use references possibilities for male–male coupling and conception that could produce that sodomitical figure of invective to be found in satires such as Michael Drayton's *The Moone-Calfe* (pub. 1627).

Similar arguments can be made about Palador, whose devotion to books and artifice denotes the dangers of love, and whose obsession with Parthenophill represents a highly artificial and problematic masculinity that stands, like Thamasta's desire for Parthenophill, in opposition to normative gender structures and appropriate marital alliance. Both Cuculus and Palador represent artificial, unnatural, and unhealthy conditions that must be corrected: in Cuculus's case through ridicule and his safe confinement in the subplot, and in the prince's case through the careful medical correction that provides the driving action of the main plot. *The Lover's Melancholy,* like *King Lear* or *Pericles,* dramatizes a diseased mind recovering the source of its sanity in the incremental perception of that which has been lost to it. With its story of a prince whose kingdom has been damaged by his father's political and sexual misconduct and who is himself unable to restore effective order, this romantic tragicomedy does suggest something of a political allegory. But it also articulates a specific sexual politics in its tale of Palador's brief flirtation with homoerotic desire and his eventual awakening to a heteroerotic alliance rendered all the more normative because it presages the return of political stability. In this respect (and reversing the habit of mind by which the seemingly less important realm of sex serves as a metaphor for the political), the political play suggests something of an allegory of normatively sexualized heteroerotic alliance. Political stability, in other words, becomes the metaphor for sexual conformity.

It is not surprising, in the playwright whose most famous stage image is the literalizing of a Petrarchan metaphor in Giovanni's impaling Annabella's heart on his dagger (which, in its own way, suggests a dangerously flawed masculinity), that Palador's male dysfunction is represented as an excessive self-indulgence in books and words that signify the inessential or inconsequential. But here such indulgence is roundly criticized by the malcontent Rhetias, Palador's physician Corax, and others. When Corax encounters the prince reading a book, he exclaims,

> A book! Is this the early exercise
> I did prescribe? Instead of following health,
> Which all men covet, you pursue your disease.
> Where's your great horse, your hounds, your set at tennis,
> Your balloon ball, the practice of your dancing,
> Your casting of the sledge, or learning how
> To toss a pike?—All changed into a sonnet? (2.1.48–54)

Palador's obsession with books, words, and poetry as well as his linguistic excess mark his retreat from masculine pursuit into a realm in which art disorders nature. Yet this retreat itself signifies a perverse appropriation of masculine power, a willful and indulgent insistence on self-assertion outside the bounds of social expectation that is hinted at not simply in the subplot but also by Ford's rethematizing of a lyric trope in his introduction of Parthenophill.

Our introduction to Parthenophill occurs when Menaphon reports the supposed boy's role in a contest pitting this beautiful "boy" singer against a nightingale, a motif that has classical precedent and a contemporary analogue in Richard Crashaw's "Musicks Duell." But even though it has been remarked that only in Ford does the bird actually expire from its exertions, and that the bird's death tends to underline the fundamental disruption that has been brought about by Eroclea's banishment from Cyprus and Palador, the trope also suggests that Eroclea's appearance as a boy occasions a division between the natural world and the world of art and artifice in the play—a divide that, as I've suggested, energizes the work as a whole. Parthenophill here is a willful destroyer of nature, and that position aligns "him" in a perverse way with Cuculus. More to the point, however, it signals "his" symbolic (although not causal) role in the disruption of Palador's health and the imminent political disaster constantly predicted for his state.

The trope occurs, then, within a pattern of discursive formulations linking the disruption of Palador's sanity and the undermining of his state to an artificially induced sexual condition, and it instantiates yet another misperformance of masculinity to be distinguished from more normative, and more normatively silenced, forms in the play. Menaphon himself come close to just such a misperformance in his frustrated wooing of Thamasta once she has fallen for Parthenophill, although he ultimately articulates the type of masculine control that he comes to model for Palador: "Henceforth I will bury / Unmanly passion in perpetual silence" (3.2.194–95). Once Palador is restored to himself—that is, once he is reunited with Eroclea—he, too, gains a linguistic control formerly alien to him. Almost echoing Menaphon's words, he says to his lover, "My ecstasy of joys would speak in passion / But that I would not lose that part of man / Which is reserved to entertain content" (4.3.137–39). This model of normative, not-to-be-spoken love is the one Opie identifies in Ford, and it depends on a restraint linked to masculine reserve, one characterized by contrast with perverse masculine performance conceived in relation to noisier sodomitical constructions.

In contrasting Palador's willfully pursued sodomitical desires (in the many sexual and social senses of that word) with those of Menaphon, however, Ford does more than reveal Menaphon and Amethus as normative models. He makes clear the difference between men who are supported within homosocial alliances and those who are disempowered by them. Whereas Menaphon's frustrations in his love for Thamasta cause Amethus to side with his friend against his sister, bolstering Menaphon's sense of masculine identification against the threats of female passion and mutability, Palador's father undermines the security of his son's identity by interfering with the marital alliance that he had already set up and denying Palador the only type of sexual self-determination allowed a prince in his circumstances. It may seem difficult to sympathize with Palador, whose class position privileges him and whose seeming willfulness jeopardizes all. But his disempowerment at the hands of his father makes him a model of failed manhood that Ford explores in the perverse, sodomitical terms available to him. The play does not stigmatize masculine desire, for that is nobly represented in Amethus and Menaphon. It does, however, rely on the possibilities for stigmatizing that desire as sodomitical to examine and ultimately police (however ineffectively) its prince, who, Ford recognizes, is able to make his own separate sexual peace outside the normative structures of homosocial bonding and heteronormative alliance that have been denied him so long in Eroclea's absence from the kingdom.

Consequently, we might say that Palador's brief flirtation with homoerotic desire, like Cuculus's, represents a type of (both sexual and social) resistance—in Palador's case to the emasculation he has suffered at the hands of his father. Palador himself claims to be unaware of his father's perfidy (2.1.144–47), but he is clear that his melancholic withdrawal from life at court is linked to the loss of Eroclea subsequent to her flight from Agenor. Indeed, Palador's melancholic withdrawal is mirrored in the play by that of Eroclea's father, Meleander, whose mind has also become diseased by his banishment from the court subsequent to his rescuing Eroclea from Agenor and sending her to safety in Athens. In both cases, Ford echoes precepts set out in Robert Burton's *Anatomy of Melancholy* (1621) by suggesting that the diseased mind pursues a willful resistance to normative practice.[24] More to the point, Palador is direct in insisting on his desire for Parthenophill, which he expresses in quite willful language: "Parthenophill is lost, and I would see him" (4.3.28). Having lost Eroclea, Palador seems unwilling to resume his proper role as a man and head of state. Once he reveals to Rhetias that the loss of Eroclea is, in fact, the source of his melancholy, he swears his servant to silence with the claim that he has taken care of business by advancing "Sophronos [a councilor] to the helm / Of government" (2.1.217–18). But Rhetias senses that only the return of Eroclea will cure the prince, both of his melancholy and of his seemingly homoerotic obsession. And Rhetias is correct, for Palador, like Giovanni, insists on defining his own sexuality, however perversely.[25]

What we initially find in Palador, then, is not only his inability but even perhaps his refusal to be a proper man, to negotiate appropriate distinctions of male bonding, to assume an appropriate role as prince, and to take responsibility for keeping order over male–female affections in his kingdom. The play alludes to a kind of perversity in its representation of Palador—a perversity that (like modern homosexuality) is signified as a prohibited form of inadequate or flawed masculinity. While these prohibitions are registered within the dynamics of sex and gender typical of Ford's period, not our own, the play's representation of failed masculine desire is clearly linked to an excessive self-expression, which is the very thing that signifies its willfulness and perversity—and it is here that Ford comes closest to being what Havelock Ellis long ago claimed for him, "the most modern of the tribe to whom he belonged."[26] Ford signals Palador's perversity not simply—and perhaps not even most essentially—as a sexual difference; he reveals it as a linguistic difference that marks the assumption of individualizing social agency where it does not—where it will not be allowed to—belong, at least in the Renaissance.

What is prohibited is speech about desire outside the systems that normatively obscure such desires, as well as the desire to speak in ways conducive to individual sexual self-regulation. Such prohibitions on the speaking of masculine desire as we find in the play reveal by contrast the structure of normative, silenced assent both to heteronormative and homosocial bonding that is assumed in empowered, dominant masculinity. If, that is, the noble bonding of Menaphon and Amethus implies the possibility of erotic relationship, then that possibility is not simply allowed by but is dependent on their silence about its sexual manifestations—just as women's silence about sex seemingly enforced their consent to normative patriarchal structures, so, too, does men's. Amethus and Menaphon do not articulate the eroticism always perhaps implicit in masculine friendship because such friendship is privileged as a, perhaps *the,* site at which sodomy cannot be spoken. But Palador, seeking a private accommodation outside social normativity, is represented as articulating a passionate and erotic attraction that marks him as perverse. Attending to the structures of masculine perversity in Ford, we are therefore brought full circle to one of the paradoxes of a modern sexuality in which categories of distinction between men are defined both in terms of sexual activity or erotic preference and within the normative structures of power through which one is or is not allowed to speak of those activities. It is this insight that Ford explores so brilliantly in *Perkin Warbeck,* a play that has been understood in relation to sodomy but that may be given a more nuanced interpretation by exploring the ways it creates the perverse as a valorized aspect of the struggle around masculine self-assertion in a rigidly hierarchical male society.

Lisa Hopkins has claimed that at its heart, Ford's sole history play encodes a sodomitical secret linked to the Castlehaven scandal.[27] However, apparently taking for granted an anachronistic idea that sodomy is primarily associated with male–male buggery, Hopkins does not analyze what the idea may have signified in Ford's theater, especially in light of the gender transgressions Jean Howard finds in the play's male characters. Howard argues that Perkin is marked as "effeminately dolent" by his too-close dependence on his wife, Katherine Gordon, and his multiple failures to live up to the model of dominating masculinity represented by Henry VII and the Lancastrian kings of Shakespeare's history cycle.[28] Building on Howard's thesis about the feminization of Warbeck, we might also say that Warbeck transgresses within his own gender in ways that might seem to be distortions—indeed perversions—of normatively silenced, eroticized masculine hierarchies that are themselves symbolized by political relations in the play. Warbeck mounts a powerful and perhaps fully realized effort to define himself in a hierarchical regime in which men's places are rigidly controlled by the privileged few. He may not behave aggressively on the battlefield, but in both Scottish James's and English Henry's courts, he claims an unequivocal right to name himself that, at the very least, unsettles normative assumptions about the privilege of male aristocrats to define masculinity and the structure of male relations.

Writing before the proliferation of knowledge about the centrality of male homosocial relations and their erotic potential in the English Renaissance, Howard characterizes Warbeck as resigned and adopting a feminine pose of "patient suffering."[29] Rather more to the point, the power of Warbeck's speech becomes analogous to the prohibited voices of powerful women in the period in its ability to disrupt and so becomes an alternative discourse of masculine resistance to dominant forms of homosocial relations. His association with monstrous women such as Margaret of Burgundy, who is imaged as a witch and the producer of unnatural children such as Warbeck, and with that other pretender to Henry's throne, Lambert Simnel, brings Warbeck within the realm of the perverse, the monstrous, and even the sodomitical, although the play works to contain this perversion in its reproduction of the "known," "famous," and "true" history in which Warbeck is ultimately executed for his treason (Prologue 15–16). Still, as is often noted, in defiance of all its historical sources the play never falters in characterizing Warbeck as a potentially legitimate monarch. Indeed, famously, Warbeck never admits to being anyone other than Duke of York, the son of Edward IV and brother of Henry's Queen Elizabeth, and the self-composure that is the seemingly surest sign of his royal birth never wanes.[30]

One might therefore argue that Warbeck does not merely play the woman's part; he transforms that part into his own private idea of masculinity through his amazingly virile linguistic assertion, especially at the end, where Ford's notable poetic genius is never better evidenced than in the mouth of this character who brilliantly asserts his capacity to define the meaning of his own life even in the face of his enforced death:

> Death? Pish, 'tis but a sound, a name of air,
> A minute's storm, or not so much. To tumble
> From bed to bed, be massacred alive
> By some physicians for a month or two
> In hope of freedom from a fever's torments,
> Might stagger manhood; here, the pain is passed
> Ere sensibly 'tis felt. Be men of spirit!
> Spurn coward passion! So illustrious mention
> Shall blaze our names, and style us Kings o'er Death. (5.3.198–206)

The play fails to contain the most subversive aspect of Warbeck's character, and his almost tragic sense of integrity grows stronger with each degree of his humiliation by the play's two crowned monarchs: James (who deserts him) and Henry (who defeats him militarily). Once again, we find disruptive masculine homosocial behavior positioned on a continuum with tragic self-assertion and political disorder. But the overarching historical structure of the play seems even less capable of containing the protagonist's threat than the heteronormatively weighted tragicomic ending of *The Lover's Melancholy.*

As Susannah Breitz Monta reminds us, by altering his sources to emphasize Katherine Gordon's exceptional loyalty to Warbeck, Ford does not so much effeminize his character as use Warbeck to prevent "the consolidation of domestic and political loyalties behind one figure [Henry], and create a degree of unsettling sympathy for a traitor who, in the play's sources, enjoys none."[31] So, we might argue that Warbeck finally becomes the most powerful voice in the play, even if he does not cut the most normatively masculine figure. As James says about him, "He must be more than subject who can utter / The language of a king" (2.1.103–4), and Warbeck's language never fails him. It is not, then, Warbeck's "feminization" alone that reveals the substance of his challenge to established authority but his linguistic performance of differences within masculinity that were threatening and usually not articulated in the period. What Warbeck destabilizes is not merely a difference between men and women but the assumed natural differences between and among men.

Alan Bray argued long ago that in Renaissance England, one might use sodomy as a weapon by deliberately confusing the signs of normative masculine relations such as friendship with sodomitical constructions, especially if it seemed that otherwise usual orders of hierarchy were being transgressed in the friendship relations.[32] *Perkin Warbeck* explores this potential confusion of signs not as a weapon to be used by others but as a source of power to be exploited by otherwise disempowered men, for within his shaping of a history play, Ford represents the institutions of male authority and preferment not as natural structures of political order but as social structures potentially subject to sexual industry. The point is made literally clear in the chorus of working men who follow Warbeck, and it is given linguistic vitality in a brief snatch of dialogue between Heron and Sketon:

> HERON. Hopes are but hopes; I was ever confident, when I traded but in remnants, that my stars had reserved me to the title of a viscount at least. Honour is honour, though cut out of any stuffs.
>
> SKETON. My brother Heron hath right wisely delivered his opinion; for he that threads his needle with the sharp eyes of industry shall in time go through-stitch with the new suit of preferment. (2.3.109–14)

Typically, Ford has not been credited with the brilliance that leads him, in these few short lines, to sum up those social structures in the period that misshape expectation, even as he dramatizes the cunning and ingenuity of those determined not to be bound to those expectations.[33] Heron, recognizing that honor is not linked to social class, is thereby able to identify social distinction as being a matter of fortune to which he himself may aspire. However much he sees himself as trading in "remnants," an image redolent of the type of social disdain to which these men are subject throughout the play, he nevertheless manifests the kind of hope that propels Warbeck himself.

More to the point, Sketon, in a witty, materialist, and, perhaps, sodomitical reimagining of Heron's classed thinking, seems to reveal what was otherwise protected by a veil of silence in the period: the place sex rather than fortune might play in one's social advancement. Preferment could depend on one's willingness to thread one's needle with a clear eye to social advancement—or to thread someone else's. Proverbial jokes about tailors emphasized their assistance in and benefit "from the illegitimate activities involved in social climbing," and while such jokes tended to "portray [tailors] both as heterosexually lecherous and (mainly) effeminate," as Simon Shepherd has argued, the sexual nature of these jokes linked tailors' supposed failures in normative marital alliances to their social disruptions.[34] Hence Sketon's lines seem at the least deliberately phallic and, perhaps in context, refer specifically to male–male buggery. In any event, they evoke the sexualized social disorder that could always be signified as sodomy.

It is at just such a point that Ford's play seems most transgressive, not for making clear the role of sex in masculine advancement but for revealing the ways a master's man might understand and exploit that role. What is shocking here is the facility and ease with which Sketon speaks about practices typically revealed only in the most scurrilous satires of the period. Warbeck himself does not, so far as we see at least, ingratiate himself with King James in this literally sodomitical way, but he insinuates himself into the aristocratic body of the state in several ways, and not only through his courtship of and love for Katherine Gordon, which is not the only or primary aspect of eroticism in the play. Ford also represents in Perkin that genuine erotic frisson for male bonding that is typically contained within the structures of authority and hence typically represented as orderly social assent, although now that erotic desire is being created, controlled, and authorized by a questionable figure, Warbeck himself. In this regard, we might usefully compare Ford's deft placement of twin scenes, the first being one in which Warbeck is introduced to James, and woos the Scottish king into something of a marriage between "two kingdoms in a love / Never to be divorced while time is time" (2.1.88–89). Here Warbeck not only gains the trust of James but lures him toward such intimacy that James is almost forced to acknowledge him "Cousin of York" to maintain the decorum suitable to his own comportment (2.1.108). Indeed, in these scenes in which Warbeck woos James, Katherine's own passions for him are excited: "Beshrew me, but his words have touched me home, / As if his cause concerned me" (2.1.118–19).

This scene is followed immediately by one in which Henry VII passionately laments the loss of his friend when Stanley defects to Warbeck. By acknowledging that he has been unable to see into Stanley's heart, Henry not only warns against trusting the intimacy Warbeck has just assumed with James but also makes clear that such intimacy and secrecy is the basis of love between men and a loyalty between king and subject that is not necessarily subject to apparent political hierarchies. In this respect, Warbeck's integrity contrasts with Stanley's, and even as the manipulation of love and loyalty revealed in Stanley's actions represents an unattractive political aspect of male betrayal, that kind of political betrayal can never really be made to stick to Warbeck. It is James who finally divorces Warbeck, whose own actions might be seen to stand for a true love for his fellow that James will sacrifice to political expediency.

In this way, *Perkin Warbeck* becomes a love story of another sort. It is not about sodomy in the literal sense of male buggery but a story in which Warbeck foregrounds male desire as the key to his own assumption of superior place. To be sure, Ford is not deceived about the practices of social deception—as when, at the end of the scene between Heron and Sketon I cited earlier, he has Frion reveal his "toil" in "humouring this abject scum of mankind! / Muddy-brained peasants!" (2.3.176–78). But Warbeck, it seems, is master of a love more profound, one that never accedes to itself as anything but genuine, although history itself tells a different story. That the historical James's support of Warbeck served his political ends is not irrelevant to Ford's play, but Ford dramatizes the two men's relationship rather more warmly than we might imagine if politics alone were at issue. James seems genuinely convinced by Warbeck, and to the extent he is, Ford reveals once again the potential instabilities of a social order based in masculine bonding.

Ever so subtly, Warbeck's actions expose the difference between two kings (rendered literal in the war between England and Scotland) rather than reinforcing their mutual identifications as masters of authority and desire. Almost immediately, Warbeck's presence in both courts begins to unravel the bonds of masculine desire and alliance that undergird the structure of those courts. Katherine's father Huntly understands implicitly that in supporting Warbeck's marriage to his daughter, James "pulls down / What old desert hath builded" (2.3.56–57). To James's response that he "violate[s] no pawns of faith . . . on private loves" (2.3.58–59), Huntly points aptly toward those of his "subjects' hearts" the king will cause to bleed (2.3.66). The love between a subject and his king, Huntly seems to suggest, is under attack.

This point is never clearer, perhaps, than in the scene in which Henry laments the defection of Stanley to Warbeck. With a display of passion usually foreign to this King of England, Henry refuses to speak to Stanley because he fears that his love is so strong he "could deny him [i.e., Stanley] nothing" (2.2.43). It is Henry who appeals to the Bishop of Durham for a reason to excuse his erstwhile friend and Durham who attempts to maintain a normative structure of order by telling the king that a show of mercy would "persuade your subjects that the title / Of York is better, nay, more just and lawful / Than yours of Lancaster" (2.2.15–17). Indeed, Durham aptly notes the provisionality of rule that Warbeck has introduced into the kingdom when he argues that if Stanley's belief in Warbeck's legitimacy is true, then the loyalty of all Henry's supporters is false and "Stanley true alone to Heaven" (2.2.23). A normative social order supported by one kind of erotic identification is being replaced in Scotland and threatens to be replaced in England with one based on the personal charisma of Warbeck.

That we might read this new erotic order rather perversely is perhaps apparent in the scope with which Warbeck troubles the political relations of Europe. Not only do his actions promise trouble between Scotland and England but they threaten the alliance King Henry is creating with Spain, as Hialas, the ambassador of Ferdinand and Isabel, suggests that

Henry's court may be too unstable for such an alliance so long as the Yorkist pretender remains to trouble it. On one hand, it seems that Warbeck's pretense undermines political order; on the other hand, we can understand the political disorder in Henry's kingdom as pointing toward Warbeck's genuine powers of self-definition, erotic and otherwise. The surprise of the play comes when the political action turns against Warbeck and he manages to maintain those powers of self-definition. In this way, Ford creates a scapegoat for political disorder, but only by shaping Warbeck into a perverse self who is other to those bonds between men that are themselves so normative as to typically need no elaboration. Male sodomitical desire comes into view as Warbeck's tragic determination to define his own place in an eroticized order between men. Indeed, so powerful is his self-fashioning that he begins to reveal sodomitical desire as that type of male desire that would presume to shape its own social and sexual destiny. If such desire lacks a proper name, its emergence in dialectical opposition to normative social values nevertheless puts it into play in ways similar to those pejorative designations of unauthorized female sexuality that helped police heteronormative gender roles in the period. The play does more than reveal the pleasures or instabilities of male homosocial desires: it reveals the ways those desires depended on the stabilizing function of prohibition, the explicit recognition of what was not to be allowed to be spoken as the proof of what it was not necessary to say about men and their relations.

What Ford's plays suggest to us, then, is that sodomy or disorderly male sexuality was coming into focus as male desire that could in certain respects be spoken or articulated by men conceived in perverse opposition to normalizing structures for controlling sexuality. In both *The Lover's Melancholy* and *Perkin Warbeck*, male characters evoke configurations of same-sex desire in highly elaborated rhetorical or theatrical constructs that do not point to their sexual identities but that certainly do seem to refer to their conspicuous articulation of sex or desire as a site of resistance to normative social constructions. Conceived with differing levels of prohibition, Cuculus, Palador, and Warbeck all assert with clearly articulated voices their desire to shape themselves over and against normative structures of social and sexual ordering, and it is precisely these voices, metatheatrical or even seemingly extralinguistic, that allow Ford to focus on aspects of masculine perversion to be contained and controlled. In this respect, male–male sexual disorder is linked, as was women's sexual disorder, to the failure to speak appropriately, in one's proper turn, in place, in the voices allotted one by the dominant social system. If Ford's plays are taken as evidence, inter-male desire per se was not prohibited so much as the desire of some men to speak for themselves and thus control that desire and everything it might come to stand for. Male–male eroticized desire was increasingly located as a potential site of social resistance in Ford's plays precisely because it enabled men who were not otherwise entitled to do so to articulate their own desire for self-control.

As any number of commentators have made clear, masculine desire was enabled by the multiple homosocial structures that privileged men in the period—indeed, structures of homosocial desire often lubricated the machinery of Renaissance social relations. But those same structures were hierarchically arranged to privilege normatively empowered men whose explicitly sexual or erotic desires may have been obscured, even seemingly rendered silent, in contrast to noisier articulations of sex, desire, and self-promotion. Such an arrangement ensured that only the few could control desire and its sexual effects within the usually not sexually specific social discourses in which they might be legitimately expressed. Rather than valorize the potential eroticism of male homosocial bonds in Shakespeare's England, we need to be more concerned with those disparities of class and gender position that might distinguish remarkable perversions from authorized erotic activities. If this conclusion seems like a simple one, then we might well wonder why so many recent formulations of male–male desire have been so little attentive to the power disparities by which disempowered voices bear the brunt of the period's animus toward sodomy and male sexual disorder.

Indeed, we might wonder the same thing in the modern period as well, for such representations of the sexually disempowered as we find in Ford remind us of a continuing fear of empowering those whose minority sexuality is specifically available as an articulate location of identity. Ford's plays do not in any simple way validate modern homosexual subjectivities as a stable location for negotiating power, but they help make clear how privileged, normative (even silently eroticized) male bonds have come to be understood as fundamentally different from deprivileged, explicitly sexual or erotic ones. The plays suggest that it is not acts that distinguish men so much as the differences in their relation to the privileges of articulating and controlling desire itself and the relation of these differences to the silently enforced privileges of manhood. So they do help make clear some of the ways minority subject positions figure into more comprehensive discursive patterns of minoritizing and universalizing notions of sexual identity and thus perhaps provide a nuanced understanding of the interaction of both in the construction and consolidation of social power dynamics. They do not, in other words, invalidate modern sexual subject positions by suggesting that sexuality is only incoherent and sexual identities are always recuperative.

Reading Ford's plays suggests that there is no "before sex" at all. There is only the (mis)apprehension of what is not to be named in the words we have to name it. Before homosexuality—at least in *The Lover's Melancholy* and *Perkin Warbeck*—there was speech between men that articulated various forms of eroticism and embodied desire. Those characters whose speech exposed or exploited the power to fashion themselves outside the status quo are represented as drifting toward a recognizable (at least to us) and prohibited discourse of male homoerotic desire. These figures, and Ford himself, might be said to sodomize the fabric of male–male relations—to reveal the sodomitical possibilities in all male erotic relations—by revealing and reveling in what otherwise remained unspoken, just as, perhaps, the modern critic does who gives a name to the workings of sodomy and perversion in texts that otherwise have no name for either. But such sodomitical *jouissance* as Ford uncovers or the modern critic replicates cannot stand simply in place of recognizing those material and discursive structures that misshape the expectations both of Ford's perverse male characters and of his modern homosexual readers. We might learn from Ford's plays that "silence" about male erotic desire is a means to enable it in some, while we quash it in those whose relation to social power is not guaranteed. Reading strategies that do not account for these minoritized voices, that enfold sexually minoritized men unproblematically into the larger category of men or imagine them as monolithically empowered over and against other categories of identification, may assume the same relation to power as those authorized in Ford's plays not to speak their desires disruptively—and the word for that silence is a quintessentially modern one: *homophobia.*

Notes

1 Michel Foucault, *The History of Homosexuality,* vol. 1, *An Introduction,* trans. Robert Hurley (New York: Random House, 1978), 43.

2 Graham L. Hammill, *Sexuality and Form: Caravaggio, Marlowe, and Bacon* (Chicago: University of Chicago Press, 2000), 3.

3 Madhavi Menon, *Unhistorical Shakespeare: Queer Theory in Shakespearean Literature and Film* (New York: Palgrave Macmillan, 2008), 3.

4 Eve Kosovsky Sedgwick, *Epistemology of the Closet* (Berkeley: University of California Press, 1990), 1.

5 Although the chapter seeks new ways to "combat the restrictions of a historicist approach" to Renaissance studies as this goal has been defined by Stephen Guy-Bray, Vin Nardizzi, and Will Stockton in the introduction to *Queer Renaissance Historiography: Backward Gaze* (Burlington, Vt.: Ashgate, 2009), 1, my argument relies primarily on my earlier analysis of the ways men's different social positions in the early modern period shaped legal and literary representations of their erotic interactions. See Nicholas F. Radel, "Can the Sodomite Speak? Sodomy, Satire, Desire, and the Castlehaven Case," in *Love, Sex, and Intimacy between Men, 1500–1800,* ed. Katherine O'Donnell and Michael O'Rourke, 146–65 (New York: Palgrave Macmillan, 2002). Also relevant is Alan Sinfield's materialist concern with recovering "subordinated voices" of male same-gender desire in early modern England whose relationship to modern homosexuality may be found more in the strategies by which they have been subordinated than in any assumed identifications. Sinfield, *Shakespeare, Authority, Sexuality: Unfinished Business in Cultural Materialism* (New York: Routledge, 2006), 25. Ultimately, I reject the exclusionary force of arguments setting theory against history in the work of Menon and others not to reinscribe heterotemporality and historical difference but to investigate more precisely how the past destabilizes the present. For an analysis of and response to the often unclear "theoretical rationales and political stakes" of queer scholarship's recent concern with temporality, see Valerie Traub's "The New Unhistoricism in Queer Studies," *PMLA,*

forthcoming. I am grateful to Professor Traub for sharing her unpublished work with me.

6 My argument is indebted to Carla Freccero's similar argument about minoritizing views of women in the period that I discuss at greater length later in the essay. See Freccero, *Queer/Early/Modern* (Durham, N.C.: Duke University Press, 2006), 36.

7 Eve Kosofsky Sedgwick, *Between Men: English Literature and Male Homosocial Desire* (New York: Columbia University Press, 1985), 86.

8 "It is imperative," Alexandra Shepard writes, "that we approach masculinity . . . in multi-relational terms. This means not only considering the ways in which maleness was defined in relation to femaleness . . . but also exploring the ways in which concepts and experiences of masculinity were premised on differences among men." Shepard, "From Anxious Patriarchs to Refined Gentlemen? Manhood in Britain, circa 1500–1700," *Journal of British Studies* 44, no. 2 (2005): 289. Although Shepard's point is now commonplace in masculinity studies, my understanding that masculinity is a varied discursive category subject to differential interpellation is indebted to early feminist analysis of vectors of social power that troubled categories such as "woman" and "women." See, e.g., Monique Wittig, "One Is Not Born a Woman," in *The Straight Mind and Other Essays* (1981; repr., Boston: Beacon Press, 1992), 9–20, which posits that a "materialist feminist approach to women's oppression destroys the idea that women are a 'natural group'" (9), or—more to the point of specific social differences—Audre Lorde, "Age, Race, Class, and Sex: Women Redefining Difference," in *Literary Theory: An Anthology,* 2nd ed., ed. Julie Rivkin and Michael Ryan, 854–60 (1984; repr., Oxford: Blackwell, 2004), which argues that "differences of race, sexual preference, class, and age" (855) shape particular experiences of gender oppression. For a theoretical elaboration of the issues, see Denise Riley, "Am I That Name? Feminism and the Category of 'Women' in History," in *Feminisms,* ed. Sandra Kemp and Judith Squires, 241–46 (1988; repr., Oxford: Oxford University Press, 1997).

9 A full analysis of the handling of male sex, masculine eroticism, and perversity in Ford's major plays would necessarily include detailed consideration of Giovanni in *'Tis Pity She's a Whore* and the sadomasochistic elements in the relations of Orgilus and Ithocles in *The Broken Heart.* I omit these for reasons of space.

10 Mario DiGangi demonstrates that "homoeroticism" was a "prevalent . . .

component of male relations in early modern society" in *The Homoerotics of Early Modern Drama* (Cambridge: Cambridge University Press, 1997), 12. I am working to bring his crucial insights into dialectical relation with Jonathan Goldberg's investigations into sodomy as a confused category of social and political dislocation in *Sodometries: Renaissance Texts, Modern Sexualities* (Stanford, Calif.: Stanford University Press, 1992), 18ff. My dialectical focus has largely been shaped by Jonathan Dollimore, who argues for the need to explore "the history of perversion . . . to see how culture is not only formed, but consolidated, destabilized, and reformed" through the workings of a "perverse dynamic" in which perversion is "intrinsic to social process" and "emerge[s] within the selfsame conformist orders that proscribe" it. Dollimore, *Sexual Dissidence: Augustine to Wilde, Freud to Foucault* (Oxford: Oxford University Press, 1991), 104, 228.

11 Alan Bray, "Homosexuality and the Signs of Male Friendship in Elizabethan England," in *Queering the Renaissance*, ed. Jonathan Goldberg, 40–61 (Durham, N.C.: Duke University Press, 1994).

12 See Gail Kern Paster on the overlap between threatening female independence, talkativeness, and bodily disorder in *The Body Embarrassed: Drama and the Disciplines of Shame in Early Modern England* (Ithaca, N.Y.: Cornell University Press, 1993), 25. Paster traces her own argument to Peter Stallybrass, "Patriarchal Territories: The Body Enclosed," in *Rewriting the Renaissance: The Discourses of Sexual Difference in Early Modern Europe*, ed. Margaret W. Ferguson, Maureen Quilligan, and Nancy J. Vickers, 123–42 (Chicago: University of Chicago Press, 1980), who writes that "silence, the closed mouth, is made a sign of chastity" (127) in early modern texts.

13 Freccero, *Queer/Early/Modern*, 36. Interestingly, Freccero's comments, which occur as part of an argument with David Halperin, seem also to suggest that although it is important not to erase the varied proscriptions on the experience of women in the Renaissance, homosexuality might be construed as a monolithically unavailable category of masculine desire in the period. So while her materialist commitments to women's experience seem to win out when she places perversion back into equations of gender, her lack of concern with possible multiple homosexual subjectivities perhaps blunts some of the point of her argument with Halperin.

14 Mario DiGangi, "John Ford," in *A Companion to Renaissance Drama*, ed. Arthur F. Kinney (Oxford: Blackwell, 2004), 571. Indeed, that the promise of political stability is fully encoded onto the prince's eventual

happy reuniting with his beloved, Eroclea, may recall the widely perceived ill effects of Buckingham's influence on the new King Charles I and reflect concerns about sodomy that arose in relation to his father James I's troubling male relationships. On history and politics in Beaumont and Fletcher, see Phillip J. Finkelpearl, *Court and Country Politics in the Plays of Beaumont and Fletcher* (Princeton, N.J.: Princeton University Press, 1990), and Gordon McMullan, *The Politics of Unease in the Plays of John Fletcher* (Amherst: University of Massachusetts Press, 1994).

15 Brian Opie, "'Being All One': Ford's Analysis of Love and Friendship in *Loues Sacrifice* and *The Ladies Triall*," in *John Ford: Critical Re-visions*, ed. Michael Neill (Cambridge: Cambridge University Press, 1988), 242.

16 DiGangi, "John Ford," 573.

17 References to Ford's plays are to the Oxford World's Classics edition, *John Ford: 'Tis Pity She's a Whore and Other Plays*, ed. Marion Lomax (Oxford: Oxford University Press, 1995), and will be cited in the text.

18 Sinfield, *Shakespeare, Authority, Sexuality*, 117.

19 On the differences between Shakespeare's and Fletcher's handling of these plots, see Bruce R. Smith, "Making a Difference: Male/Male 'Desire' in Tragedy, Comedy, and Tragi-comedy," in *Erotic Politics: Desire on the Renaissance Stage*, ed. Susan Zimmerman, 127–49 (London: Routledge, 1992), as well as Nicholas F. Radel, "Fletcherian Tragicomedy, Cross-dressing, and the Constriction of Homoerotic Desire in Early Modern England," *Renaissance Drama* 26 (1995): 53–82.

20 Walter Cohen suggests that "in so far as reconciliation implies incorporation rather than exclusion . . . one may occasionally hear marginal or oppositional voices" in tragicomedy. Cohen, "Prerevolutionary Drama," in *The Politics of Tragicomedy*, ed. Gordon McMullan and Jonathan Hope (New York: Routledge, 1992), 127. For an elaboration of Cohen's ideas in specifically sexual terms, see Nicholas F. Radel, "Homoeroticism, Discursive Change, and Politics: Reading 'Revolution' in Seventeenth-Century English Tragicomedy," *Medieval and Renaissance Drama in England* 9 (1997): 162–78, which also explores the ways the endings of Fletcher's tragicomedies fail to contain the plays' provocative political and sexual implications.

21 Bruce R. Smith makes clear that "masculinity" in Renaissance England was "a matter of contingency, of circumstances, of performance" that occasioned considerable anxiety about the correctness of its performance. Smith, *Shakespeare and Masculinity* (Oxford: Oxford University Press,

2000), 4. See also Mark Breitenberg, *Anxious Masculinity in Early Modern England* (Cambridge: Cambridge University Press, 1996), who writes that "masculine subjectivity constructed and sustained by a patriarchal culture—infused with patriarchal assumptions about power, privilege, sexual desire, the body—inevitably engenders varying degrees of anxiety in its male members" (1).

22 DiGangi, "John Ford," 572–73. Nevertheless, DiGangi does not concur with my reading of the Cuculus subplot as reflecting Palador's condition. For DiGangi, this subplot serves as a "foil" action to the main plot, an idea also noted by Lisa Hopkins in *John Ford's Political Theatre* (Manchester, U.K.: Manchester University Press, 1994).

23 Gregory W. Bredbeck, *Sodomy and Interpretation: Marlowe to Milton* (Ithaca, N.Y.: Cornell University Press, 1991), 33–34.

24 R. F. Hill, in the introduction to The Revels Plays edition of *The Lover's Melancholy* (Manchester, U.K.: Manchester University Press, 1985), writes that melancholy is "not inevitable" but proceeds "from the indulgence of the passions that can and should be controlled by reason" (6). The classic account of Burton's influence on Ford is S. Blaine Ewing, *Burtonian Melancholy in the Plays of John Ford* (Princeton, N.J.: Princeton University Press, 1940).

25 In "Staging Passion in Ford's *The Lover's Melancholy*," *Studies in English Literature* 45, no. 2 (2005): 443–59, Lisa Hopkins argues that while this play seems on the surface to be different from Ford's other work, its concern with the careful staging of emotional passion represents not absolute difference but an earlier stage in Ford's dramatic development (445). I am suggesting that, like *'Tis Pity She's a Whore,* the play dramatizes an earlier, and perhaps more ambiguous, exploration of a character represented as simultaneously perverse and to be admired.

26 Havelock Ellis, introduction to *John Ford: Five Plays,* ed. Havelock Ellis (1888; repr., New York: Hill and Wang, 1957), xvi.

27 If, that is, we take the date of the play to be circa 1632, the one traditionally ascribed to it. For arguments dating the play to the last years of James I's reign, see Peter Ure's Revels edition (Manchester, U.K.: Manchester University Press, 1968). For Hopkins, see "Touching Touchets: *Perkin Warbeck* and the Buggery Statute," *Renaissance Quarterly* 52, no. 2 (1999): 384–401.

28 Jean Howard, "'Effeminately Dolent': Gender and Legitimacy in Ford's *Perkin Warbeck,*" in *John Ford: Critical Re-visions,* ed. Michael Neill (Cambridge: Cambridge University Press, 1988), 261.

29 Ibid., 270.

30 In "Acting the Self: John Ford's *Perkin Warbeck* and the Politics of Imposture," *Cahiers Elisabethains* 48 (1995): 31–36, Lisa Hopkins argues that Ford may have suggested that Warbeck "was not an impostor at all," a theory that "while unacceptable to historians now, would by no means have been out of the question in the mid-seventeenth century" (32). Providing another take on the collision between historical truth and Warbeck's claims, Miles Taylor suggests that Ford explores how new understandings of history in the Stuart age effectively put an end to the English history play by locating truth in "immutable laws governing human affairs" rather than "individual agency." Taylor, "The End of the English History Play in *Perkin Warbeck*," *Studies in English Literature* 48, no. 2 (2008): 400.

31 Susannah Breitz Monta, "Marital Discourse and Political Discord: Reconsidering *Perkin Warbeck*," *Studies in English Literature* 37, no. 2 (1997): 392.

32 Bray, "Homosexuality and the Signs of Male Friendship," 51–52.

33 The point was not lost, however, on one student in my senior seminar in history, sexuality, and Ford's drama in winter 2006. In an analysis to which my own work owes a debt, Graham Salzer argued that Warbeck's actions in the play "sodomize the fabric of male friendships," a point he defended by his reading of the phallic imagery of these lines.

34 Simon Shepherd, "What's So Funny about Ladies' Tailors? A Survey of Some Male (Homo) Sexual Types in the Renaissance," *Textual Practice* 6, no. 1 (1992): 16.

5

The Erotics of Chin Chucking in Seventeenth-Century England

WILL FISHER

Robert Herrick's "The suspition upon his over-much familiarity with a Gentlewoman" is, as its title implies, a poem in which the speaker responds to rumors about the nature of his relationship with "a Gentlewoman."[1] The speaker reassures his beloved—and anyone who happens to read the poem—that they do not have to worry about their behavior because they know that they have been "innocent" (5) and "faultless" (11): as he puts it, "where no sin / Unbolts the doore, no shame comes in" (12–13). In the following lines, the speaker claims that even though he and his beloved have "embrac't" (26), they have not been "for that unchaste" (27). He also suggests that he and his beloved have engaged in the act of chin chucking. He justifies this behavior by exclaiming, "Love makes the cheek and chin / A sphere to dance and play in" (21–22). Chin chucking is a gesture in which one person gently strokes or pinches the chin or cheek of another.[2] It was generally considered a sign of affection or a form of erotic persuasion. As Gordon Williams puts it in *A Dictionary of Sexual Language and Imagery in Shakespearean and Stuart Literature,* it was a common "amatory signal."[3]

I begin with Herrick's allusion to chin chucking for two reasons. First, I simply want to call attention to the existence of this gesture.[4] Most people today have never heard of chin chucking and will therefore be surprised to find that there are almost a hundred different texts from the sixteenth and seventeenth centuries that make reference to it, as well as many different erotic paintings and illustrations from the same period that depict it (see Figure 5.1). This remarkable archive is the basis for my analysis here. My argument is that in the aggregate, these

FIGURE 5.1. Giulio Romano, *Jupiter Seducing Olympia,* fresco, 1527, Palazzo Te, Mantua, Italy. Courtesy of Comune di Mantova.

texts worked to socialize chin chucking. That is to say, they helped to produce and circulate information about the practice, including how it was performed and who should perform it. In addition, they helped to establish the gesture's meanings or connotations.

Second, I begin with Herrick's allusion to raise a question: was chin chucking considered a "sexual" act? Herrick's speaker insists that his "desire" is "chaste" (33), even though he also acknowledges that others would disagree: after he states that "Love makes the cheek and chin a sphere to dance and play in," he quips that "Suspicion questions every hair" (23). Moreover, the speaker himself admits that chin chucking is amorous or flirtatious (something people do when they are in "love"). Other writers from the period made similar claims about the amorous nature of the act. John Bulwer states in his seventeenth-century study of gestures titled *Chirologia: or The Natural Language of the Hand* that "we . . . stroke them gently with our hand whom we make much of . . . or affectionately love." He explains that the gesture of chin chucking is performed by "drawing our Hand with sweetening motion over the . . . face of the party to whom we intend this insinuation."[5] He then goes on to say that "lovers, I know not by what amorous instinct . . . [are wont to] direct their passionate respects to the [face] of those they love."[6]

But if both Herrick and Bulwer depict chin chucking as an amorous gesture, the question remains about whether it was considered to be sexual. We might ask, too, what counts as sexual in the first place. Even though Herrick insists that chin chucking is "chaste," others certainly saw it as much less innocuous.[7] Indeed, the Puritan clergyman Daniel Rogers warns people about this act in his 1642 treatise *Matrimonial Honour.* As the title implies, Rogers's text offers advice about "the right way to preserve the honour of marriage unstained," and one of the things that he insists husbands must refrain from is "stroking [women's] cheeks . . . with Wantonnesse." According to Rogers, "whatsoever savors of carnall and sensuall desire . . . cannot . . . but threaten mischeefe." Rogers insists that this type of behavior not only stains the "honour" of marriage but will eventually bring "judgment," either "from man, or just with God."[8]

This wasn't an idle threat. Chin chucking did help to bring judgment in cases of adultery from the period. David Turner points out that witnesses sometimes mentioned this gesture as evidence of infidelity. He notes that the witnesses described a wide range of "'freedoms' and 'familiarities,'" and when viewed together, the testimonies in these cases give us some insight into what people understood "adulterous conduct" to be.[9] For my purposes, the crucial point is that chin chucking is one of the types of "over-familiarity" (to return to Herrick's phrase) that deponents mentioned. In a case from 1690 in Hillsden, Buckinghamshire, for instance, Alexander Denton sued for separation from his wife, Hester, alleging that she had "conversed scandalously and incontinently" with their neighbor, Thomas Smith. During the trial, one of the Dentons' maidservants, Martha Ryland, testified that Thomas Smith had visited the house when Alexander was away and that he and Hester had gone into the parlor and shut the door behind them. Ryland said she peered through a hole in the door and observed the following scene:

> Hester Denton [did] seat her selfe in a chayr and the said Mr Smith came p[re]sently to her And standing over her with his face towards hers seated himself in her lap and continued . . . a quarter of an hour in that posture kissing and stroaking her upon ye face and sometimes c[h]ucking her under ye chin.[10]

Hester Denton and Thomas Smith allegedly engaged in other types of overly familiar behavior as well, including "kiss[ing] and embrac[ing]." Ryland also noted that Smith put his "armes sometimes about her Neck and at other times about her waist," and one witness even imputed that they may have had intercourse in the house of a friend in London.[11] In the end, all these different acts served as evidence of their affair; the two were eventually found guilty, and Alexander Denton was granted a separation.

There are other cases of adultery from the period that mention chin chucking. One is the case of John Jopling and Elizabeth Myres of Durham City from 1674. Jopling was married and had been entrusted with helping Myres manage her affairs after the death of her husband. One of the servants in Myres's house, Eleanor Green, testified that she witnessed Myres and Jopling kissing and embracing "like man and wife." This included one occasion on which Green saw Myres "go unto [Jopling] and sit upon his knee and kiss him and stroke his cheeks and call him her dear and her Joy and Comfort." On another occasion, Green testified that she saw Jopling join Myres in her bed. The servant slept in a truckle bed in her mistress's bedchamber, and Jopling apparently came into the room and had Green help him "pull off his shoes" before he went "onto the bed where [Myres] was lying . . . and pulling the curtains close[,] hath stayed there all the night, during which time this examinate . . . hath heard very kind words and expressions of Love pass between them."[12]

While the witnesses in these cases allude to a range of activities—from kissing and embracing to sharing a bed and engaging in intercourse—the fact that they mention chin chucking alongside these other types of behavior implies that they considered the gesture to be erotic and therefore inappropriate. At the same time, it is also significant that the witnesses in these cases mention chin chucking *in conjunction with* these other sexualized behaviors, as this conjunction suggests that it might not have been considered adulterous on its own. In fact, we might say that what counts as "unchaste" behavior in these cases is somewhat contextual: the entire constellation of activities seems to determine whether the behavior was deemed adulterous.[13]

There is, however, one text from the seventeenth century that suggests that chin chucking alone might be enough to convince someone that his or her spouse had been unfaithful. This text offers a history of the Brome family of Warwickshire during the sixteenth century. It recounts an incident that occurred during the life of Nicholas Brome, one of the heirs of the family. Brome apparently came home one evening and "found the Parish-Priest" in the parlor of the family home "chocking his wife under the chin." He was "so enraged" by the priest's behavior that "he presently kil'd him." Afterward, Brome was forced to "obtain . . . the King's pardon" for his actions, and "he was enjoyn'd to do something toward the expiation thereof."[14]

Literary texts tend to figure chin chucking as a much more ambiguous gesture. Some of them certainly do suggest that it is "erotic" and that it is an indication of adultery. Indeed, some of the incidents in plays and poems mirror the incidents in the court cases quite closely. In Thomas D'Urfey's *A Fond Husband,* one of the characters, Ranger, tries to convince his friend, the fond husband of the play's title, that his wife, Emilia, is having an affair with a man named Rashley. The husband, however, is "A credulous fond Cuckold" and refuses to believe him. Thus, as "evidence," Ranger tells the husband that he has seen Emilia "kiss him, play with his Nose, and clap his cheeks, and laugh till her whole Frame shook with Titulation."[15] Later in the play, Ranger claims to have witnessed still another scene that he says he cannot "be silent" about: he says that he "discovered" the adulterous couple at the "Backside of the Kitchin into the Parlour" and that the wife had "with a fond passion strok'd [Rashley's] Cheeks, and dalli'd with his hair."

Still, literary texts do not always figure chin chucking as such a serious infraction. In Shakespeare's works, the gesture is portrayed as problematic in some instances and completely innocuous in others. Hamlet, for example, admonishes Gertrude not to "let the bloat king tempt you again into bed" or "Pinch wanton on your cheek" (3.4.166–67), whereas in *Venus and Adonis,* Venus "stroke[s] [Adonis's] cheek" (45) the first time she sees him.[16] Although her actions are amorous, they are hardly wanton or indecent. Interestingly, however, Venus repeats the gesture later in the poem, and this second chin chuck is more erotic: Venus begins by "kneel[ing]" down next to Adonis "like a lowly lover" (350), and with one hand she "heave[s] up his hat" (351) and with "Her other tender hand . . . his fair cheek feels" (352). Moreover, "His tenderer cheek receives her soft hand's print, / As apt as new-fall'n snow takes any dint" (353–54). The receptivity of Adonis's cheek here is significant, for later in this scene, Adonis responds for the first time to Venus's overtures, and the two engage in a "sweet embrace"—"incorporate they seem; face grows to face" (540–41).

It is worth pointing out that there are instances in which chin chucking is performed in same-sex contexts as well. Although there do not seem to be any visual representations of same-sex chin chucking in early modern English sources, there are certainly examples from the continent. In his Jupiter and Cupid fresco in the Villa Farnesia (1518–19), Raphael depicts Jupiter chucking Cupid's chin. Rubens paints Jupiter as a woman doing the same to Callisto (Figure 5.2). Moreover, quite a few literary texts from early modern England show the gesture being performed between partners of the same sex. In Marlowe's *Hero and Leander,* for instance, Neptune "clapp[ed Leander's] plump cheeks, and with his tresses played / And smiling wantonly, his love betray'd" (449).[17] Likewise, in Marlowe's *Edward II,* Isabella complains that Edward "claps [Gaveston's] cheek and hangs about his neck" (1.2.52). Finally, in James Shirley's *The Doubtful Heir,* Queen Olivia attempts to seduce Rosania, who is disguised as a male page. During their initial encounter, Olivia "playes with [Rosania's] hair, and smiles . . . [and] strokes [her] cheek."[18] Later, Olivia arranges an assignation in her bedchamber, where she continues her seduction: she proposes that they kiss and "finde out pleasure by warm exchange of souls from our soft lips" (49). The connotations of chin chucking in these scenes vary, just as they do in the scenes where the gesture is used in a heterosexual context. Although the interactions of Neptune–Leander and Olivia–Rosania are relatively playful and decorous, Isabella's complaints about Edward's behavior with Gaveston resonate with the complaints of wronged spouses from the adultery trials.

I want to discuss one final instance of chin chucking to illustrate

FIGURE 5.2. Peter Paul Rubens, *Jupiter and Callisto*, 1613.

the point about the ambiguous eroticism of the gesture. It comes from Samuel Pepys's diary. Pepys actually mentions stroking the cheeks of three different women in his diary, but I want to focus on one of these women here because Pepys goes on to develop an adulterous relationship with her and charts its progress in some detail. Pepys refers to this woman only as "Bagwell's wife." He had apparently known both Bagwell and his wife for some time and admits as early as July 1663 that he thought that the wife was "very pretty." In fact, he says that he purposefully sought out her husband so that he might contrive some "occasion" to "forc[e] her to come to [his] office" (4.222).[19] He eventually managed to do just that, and on February 27, 1664, Bagwell's wife paid a visit to Pepys in his office to speak with him on behalf of her husband. Pepys notes that during her visit, he "stroked her under the chin." He adds that he did not "offer her" anything "uncivil" because he did not want to offend her—"she [is]," as he puts it, "a very modest woman" (5.65–66). Nevertheless, a couple of months later, when the woman came to visit Pepys again, he took her "into the office" and this time he "kissed her." She apparently "rebuked [him] for doing [so]" (5.287), but she continued to come see him because he was "getting her husband a place" at sea (5.301–2). On still another visit, Pepys says that he "caresse[d] her" (5.313). Finally, on November 15, 1664, they ate and drank together in a "blind alehouse" and afterward consummated their relationship. As Pepys says, "I did arrive at what I would, with great pleasure" (5.322). The two went on to become lovers, with their affair continuing for three years.

Pepys's diary entries are helpful because they place the gesture of chin chucking in the context of a developing relationship. Moreover, the diary entries reinforce the point I have been making here about the ambiguous eroticism of the gesture. On one hand, Pepys implies that chin chucking is simply an innocent form of flirtation since he claims that when he stroked the woman's chin, he didn't "offer" her anything "uncivil." It is impossible to know what Bagwell's wife thought of Pepys's actions (especially considering that the whole relationship developed under extremely coercive circumstances), but it is interesting that she did not rebuke Pepys for stroking her chin in the way she later did when he kissed her. The absence of rebuke suggests that chin chucking might have in fact been viewed as relatively innocuous. But at the same time, when we look at diary entries together, they situate the gesture along an erotic continuum. Pepys's "seduction" begins with him stroking the woman's chin, and then he kisses and caresses her, before he finally "arrives" at "what [he] would." It is also worth pointing out that the "freedoms" that Pepys mentions in his diary are remarkably similar to those mentioned in the adultery cases. In the end, chin chucking may not, therefore, seem as chaste or "civil" as Pepys implies.

When the references to chin chucking in Pepys's diary are viewed in relation to the references to the gesture in court cases, literary texts, and books on gesture, it is clear that the social meanings of chin chucking were at least somewhat ambiguous or contested. As a result, it is impossible to give a definitive answer to the question about whether chin chucking was imagined to be a "sexual" act. Still, these collective references demonstrate that the boundaries of "the sexual" were always in the process of being defined or negotiated. This process is apparent in many of the texts I have discussed. In the trials for adultery, for instance, the verdict often hinged on whether an act like chin chucking or embracing was defined as chaste or unchaste. Likewise, the rebuke that Bagwell's wife gave to Pepys was a way of defining his behavior as "immodest" or "uncivil." Finally, the rumors that Herrick mentions in his poem were also an attempt to define the couple's behavior as "overfamiliar," while the speaker's response to those rumors attempts to contest that definition. Printed texts like Bulwer's book on gesture or Herrick's poem are particularly important in this regard because they did not simply reflect ideas about the meaning and performance of this gesture but actively helped to shape them.

Once we acknowledge that categories like "the sexual" or "the chaste" are socially constructed, three important points follow. First, despite their constructedness, these categories nevertheless served important social-regulatory functions. As we have seen, labeling a couple's behavior as "sexual"—or more precisely as "unchaste" or "adulterous"—could have severe consequences, and the threat of these labels undoubtedly led people to restrict their own behavior. Second, we need to resist assuming that we know what counts as sexual, whether in early modern English culture or in our own time. Third, behaviors that are considered sexual or amorous at one historical moment are not necessarily viewed that way in others. The gesture of chin chucking illustrates this third point quite well because today, it is not generally considered to be a sexual act. In fact, one of the interesting things about chin chucking is that it is not really recognized as an act at all. This absence of notice suggests that not only is the category of "the sexual" subject to transformation but erotic behaviors themselves are as well. The art historian Leo Steinberg makes an analogous point when he claims that chin chucking "has suffered gradual debasement since the seventeenth century" and that today "modern lovers [no longer] . . . localize [their] erotic fantasies at the chin."[20] While it is an overstatement to say, categorically, that modern lovers no longer "localize their erotic fantasies at the chin," it is nevertheless true that the gesture and its corresponding erotic fantasies are no longer socialized today in quite the same way as they were in earlier eras.

In the remainder of this essay, I want to explore *how* the texts from the seventeenth century construct the act of chin chucking. How did they imagine the gesture to be performed? Were there any social rules or conventions that governed its performance? At first glance, there do not appear to have been any such rules. Chin chucking seems to have been performed by all sorts of different people and on all sorts of different people. With regard to gender, for example, we have already seen instances in which males chuck the chins of females, females chuck the chins of males, males chuck the chins of other males, and females chuck the chins of other females. But if the gender of the participants does not seem to have restricted or enabled the act, there does nevertheless appear to be a logic underlying these representations. For starters, the chucker generally seems to be portrayed as the active or dominant partner. In the visual representations, the chucker stands over the person who has his or her chin chucked. Moreover, the person who receives the gesture is generally portrayed as passive or subordinate. Bette Talvacchia similarly remarks that the chucking gesture is usually "allotted to the seducer."[21]

Virtually all the literary depictions that I have mentioned figure the act in this way. Claudius is the one who pinches Gertrude's cheek, Neptune claps Leander's cheek, Edward claps Gaveston's cheek, and Olivia strokes Rosania's cheek. Shakespere's Venus is particularly interesting in this regard because she offers an example of a woman who takes the active role. Indeed, Venus's sexual assertiveness is one of her defining characteristics. It is established in the opening lines of the poem, which describe how "the bold faced suitor" begins to "woo [Adonis]" (6). Venus's dominance is then reinforced later in the poem, when Venus positions herself over Adonis as she strokes his cheek. This positioning corresponds with many of the visual representations of the act.

If the seventeenth-century depictions of chin chucking thus tend to construct it as an act in which an active partner attempts to seduce a more passive partner by stroking his or her chin or cheek, then these depictions might be seen as giving credence to Lisa Jardine's argument that activity and passivity were the main conceptual rubrics that people used to understand sexual relations at the time. As Jardine puts it, "eroticism, in the early modern period, is not gender-specific, is not grounded in the sex of the possibly 'submissive' partner, but is an expectation of that very submissiveness."[22] In my opinion, scholars working on sexuality in early modern England have not adequately considered Jardine's thesis, especially given that historians focusing on other European countries have insisted on the centrality of these rubrics.[23] Michael Rocke, for instance, contends that "Florentines . . . were very alert to the [active–passive] oppositions in sexual roles . . . and to the conventional links between those roles and age," despite the fact that they "showed little concern about distinguishing sharply between 'heterosexuals' and 'homosexuals.'" In fact, Rocke says that one of the "central argument[s]" of his book "is that these conventions mattered . . . greatly to Florentines."[24]

These conventions seem to have mattered greatly to the English as well. The terms that were generally used to refer to the active and passive partners were "agent" and "patient." (The terminology that Jardine uses—"dominant" and "submissive"—is drawn from the modern BDSM movement, and while this terminology was not used in the seventeenth century, it is not entirely inappropriate either.) Thus the popular legal writer Giles Jacob explains in his discussion of the Henrican sodomy statute that sodomy "is Felony both in the Agent and the Patient consenting."[25] The influential jurist Sir Edward Coke had stressed this same point earlier; he notes that "both the agent and the consentient are felons."[26] It was not just same-sex relations that were viewed this way, however. Medical writers consistently figured heterosexual intercourse in precisely these terms. Thus the physician John Sadler notes that "in the act of conception there must be an Agent and a Patient . . . he is the agent, she is the Patient."[27] Jane Sharp echoes this logic in *The Midwives Book* when she writes that "man in the act of procreation is the agent and tiller and sower of the ground, woman is the patient or ground to be tilled."[28]

But if erotic relations in early modern England were frequently imagined to involve an active and passive partner in a way that seems to corroborate Jardine's argument, I believe that her thesis nevertheless needs to be revised in several important ways. First, Jardine implies that the distinction between agents and patients was the only one through which desire gained cultural intelligibility. Thus she seems to imagine that there was a notion of sexual orientation in place in the earlier period that is similar to the modern notion of sexual orientation, but that the former was organized around the agent–patient distinction as opposed to the homosexual–heterosexual distinction. In other words, she seems to envision people's activity or passivity defining them in a way that is similar to the way that homosexuality or heterosexuality defines people today. I propose instead that desire was structured by a range of different distinctions, all of which were central or constitutive.

Activity–passivity was certainly one of these, but other important rubrics included gender, age, and status.[29] Moreover, these distinctions often worked together and were mapped onto one another so that the active partner, for instance, was regularly portrayed as being male, older, and of higher status. At the same time, fault lines regularly emerged in these ideologies, since sexual role, gender, age, and status were not mapped seamlessly onto one another. As we've seen with Shakespeare's Venus, for instance, women were sometimes imagined to be sexual agents, although in her case, she is also older and of higher status than her partner. Finally, I would revise Jardine's thesis by suggesting that these definitional vectors appear to be more relational than ontological in early modern texts. That is to say, people's desires were not generally seen as being fixed exclusively on individuals of a particular gender, role, age, or status because all these things were at least to some extent defined in relation to others and could change over time or with different partners or circumstances.[30]

Pepys's chin chucking conforms to what we might call the "dominant" model. As a male, he consistently takes the active role with his female partners and strokes their cheeks and chins. In addition, he is invariably older and of higher social standing than his partners. The distinctions of social status permeated his relationship with Bagwell's wife, but these permeations were also present in his relationships with two other women whose chins he chucked—they were both young servants in his household. Literary texts, too, often figure the gesture according to this dominant model, and unlike Pepys's diary, they would have helped to reinforce the social logic of the act through their publication and performance. Marlowe's account of Neptune stroking Leander's cheek offers one example. Even though this encounter involves two males and therefore does not seem to be structured by issues of gender, it does reinforce the hierarchies of age and status insofar as Neptune is both older than Leander and of higher social standing. When Leander resists Neptune's advances by saying that he is not a woman, the god responds by telling him a story of love featuring a "shepherd . . . [that] played with a boy so lovely fair and kind" (449–50). Critics have noted that Neptune's speech here is meant to alert Leander to the possibilities of male–male love by alluding to the homoerotic pastoral tradition from classical antiquity paradigmatically expressed in Theocritus's *Idylls* and Virgil's *Eclogues*, but in doing so, Neptune also invokes a very specific type of homoerotic relationship: one based on age and power asymmetries, where the older shepherd actively "plays" with "a *boy* so lovely [and] fair." This asymmetry is further reinforced by the fact that Neptune mistakes Leander for "Ganymede" (413)—a figuration that again emphasizes Leander's youth as well as his subordinate place in the social hierarchy.[31]

If Marlowe's description of the gesture of chin chucking in *Hero and Leander* follows—and would have helped to (re)produce—some of the dominant social logics that I outlined earlier, not all the literary representations did so. A number of texts from the period, for instance, portray women taking the active role and chucking the chins of their male partners.[32] Shakespeare's Venus is particularly important in this regard because she seems to have become an archetype of the female seducer.[33] Indeed, when the narrator of a late-seventeenth-century ballad describes how an alehouse hostess would "chuck [him] under the chin, / and perhaps . . . give [him] a kiss," he adds that she did this "As Venus drew Adonis in."[34] Likewise, Queen Olivia from James Shirley's *The Doubtful Heir* compares herself to Venus during her seduction of "Tiberio." This scene is complicated by the fact that Tiberio is really the character Rosania in disguise, but the crucial thing for my purposes is that Olivia is positioned as the wooer in the encounter: she not only "strokes his cheek" but also invites him to her chamber, where she kisses him and declares her love for him.

These literary depictions literalize Natalie Zemon Davis's notion of "women on top" and seem to transgress the assumptions about men taking the active role in performing the gesture (and in wooing more generally).[35] Put differently, we might say that they socialize the gesture in an alternate way, opening up fault lines in the social logic governing its performance. There are at least two possible explanations for this alternative socialization. One would be that the gender transgression was somehow "offset" by the fact that these representations simultaneously reinforced the assumptions about the older, more elite, partner (Venus, Queen Olivia) being active.[36] Shirley consistently highlights the distinctions of age and status underwriting the queen's relationship with her page. Olivia refers to Tiberio as "pretty youth" at one point and as a "proud boy" at another. The king also views their relationship in this way. After observing the queen stroking Tiberio's cheek, he says that she seems to "want / A Ganimed" (36). This comparison does not simply emphasize that the queen is besotted with Tiberio; it also emphasizes the asymmetries of age and status between the two in much the same way that Neptune's mistaking Leander for Ganymede does in Marlowe's *Hero and Leander.* It may at first seem odd that the king makes this comparison given that the queen's relationship with Tiberio is ostensibly "heterosexual." Possibly, the king's comment hints at the underlying homoeroticism of the scene, but it is also possible that he is using the term "Ganymede" in a heterosexual way. Other texts from the period use the term in reference to a young male who is the servant—and erotic object—of an older, more powerful woman.[37]

Even though neither Shakespeare nor Shirley demonize their female protagonists for their chin chucking (or for their sexually assertive behavior), other writers from the period certainly did. These writers often, for instance, revile prostitutes for their behavior in stroking the chins of their prospective clients.[38] In the ballad *A New Ballad of a Finical Monsieur* (circa 1685–88), the titular Frenchman describes how his "whore" would "chuck a my chin" and "kiss a my Cheek," and he adds that "Her Impudent actions do make a me sick."[39] Likewise, in *Strange Newes from Bartholomew-Fair, or the wandering-whore discovered,* the eponymous character reveals the ploys she would use to "entice young punys." She says she would give them "a wink, a smile and a chuck under the Chin" and that she would "clap... [her] hand on [her] market-place, and say... here's your Ware boys."[40] In both these cases, the women's behavior is implicitly condemned. While this may be on account of their sexual assertiveness, it is also significant that these women are both imagined to be of lower social standing than their partners. Thus these female characters do not simply transgress gendered hierarchies by taking the role of the seducer but also transgress the hierarchies of status in doing so. This transgression is complicated even further in the example from *Strange Newes* because the prostitute refers to her potential customers as "boys," thus emphasizing—or imagining—a distinction based on age. Perhaps for this reason, the "wandering whore's" behavior is not so harshly condemned as that of her counterpart in the ballad: her behavior is certainly portrayed as crass (even grotesque), but it is also portrayed as somewhat comical. A number of different relational vectors thus appear in these two examples, but both texts suggest that it is inappropriate for women to take the active role in performing chin chucking. As a result, the representations of chin chucking in the texts differ in their overall effect from the representations of Shakespeare and Shirley. The former would have socialized the gesture of chin chucking in a much more "normative" way than the latter.

There is, however, still another possible explanation for why Shakespeare and Shirley do not stigmatize their female protagonists' behavior to a greater degree. It is possible that women's sexual agency—and their chin chucking—was accepted to a certain extent, or at least in certain circumstances. Given the patriarchal nature of early modern English culture, this might seem somewhat surprising, but it would help explain why the texts that socialized chin chucking did so in such a conflicted or contradictory way. A seventeenth-century ballad seems to address this issue directly. In it, the male narrator states, "If my Lady . . . bidd mee Kisse and play, Shall I shrinke? Cold Foole away. If Shee clap my Cheekes and spye little Cupids in my eye, gripe my hand and Stroake my haire, shall I like a faint heart feare? No, no, no." The narrator here assumes that many people find women's "kissing" and "clapping" troubling and "shrinke" from it or "feare" it, but he insists that he finds it attractive and that others ought to do so as well. Yet if the speaker thus advocates the acceptance of women's sexual agency, there are some limits to this acceptance. He does not, for instance, imagine himself as completely passive—so he is not describing a complete role reversal along the lines of what happens in Shakespeare's *Venus and Adonis.* In the final line of the poem, he says that "Hope makes me Hardy, and so does Shee." The speaker's formulation here is carefully calibrated: he figures himself as a "hardy" lover (read "active," with the obvious bawdy pun), but at the same time, he acknowledges that the sexually aggressive behavior of "his lady" helps to make him that way.[41]

A remarkably similar dynamic appears in one of the pornographic prints appended to Nicholas Chorier's *Satyra Sotadica de Arcanis Amoris et*

Veneris (Figure 5.3). One of the best-known works of pornography from the seventeenth century, *Satyra Sotadica* was first published in 1660, and this particular image is one of twenty-eight woodcuts that were added to the 1690 edition of the text.[42] The woodcuts illustrate a range of different erotic practices and positions and are somewhat reminiscent of Aretino's *I Modi (The Ways),* which describes sixteen different "ways" of making love.[43] For my purposes, the first thing to say about the engraving of the woman chucking her male partner's chin is that the male in the scene is plainly coded as the active partner: he is not only about to penetrate the woman, he is also situated above her, and she lies in a precarious position with her legs on his shoulders. Given that the woman is visually subordinated, it is surprising that she is the one who chucks his chin rather than vice versa. The act creates a secondary power dynamic, stressing her active participation in the encounter. The overall active–passive dynamics are therefore virtually identical to those presented in the ballad. In both cases, the woman's sexual agency is accepted or even embraced, but it is also situated in a context where the man is still ultimately dominant. Indeed, the women's agency and their chin chucking may be intended to make their partners—or indeed some male viewers—more "hardy."

At the very least, these representations of women chucking the chins of their male partners would have potentially expanded the accepted ways that the gesture could be performed. It is likewise possible that women's erotic agency as chin chuckers was condoned to some extent and that that condoning was more likely if the act ended up reinforcing other social hierarchies such as those of age and status. Lisa Jardine's thesis that early modern eroticism was structured around "expectations of submissiveness" is thus to some extent corroborated by the depictions of chin chucking that I have surveyed, although other sexual dynamics structure them as well. These depictions foreground the importance of age and gender hierarchies. Jardine's thesis usefully distinguishes early modern eroticism from a modern notion of sexual orientation that is grounded on the sex of the person one desires (if not exactly the sex of the submissive partner), but her formulation is also potentially misleading because the active–passive distinction was not the only basis on which erotic interactions were structured.

FIGURE 5.3. Engraving appended to Nicholas Chorier's *Satyra Sotadica,* circa 1690, copyright British Library Board, P.C.30.i.10.

So far, I have been exploring what these depictions of chin chucking tell us about the gendered conventions surrounding the active partner, but there seems to have been a similar set of conventions regarding the gender of the passive partner. It is true, of course, that both males and females have their chins chucked, but the males who are placed in the subordinate position are often beardless. In other words, they are coded as being boys or youths.[44] Shakespeare's Adonis, for instance, is explicitly described as having a "hairless face" (487), and Leander is also sometimes portrayed as being "beardless."[45] In Shirley's *The Doubtful Heir,* "Tiberio" is undoubtedly intended to be beardless, given that he is really a woman in disguise, and he is also repeatedly referred to as a "boy" or "youth." Arguably, the figures' ages help rationalize their subordination, but their genders do so as well. Another way of thinking about this rationalization would be to say that age and gender are so tightly linked that boys are almost a different gender from men.[46]

There are a few instances in which bearded men have their chins chucked and are placed in the passive role. These instances are quite rare, and when they do occur, they are usually marked as transgressive. In Edward Ward's *The Miracles Performed by Money,* for instance, the narrator describes the behavior of the young bride in a May–December marriage:

> With what Impatience have I often seen,
> A *Youthful Bride,* who never saw Eighteen,
> Running with nimble haste to opening Door,
> To meet her *Good old Man* of Sixty-four,
> Clap her Warm, Soft, Plump, Rosy Cheek to his,
> And nestle through his Beard to get a Kiss?
> Play with her Hand upon his Grisly Chin,
> And softly say, my *Dear where have you been?*[47]

These lines do not simply depict the young bride chucking the chin of her older husband; they also suggest that this behavior is somewhat ridiculous. In fact, the speaker purposefully juxtaposes the wife's "Soft, Plump, Rosy cheek" (which is eminently chuckable) with the "Grisly [bearded] Chin" of her "Good old Man" to highlight the preposterousness of the wife's actions.[48] As with the earlier depictions of prostitutes chucking the chins of her male clients, this representation involves the transgression of both age and gender hierarchies. Moreover, the narrator's derision of the wife's behavior would likely have worked to discourage people from performing the gesture in this way.

If all the texts examined here helped to socialize chin chucking, and to shape or regulate its performance, my hope is that this examination has also provided some insight into the broader ways in which erotic relations were constructed in early modern England. This hope assumes, of course, that a seemingly insignificant gesture like chin chucking has encoded within it an entire "micro-physics of power" or that it has the ability to instantiate a range of different ideologies.[49] In the end, the main thing that my analysis has suggested is that activity and passivity were indeed central terms through which desire gained cultural intelligibility but that they also intersected in complex and sometimes contradictory ways with distinctions based on age, status, and gender. As a result of these multiple and interlocking investments, the way the gesture of chin chucking is performed may, at first glance, appear to be completely arbitrary or fluid, especially when viewed from a modern perspective, but this fluidity can also be seen as the by-product of the conflicting investments. By comparison, the modern notion of sexual orientation seems much less polyvalent. It is, of course, organized around a single issue—the gender of the individuals to whom one is attracted. Eve Sedgwick calls attention to the peculiarity of this notion of sexual orientation in *Epistemology of the Closet*: "It is a rather amazing fact that, of the . . . many dimensions along which the genital activity of one person can be differentiated from that of another . . . precisely one, the gender of object choice, . . . [has become] the dimension denoted by the now ubiquitous category of 'sexual orientation.'" Yet Sedgwick then goes on to list some alternate ways we think of sexuality being "oriented," including a preference for "a certain species," "a certain number of participants," or "a certain relation of age or power."[50] She insists, moreover, that although these other possible ways of categorizing people's sexual impulses do not have the "diacritical potential for signifying [a particular type of sexuality]," they do nevertheless exert a "definitional force."[51] As a result, sexuality should not be viewed as a "coherent definitional field" but as "a space of overlapping, contradictory and conflictual definitional forces"—one that is ultimately characterized by the "unrationalized coexistence" of different models.[52]

Building on Sedwick's analysis, I want to point out that the early modern erotic logics that I've been analyzing here continue to exert some "definitional force" today. For instance, the early modern distinction between agents and patients might be linked to the modern distinction between "tops" and "bottoms" or "dominants" and "submissives." Although today, these terms are used primarily by minority groups like gay men and members of the BDSM community, one could argue that they have a much more pervasive influence. Likewise, age and status continue to be part of the way people imagine their sexual preferences, although again, their "definitional force" is occluded—or rendered ancillary—by the hegemony of the homosexual–heterosexual model. The fact that these earlier models persist today is not surprising. David Halperin argues that what Sedgwick calls "the unrationalized coexistence of different models [of sexuality]" ought to be understood as "the cumulative effect of a long process of historical overlay and accretion . . . [in which] we have preserved and retained different definitions of sex [or ways of conceptualizing it] from our pre-modern past, despite the logical contradictions among them." Thus, according to Halperin, the "definitional incoherence at the core of the modern notions of [sexuality]" results from the way that our "modern" thinking has "incorporated—without homogenizing—[these] earlier models [of sexual relations], models that directly conflict with the [modern thinking about sexuality] that has nonetheless absorbed them."[53] When seen from this perspective, what I have been exploring here is only a small piece of this much larger "process of historical overlay and accretion," but it is nevertheless a significant piece in that it offers a glimpse into the workings of these larger cultural and historical processes.

Notes

1 Robert Herrick, "The suspition upon his over-much familiarity with a Gentlewoman," in *Hesperides* (London, 1648), 52.

2 Leo Steinberg's *The Sexuality of Christ in Renaissance Art and in Modern Oblivion* (New York: Pantheon Books, 1983) contains a fairly extensive discussion of this gesture (3–4, 110–16). Steinberg provides the following description of the act itself: "What I have summarily called the chin-chuck should be understood to include any reaching for . . . touching, fingering, pinching, caressing, cupping, or clasping [of the cheek or chin]" (110). Other art historians have also briefly mentioned the gesture. See, e.g., James Saslow, *Ganymede in the Renaissance: Homosexuality in Art and Society* (New Haven, Conn.: Yale University Press, 1988), 132, and

Bette Talvacchia, *Taking Positions: On the Erotic in Renaissance Culture* (Princeton, N.J.: Princeton University Press, 2001), 44–45.

3 Gordon Williams, *A Dictionary of Sexual Language in Shakespearean and Stuart Literature* (Atlantic Highlands, N.J.: Athlone Press, 1994), 238. Leo Steinberg likewise states that the gesture was "a token of affection or erotic persuasion" and that "no . . . artist, medieval or Renaissance, would have taken this long-fixed convention for anything but a sign of erotic communion." Steinberg, *Sexuality of Christ*, 3.

4 There is a growing body of research on the history of gesture that seeks to examine the social meanings of these acts in light of theoretical work done by writers like Marcel Mauss, Norbert Elias, Mary Douglas, and Pierre Bourdieu. See, e.g., the collection *A Cultural History of Gesture*, ed. Jan Bremmer and Herman Roodenburg (Ithaca, N.Y.: Cornell University Press, 1991), and Adam Kendon, *Gesture: Visible Action as Utterance* (Cambridge: Cambridge University Press, 2004).

5 John Bulwer, *Chirologia, or, The naturall language of the hand composed of the speaking motions, and the discoursing gestures thereof* (London, 1644), 78.

6 Ibid., 117. What Bulwer actually says is "lovers, I know not by what amorous instinct, next to the face, direct their passionate respects to the Hand of those they love." Implicit is the idea that lovers first direct their attentions to the face and secondarily to the hand, so I've transposed the words to make the meaning clearer for my purposes.

7 In addition to claiming it is not "unchaste," Herrick links it rhetorically with "non-sexual" activities like "danc[ing]" and "play[ing]." The kinds of rhetorical linkages that Herrick makes in his poem are by no means universal, however. In one of his other poems, "On Himselfe," Herrick discusses the gesture in a much more sexualized context: "Young I was, but now am old, / But I am not yet grown cold; / I can play, and I can twine / Bout a Virgin like a Vine: / In her lap too I can lye / Melting, and in fancie die: / And return to life, if she / Claps my cheek, or kisseth me; / Thus, and thus it now appears / That our love out-lasts our yeeres." Herrick, *Hesperides*, 15. Other authors from the period also associate chin chucking with much more explicitly sexual activity. In the ballad *A New Song, Call'd the Old Man's Wish* (1691), for instance, the titular character laments, "O that I were but Young again, / Then I would chuck her under the Chin; / Under the chin, and t'other Thing too, / Oh that I were but Young for you." Likewise, in another ballad from the period, *The*

St. James's Frolick (circa 1683–1703), a barber "chucks" a women "under the chin" and then "straight away did trim her / far better than e're she had been." Throughout this chapter, I draw heavily on ballads from the period because they frequently mention chin chucking and also because they can provide an excellent window into popular perceptions of the gesture. Unless otherwise noted, all references are from the English Broadside Ballad Archive. Both are originally from the Pepys Collection: *The Old Man's Wish* is Pepys 5.186 and *The St. James's Frolick* is Pepys 3.243.

8 Daniel Rogers, *Matrimoniall honour, or, The mutuall crowne and comfort of godly, loyall, and chaste marriage wherein the right way to preserve the honour of marriage unstained is at large described, urged, and applied* (London, 1642), 358–59.

9 David Turner, *Fashioning Adultery: Gender, Sex and Civility in England, 1660–1740* (Cambridge: Cambridge University Press, 2002), 165.

10 Ibid., 148, 160.

11 Ibid., 166.

12 This case has been discussed by several historians, including Laura Gowing and Joanne Bailey. The transcriptions of Green's testimony are from Laura Gowing's *Common Bodies: Women, Touch, and Power in Seventeenth-Century England* (New Haven, Conn.: Yale University Press, 2003), 105. Also see Bailey's *Unquiet Lives: Marriage and Marriage Breakdown in England, 1660–1800* (Cambridge: Cambridge University Press, 2003), 148, 159, and 189.

13 My thanks to Jim Bromley for this formulation.

14 Sir William Dugdale, *The antiquities of Warwickshire illustrated from records, leiger-books, manuscripts, charters, evidences, tombes, and armes* (London, 1656), 711. While this last detail implies that Brome's decision to take the law into his own hands was considered rash and inappropriate, the fact that he was pardoned might also suggest that his actions were not completely unacceptable.

15 Thomas D'Urfey, *A Fond Husband* (London, 1677), 26. At another point in the play, Ranger makes a similar accusation. He says that he peeked through the keyhole and saw the two of them together in a parlor on the backside of the kitchen and that Rashley allegedly had "his Head . . . in her Lap,—whilst she with a fond passion strok'd his Cheeks, and dalli'd with his Hair" (55). Thomas Bayly's fictionalized "history" of Rome, *Herba Parietis or, The wall-flower* (London, 1650), offers an interesting counterexample. One of Bayly's chapters tells the story of Honoria, a

Roman princess and a ward of Maximanus, who ends up falling in love with her. Maximanus is led to believe, however, that she has been seduced by Hortensia (the gardener). Thus the spies of Maximanus "inform'd [him] that they had seen them as good as naught together" and that "they had seen them court one another extreamly." The spies admit that "the[ir] words . . . they could not hear well, but their actions were too palpable." They point out, for instance, "that she stroakt him under the Chin, clapt his Cheeks, thrust her fingers into his Bosome, smil'd him in the Face." With this information "being so confidently related by so many witnesses" to Maximanus, it "made him believe (as it did too many others) that it had been so indeed." But in this instance, the narrator makes it clear that Maximanus's spies are mistaken and that they have "misread" the gestures and relationship of Honoria and Hortensia. So when Honoria supposedly strokes the gardener's cheek and "thrust[s] her fingers into his Bosome," for instance, what actually happens is that Honoria spies "an Earwig ready to creep into Hertensius ear, endeavouring to strike it off with her hand, she strikes it into his Neck; and perceiving it to be there, thrust her fingers into his Coller to take it thence" (28).

16 All references to Shakespeare are from *The Norton Shakespeare,* ed. Stephen Greenblatt, Walter Cohen, Jean E. Howard, and Katharine Eisaman Maus (New York: W. W. Norton, 1997). Another example of this gesture from Shakespeare's works is Cressida stroking the cheek of Diomedes in *Troilus and Cressida* (5.2.49).

17 All references to Marlowe's works are from *The Complete Works of Christopher Marlowe,* 2nd ed., ed. Fredson Bowers (Cambridge: Cambridge University Press, 1981).

18 James Shirley, *Six New Playes* (London, 1653), 36. These are King Ferdinand's observations. It is significant that Rosania is dressed like a page or subordinate. Interestingly, the king says "she does want / A Ganimed" (36) and thus evokes the male homoerotic context, though the term *ganymede* was also sometimes used in a heterosexual context in the period, when a young man became the sexual object or servant for an older, more powerful woman. See Denise Walen's discussion of this scene, and of the complex (homo)erotics of the play, in *Constructions of Female Homoeroticism in Early Modern Drama* (New York: Palgrave Macmillan, 2005), 88–92.

19 All references to Pepys's diary are by volume and page number to the eleven-volume *Diary of Samuel Pepys: A New and Complete Transcription,*

ed. Robert Latham and William Matthews (Berkeley: University of California Press, 1971).

20 Steinberg, *Sexuality of Christ,* 110–11. The medieval practice of wearing wimples and chin bands (also known as a "chin-cloths" or "chin-clouts") strikes me as an important testament to the erotic power of the chin, though an analysis of this phenomenon lies outside the purview of this essay.

21 Talvacchia, *Taking Positions,* 44.

22 Lisa Jardine, "Twins and Travesties: Gender, Dependency and Sexual Availability in *Twelfth Night,*" in *Erotic Politics: Desire on the Renaissance Stage,* ed. Susan Zimmerman (New York: Routledge, 1992), 34.

23 Even the best studies of early modern English (homo)sexuality have tended to downplay the cultural significance of the active–passive rubrics and, by extension, the importance of age-graded relationships. Alan Bray's *Homosexuality in Renaissance England* (1995; repr., New York: Columbia University Press, 1996) is still arguably the best introduction to this subject, but as Michael Rocke points out, Bray "curiously fails to emphasize the predominance in Renaissance England of the adult–boy model, even though a great deal of [the] evidence he presents points in this direction." Rocke, *Forbidden Friendships: Homosexuality and Male Culture in Renaissance Florence* (Oxford: Oxford University Press, 1998), 281. Bruce Smith acknowledges the existence of these rubrics to a much greater degree than Bray, but he, too, tends to downplay their significance in literary texts, ultimately contending that "age-graded homosexuality" and "egalitarian homosexuality" were both equally "possible ways of enacting male bonds among Shakespeare and his contemporaries." Smith, *Homosexual Desire in Shakespeare's England: A Cultural Poetics* (Chicago: University of Chicago Press, 1991), 76.

24 Rocke, *Forbidden Friendships,* 13. Rocke explains that these conventions "were tightly bound up with what it meant to be a male. . . . The 'active' and usually penetrating role substantially conformed to the behaviors and ideas that were defined as virile, and consequently a man's sexual relations with a boy, when enacted within these conventions, did not call into question his status as a 'normal' and masculine male. To take the 'passive' role in sex with a male, however, was deemed 'feminine' and dishonorable, but since this role was in effect limited to the biological period of adolescence it was only a temporary and wayward turn on a boy's path to full-fledged manhood" (13).

25 Giles Jacob, *New Law Dictionary* (London, 1729), n.p.

26 Sir Edward Coke, *The Third Part of the Institutes of the Laws of England* (London, 1644), 59.

27 John Sadler, *The Sicke Woman's Private Looking-Glasse* (London, 1636), 12.

28 Jane Sharp, *The Midwives Book* (London, 1671), 33.

29 I am focusing on these particular rubrics here because they are the ones that emerge most clearly in the sources that discuss chin chucking, but I do not mean to imply that they were the only terms structuring desire in the period. Race, religion, and species (to name but a few) were also extremely important.

30 Another way of making this point would be to say that although these factors were constitutive and shaped individuals' sexual relations, they do not seem to have coalesced to form any kind of erotic identity. The schema that I am imagining here might be compared to the one that David Halperin maps in *How to Do the History of Homosexuality* (Chicago: University of Chicago Press, 2004), although the terms that he uses are somewhat different.

31 The dynamics in the relationship between Edward and his minion, Gaveston, in Marlowe's *Edward II* are similar, although a little more complex. Edward is the one who allegedly "claps [Gaveston's] cheek and hangs about his neck," and while this gesture might be understood to reinforce the gulf in social status between them, this reading is complicated by the fact that Edward also "hangs" about Gaveston's "neck." This particular posture could be understood to imply a kind of overattachment that is inappropriate for someone of his status. My reading of this relationship differs somewhat in its emphasis from Jonathan Goldberg's. Goldberg contends that Gaveston and Edward are "equals" and that "Gaveston has been raised from his lower-class position to be Edward's equal." Goldberg, *Sodometries: Renaissance Texts, Modern Sexualities* (Stanford, Calif.: Stanford University Press, 1992), 121. What matters to the Mortimers, according to Goldberg, is not that Edward is having sex with Gaveston but that Gaveston is not Edward's subordinate. Although I find Goldberg's analysis fascinating, I think more attention still needs to be paid to the complexities of the active–passive dynamic in Edward and Gaveston's relationship.

32 Of the eighty-five representations of the act that I have examined, forty-four depict women chucking the chins of men, and thirty-three depict men chucking the chins of women. (The others depict same-sex couplings.)

In approximately half of the instances in which women take the active role, however, they are criticized for this behavior (either explicitly or implicitly). In the aggregate, I would therefore still maintain that the primary way that these texts socialize this gesture is with men taking the active role.

33 Thomas Heywood presents a vignette of Venus wooing Adonis that echoes Shakespeare's poem: "Pre'thee be wanton; let vs toy and play, / Thy Icy fingers warme betweene my breasts; / Looke on me Adon with a stedfast eye, / That in these Christall glasses I may see / My beauty, that charmes Gods, makes men amaz'd, / And stownd with wonder: doth this roseat pillow / Offend my loue? come, wallow in my lap, / With my white fingers I will clap thy cheeke, / Whisper a thousand pleasures in thine eare." Heywood, *The Brazen Age* (London, 1613), sig. C3r.

34 The ballad, *A Caveat for Young Men* (Pepys 2.22.), is intended as a warning to young men not to be lured in by the advances of such women. The narrator describes his own "downfall": "She'd chuck me under the chin, / and perhaps would give me a kiss, / As Venus drew Adonis in, / my Hoastis would never miss: / She'd tell me it was too early, / or else it was too late, / until by the Oyle of Barely, / they had gotten my whole estate." Unlike Venus, the hostess here seems to be of the same rank as her "customer," and this fact may help to explain why her behavior is implicitly criticized. At the same time, she does seem to be older and more agential than the young man, as she takes advantage of him.

35 See Natalie Zemon Davis, "Women on Top," in *Society and Culture in Early Modern France: Eight Essays* (Stanford, Calif.: Stanford University Press, 1975), 124–52.

36 This type of behavior was not just something presented in literary texts. In the court case of Elizabeth Myers from 1674, Myers is the one who allegedly "stroked" the cheeks of her lover John Jopling. Interestingly, she was a widow of one of the aldermen from the city of Durham and thus seems to have been of slightly higher status than Jopling, who was nevertheless, according to the court documents, a "gentleman."

37 In *The Seven Deadly Sins of London* (London, 1606), for instance, Thomas Dekker personifies money as a queen and imagines "riot" as her "smooth-fac'd Ganimed" (sig. C3v). An even more interesting example is the satire of a Puritan wife, Mistress Simula, in Richard Corbet's 1611 *The Times' Whistle* (London: Early English Text Society, 1871). Simula is a typical religious hypocrite. Although she is "ready to faint if she an oth but

hear," in reality, she is "Living in sinne & sensual delight": "For, would you think it? she was ta[ke]ne in bed / With a yong, tender, smoothfacd Ganimed, / Her husbands prentice" (733–41). This passage emphasizes that Mistress Simula's "Ganimed" is both younger than her ("young, tender, [and] smoothfacd") and also subordinate to her (by virtue of being "her husbands prentice"). Although Corbet uses the term "Ganimed" here in a heteroerotic context, Corbet was certainly aware of its homoerotic usages, too, for later in the book, there is a satirical portrait of "Sodomeo" who finds "all his joy . . . in a rarely featured lively boy, / With whom (I shame to speake it) in his bed / He plays like Jove with Phrigian Ganimede" (2467–70).

38 As Ruth Mazo Karras argues in *Common Women: Prostitution and Sexuality in Medieval England* (Oxford: Oxford University Press, 1998), prostitutes were defined less by the transactional–economic nature of their relationships than by the inordinate nature of their desires. Karras makes this point about prostitution in the Middle Ages, but I believe that it holds true for the early modern period as well.

39 *The Difficult French-Man's Unsuccessful Adventers; Or, A New Ballad of a Finical Monsieur* (Pepys 3.136). There are many examples of prostitutes behaving in similar fashion. A 1620 ballad warns men to "take heed" not to "trust . . . a whore," detailing the methods they use to lure men in: "Shee'l stroke your cheeks shee'l stroke your chin, / Shee'le fling her armes abou' you. / And sh'eele protest with vowes and oaths, / She cannot dieu withou' you." *A Caveat or Warning. / For all sortes of Men both young and olde to avoid the / Company of lewd and wicked Woemen / To the tune of Virginia* (Pepys 1.46–47). In *The Rogue: or The Life of Guzman de Alfarache. Written in Spanish by Matheo Aleman* (London, 1623), the rhetoric condemning the prostitute's behavior is even more vituperative. The main character explains that he told the woman he was "of Sevill," and "with that, she came neerer unto me, and giving me a chocke under the chin, she said unto me; Now you little wanton foole, whither wander you?" He later comments that "her stinking breath" annoyed him and that "with her very touching of me, me thought . . . that the utmost of evils had now lighted upon me in meeting with such a filthy unsavoury Slut" (31).

40 *Strange Newes from Bartholomew-Fair, or the wandering-whore discovered* (London, 1661), 3.

41 *Cheerfull ayres or ballads first composed for one single voice* (London, 1660), 73–75.

42 I am aware of only one extant copy that still contains these pull-out images: *Joannis Meursii Elegantiae Latini Sermonis* at the British Library, P.C.30.i.10. It is also not clear if these images originally appeared in all the copies of the 1690 edition or if they were appended to earlier editions as well but later removed. The woodcuts do not seem to be directly related to the text itself: they are not, for instance, illustrations of specific scenes from the narrative.

43 A facsimile and a translation of *I Modi* appear in Talvacchia, *Taking Positions.*

44 Much excellent scholarly research on early modern boyhood has addressed both the gender and sexuality of boys. For a few influential examples, see Stephen Orgel, *Impersonations: The Performance of Gender in Shakespeare's England* (Cambridge: Cambridge University Press, 1996); Bruce Smith, *Shakespeare and Masculinity* (Oxford: Oxford University Press, 2000); Gina Bloom, "Squeaky Voices: Marston, Mulcaster, and the Boy Actor," in *Voice in Motion: Staging Gender, Shaping Sound in Early Modern England* (Philadelphia: University of Pennsylvania Press, 2007), 21–66 ; Gina Bloom, "'Boys Eternal': Aging, Games and Masculinity in *The Winter's Tale,*" *ELR* 40, no. 3 (2010): 329–56; Jeffrey Masten, "Editing Boys: The Performance of Gender in Print," in *Redefining British Theatre History: From Performance to Print,* ed. Peter Holland and Stephen Orgel, 113–34 (New York: Palgrave Macmillan, 2006); and Lucy Munro, "The Humour of Children: Performance, Gender, and the Early Modern Children's Companies," *Literature Compass* 2, no. 1 (2005): 1–26.

45 At another point in Shakespeare's poem, Venus calls attention to "The tender spring upon [his] tempting lip," which "shows thee unripe: yet mayst thou well be tasted" (127–28). The different stages of manhood were sometimes divided according to the growth of facial hair. Manhood is signaled by the development of a full beard, whereas stages like infancy, boyhood, and youth all precede this development. See my chapter "'His Majesty the Beard': Beards and Masculinity," in *Materializing Gender in Early Modern English Literature and Culture,* 83–129 (Cambridge: Cambridge University Press, 2006), esp. 88. Marlowe's Leander is clearly an adolescent, but he is not specifically said to be beardless. There is, however, a reference to "Beardless Leander" in the earlier play *The Raigne of King Edward the third* (London, 1596), sig. D4v. For the argument that Marlowe wrote several scenes of *Edward III,* see Thomas Merriam, "Marlowe's Hand in *Edward III,*" *Literary and Linguistic Computing* 8, no.

2 (1993): 59–72, and "Marlowe's Hand in *Edward III* Revisited," *Literary and Linguistic Computing* 11, no. 1 (1996): 19–22.

46 I argue in "His Majesty the Beard" that one of the ways that this gendered distinction was materialized was through facial hair. More recently, Bloom, "Squeaky Voices," has discussed the way that this distinction was materialized through the voice.

47 Edward Ward, *The Miracles Performed by Money* (London, 1692), 16.

48 A passage in Thomas Carew's masque *Coleum Britanicum* (London, 1633) resonates with this one. The character Momus, the god of mockery, describes how all the Roman gods have reformed their adulterous behavior after being inspired by the relationship between Charles I and Henrietta Maria. Momus claims that even "Venus hath confest all her adulteries, and is receiv'd to grace by her husband, who conscious of the great disparity betwixt her perfections and his deformities, allowes those levities as an equall counterpoize; but it is the prettiest spectacle to see her stroaking with her Ivory hand his collied cheeks, and with her sinowy fingers combing his sooty beard" (8). In this passage, Venus's act of stroking Vulcan's "collied" cheeks and sooty beard is clearly meant to be seen as unorthodox, but, as I noted earlier, Venus is often held up as the archetype of the sexually agential woman, and in this instance, her chin chucking is certainly meant to be an index of her libidinal nature (which Vulcan has agreed to tolerate, along with her adultery).

49 "Micro-physics of power" is Michel Foucault's phrase in *Discipline and Punish: The Birth of the Prison* (New York: Random House, 1979), 26. My second formulation echoes a point that Pierre Bourdieu makes in *Outline for a Theory of Practice* (Cambridge: Cambridge University Press, 1977), namely, that "injunctions as insignificant as 'stand up straight' or 'don't hold your knife in your left hand'" can inculcate "a whole cosmology, an ethic, a metaphysic, [or] a political philosophy" (94).

50 Eve Kosofsky Sedgwick, *Epistemology of the Closet* (Berkeley: University of California Press, 2008), 8.

51 Ibid., 9.

52 Ibid., 45, 48.

53 Halperin, *How to Do the History of Homosexuality,* 12. I have adapted Halperin's point here. He's talking specifically about homosexuality, but as my adaptation demonstrates, his point can applied to sexuality—and especially the modern notion of sexual orientation—more generally.

6

Rimming the Renaissance

JAMES M. BROMLEY

Ben Jonson's *The Alchemist* (1610) begins with a perhaps notorious quarrel in which the title character Subtle tells Face, "I fart at thee" (1.1.1), and directs him to "Lick figs / Out at my—" (1.1.3–4).[1] With the "fart" directing us to the backside of the body, we can safely supply the missing conclusion of "arse," which, with the command to lick, makes the barb akin to the modern "kiss my ass."[2] As with many insults, such as "jerk," "kiss my ass" draws on and intensifies meanings associated with a sexual practice—in this case, anilingus, or colloquially rimming or rimjobs—which may be objectionable to some but pleasurable to others. Mapping references to anilingus in early modern texts, this chapter examines what work these references might do in gesturing toward alternate organizations of bodies, pleasures, and subjectivities even in contexts that load them with negative affect. Like *sex, anilingus* and *rimming* are anachronistic terms for the early modern period despite the existence of references to the acts those terms name, but this anachronism can be productive in linking early modern and modern interruptions in the abstraction of sexual identities from sexual practices.

During the early modern period, the circulation of sexual knowledge about anilingus is partly connected to the conventional association of figs and the anus, an association that I partly draw out of the history of the gesture known as the *fico.* Bringing the history of gesture to bear on the history of sexuality, I show that in the early modern period, anilingus receives negative charge when the practice is invoked in the domains of waste, foreignness, bestiality, flattery, and gender, but in those domains, references to rimming are insufficient to erect the boundaries they are marshaled to support. Cary Howie's recent provocative work on medieval literature prompted me to attempt in this chapter to situate references to anilingus in the history of sexuality and in other early modern discourses. Howie calls for the development of "a poetics of rimming and limning" that resists thinking of binaries, such as virtue and vice, as collapsing into "immanent unity or selfsameness" and that instead aesthetically and ethically appreciates "what refuses to be assimilated."[3] The act of rimming plugs a hole with the tongue by penetrating it, or as Howie puts it, "a tongue has intervened to preserve the enclosure and, simultaneously, to open it up."[4] Howie's work revels in ambivalences about corporeal and other boundaries encoded in rimming that are similar to those concerns with which this chapter tarries.

In addition to historicizing the practice, I want to articulate an ethics from these references. Saturated as they are by condemnation, early modern references to anilingus imagine the possibility and the pleasures of depersonalized intimacy. Thus I seek to attend to a particular sexual practice's history while avoiding abstracting from that practice further taxonomies or an identity-based schema for organizing early modern sexual practices. Rimming's relationship to modern forms of sexual identity is tenuous at best. While popularly associated with gay men, rimming is neither constitutive of their identity nor exclusive to them as a practice. As such, it can figure, I suggest, the interruption of linkages between identity and sexual practice that organize power relations and restrict pleasures. For queer historiography, rimming reveals ways of thinking about sexuality that do not align acts with the past and identities with the present. In the second half of this chapter, then, I argue that both the gender indeterminacy of early modern references to anilingus and the practice's oblique relation to passive and active roles offer ways to rethink the relationship of sexuality and subjectivity as scholars currently articulate it for the early modern period and as that relationship works under modern heteronormativity.

The Boundary Work of Anilingus

The entries for *fig* in multiple historical dictionaries of slang and sexual language mention the word's use as genital and anal euphemism, and because *fico* is Italian for "fig," they occasionally cross-reference the *fico* gesture, where a person conveys contempt by putting his or her thumb between his middle and index fingers.[5] According to John Bulwer's *Chirologia, or the Naturall Language of the Hand* (1644), the *fico* comes to England by way of the Spanish, who derived it from the Greek. Bulwer reports that the Spanish mean by it "*paedicavi te,*" or "go sodomize yourself."[6] The fig acquires a specifically anal resonance partly through the many textual iterations of an apocryphal story about Frederick Barbarossa's siege of Milan in 1161.[7] Incited by the pope to rebel against Barbarossa's authority, the Milanese placed Frederick's wife backward on the back of an ass, forcing her to use the tail as a bridle. Ruth Melinkoff reminds us that such an arrangement would frequently force the face of the rider into the anal cleft of the animal.[8] Thus the *contrapasso* punishment Barbarossa inflicted on the people after subduing the rebellion: according to Peter Heylyn's political geography *Mikrokosmos: A Little Description of the Great World* (1625), Barbarossa "adjudged all the people to dye, save such as would undergoe this ransome. Betweene the buttocks of a skittish Mule, a bunch of Figges was fastned; and such as would live, must with their hands bound behind, runne after the Mule, till with their teeth they had snatched out one or more of the Figges."[9] In *Pantagruel,* François Rabelais adds this flourish: "These, after pulling out the fig with their teeth, displayed it clearly to the hangman, saying: *Ecco lo fico.*"[10] James T. Henke cautions us that the Barbarossa story is not the origin of the *fico* gesture but "may represent the attempts of some later scholar to account for the Greek sense of the gesture."[11] Such a hypothesis does not preclude a meaningful connection between the anus and the gesture for people in the sixteenth and seventeenth centuries. Even if the Barbarossa story is an afterthought, the humiliation the Milanese and Barbarossa practiced on each other involves anal–oral contact. Bringing the *fico* and the Barbarossa story together also will caution us against assuming, as Gordon Williams does, that "a genital explanation is more likely" for the sexualization of the fig.[12] I am not simply quibbling with a dictionary entry here. If we default to or merely prefer a genital explanation when at the very least the fig is overdetermined by competing genital and anilingual meanings, then our historical dictionaries, as well as our footnotes and glosses in critical editions and our critical analyses of literary texts that draw on such dictionaries, will map a genital, even reproductive, often heterosexist reading onto usages that are more complex. These readings can, in turn, ramify outward such that the more complex parsings of sexual acts in the culture are reduced to a system organized around reproductive, genital heterosexuality at the exclusion of all other sexual practices. If, as scholars have repeatedly shown, gestures, even those of contempt, reflected and shaped social relations in the early modern period, then the important cultural sites in which the *fico* was implicated were also in some sense shaped by anilingus.[13]

Part of the force of the Barbarossa story comes from the erosion of the boundary between consumption and excretion, a boundary central to the civilizing process. As many cultural historians, theorists, and critics have noted, such erosion testifies to the way that civilized consumption requires an abjected, purged, excremental other to give definitional contour to the category of civility.[14] In the quotation from *The Alchemist* with which this essay began, Subtle's reference to the Barbarossa story subordinates Face by imagining Face's oral contact with his anus. What is more, if Williams is correct that the figs refer to hemorrhoids, when Subtle transforms the mouth's role in consuming food, such as figs, into an image of anilingus, the breakdown of the boundary between food and waste is indexed by a reference to disease.[15] That is, the insult is even more humiliating in its intent because it combines the stigma of the "incorrect," uncivil use of a body part and illness and even suggests a continuity between them.

More broadly, then, rimjobs were good to think with in Renaissance texts, but thinking with them in boundary-enforcing, stigmatizing ways often inadvertently produced queer boundary-blurring effects. In Shakespeare's *Midsummer Night's Dream* (1595), the fig is not explicitly present, but rimming's association with waste produces hierarchies of civility. In the staging of "Pyramus and Thisbe" by the "rude mechanicals," Bottom, whose anality has been frequently remarked, refers to the wall that separates his Pyramus from Flute's Thisbe as "vile" (5.1.99).[16] While the wall may be vile because it keeps the lovers apart, its physicality too is vile because of what Flute, as Thisbe, has been doing with the wall: "My cherry lips have often kissed thy stones, / Thy stones with lime and hair knit up in thee" (5.1.189–90). The kissing of stones immediately conjures the testicles, but as Bruce Thomas Boehrer reminds us, the plaster for walls was made of a mixture that included animal dung.[17] Even though the wall is played by a human, Snout, and even though Flute only mentions hair and lime, not dung, the kissing staged in "Pyramus and Thisbe" gestures toward rimming as a part of the humor of the performance by substituting a hole in the wall for Bottom. Though the wall keeps the lovers apart, it blends waste with the human labor that constructed the wall to divide the property of the lovers' parents, and the demarcation of property is often taken as a hallmark of civilization. Such mingling of waste and civility are central to representations of anilingus. Furthermore, the actors' inadvertent, out-of-place reference to anilingus in the space of the court and Theseus's marital celebrations here help articulate the class distinction between the "rude mechanicals" and the more refined audience of other characters watching "Pyramus and Thisbe," and this performance creates an anilingual counternarrative to the play's movement toward the harmonious incorporation of characters of different social strata. Even as the ending of the play suggests the totalizing grasp of the reproductive, marital order into which Theseus and Hippolyta, Lysander and Hermia, and Demetrius and Helena have just entered, the references in "Pyramus and Thisbe" to anilingus cite sexual practices not fully accounted for in that order.

Much like the wall is a kind of failed boundary in *Midsummer Night's Dream,* the fig, *fico,* and anilingus erect and break down ethnic and national divisions in early modern texts. The *fico* and the Barbarossa story are themselves foreign imports from Spain and Italy, respectively. Further emphasizing foreignness, in Rabelais's version of the Barbarossa story, the mule is named *Thacor,* which Rabelais glosses as Hebrew for "fig in the fundament."[18] These foreign associations apply to references to rimming in part through the conflation of waste and consumption. In Ben Jonson's *Masque of the Gypsies Metamorphosed* (1621), the Jackman tells the story of the gypsy Cock Lorel, who feasts with the devil in a cave known as the Devil's Arse. The sodomitical "cock in arse" joke is obvious, but the feasting suggests an oral–anal connection too. Though the gypsies are racialized as others in the text, the feast takes place in Derbyshire—that is, in England—and its culmination with Cock Lorel's fart in the Windsor version of the masque further breaks down the barrier between English and non-English.[19] His fart becomes

> tobacco, the learned suppose,
> Which since in country, court, and town,
> In the devil's glister-pipe smokes at the nose
> Of polecat and madam, of gallant and clown. (1171–74)[20]

In this description of smoking, the nose and the glister-pipe, or enema tube, bring together the face and the anus to describe another practice's popularity among the English, not the racial others that populate this story of tobacco's origins.

In *The Alchemist*'s similar blending of English and non-English, Surly comes disguised as a Spaniard to undo Subtle's con game, and Subtle responds to his offer to kiss their hands, "would you had stooped a little and kissed our *anos*" (4.3.23). Substituting *anos* for *manos*, or hand, Jonson conveys anti-Spanish sentiment by showing how easy it is, in the Spanish language, to go from civility to anilingus.[21] The mockery does come from a con artist, and Surly ultimately does not foil the alchemy swindle, which perhaps undermines the sentiment or couches it safely at a time when Spanish–English relations were delicate. In taking on his disguise, Surly assumes that the gap between English and Spanish is bridgeable. In that he is unsuccessful, the play seems to reify difference, but Surly fails not because anyone sees through his disguise (he has to reveal himself to other characters, such as Dame Pliant), so this Englishman does effectively pass as Spanish. Thus, in another reference to anal–oral contact, a boundary is simultaneously constructed and deconstructed. At the level of theatrical practice, all such national and ethnic crossings on the English stage are as feigned as Surly's attempt in that an English actor pretends he is someone of another ethnic background; that is, the actor attempts to produce a foreign body out of an English one. The theater, even as it seeks to construct national difference, requires the boundaries it erects to be permeable.[22]

The importation of the *fico* gesture into England is only possible because of a boundary crossing we might call intellectual, and the blending of the *fico* and the Barbarossa story is implicated in English national difference. In its various iterations, the Barbarossa story is one of defiance against papal authority. The story may have flattered English religious nationalism; as a story about standing up against the pope, it complements a view of the English Reformation as an act of casting off of the foreign domination and influence of Catholicism. In a more secular context in *Henry IV,* part 2 (1597), Pistol invokes the national implications of the *fico* gesture when he brings news that Hal has been crowned King. To assure his auditors he is telling the truth, he says, "When Pistol lies, do this *(making the fig)* and fig me, / Like the bragging Spaniard" (5.3.118–19). The *fico* tells us that the Spanish are false braggarts, in contrast to the true report of the accession of the King who will unite a divided Britain, but Pistol's assertion of Spanish difference contains the specter of potential similarity encoded in "like." In *Henry V* (1599), Pistol finds himself on the wrong side of the move to British unity when, after Fluellen insists on the rightness of executing Bardolph, he merges the *fico* and Barbarossa stories:

> PISTOL. Die and be damned! and *fico* for thy friendship.
> FLUELLEN. It is well.
> PISTOL. The fig of Spain.
> FLUELLEN. Very good.
> PISTOL. I say the fig within thy bowels and thy dirty maw. (3.6.55–59)[23]

Calling Fluellen both the ass holding the fig and the person who retrieves it, Pistol explicitly mixes waste and consumption, as well as the anus and the mouth, as he tries to subordinate the Welshman. Later, Pistol does not recognize Henry, who presents himself as Welsh, drawing on his past as Prince of Wales, which is, ironically, the title Henry had when he and Pistol spent time together. At 4.1.61, Pistol gives Henry the *fico* when he mentions he is friend and countryman to Fluellen, and this exchange is one of several to underscore that the "national" about which this play is anxious is archipelagic, not just English. The *fico* and its connection to anilingus via the eating of excrement have a clearly vexed and changing relationship to the discourse of nationality in the period.

The Barbarossa story also shows the human–animal divide as structured and deconstructed by anilingus. Barbarossa's wife and the Milanese captives are forced into improper relations with the anus of an ass (or mule in some versions), pairing bestiality and rimming. Furthermore, the *fico* gesture is performed with the hand, which Jonathan Goldberg has argued is a central site for figuring humanity because of the hand's opposable thumbs, its performance of manual labor, and its role in writing.[24] Thus, if the *fico* is conflated with the Barbarossa story in the period and is thereby implicated in the bestial, it employs a site that produces an animal–human boundary to undo that boundary. The Barbarossa story itself brings immediately to mind *A Midsummer Night's Dream* and Titania's encounter with Bottom, whose ass's head has been discussed in the context of anality and bestiality by Gail Kern Paster and Bruce Boehrer, respectively.[25] Shakespeare makes perhaps a more explicit connection of the bestial to anilingus in this famous exchange from *The Taming of the Shrew* (1591):

> PETRUCCIO. Come, come, you wasp, I'faith you are too angry.
> KATHERINE. If I be waspish, best beware my sting.
> PETRUCCIO. My remedy is then to pluck it out.
> KATHERINE. Ay, if the fool could find it where it lies.
> PETRUCCIO. Why knows not where a wasp does wear his sting? In his tail.
> KATHERINE. In his tongue.
> PETRUCCIO. Whose tongue?
> KATHERINE. Yours, if you talk of tales, and so farewell.
> PETRUCCIO. What, with my tongue in your tail? Nay, come again, Good Kate, I am a gentleman. (2.1.209–17)

Kate here figures herself as an insect, in a play that repeatedly associates her with small mammals, beasts of burden, and birds of prey, and through this figuration, she suggests sexual inadequacy in Petruccio's inability to find her "sting."[26] Even as Petruccio is trying to subordinate her linguistically by further developing her animal image, he ends up suggesting his own participation in an improper anal–oral relation with an animal, which, as in the Barbarossa story, is a form of humiliation.[27] Anilingus is titillating and comic, part of the sexualized wordplay of this couple's version of courtship, but Petruccio quickly distances himself from his own suggestion of providing Kate with anal–oral pleasure as an act both ungentlemanly and uncivil, which puts him right back into the realm of sexual nonperformance suggested by the fool who cannot find the wasp's sting.

Rimming and the Politics of Adjacency

Given the work that references to rimming queerly do and undo in early modern texts, how might rimjobs be good for literary critics, historians of sexuality, and queer theorists to think with? To get a better purchase on the ethical possibilities of the invocation of rimming in Renaissance texts without proliferating further taxonomies of sexual practice, I want to supplement a critical focus aimed at improper forms of boundary crossing—whether through incorporation or consumption or penetration—with a recognition of what I am calling rimming's politics of adjacency, or the way that, as a nonpenetrative, nongenital practice, rimming is not organized around subjectivity. Inquiry into the history of sexuality has been limited insofar as it has been based on a model of transgression—a word that derives from the Latin for "to step across." In this way, transgression is a penetrative practice. As a model, then, a focus on transgression is not calibrated to moments where abutment and juxtaposition can also do political work.

This transgression model was articulated in Peter Stallybrass and Allon White's influential *The Politics and Poetics of Transgression,* which offers a systematic discussion of the interdependence of high and low culture. Stallybrass and White argue that even as the top attempts to cast the low as Other, "the top includes [the] low symbolically as a primary eroticized constituent of its own fantasy life."[28] Turning to subjectivity, they go on to indicate that "the bourgeois subject continuously defined and re-defined itself through the exclusion of what it marked out as 'low'—as dirty, repulsive, noisy, contaminating. Yet that very act of exclusion was constitutive of its identity. The low was internalized under the sign of negation and disgust."[29] This rhetoric of inclusion and exclusion, incorporation and abjection, has structured much criticism about the early modern body, but because it is designed to make legible the crossing of boundaries between inside and out, it problematically resembles the process by which sexual subjectivities were formed through the "incitement to discourse," "deployment of sexuality," and "implantation of perversions" that Michel Foucault located in the eighteenth and nineteenth centuries.[30] In the various sites where I have showed anilingus to be performing other kinds of boundary work—waste, foreignness, and bestiality—sexual practice is put into discourse in a way that seems transgressive but at least partially underwrites hegemony. By viewing them in this manner, these references to anilingus anticipate the historical process of which Foucault writes. But what about early modern references to sex that do not anticipate this future? Stallybrass and White's model is more complicated than has often been recognized, for they call for a critical practice that is supposed to be calibrated to "oppositions, interpenetrations, *and* transgressions of high and low," three terms that do not describe the same kind of relationship, especially if they are mapped onto bodies having sex.[31] Anilingus does not necessitate penetration or crossing of an orificial boundary, though in modern pornography, it often is a precursor to it. Thus interpenetration and transgression cannot fully attend to the implications of references to rimming. More generally, the history of sexuality has paid much more attention to boundary crossing than to contact through abrasion and opposition, and such a focus has often led to reproducing the power relations that the transgressions under investigation seem to undermine.

For even as references to anilingus frequently produce unintended meanings, the counterhegemonic work these references might do can only be measured from the vantage point of hegemony, at least under a methodology calibrated only for the transgressive. Valerie Traub puts it another way when she writes, "Because notions of norms and their transgression are structured by a binary of the licit and the illicit, they necessarily are indexed to the dominant social orthodoxy—even when the intention is to uncover the existence of those who would defy it."[32] When calibrated to moments of transgression, critical inquiry participates in the incitement to discourse, probing into texts to discover and speak the "truth" about transgressive sexuality in the past to organize those sexualities into categorical schema and subject them to the critic's or historian's mastery and the disciplinary mechanisms of academic discourse.[33] Roy Porter and Lesley Hall have written that in sex advice manuals in the seventeenth through nineteenth centuries, "sexual discourse has aimed to limit and create closures in sexual identity."[34] This assertion equally applies to some critical discourse on sexuality, even when critics are motivated politically to liberate texts from previous readings that repress sexual meanings. Practices that taxonomize early modern sexuality, those that seek the origins of a supposedly inevitable and preferable modern regime of sexuality, or those for whom evidence of queerness in the past is evidence of essentialized, transhistorical gay and lesbian subjectivities have "always unfolded within the deployment of sexuality, and not outside it or against it."[35] Critical practice has heretofore made significant, politically efficacious contributions to our understanding of sexuality in the past—for instance, the work of historians of sexuality was cited in the opinion *Lawrence v. Texas,* which overturned state sodomy laws. It may not be possible as critics to stand entirely outside the deployment of sexuality, nor is it politically advisable, in terms of this chapter's content, to ignore moments in which that deployment picks up on anilingus for its own conservative ends. But would a practice less indexed to transgression also be less complicit in the deployment of sexuality and incitement to discourse, and therefore, would it be more attuned to sexual practices that both do not map neatly onto forms of selfhood and provoke us to rethink embodiment and pleasure?

Leo Bersani and Guy Hocquenghem have shown how libidinal investment in the anus avoids the type of indexing to dominant culture's terms, institutions, and goals that goes along with transgression, and I would argue that anilingus similarly sidesteps such indexing in its irreducibility to penetration.[36] Here is where I part company with Howie's particular formulation of a poetics of rimming, for he expresses interest in the contact that takes place in liminal zones but employs an overarching rubric of enclosure–disclosure and "the participation of tongues *in* holes."[37] He thereby resorts to a transgression and penetration model that is partly indexed to the hegemonic. According to this model, references to anilingus exceed or are insufficient to the purposes for which they are invoked; they fail to respect the boundaries set up by dominant culture. What these failures have in common is a resistance to playing a role in different kinds of subjectivity, whether based in class, nation, or even species. But in the instances to which this chapter attends, perverse and other kinds of implantation neither penetrate the threshold of the body to fashion deep subjectivity nor threaten to contaminate other bodies with deviant subjectivities by transgressing their boundaries. Instead, these references to the adjacency of surfaces without penetration imagine the possibilities and pleasures when certain forms of subjectivity are absent or dissolved. Through a critical practice I will call "rimming the Renaissance," I will examine rimming's configuration of the body, its pleasures, and its relation to other bodies, especially as rimming refuses to resolve into sexual subjectivity.

The contact of mouth and anus in rimming decenters the genitals in sexual practice and thereby destabilizes gender. Helkiah Crooke's *Mikrokosmographia* (1616) draws on the discourse of civility to describe what Crooke perceives as the structural impurity of the lips, which combine skin and muscle "after an uncouth manner."[38] If we move beyond the *fico* gesture, the Barbarossa story, and the mouth's function in eating, we can find anilingus figured as a misuse of the already problematic mouth in its speaking function, especially as the tongue stands in for the mouth synecdochically. Encountering such images of misused speech, critics have suggested that early modern authors frequently conflate the mouth and the anus.[39] In references to the practice of anilingus, it is actually the adjacency, not the conflation, of the mouth and anus that figures the improper or inefficacious use of language. In *Have with You to Saffron Walden* (1596), part of his pamphlet war with Gabriel Harvey, Thomas Nashe writes that if he fails to rebut Harvey's charges that he is "a changer, an innovator, a cony-catcher, a rimer, a rayler, that out faceth heaven and earth"—that is, one who misuses language—then he will "give [him] his tung for a rag to wype [his] taile with."[40] If Harvey is right that he is a rimer, then Nashe will also be a rimmer. While Nashe offers anilingus as a potential humiliating punishment for his own rhetorical failure, Anthony Nixon, in *The Foot-Post of Dover* (1616), describes the invective of a malcontent as an aesthetic failure of language. The malcontent, Nixon writes, "wipeth vices taile with his tongue, and that is the reason his words are so unsavory."[41] Finally, Richard Niccols's *The Beggers Ape* (1627) inveighs against flattery, the misuse of language that persistently earned the censure of early modern writers, by defining a flatterer as "hee whose tongue the tayle of Greatnesse lickes."[42] In these passages, contamination comes from licking and wiping, not from crossing the boundaries of the body, so they are not completely assimilable to the penetrative model of transgression.[43]

Yet when Flute, as Thisbe, says in *Midsummer Night's Dream* "I kiss the wall's hole, not your lips at all" (5.1.200), the humor depends on both an anally coded opening substituting for a mouth (the wall's/Snout's "chink," itself a substitute for Bottom's Pyramus's mouth) and a mouth coming into contact with that anal opening—in short, one conflation and one juxtaposition. Still others read the tongue as phallic and penetrative, cued by passages such as the one in *Taming of the Shrew* cited earlier, in which Petruccio specifically says "tongue *in* your tail." Certainly a layer of meaning of this passage involves Petruccio neutralizing Kate's phallic, waspish, stinging tongue by, as Leonard Tennenhouse says, "assert[ing] her sexual subordination to him . . . and constitut[ing] the grotesque figure of the penetration of her body," but as I showed earlier, he draws back from that image because of its anilingual import.[44] We elide references to anilingus when we rewrite an anal–oral connection as "really" a genital connection, whether that involves transforming a tongue into a penis or an anus into a vagina. Furthermore, I would suggest that a better history of sexual practice would take early modern writers at their word, examine the various other permutations possible through such substitution, and expose the ideological motivations behind occluding certain sexual practices by substituting them for others.

Since rimming need not be indexed to penetration or genitalia, the dominant models for understanding libidinal investment in the anus in the early modern period—coprophagia and sodomy—are of limited applicability to rimming; useful as they have been in early modern sexuality studies in general, they pivot around improper crossings of the body's orificial boundaries. The early modern period's sodomy laws are indexed to penile penetration, so the examples I have discussed resist subsumption into that category. In his discussion of *Romeo and Juliet,* Jonathan Goldberg notes the nickname of the medlar, the "open-arse," involves a sexualized image of consumption sited at the anus, much in the way the fig has done in this chapter's analysis.[45] Nevertheless, the coprophagic model Goldberg employs is inapt both for Petruccio's "tongue in your tail" comment in *Taming of the Shrew* and for the "tongue-wiping-ass" image in early modern discussions of flattery, because neither develop an oral–anal contact through a reference to eating. And though it is also true that Bulwer's *Chirologia* connects the *fico* to sodomy, Heylyn's *Mikrokosmos,* perhaps drawing on the similarity of Barbarossa's wife's backward mule ride and the skimmington, notes its other sexualized meanings:

"it is counted a disgrace answerable to our English custome of making hornes to that man whom wee suspect to be a Cuckold."[46] Because of the many ways that rimming was invoked and because the practice need not require penetration, anilingus involves a kind of logistical and categorical indeterminacy to coprophagia and sodomy in the early modern period quite unlike the nineteenth-century discursive deployment of sexuality.

These critical substitutions of penetration for nonpenetration, of genitality for nongenitality, of one orifice for another, tend to mask the gender indeterminacy associated with the practice of anilingus. Williams mentions a "gender vagueness" for the word *fig* in Latin, and Jonathan Goldberg reminds us that "the locus of anal penetration, of course, is available on any body, male or female."[47] Yet because anilingus does not have to involve penetration, the sex of neither partner is written into the definition of the practice.[48] In the opening of *The Alchemist,* the reference occurs between two men, Face and Subtle, whereas in *Taming of the Shrew,* Petruccio imagines it in a heterosexual context with Kate. We might assume that in *Taming,* the "tail" is meant vaginally, just as a gynosodomitical intent is not assumed when modern heterosexual men refer to women as "a nice piece of ass" and to sexual exploits as "getting some tail" and even "tapping that ass." Still, we might ask why the backside functions as a substitute for the front side of the body in these permutations when anal eroticism, both homosexual and heterosexual, is often publicly scorned. It is true that cover is provided by a patriarchal vision of sexual mastery reflected in the doggy-style sexual position that often implicitly or explicitly is invoked through these modern phrases. A critical practice of "rimming the Renaissance" pauses on these references' literal content before we translate them into the normative intents we assume motivate them to show the libidinal investments such translations occlude when they seek to stabilize certain forms of gender relations. While male subjectivity, defined as sexual mastery, is at stake in these instances of modern slang as well as in *Taming,* the involvement of the tongue differentiates *Taming*'s reference, opens it up to an anilingual interpretation, and makes it possible to include a play so saturated by concern with gender roles in a canon of references to a practice that is not entirely determined by gender. By substituting a penis for a tongue and a vagina for an anus, a critic interpreting this passage might claim to draw on a supposedly agreed-on definition of sex. Such substitutions, however, narrow the erotic, doing the ideological work of tacitly securing the status of genital intercourse as what really counts as sex.

In *Gammer Gurton's Needle* (1553), a play whose interest in the anus has been critically noted, references to anilingus with same- and opposite-gender combinations appear together.[49] First, between two men, rimming is suggested when Hodge "kisseth Diccon's breech" in fealty after Diccon promises to help Hodge find Gammer's needle (2.1.76). When the needle turns up embedded in the seat of Hodge's breeches, there is a sodomitical reference: "Chwas almost undone, 'twas so far in my buttock," Hodge says of the needle (5.2.307). This discovery occurs when Diccon hits Hodge on the backside, and the prick of the needle first causes Hodge to make the accusation: "thou false villain, dost thou bite me" (5.2.290). Hodge images anal–oral contact prior to invoking penetration. Second, Doctor Rat breaks into Dame Chat's house by way of an anally coded "privy way" and "black hole" (5.1.187, 188) that Gail Kern Paster connects to the anus.[50] Therefore, when Dame Chat describes beating Doctor Rat with her door bar by saying "thy head and my door bar kissed" (5.2.97), she conjures an image of heterosexual rimming.

In *A Midsummer Night's Dream,* the genders of the participants are reversed and further confused when Flute, playing the female Thisbe, kisses the hole of the wall played by the male Snout as a substitute for Bottom's Pyramus. The cross-dressing of Flute as Thisbe complements the gender indeterminacy of rimming, and we might usefully juxtapose this Shakespearean instance with the scene from Thomas Middleton's *More Dissemblers besides Women* (1615), in which Cinquepace the dance instructor forces the Page, a cross-dressed pregnant woman, to dance. The Page keeps her legs together, fearing the dance will cause her to go into labor, and Cinquepace responds, "I could eat thee up, I could eat thee up, and begin upon thy hinder quarter, thy hinder quarter. I shall never teach this boy without a screw; his knees must be opened with a vice, or there's no good to be done upon him" (5.2.200–4).[51] We might be tempted to see an oblique reference to anal birth when the Page does go into labor, or we might focus on the penetrative and sodomitical "screw" and "vice." However, we should not miss Cinquepace's expressed wish to put his mouth to the backside of the boy–woman in order to dine on his–her hindquarters. It is not exactly a coprophagic reference, though, as Cinquepace mentions eating the body, not its effluvia.

The gender indeterminacy and general epistemological recalcitrance I outlined earlier is part of rimming's particular nonrelation to subjectivity. From these various references to anilingus, we would be hard-pressed to abstract a prehistory of a modern sexual identity. Rimming, then, is queer in the sense that Carla Freccero gives the term: "that which resists being ideologically materialized into the individual."[52] As Foucault claimed, sex itself was part of the deployment of sexuality; that is, instead of sexualities being organized around sexual practices, what we understand as sex derives from modern understandings of sexuality and sexual subjectivity.[53] Foucault claims also that this process was nascent in early modern Europe. As its various failures to enforce boundaries show, rimming was repeatedly called on in the early stages of the deployment of sexuality, but its failure to secure subjectivity also meant its failure to do the ideological work of subjectivity. Rimming interrupts the taxonomizing of individuals and the march toward modernity that the proliferation of such taxonomies supposedly implies.

At the same time, "rimming the Renaissance" allows us to consider new approaches to queer historiography insofar as it is locked into the debate that Traub describes as "the by now notorious distinction between acts versus identity, and its corollary, alterity versus continuism."[54] To break through the critical impasse between those interested in historical continuity and those interested in change, she proposes that we attend to recurring patterns in the history of sexuality as well as the features that make each instantiation of that pattern specific to its historical moment. Whereas Traub proposes a resolution to the temporal opposition of continuity and alterity, I seek to trouble the mapping of acts onto historical alterity and identity onto continuity. Even as references to rimming resist dominant early modern understandings of embodiment and gender, rimming can push against the limits of modern sexual politics, which too often requires sexual practices to affirm selves. This problematization of standard notions of selfhood might also help us see a way through the debate about the ethical relation of the self and the other that has emerged from Alain Badiou's critique of the work of Emmanuel Levinas. Badiou objects to Levinas's view of relationality, in which otherness is welcomed, because such welcoming is often predicated on the at least partial assimilation of the other, or as Badiou pithily puts it, "become like me and I will respect your difference."[55] Instead, Badiou suggests that ethics should be based on a plurality of truths that are nevertheless "indifferent to differences."[56] Such indifference certainly is consistent with what I argued in the first section of this chapter about the way anilingus troubles the boundaries that it is supposed to enforce in early modern texts. From the point of view of adjacency, rimming's indifference to penetration is analogous to an indifference to the implanted differences of deep subjectivity. Leo Bersani and Adam Phillips have recently written about the consequences for politics and selfhood of imagining "a world where no one is interested in penetrating—invading and possessing—any one else's desire."[57] What they call "impersonal intimacy" takes place in practices that result "in the felicitous erasure of people as persons."[58] Nevertheless, I would not dismiss Levinas's work on relationality entirely, as his work on proximity can also help us emerge from the critical model of transgression. One figure for proximity in Levinas is the caress, which he says "aims at neither a person nor a thing" and "loses itself in a being that dissipates as though into an impersonal dream, without will and even without resistance."[59] Expanding on this idea from *Totality and Infinity* in his later *Otherwise Than Being,* Levinas writes that "to be in contact is neither to invest the other and annul his alterity, nor to suppress myself in the other."[60] Contact and proximity here are apt terms for anilingus's politics of adjacency. It is true that the pathos here in Levinas has the potential to devolve into a self-serving, narcissistic pleasure in the proximity of otherness that only reinforces dominance over the other, as Badiou cautions.[61] I would, however, point to the way contact and proximity are nonsubjective and impersonal: Levinas's description of them is akin to the kind of impersonal relational innovations that Bersani and Phillips call for and is consistent with the indifference to differences on which Badiou insists.

An impersonal, nonsubjective contact and proximity is a feature of the various invocations of anilingus in early modern texts that I have traced. When Hodge, from *Gammer Gurton's Needle,* says he is "almost undone" when he thinks Diccon has bit him in the butt, he gestures toward the possibility that anilingus undoes subjectivity. It is this same deconstruction of subjectivity that Petruccio resists when he rejects anilingus by claiming his gentry status. Instead of the face-to-face encounter with the Other around which Levinas organizes his ethics, anilingus involves impersonal intimacy, as Bersani and Phillips define the term and insofar as the face indexes selfhood. From a logistical point of view, the one who does the licking presses his or her face onto the backside of another, whose face is momentarily irrelevant. In *The Alchemist,* Subtle invests this irrelevancy of the face in rimming with negative affect when he says "lick figs" to Face, whose name compounds the effect of the command. As Doll reminds the men, their argument threatens a dissolution of their fraudulent selves and a return to a state of degradation in the "dunghills" and "the heat of horse-dung" they experienced before they "countenanced," a synonym of "faced," each other (1.1.34, 84, 22). Rimming here hardly indexes a threatened return to true selfhood for these characters, however, as there are no characters whose selfhood remains untouched by and ungrounded in fraudulence by the play's end. The texts that inveigh against flattery also invoke rimming to mark a threatening departure from supposedly true selfhood. Anilingus thus does not always provide the anal foundation of selfhood that, as Jeffrey Masten has convincingly demonstrated, the "fundament" does in many early modern texts.[62] Though it appears in conjunction with sodomy and has some similar effects, rimming is not the same as sodomy in the period.

If we approach these early modern references to anilingus through a hermeneutics of suspicion, we might infer that the negative affect surrounding rimming provokes the necessary anxiety to shore up subjectivity. Symptomatically, anilingus could represent a persistent yet only partially articulable disturbance of selfhood and early modern sexuality in these texts. However, I would like to conclude in the spirit of Eve Sedgwick's notion of "reparative reading" by briefly focusing on and lingering over the possibilities for pleasure that representations of rimming can activate.[63] Anilingus blurs the lines between active and passive sexual roles and their usual social meanings on which various early modern forms of subjectivity battened. This blurring produces and circulates knowledge about pleasure. Linda Williams notes that in modern pornography, the mouth is often differentiated from the genitals because it can give and receive, be an active participant or a passive receptacle.[64] Active and passive roles are not stable in the practice, at least in relation to pleasure. We have seen references in which the practice is organized around the pleasure of the person licking, as when Cinquepace imagines eating up the Page's hindquarters in *More Dissemblers besides Women*; some references focus on the pleasures of the recipient, as when Hodge kisses Diccon's breeches and swears "to work that his pleasure is" (2.1.77). When Flute as Thisbe and Bottom as Pyramus kiss the wall, the pleasures of both are the goal, even if the scene ends in the performance's failure—in the sense that the lovers' lips never make contact and that the rude mechanicals' serious intents yield a comic product. This independence of position-dependent pleasure conflicts with the hierarchies of bodies and pleasures that official early modern culture spun out of missionary-position heterosexual congress, just as it contrasts with modern culture's investment in abstracting identities from sexual acts.

This chapter has not been a positivist history of the extent of anilingus's practice in the early modern period. I have sought instead to explore the cultural contexts in which rimming was invoked and the consequences of its instability and indeterminacy for subjectivity and historiography. Most early modern references to anilingus do occur in contexts that convey a negative charge, as if discourse was proliferating to tamp down on the practice and foster anxiety about it. Yet this proliferation also enables the circulation of knowledge about rimming's effects of self-erasure that can provide subversive forms of pleasure and create new possibilities for nonsubjective relationships and community. As scholars of sexual history, we should not only attend to such alternative relations in the past but should also develop alternative relations with the literary and historical material we study to minimize our participation in the ideological projects against which we would define our critical practice.

Notes

1 Ben Jonson, *The Alchemist*, in *The Alchemist and Other Plays*, ed. Gordon Campbell, 211–326 (Oxford: Oxford University Press, 1995).

2 The concern with anality in this play has been usefully traced by Gail Kern Paster, *The Body Embarrassed: Drama and the Disciplines of Shame*

in Early Modern England (Ithaca, N.Y.: Cornell University Press, 1993), 143–62, and John W. Velz, "Scatology and Moral Meaning in Two English Renaissance Plays," *South Central Review* 1, nos. 1–2 (1984): 11–17.

3 Cary Howie, *Claustrophilia: The Erotics of Enclosure in Medieval Literature* (New York: Palgrave Macmillan, 2007), 6.

4 Ibid., 10.

5 See J. S. Farmer and W. E. Henley, *Slang and Its Analogues,* vol. 2 (New York: Arno Press, 1970); James T. Henke, *Courtesans and Cuckolds: A Glossary of Renaissance Dramatic Bawdy (Exclusive of Shakespeare)* (New York: Garland, 1979), 91; Eric Partridge, *Shakespeare's Bawdy,* 3rd ed. (New York: Routledge, 1968), 105; and Gordon Williams, *A Dictionary of Sexual Language in Shakespearean and Stuart Literature,* vol. 1 (London: Athlone Press, 1994), 480–81.

6 John Bulwer, *Chirologia, or The Naturall Language of the Hand* (London, 1644), 183. When using early modern editions, I have silently modernized *i/j* and *u/v*. On Bulwer, and especially his involvement in the seventeenth-century universal language movement, see Stephen Greenblatt, "Toward a Universal Language of Motion: Reflections on a Seventeenth-Century Muscle Man," in *Choreographing History,* ed. Susan Leigh Foster, 25–31 (Bloomington: Indiana University Press, 1995), and Jeffrey Wollock, "John Bulwer (1606–1656) and the Significance of Gesture in Seventeenth-Century Theories of Language and Cognition," *Gesture* 2, no. 2 (2002): 227–58.

7 See John of Hainault, *The Estate of the Church,* trans. Simon Patrike (London, 1602), 332–35; Peter Heylyn, *Mikrokosmos: A Little Description of the Great World* (London: 1625), 214; and François Rabelais, *Pantagruel,* vol. 4, *The Complete Works of François Rabelais,* trans. Donald M. Frame (Berkeley: University of California Press, 1991), 533–35.

8 Ruth Melinkoff, "Riding Backwards: Theme of Humiliation and Symbol of Evil," *Viator* 4 (1973): 160, 174–75.

9 Heylyn, *Mikrokosmos,* 214.

10 Rabelais, *Pantagruel,* 534.

11 Henke, *Courtesans and Cuckolds,* 91.

12 Williams, *Dictionary of Sexual Language,* 481.

13 On the social importance of gesture, see David Bevington, *Action Is Eloquence: Shakespeare's Language of Gesture* (Cambridge, Mass.: Harvard University Press, 1984); Michael Neill, *Putting History to the Question: Power, Politics, and Society in English Renaissance Drama* (New York:

Columbia University Press, 2000), 179–203; and John Walter, "Gesturing at Authority: Deciphering the Gestural Code of Early Modern England," in *The Politics of Gesture: Historical Perspectives,* ed. Michael J. Braddick, 96–127 (Oxford: Oxford University Press, 2009).

14 On the civilizing process and excrement in culture generally, see Norbert Elias, *The Civilizing Process,* rev. ed., trans. Edmund Jephcott (Oxford: Blackwell, 2000), and Mary Poovey, *Purity and Danger: An Analysis of the Concept of Pollution and Taboo,* 2nd ed. (New York: Routledge, 2002). For work on the civilizing process, with particular attention to consumption and excrement in Renaissance texts, see Bruce Thomas Boehrer, "The Ordure of Things: Ben Jonson, Sir John Harington, and the Culture of Excrement in Early Modern England," in *New Perspectives on Ben Jonson,* ed. James Hirst, 174–96 (Madison, N.J.: Fairleigh Dickinson University Press, 1997); Ben Saunders, "Iago's Clyster: Purgation, Anality, and the Civilizing Process," *Shakespeare Quarterly* 55, no. 2 (2004): 148–76; Will Stockton, *Playing Dirty: Sexuality and Waste in Early Modern Comedy* (Minneapolis: University of Minnesota Press, 2011); and Frank Whigham, "Reading Social Conflict in the Alimentary Tract: More on the Body in Renaissance Drama," *ELH* 55 (1988): 333–50.

15 Williams, *Dictionary of Sexual Language,* 480–81.

16 William Shakespeare, *A Midsummer Night's Dream,* in *William Shakespeare: The Complete Works,* ed. Gary Taylor and Stanley Wells, 401–24 (Oxford: Clarendon Press, 1988). References to Shakespeare's plays come from this edition.

17 Boehrer, "Ordure of Things," 180.

18 Rabelais, *Pantagruel,* 602. On Jews and anality, see Jonathan Gil Harris, *Foreign Bodies and the Body Politic: Discourses of Social Pathology in Early Modern England* (Cambridge: Cambridge University Press, 1998), 79–106.

19 On the breakdown of ethnic distinctions in the masque, see Mark Netzloff, "'Counterfeit Egyptians' and Imagined Borders: Jonson's *The Gypsies Metamorphosed,*" *ELH* 68, no. 4 (2001): 763–93.

20 Ben Jonson, *The Masque of the Gypsies Metamorphosed,* in *Masques of Difference: Four Court Masques,* ed. Kristen McDermott, 141–204 (Manchester, U.K.: Manchester University Press, 2007).

21 This scene is reminiscent of Iago's infamous aside in *Othello* (1604), where he imagines Cassio's fingers as "clyster pipes" when Cassio kisses them as a gesture of courtesy to Desdemona (2.1.180). See Saunders,

"Iago's Clyster," for the way Iago's comment is embedded in the play's larger concerns with purgation and civility.

22 On this interplay, see Lloyd Edward Kermode, *Aliens and Englishness in Elizabethan Drama* (Cambridge: Cambridge University Press, 2009).

23 On Pistol's failure to conform to the play's figuration of masculinity as testicular, see Rebecca Ann Bach, "Tennis Balls: *Henry V* and Testicular Masculinity, or, According to the *OED*, Shakespeare Doesn't Have Any Balls," *Renaissance Drama* 30 (2001): 3–24.

24 Jonathan Goldberg, *Shakespeare's Hand* (Minneapolis: University of Minnesota Press, 2003), 106.

25 See Thomas Boehrer, "Economies of Desire in *A Midsummer Night's Dream*," *Shakespeare Studies* 32 (2004): 99–117, and *Shakespeare among the Animals: Nature and Society in the Drama of Early Modern England* (New York: Palgrave Macmillan, 2002), 41–70. See also Paster, *Body Embarrassed*, 125–43.

26 On animal imagery in *Taming of the Shrew*, see Jeanne Addison Roberts, "Horses and Hermaphrodites: Metamorphoses in *The Taming of the Shrew*," *Shakespeare Quarterly* 34, no. 2 (1983): 159–71, and LaRue Love Sloan, "'Caparisoned Like the Horse': Tongue and Tail in Shakespeare's *The Taming of the Shrew*," *Early Modern Literary Studies* 10, no. 2 (2004), http://purl.oclc.org/emls/10-2/sloacapa.htm.

27 We should also not forget the anal origins given to Petruccio in the first four folios when his father is named "Butonio" (TLN 756). Modern editors amend it to Antonio, which he uses at TLN 620.

28 Peter Stallybrass and Allon White, *The Politics and Poetics of Transgression* (Ithaca, N.Y.: Cornell University Press, 1986), 5.

29 Ibid., 191.

30 Michel Foucault, *The History of Sexuality*, vol. 1, *An Introduction*, trans. Robert Hurley (New York: Random House, 1990).

31 Stallybrass and White, *Politics and Poetics*, 4; emphasis added.

32 Valerie Traub, "The Joys of Martha Joyless: Queer Pedagogy and the (Early Modern) Production of Sexual Knowledge," in *The Forms of Renaissance Thought: New Essays in Literature and Culture*, ed. Leonard Barkan, Bradin Cormack, and Sean Keilen (New York: Palgrave Macmillan, 2009), 179.

33 For a similar critique, see Carla Freccero, *Queer/Early/Modern* (Durham, N.C.: Duke University Press, 2006), 31–50.

34 Roy Porter and Lesley Hall, *The Facts of Life: The Creation of Sexual Knowledge in Britain, 1650–1950* (New Haven, Conn.: Yale University Press, 1995), 11.

35 Foucault, *History of Sexuality,* 131.

36 Leo Bersani, "Is the Rectum a Grave?" *October* 43 (1987): 197–222; Guy Hocquenghem, *Homosexual Desire,* trans. Daniella Dangoor (Durham, N.C.: Duke University Press, 1993), 93–112.

37 Howie, *Claustrophilia,* 6; emphasis added.

38 Helkiah Crooke, *Mikrokosmographia* (London, 1616), 621.

39 See Maurice Hunt, "The Backward Voice of Coriol-anus," *Shakespeare Studies* 32 (2004): 220–39, and Paster, *Body Embarrassed,* 126–27.

40 Thomas Nashe, *Have with You to Saffron Walden* (London, 1596), sig. S3r.

41 Anthony Nixon, *The Foot-Post of Dover* (London, 1616), sig. F2r.

42 Richard Niccols, *The Beggers Ape* (London, 1627), sig. B4r.

43 I have written elsewhere about not assuming sexuality was organized around penetration when we read early modern texts. See my "'Let It Suffise': Sexual Acts and Narrative Structure in *Hero and Leander,*" in *Queer Renaissance Historiography: Backward Gaze,* ed. Stephen Guy-Bray, Vin Nardizzi, and Will Stockton, 67–84 (Burlington, Vt.: Ashgate, 2009).

44 On the phallic tongue in this passage, see Leonard Tennenhouse, *Power on Display: The Politics of Shakespeare's Genres* (New York: Methuen, 1986), 49. On the vexed gendering of the tongue as phallic and feminine, see Carla Mazzio, "Sins of the Tongue," in *The Body in Parts: Fantasies of Corporeality in Early Modern Europe,* ed. David Hillman and Carla Mazzio, 53–80 (New York: Routledge, 1997).

45 Jonathan Goldberg, "Romeo and Juliet's Open Rs," in *Queering the Renaissance,* ed. Jonathan Goldberg, 218–35 (Durham, N.C.: Duke University Press, 1994).

46 Heylyn, *Mikrokosmos,* 214.

47 Williams, *Dictionary of Sexual Language,* 480; Goldberg, "Romeo and Juliet's Open Rs," 230.

48 Of course, the same could be said for penetrative practices if they involve prostheses. See Valerie Traub, *The Renaissance of Lesbianism in Early Modern England* (Cambridge: Cambridge University Press, 2002). Though I do not discuss an example involving two women, I would not presume to say anilingus would be unimaginable between two women in the period, only that I have not yet found a reference to it.

49 *Gammer Gurton's Needle,* 2nd ed., ed. Charles Whitworth (London: A&C Black, 1997). On the anus in *Gammer Gurton's Needle,* see Paster, *Body Embarrassed,* 116–25, and Velz, "Scatology," 4–11.

50 Paster, *Body Embarrassed,* 116.

51 Thomas Middleton, *More Dissemblers besides Women,* ed. John Jowett,

in *Thomas Middleton: The Collected Works,* ed. Gary Taylor and Sohn Lavagnino, 1034–73 (Oxford: Clarendon Press, 2007).

52 Freccero, *Queer/Early/Modern,* 20.

53 Foucault, *History of Sexuality,* 155.

54 Valerie Traub, "The Present Future of Lesbian Historiography," in *A Companion to Lesbian, Gay, Bisexual, Transgender, and Queer Studies,* ed. George E. Haggerty and Molly McGarry (Oxford: Blackwell, 2007), 124.

55 Alain Badiou, *Ethics: An Essay on the Understanding of Evil,* trans. Peter Hallward (London: Verso, 2001), 25.

56 Ibid., 27.

57 Leo Bersani and Adam Phillips, *Intimacies* (Chicago: University of Chicago Press, 2008), 41.

58 Ibid., 38.

59 Emmanuel Levinas, *Totality and Infinity: An Essay on Exteriority,* trans. Alphonso Lingis (Pittsburgh, Pa.: Duquesne University Press, 1969), 259.

60 Emmanuel Levinas, *Otherwise Than Being: Or Beyond Essence,* trans. Alphonso Lingis (Pittsburgh, Pa.: Duquesne University Press, 1998), 86.

61 Badiou, *Ethics,* 34.

62 Jeffrey Masten, "Is the Fundament a Grave?" in *The Body in Parts: Fantasies of Corporeality in Early Modern Europe,* ed. David Hillman and Carla Mazzio, 129–46 (New York: Routledge, 1997).

63 Eve Kosofsky Sedgwick, "Paranoid Reading and Reparative Reading, or, You're So Paranoid, You Probably Think This Essay Is about You," in *Touching Feeling: Affect, Pedagogy, Performativity* (Durham, N.C.: Duke University Press, 2003), 123–52.

64 Linda Williams, *Hard Core: Power, Pleasure, and the "Frenzy of the Visible"* (Berkeley: University of California Press, 1989), 172.

7

Animal, Vegetable, Sexual: Metaphor in John Donne's "Sappho to Philaenis" and Andrew Marvell's "The Garden"

STEPHEN GUY-BRAY

It is generally accepted that human reproduction is both necessary and good: the problem is the means employed. This problem would have seemed particularly evident to a culture like Renaissance England, in which the similarities between human and animal sexuality were taken as indications that sex was an unworthy activity for creatures believed to have immortal souls. Sex was something that connected humans to what were then regarded as the lower orders of creation. This attitude has not disappeared, but for my purposes here, what is most remarkable about the difference between contemporary and Renaissance sexualities is that while we still frequently use animal metaphors in talking about human sexual activity, both in praise and in condemnation, in the Renaissance, the resemblances between human and animal sexuality were more seriously pondered.[1] As we shall see, some poets approached these questions through a consideration of metaphor itself; that is, instead of merely making a metaphorical equivalence between a certain kind of human and a certain kind of animal, some poets would attempt to rethink their sense of the connections between humans and animals by rethinking the very concept of metaphor itself in ways that had a number of implications for their poems.

In what follows, I want to look at a number of Renaissance attempts to think human sexuality through animals—and through plants as well: although we recognize plants as living beings, we are not likely, I think, to consider them as models for our own behavior (sexual or otherwise) in either a good or bad way. In contrast, in the Renaissance, both the boundaries among various kinds of living organisms and the boundaries that structure our contemporary sexual taxonomy were largely unfixed.[2] One of the best-known Renaissance examples of thinking human and vegetable sexuality together comes from Sir Thomas Browne's *Religio Medici*:

> I could wish that we might procreate like trees, without conjunction, or that there were any way to perpetuate the world without this triviall and vulgar way of coition; It is the foolishest act a wise man commits in all his life, nor is there anything that will deject his cold imagination more, then when he shall consider what an odde and unworthy piece of folly he hath committed; I speak not in prejudice, nor am averse from that sweete sexe, but naturally amorous of all that is beautifull; I can looke a whole day with delight upon a handsome picture, though it be but of an Horse.[3] (140)

Once he states his wish, Browne's concern is to clear himself of the imputation of misogyny, but the way in which he does so should strike us as curious. His fondness for the "sweete sexe" turns out to be part of a larger love for beauty, and rather than speak of a desire for the company of women, he turns to pictures, and his specific example is a picture of a horse, although he clearly implies that this is a relatively inferior kind of painting.

What is most striking to me in this passage is Browne's clear distinction between aesthetics and reproduction. There is no sense here that his pleasure in a beautiful woman might lead him to have sex with her; instead, while reproduction is, at least implicitly, a necessity (he does not question it anywhere in the *Religio Medici*), the pleasure he takes in a beautiful woman is only part of his general pleasure in beauty. This pleasure may be different in degree from his pleasure in paintings or animals, or indeed paintings of animals, but it is apparently not different in kind, just as Browne himself is not different in kind from either the trees that begin the passage or the horse that ends it. Browne collapses two oppositions that are crucial to our sense of our selves and of our place in the world: the opposition between human and animal and the opposition between the natural and the artificial. To me, that he makes this rhetorical move in the course of a consideration of human reproduction suggests that we could see human sexuality itself as something that might not be restricted either to humans or to what we would now call sexual acts.

This expansive sense of sexuality is part of Browne's general sense of himself in his environment. Throughout *Religio Medici,* he stresses his connection to the world around him. Early on, for instance, he avers that "*Natura nihil agit frustra,* is the onely and indisputable axiome in Philosophy, there is no *Grotesco* in nature" (24), and he goes on to praise "Bees, Aunts, and Spiders" (25) as being in many ways wiser than we are. Nor is Browne merely concerned to compare humans with the animals around them: he describes a human being as "a rude masse" (64) and argues that we live the lives of plants and animals as well as our own human lives; he goes on to say that "we are all monsters, that is, a composition of man and beast" (106). A member of the "sweete sexe," a spider, a horse, Browne himself—all are not only adjacent or even connected but related, and I would argue that he extends this relation to representations of these things. Thus, while the passage in which Browne wishes we could "procreate like trees" is often discussed out of context as an example of his morbidity or peculiarity, I want to make the point that it is actually entirely of a piece with his thinking throughout the book.

The centrality of this passage to *Religio Medici* as a whole is the subject of Marjorie Swann's excellent essay on Browne, which is one of the few discussions of this much-discussed passage to take it seriously. Swann relates his concern with arboreal reproduction to his concern with friendship, and it is to this aspect of the book that I now turn.[4] In writing about true friendship, Browne states that "united soules are not satisfied with embraces, but desire to be truly each other, which being impossible, their desires are infinite, and must proceed without a possibility of satisfaction" (131). Later on, he returns to the topic and says "that part of our loving friends that we love, is not that part that we embrace; but that insensible part that our armes cannot embrace" (156). The friends do embrace, but this is to be seen as a symbol of that more perfect union that cannot be achieved. At this point we should remember that Browne identifies the superiority of arboreal reproduction as its lack of conjunction. The conjunction that is sex is bad not primarily because it is "triviall and vulgar," but because it, like the friendly embraces which we can see as its less energetic form, can never be anything but an imperfect substitute for the state of mutual identity that true friends seek.

Browne regrets that this state of perfect mutual union is impossible for humans, but as Raphael tells Adam in *Paradise Lost,* it is possible for angels. Whatever humans enjoy sexually, angels

> enjoy
> In eminence, and obstacle find none
> Of membrane, joint, or limb, exclusive bars:
> Easier than Air with Air, if Spirits embrace,
> Total they mix.[5] (8.623–27)

In their sexuality, angels achieve what Browne identifies as the desire of friends "to be truly each other." In contrast, postlapsarian human sexual intercourse—conjunction—can only ever be a metaphor for this true conjunction. Browne wants humans to procreate like trees so that they can avoid what he sees as the debased metaphor that is human sexual activity. In this context, I want to return to the fact that he cites "a handsome picture, though it be but of an Horse" as something that he would take pleasure in contemplating. For Browne, sexuality is part of aesthetic pleasure, and in his gazing, he apparently makes no distinction between the natural and the artificial. Though sexual activity is a metaphor, it seems that artistic representation, at least from an aesthetic point of view, has the same status as the thing represented.

Although Browne's ideas about sex and about art may seem idiosyncratic to us now (and this has certainly been the assumption in critical writing on the *Religio Medici*), I believe that they were less unusual in a seventeenth-century context and that a number of authors who were more or less his contemporaries were thinking along similar lines. My specific examples here are John Donne in "Sappho to Philaenis" and Andrew Marvell in "The Garden." I am not making an argument about influence—that is, I am not arguing that Browne had Donne in mind when he wrote *Religio Medici* or that Marvell was thinking of Browne when he wrote "The Garden"—instead, I think that all three authors were interested in what sex did and meant and in the relationships between humans and the world in which they live, on one hand, and between art and nature, on the other. We could say that my argument in this essay is that the contrasting hands in the previous sentence are our contemporary hands and that where we see—and, indeed, depend on—binary oppositions (both the ones I mentioned in the previous sentence and the opposition between sexual activity as the "triviall and vulgar way of coition" and the friendship as the embraces we give our friends and that represent the perfect union we cannot attain), seventeenth-century writers were more likely to see overlapping and shifting continuums.

One way to understand Donne's "Sappho to Philaenis" is to say that Donne makes Browne's largely implicit consideration of the connection between metaphor and sexuality explicit. William N. West has argued persuasively that metaphor is one of the poem's main subjects: "Starting from a prohibition of metaphor, a trope connected in the seventeenth century with male language and thought, Donne tries to devise alternative strategies of speaking that will give Sappho a voice that is, in the terms of Jacobean England, recognizably feminine without reducing her to silence or ineffectuality."[6] Sappho rejects metaphor early on in the poem:

> Thou art not soft, and cleare, and strait, and faire,
> As *Down,* as *Stars, Cedars,* and *Lillies* are,
> But thy right hand, and cheek, and eye, only
> Are like thy other hand, and cheek, and eye.[7] (21–24)

This is at once poetic praise—Philaenis's beauty exceeds conventional poetic methods—and, it will turn out, a comment on sexuality: Sappho aspires to the becoming-one-another that Browne identifies as the goal of friendship.

Sappho's attitude here and her use later in the poems of images of mirroring in which, as she says, "Me, in my glasse, I call thee" (55) present her and Philaenis as, at least ideally, the same as each other. Readers now will classify their love as what we have come to call homonormativity, but Sappho is actually more ambitious than that. As Janel Mueller commented in her essay on the poem, it is as if Donne asks, "What if we try to synthesize the unitive perfections of marriage and friendship between equals? What would the resulting relation look like?"[8] We could say that while homonormativity is the theory, lesbianism is the practice; another way to put it would be to say that Donne is gesturing toward a same-sex union. In the terms of the *Religio Medici,* Sappho and Philaenis's love would be a literal version of the metaphorical embraces between friends that would also include the coition he deplores. In the poem itself, Sappho seems doomed to disappointment, but I do not think we should read this as a criticism of her desire, just as the fact that humans lead their lives as if they were unitary and unified should not be taken to mean that either Browne's idea of a merging of friends or his sense of each human as a mixture of human and animal is mistaken.

For this reason, although I agree with Paula Blank's view in her perceptive article on the poem that "Donne presents Sappho's version of homo-sexuality . . . as a figure of language that can never materialize in any other form," I do not think the limitation matters.[9] Instead, I would argue that Donne's concentration on linguistic processes and strategies anticipates much recent queer theory. In this connection, I have in mind Lee Edelman's comment that "'homosexuality' is constructed to bear the cultural burden of the rhetoricity inherent in 'sexuality' itself; the consequence . . . is that a distinctive literariness or textuality, an allegorical relation to the possibility—and, indeed, to the mechanics—of representation, operates within the very concept of 'homosexuality.'"[10] An extreme version of this statement would be the view that sexuality exists only as a discourse, as a linguistic mode of representation that stands in for, and ultimately displaces, the sexual activity it is intended to represent. Arguably, this is precisely what Donne has in mind, as the words of which the poem is composed as well as the mirrored reflections to which Sappho refers within the poem have to substitute for the sexual encounter that seems unlikely by the end of "Sappho to Philaenis."

In refusing the traditional metaphors of erotic poetry and thus exposing the rhetoricity of sexuality, Sappho attempts to construct a discourse of sexuality founded on sameness, a sameness that operates not only between the lovers but also on the linguistic level itself. Sappho rejects the cultural burden to which Edelman refers and tries to unite the representation with the thing represented. Browne presents a picture of a horse as a beautiful object on a level with the notional beautiful woman who would be presumed to be the cause of his aesthetic pleasure (although apparently not of his sexual desire): to use more modern terms, he equates signifiers and signifieds. Sappho goes one step further by insisting on an absolute equivalence between her (artistic) signifier and the woman it signifies. The rhetoricity of her sexuality—her use of figures of sameness—is not something added to her desire but rather something that is simultaneously natural, insofar as it accurately conveys her feelings, and artificial, insofar as it is speech, and highly ordered speech at that. To use an image from the poem, in "Sappho to Philaenis," language is intended to be like a mirror, something that merely reflects what exists rather than an artifact that potentially falsifies what it purports to represent.

I have just written that Sappho refuses the traditional metaphors of erotic poetry, but in one sense, her discourse in this poem exhibits a version of the erotic similitude that Valerie Traub has identified as "a defining trope of female homoerotic desire in the early modern period."[11] In this fairly common trope—the best example is probably John Lyly's *Galathea*—an absolute similarity between women is seen as a site of erotic potential rather than as a fact that rules out sex altogether. This kind of similitude is presented as the thing that makes an erotic connection between women possible. The situation is different in Donne's poem, however. Whatever similarity might exist between the two women is not at issue in the poem, and neither is the similarity of metaphor between a beautiful woman and down, stars, cedars, and lilies that Donne explicitly rules out. Instead, it is Philaenis's similarity to herself that makes her so powerfully erotic. In this way, Donne uses a trope that, as Traub has demonstrated, is one of the traditional aspects of a certain kind of erotic poetry and refashions it to pay tribute to Philaenis's singularity—a singularity that is a problem poetically in that it makes her difficult to describe. The figurative language on which lovers and poets rely does not seem to apply to Philaenis.

Sappho does not refuse figurative language altogether, of course. For instance, while her erotic persuasion is based on the equivalence between her and Philaenis—each is the other, as in Browne's version of what true friends desire—readers are more likely to take this as a metaphor in which each can stand in for the other. As well, when

Sappho talks about sexuality, she uses a number of metaphors from the natural world that I want to consider now. Perhaps most noticeably, men and heterosexuality are associated with changes to the landscape, whereas women are associated with the landscape itself. After saying that Philaenis's body is "a naturall *Paradise,*" Sappho presents agriculture as something that represents a fall from grace. Referring to Philaenis's body as "unmanur'd" (36), she asks "why shouldst thou than / Admit the tillage of a harsh rough man" (37–38)? The agricultural metaphor picks up the earlier criticism of the boy whose "chinne, a thorny hairy unevennesse / Doth threaten, and some daily change possesse" (33–34). Now this daily change is metaphorically equated with the agriculture that transforms the natural world. Sappho intensifies the metaphor by adding that "Men leave behinde them that which their sin showes, / And are as theeves trac'd, which rob when it snows" (39–40).

Donne presents masculinity here as change, and it is always a change for the worse. Indeed, the metaphors he uses go from agriculture, which is usually seen as praiseworthy, to theft, suggesting the downward trend of male sexuality. In contrast, femininity, and specifically feminine sexuality, is characterized by the stasis of perfection, of a never-ceasing identity with oneself and with the woman one loves. As Sappho asks when comparing her body to Philaenis's, "the likenesse being such, / Why should they not alike in all parts touch" (47–48)? The sex that results from this perfect congruity will cause only a momentary and soon effaced change:

> of our dallyance no more signes there are,
> Then *fishes* leave in streames, or *Birds* in aire.
> And betweene us all sweetnesse may be had;
> All, all that *Nature* yields, or *Art* can adde. (41–44)

In Donne's formulation, it is masculine desire for women—what we now call heterosexuality—that is unnatural, whereas sex between women recalls the natural behavior of animals and unites both nature and art.

I have just written that agriculture is usually seen as praiseworthy—it goes without saying—but this is not the case in "Sappho to Philaenis." Sappho's erotics of sameness extend beyond the sameness of two female bodies to encompass the world itself. The ideal in this poem is a world in which nothing changes and, in fact, nothing happens: no agriculture, no children. In this respect, Donne goes beyond the *Religio Medici.* While Browne disapproves of the act of coition, he appears resigned to reproduction itself and, by extension, to the manipulation of the physical world that we call agriculture and on which the human population depends. In going beyond the *Religio Medici,* Donne anticipates Marvell's "The Garden," but Marvell goes beyond Donne in questioning the point of humanity altogether. As the Body bitterly remarks at the conclusion of "A Dialogue between the Soul and Body,"

> What but a Soul could have the wit
> To build me up for Sin so fit?
> So Architects do square and hew,
> Green Trees that in the Forest Grew.[12] (41–44)

In many of Marvell's poems, and perhaps most notably in "The Garden," it is the creation of the human race that is the problem, and human sexuality can never be the solution.

Marvell begins this poem by drawing our attention to what were almost dead metaphors in the poetry of his time:

> How vainly men themselves amaze
> To win the Palm, the Oke, or Bayes;
> And their uncessant Labours see
> Crown'd from some single Herb or Tree. (1–4)

Marvell restores the rewards for military, civic, or poetic glory to their status as actual plants and thus demonstrates a refusal of metaphor that recalls Sappho's. Unlike Donne, however, Marvell does not contrast activity and stasis. Instead, the plants themselves are active. Marvell tells us that the tree whose leaves are plundered for a wreath "Does prudently their [i.e., men's] Toyles upbraid" (6)—the verb he uses here sets up the comparison between human and vegetable weaving—and then that "all Flow'rs and all Trees do close / To weave the Garlands of repose" (7–8). In a way that will turn out to be paradigmatic for the poem as a whole, the plants in the garden do all the things that people do, but they do those things better.

In the third stanza, Marvell reveals that the plants are not only better at making garlands but are also to be preferred to human lovers: "No white nor red was ever seen / So am'rous as this lovely green" (17–18); that is, the flowers are not just beautiful but also lustful: they are both the cause of lust in others (and in this respect, it is significant that Marvell uses the names of the colors associated with a beautiful complexion rather than the metaphorical lilies and roses traditional in English poetry) and, as eventually becomes clear, they feel lust themselves. The former meaning predominates in the poem. Later in this stanza, Marvell alludes to the practice of carving one's beloved's name in the bark of a tree, and after declaring that the trees are more beautiful than the women whose names they are forced to bear, he makes a promise to them: "Fair Trees! where s'eer your barkes I wound, / No Name shall but your own be found" (23–24). Instead of being pressed into service in poems that tell of humans' love for other humans, the trees now occupy the center of a poem's world, not as a metaphor but as the things themselves. Marvell's point here and elsewhere in the poem—and in many of his other poems as well, if not to the same degree—is that poets who use images from the natural world have confused the tenor and the vehicle.

There remains, of course, the question of what the names of the trees are. After all, the word *oak,* for example, is only a symbol or metaphor for the tree itself. In his discussion of the poem, Robert N. Watson has suggested that "Marvell may even be pushing the nominalist mistrust of the categorical functions of language towards post-structuralism, by suggesting that many words presumed to refer legitimately to things rather than delusively to abstractions are still false impositions of the human mind on the material universe."[13] I think this is exactly what Marvell is doing. He is going beyond Browne's idea that our lives are also animal and vegetable lives and seeking to become one with the animals and vegetables. Marvell's clearest statement of this wish comes in "Upon Appleton House," when he says that "little now to make me, wants / Or of the *Fowles,* or of the *Plants*" (563–64). Indeed, just after this, he says "turn me but, and you shall see / I was but an inverted Tree" (567–68), thus implying that his humanity has been a mere trick of perspective after all, and "Already I begin to call / In their most learned Original" (569–70). For Marvell, experiencing nature is a question of experiencing it in oneself and of experiencing oneself as the same as nature, even to the extent of speaking the language(s) of nonhuman living beings.

The merging with each other that friends desire is arguably the highest good in the *Religio Medici*; in "The Garden," however, this merging is with the natural world itself, and it is famously, or perhaps notoriously, expressed in part in sexual terms. Instead of wanting to procreate like trees, the speaker of Marvell's poem wants to have sex with them. Discussions of the sexual aspects of "The Garden" have been hampered by the unwillingness to take seriously the idea that the human experience of nature could be a sexual experience.[14] To Marvell, however, this idea is obvious. In fact, for him, the sexual desire for plants is the true story of some of the most famous myths:

> *Apollo* hunted *Daphne* so,
> Only that She might Laurel grow.
> And *Pan* did after *Syrinx* speed,
> Not as a Nymph, but for a Reed. (29–32)

While we traditionally see the laurel and the reed as substitutes for the women the gods desired, Marvell's point is that the women were actually the substitutes and that the stories thus end happily rather than in sexual frustration.

Marvell's point about substitution here resembles but inverts the refusal of metaphoric substitution in Donne's poem. Sappho rejects the idea of comparing Philaenis to down, stars, cedars, or lilies because Philaenis is the real thing, but although Marvell also rejects this sort of metaphor, he does not do so because of a belief in the essential and incomparable human identity of the beloved but because the beloved in this poem is not human. In other words, he thinks that it is not the conventional poetic expression of human love that is metaphoric but rather the love itself insofar as that love is directed at another human. Human desire in "The Garden" is directed toward real plants rather than toward human beings, who could be said to resemble those plants in one way or another. If Browne wants to procreate like trees, Marvell wants to copulate like gods, and while this is quite a common wish (implicitly or explicitly stated) in Renaissance poetry that makes use of classical myths, here to have sex like a god would mean to have sex with plants. Thus, for Marvell in "The Garden," neither Daphne's metamorphosis into a tree nor Syrinx's into a reed is, properly speaking, a metaphoric substitution at all; instead, both are moments in which the truth of a situation is revealed.

As is the case with Sappho's refusal of metaphor, Marvell's assertion that the truth of these classical myths is that the gods lusted after plants has implications for poetry. Both of the original stories are connected with poetry because the laurel, which is equivalent to the "Bayes" of the first stanza, is a reward for a true poet, and the reed is the musical instrument that synecdochically represents poetry in general, and particularly the pastoral genre that could be said to include "The Garden." The connection with poetry may be the reason that Marvell chose these stories rather than, for instance, the stories of Hyacinth and Narcissus, in which divine love for humans also ends in human metamorphosis into plants. Arguably, then, as both the means and the end of poetry are associated with these tales of metamorphosis, of the substitution of a plant for a woman, poetry itself is figured as a kind of substitution, and metaphor, the trope of substitution, becomes its central and most characteristic figure.

For Marvell, however, human beings are the substitute for plants, and in entering the garden, he has entered a world that has no further need of metaphor. One signal of this change is that the garlands that work as metaphors for human achievement and that he mentions at the beginning of the first stanza are replaced by the real garlands created by "all Flow'rs and all Trees" at the end of the stanza. To demonstrate that metaphor is no longer necessary, Marvell writes the poem's fifth stanza, in which the poet is surrounded by fruit. I shall quote it in full:

> What wond'rous Life in this I lead!
> Ripe Apples drop about my head;
> The Luscious Clusters of the Vine
> Unto my Mouth do crush their Wine;
> The Nectaren, and curious Peach,
> Into my hands themselves do reach;
> Stumbling on Melons, as I pass,
> Insnar'd with Flow'rs, I fall on Grass. (33–40)

This stanza describes the richness of nature and its ability to nourish humans; the fact that the poet enjoys this nourishment without any effort on his or anyone's part means that the stanza recalls the negative attitude toward agriculture in "Sappho to Philaenis."

Commentators have tended to see sinister implications in Marvell's depiction of natural abundance, however. For instance, they have understood the apples as a reference to the fruit that caused the expulsion of Adam and Eve from Eden. The stanza's final line has seemed to confirm this reading. The poet, they argue, is "Insnar'd" in the sense of having become subject to sin. What is more, they have read "fall" as equivalent to "fall from grace" and "Grass" as a reference to the phrase "all flesh is grass." In other words, critics have read the plants of this stanza metaphorically and have used them to construct the argument that the garden is a fallen garden, an allegorical representation of the world in which the poet experiences a fallen and sinful sexuality. I shall return to the question of Marvell's attitude toward human–human sexuality; for now, I want to suggest that this stanza should not be read exclusively allegorically or, in other words, that the stanza depicts a human sexuality that is directed toward plants. That is, the apples, grapes, melons, and grass of the garden do not stand in for human flesh or human attitudes toward sexual experience but should rather be understood as the real objects of the poet's desire. Now that the poet has dispensed with metaphor, the plants of the garden are simultaneously signifiers and signifieds, like Philaenis's body in Donne's poem.

Of course, Marvell, like Donne in "Sappho to Philaenis," has not dispensed with metaphor altogether, and neither has he dispensed with the view that sexuality is not an especially exalted pastime: "Mean while the Mind, from pleasure less, / Withdraws into its happiness" (41–42). Sexuality, even with plants, is less important than mental activity. The mind here is an active force, and to describe it, Marvell returns to figurative language: the mind is an "Ocean where each kind / Does streight its own resemblance find" (43–44). The figure here is not metaphor but metonymy, however, or, we could say, a preexisting sameness rather than a sameness created by the poet's vision. What is more, the mind's activity—it is able to create "Far other Worlds, and other Seas" (46)—leads to the extinction of difference altogether: "Annihilating all that's made / To a green Thought in a green shade" (47–48). A "green Thought" is at once a thought about plants, the sort of thought that a plant would have, and, given the medieval and Renaissance use of green to represent love and sexuality, a sexual thought.[15] But this is not a sexual thought that leads to what we think of as sexual activity; instead, a universal greenness covers all. The stasis that Sappho prized in Philaenis's body in contrast to the activity associated with masculine sexuality has become general.

For Marvell, the true goal is metaphorically presented as the soul's "Casting the Bodies Vest aside" (51) and becoming like a bird that waits until it is "prepar'd for longer flight" (55). This spiritual transcendence of the body and of sexuality is conventional, but Marvell's return to the description of the paradisiacal garden is utterly unconventional: "Such was that happy Garden-state, / While Man there walk'd without a Mate" (57–58). Marvell situates the fall of man not at the moment at which Adam and Eve are forced to leave Eden but rather at the moment at which Eve is created:

> But 'twas beyond a Mortal's share
> To wander solitary there:
> Two Paradises 'twere in one
> To live in Paradise alone. (61–64)

As was the case with Browne in his desire to avoid coition, Marvell does not direct his comments against women specifically but rather against sex altogether.[16] In his vision of paradise, the human body is sexually united with the vegetation of the garden, and the human soul leaves the world altogether.

Although the soul transcends the world, the ideal for the body in "The Garden" is not to procreate like trees but rather to become a tree. Nevertheless, the poem does not conclude with a paean to trees or even with a reference to the celestial joys of the soul but rather with an image that unites the natural and the artificial in a way that might recall Browne's movement from trees to the picture of a horse: "How well the skilful Gardner drew / Of flow'rs and herbes this Dial new" (65–66). The reference to a gardener and the use of the verb *to draw*—meaning both "to sketch" and "to compel to move"—underline this floral clock's status as nature that has been transformed by conscious agency. I think it is important to note that the "Dial new" is not necessarily a floral clock in the strict sense—that is, it is not necessarily flowers planted so as to look like either a clock or a sundial. Instead, the phrase could refer to the fact that it is possible to tell the time of the year and the time of the day by looking at the leaves and flowers of plants of various kinds. In other words, the conscious agency I wrote of could be purely visual. While human time is typically measured by our system of named days, months, and years, and, on a larger scale, by the generations set up by human procreation, the time that emerges as a subject in this final stanza could be the natural time of the growing seasons of plants—the procreation of trees.

Certainly, as Marvell reminds us, we are not the only creatures who keep time: "as it works, th'industrious Bee / Computes its time as well as we" (69–70). By implication, at least, Marvell forecloses the possibility that the scientific measurement of time that was becoming increasingly important to all areas of life over the course of Marvell's lifetime could be taken as a sign of the difference between humans and animals. Bees, it turns out, tell time "as well as we," and Marvell's use of "compute" stresses timekeeping as a rational activity. What is more, as it is the bees who make the blossoming of the garden possible, it is entirely suitable to acknowledge their labors here at the poem's conclusion: the bees could even be regarded as the same as or equivalent to the "skilful Gardner" of the beginning of the stanza. With this reference to the bees, Marvell establishes his poem's trajectory from the human effect on the garden to the apian. Whereas humans tear off leaves to make garlands and carve initials in bark—we can see these things as Marvell's specific equivalent to Donne's "rough tillage"—bees perform the fertilization on which humans depend. What the poem as a whole suggests is that the proper counterpart to this insect activity is human repose.

This chapter has gone from trees to bees, from one form of asexual reproduction to another (or so they thought then: I have already mentioned the contemporary understanding of arboreal reproduction as asexual; the *locus classicus* for the asexual reproduction of bees is Virgil's *Georgics,* 4.198–201).[17] It turns out that to procreate like trees or bees means not having sex at all. Renaissance literature contains many references to sex as animalistic; in their very different ways, both Donne and Marvell reconsider the natural world as a source of metaphors for human sexuality. Both poets present human exploitation of nature as intrusive and both rule out the human reproduction that Browne takes for granted. But while Donne's Sappho positions one form of human sexuality within a landscape that it neither disturbs nor rearranges, the speaker of Marvell's poem forsakes humans altogether. In "To His Coy Mistress," the lover famously refers to his "vegetable Love" (11) to make the point that he cannot afford to have the patience of plants. We all get the joke, but my reading of "The Garden" suggests that we should perhaps take the phrase to mean not a love that grows like a plant but rather a love of plants. In what may, in this context, seem like a logical extension of Donne's points about erotic similitude, "The Garden" indicates that not only the best human sexuality but also the best human is one that makes no difference to the natural world at all.

Notes

1 In a recent article, "Botanical Shakespeares: The Racial Logic of Plant Life in *Titus Andronicus*," *South Central Review* 26, no. 1 (2009): 82–102, Jean Feerick has pointed out that "drama of the early modern period often navigates human difference by reference to botanical discourse" (83). See, esp., 84–85 for Feerick's discussion of the metaphorical links between humans and animals in Renaissance writing.

2 For an interesting discussion of the vegetative soul in Renaissance thought, see Christopher Crosbie, "*Oeconomia* and the Vegetative Soul: Rethinking Revenge in *The Spanish Tragedy*," *English Literary Renaissance* 38, no. 1 (2008): 8–12.

3 Sir Thomas Browne, *Religio Medici* (London, 1642). All references are to this first (pirated) edition of 1642. While Browne made a number of changes to the book, none of these affects my argument here. A good discussion of these changes can be found in Jonathan F. S. Post, "Browne's Revisions to *Religio Medici*," *Studies in English Literature* 25 (1985): 145–63. This passage has given rise to a great deal of commentary, much of which is covered in Marjorie Swann, "'Procreate Like Trees': Generation and Society in Thomas Browne's *Religio Medici*," in *Engaging*

with Nature: Essays on the Natural World in Medieval and Early Modern Europe, ed. Barbara A. Hanawalt and Lisa J. Kiser, 137–54 (Notre Dame, Ind.: Notre Dame University Press, 2008). For the argument that sex and death are always connected for Browne and that the passage should be read as a grim joke, see Michael Stanford, "The Terrible Thresholds: Sir Thomas Browne on Sex and Death," *English Literary Renaissance* 18, no. 3 (1988): 413–23.

4 See, in particular, Swann, "Procreate Like Trees," 148–49. Swann points out that it was not until the fittingly named Nehemiah Grew presented his botanical papers to the Royal Society in 1676 that English people understood botanical reproduction to be sexual (141).

5 John Milton, *Complete Poems and Major Prose,* ed. Merritt Y. Hughes (Indianapolis, Ind.: Odyssey, 1957).

6 William N. West, "Thinking with the Body: Sappho's 'Sappho to Philaenis,' Donne's 'Sappho to Philaenis,'" *Renaissance Papers* (1994): 68.

7 John Donne, *Poetical Works,* ed. Sir Herbert Grierson (Oxford: Oxford University Press, 1933).

8 Janel Mueller, "Lesbian Erotics: The Utopian Trope of Donne's 'Sappho to Philaenis,'" in *Homosexuality in Renaissance and Enlightenment England: Literary Representations in Historical Context,* ed. Claude J. Summers (New York: Haworth, 1992), 114.

9 Paula Blank, "Comparing Sappho to Philaenis: John Donne's 'Homopoetics,'" *PMLA* 110, no. 3 (1995): 359.

10 Lee Edelman, *Homographesis: Essays in Gay Literary and Cultural Theory* (New York: Routledge, 1994), xiv.

11 Valerie Traub, *The Renaissance of Lesbianism in Early Modern England* (Cambridge: Cambridge University Press, 2002), 328. For Traub's discussion of "Sappho to Philaenis," see 336–40. In this chapter of her book, Traub interestingly connects erotic similitude as a trope in Renaissance literature with erotic similitude as an aspect of current queer uses of medieval and Renaissance literature and history.

12 Andrew Marvell, *The Poems and Letters of Andrew Marvell,* vol. 1, ed. H. M. Margoliouth (Oxford: Clarendon Press, 1971). For a discussion of these lines with reference to "The Garden," see Harry Berger Jr., "Marvell's 'Garden': Still Another Interpretation," *Modern Language Quarterly* 28, no. 3 (1967): 285–57.

13 Robert N. Watson, *Back to Nature: The Green and the Real in the Late Renaissance* (Philadelphia: University of Pennsylvania Press, 2006), 109.

14 For a discussion of the sexual aspects of similar passages in "Upon Appleton House," including a memorable encounter with ivy, see my "No Present," in *Sex, Gender, and Time in Fiction and Culture,* ed. Ben Davies and Jana Funke, 38–52 (New York: Palgrave Macmillan, 2011).

15 See, e.g., Bruce R. Smith, *The Key of Green: Passion and Perception in Renaissance Culture* (Chicago: University of Chicago Press, 2009).

16 In any case, the presumption of heterosexuality here is unwarranted; see Paul Hammond, "Marvell's Sexuality," *Seventeenth Century* 11 (1996): 87–123.

17 Virgil, *Opera,* ed. R. A. B. Mynors (Oxford: Clarendon, 1969). For my discussion of this passage, see my *Against Reproduction: Where Renaissance Texts Come From* (Toronto, Ont.: University of Toronto Press, 2009), 31.

8

Aping Rape: Animal Ravishment and Sexual Knowledge in Early Modern England

HOLLY DUGAN

In his 1952 survey of "the sexuality of apes," H. W. Janson muses on a peculiar European literary tradition: pervasive cultural belief in interspecies rape of human females by male apes. For Janson, representations of "ape rape" raise a paradoxical question: how did this widespread European cultural belief evolve, particularly in the early modern period, before the arrival of large, biped simians in Europe? The problem is one of scale: early modern apes seem too small to pose a serious threat to humans, female or otherwise. Although he seems willing to believe that accounts of early modern ape rape involving larger simians may have been based on historical truth, he draws the line at these smaller simians:

> Who could seriously maintain this of the small and weak Barbary ape, or of the guenons? Apart from the anthropoid apes, unknown before the seventeenth century, only the baboon was strong and fierce enough to be credited with such ambitions. But when, and how, did the idea itself originate? It certainly could not have been based on actual observation[.][1]

Only anthropoid apes—apes capable of mimicking the violence of men in frighteningly embodied ways—could pose such a threat. The bodies of the "small" and "weak" Barbary apes, guenons, and even angry baboons offer no such potential. Without a material counterpoint, such accounts (at least for Janson) reveal only a peculiar early modern rape fantasy involving animals.

Janson's incredulity locates itself in the sheer improbability of the tale: certainly early modern women could defend themselves from such an attack, even if from a "strong" and "fierce" baboon with sexual "ambition." I begin with his meditation on simian and human bodies and their relationship to one another to raise questions about the role of veracity in constructing sexual knowledge and about how the category of the human—and implicit assumptions that rest on it—shapes our histories of sexual violence. What is most striking about Janson's statement is not his disbelief—many have doubted the authenticity of these tales—but rather how he articulates his doubt. His is a positivist approach: framed in this way, such attacks offer no empirical threat of bodily violence and simply cannot be true. Tales of ape rape evince only a peculiar literary history rather than an archive of sexual acts.

In this essay, I approach these examples from a different point of view to dislodge the gendered and heteronormative logic of rape that saturates approaches to sexual violence in the past. In doing so, I queer Janson's empiricism by insisting that these tales offer more than metaphoric accounts of bestial assault. As Janson's incredulity reveals, tales of ape rape are hard to believe precisely because they challenge gendered bodily norms about sexuality. Whereas human-initiated sex with animals remains a cultural taboo, bestial sexual assaults of human bodies reveal the limits in thinking sex. Our collective doubt about these tales refracts our palpable (and paradoxical) desire that sex be knowable even in moments of violence. Janson, for example, focuses on the absurdity of scale in such representations, sidestepping the ways in which the agents and victims of sexual violence remain stolidly scripted: he accepts without comment that the ambitious, angry baboon is always imagined as male and its victim as female (even within tales he deems preposterous). Such assumptions demonstrate that although these pervasive accounts are tangential to most normative histories of sexual violence, our interpretations of them remain influenced by them.[2] Consequently, these accounts of when animals attacked fit uneasily between feminist histories of rape and queer histories of bestiality. The sheer volume of these tales of ape rape raises questions about their absence within histories of sexuality. They are an unexplored penumbra within the history of rape, revealing our limits in thinking sex and violence.

Janson doubts the scale of bodily power invoked in early modern accounts of apes raping human women, not the gendered logic at work in such tales. Such a disjuncture documents the ways in which the implicit subjects and objects of rape work as definitive, rather than contested, categories: human men rape human women. Men do not rape men or animals; animals do not rape women, men, or other animals; and finally, women do not rape women, men, or animals. If the history of rape is defined in such a way, the verb *rape* orients meaning in three important ways: along gendered lines of power, through heteronormative structures of desire, and within what we might term species boundaries. Narratives of sexual violence, real or imagined, that fall outside such boundaries remain marginal to current understandings of the history of rape.[3] Yet, as numerous literary, scientific, and ethnographic examples document, premodern sexuality was often imagined as violent and inclusive of nonhuman participants. These examples explicitly call into question the definition of sex subsumed within most histories of rape.

Ravishment was a curious affective state in late medieval and early modern law and literature, often signifying submission of one's senses or seizure of one's body by a wide variety of agents, including animals. Cultural belief in early modern animal ravishment, particularly attacks by apes, was, even in Janson's terms, pervasive. These strange accounts of when animals attacked—other animals, children, women, or men—remind us that the line between men's animal desires and animals' all too human ones is repeatedly crossed in early modern literary accounts of ravishment. Here I focus on just two: Shakespeare's *Comedy of Errors* and John Donne's *Progress of the Soul.* Editors have suggested that both accounts draw on early modern naturalist texts like Konrad Gesner's *Historiae Animalium* (1551) and Edward Topsell's *History of Foure-Footed Beastes* (1607), which list numerous species of venereous apes that attack human women. These two accounts reveal a broader pattern of thinking that challenges Jansen's problem of scale and, in doing so, queers early modern tropes of sexual dominance. They offer a different vector for understanding material histories of sexual violence, estranging modern readers from the normative force of rape narratives oriented around active male bodies and passive female ones. As both Shakespeare's and Donne's texts demonstrate, the human male's position at the top of the great chain of being was precarious, resting on a paradoxical and improbable insistence that size and species do not matter when it comes to bodily penetrative power.

Comedies of Errors: Early Modern Apes and Asses

Shakespeare's *The Comedy of Errors* stages a frighteningly dissolvable self. In the play, Antipholus and Dromio of Syracuse unknowingly swap bodily knowledge, social reputations, wives, and wealth with their brothers from Ephesus. Although the experience is uncanny and, at times, nightmarish for both sets of brothers (at one point, Antipholus of Syracuse wonders if he is "in earth, in heaven, or in hell" [2.2.212]), theatrical pleasure for spectators of the play theoretically accrues around the dissolution—and ultimate restoration—of identities.[4] As Stephen Greenblatt notes in his introduction to the Norton edition, this play is, after all, a *comedy* of errors.[5] Yet in its farcical staging of doubled identities, the play posits something more sinister—that violence emerges when certain social boundaries are crossed, revealing them to be more fragile and fungible than they appear. So, too, are species boundaries: the twins' doubled identities unleash a range of bestial desires that threaten to upend Ephesus and its laws.

As Dromio of Syracuse acknowledges, part of the play's humor depends on all kinds of transformations:

> DROMIO OF SYRACUSE, *to Antipholus.* I am transformèd, master, am not I? . . .
> ANTIPHOLUS OF SYRACUSE. Thou hast thine own form.
> DROMIO OF SYRACUSE. No, I am an ape.
> LUCIANA. If thou art changed to aught, 'tis to an ass. (2.2.195–96, 198–99)

Just prior to this moment in the play, Dromio has been sexually assaulted by Nell, a woman and servant in Antipholus of Ephesus's home. In the aftermath of the assault, Dromio seeks empirical confirmation of his altered material existence. When he does not receive it, he insists that he merely "apes" his previous human form. Luciana, however, jokes that

Dromio has wandered somewhere beyond the pale of humanity and, to use contemporary terms, has slipped further down the evolutionary chain than he thinks. If Dromio has transformed, it is not into an ape, "'tis to an ass." In the Norton edition, Greenblatt glosses Dromio's use of the term *ape* to connote his status as an "imitation" or a "fool" rather than as a specific reference to an animal body. Yet Luciana's pun quickly foregrounds an important missing link related to Janson's question of scale: Dromio's experience of Nell's sexual violation alters his sense of himself, so much so that his is a diminished humanity, associated with either small, wild simians or with large, domesticated asses. Luciana's pun begs an obvious question: what is the difference between being transformed into an ape or an ass?

The answer depends on one's vulnerability to being "bridled" as a beast, demonstrating the ways in which animal bodies helped to construct emerging sexual and gendered knowledge in the period, particularly around violent encounters (rarely detailed in either literary or legal accounts of them).[6] Aping, I argue, provides a distorted, but useful, refraction of raping; the boundaries between men, apes, and asses reflect shadowy histories of early modern sexual violence. Such reflections become clearer when we consider the punch line of Luciana's joke: Dromio is an ass. Luciana's quip hints at the nature of Dromio's sexual violation: Dromio has been bridled like an ass.[7] His self-identification, however, demonstrates that apes, like asses, also connect with the sexual politics of bridling in the period. In Dromio's account, he now merely "apes" the gestures of male power and penetration; he no longer embodies them. Aping emerges as a verb of diminished male human action, refracted across species divides, a fact that Luciana's pun so cleverly utilizes. Dromio—as an ape and as an ass—is erotically defined as something other than human after his sexual encounter with Nell. His bestial transformation stems from something other than his willing participation in a sexual crime against nature.[8]

Aping was a complex term, built on early modern fascination with simian mimicry.[9] Its emergence as both a subject and a verb disoriented human subjectivity, sexual knowledge, and species boundaries. Aping, defined as a diminished animal refraction of human behavior, troubled the meanings of rape in the period. Monstrosity thus emerged through an eerie verisimilitude to humanity when simians "aped" their human counterparts. In Edward Topsell's *History of Foure Footed Beasts,* for example, the mutability of apes hinges on their likeness to men: they are creatures at once both familiar and "ridiculous" (5).[10] Topsell concludes that "as the body of an Ape is Ridiculous, by reason of an indecent likenesse and imiatation of man, so is his soule or spirit" (5). Apes thus have a remarkable ability to imitate "all" human actions, both playful and violent: they "leape, singe, driue Wagons," and are capable of "raigning and whipping the Horses very artificially" (3). Their uncanny knack for human mimicry makes them valuable, though dangerous, commodities.[11] Topsell notes, for instance, that once plucked and perfumed with "hot spices," many "diverse sorts of Apes, very like mankind" are sold to "[m]archants, who carry them about the world, preswading [*sic*] simple people that there are men in Islands of no greater stature" (5). He also notes that "rich" men equally prized these animals for "sport" and for their ability to reflect networks of social dominance: "for [apes] are kept only in rich mens houses to sport withal, being for that cause easily tamed, following euery action he seeth done, euen to his own harme without discretion" (5). Although Topsell overestimates the ease with which this domestication occurs, his descriptions of ape–human hybridity suggest that part of the "sport" of training apes involved practices of domestication that resulted in diminished echoes of their power.[12]

An ape's ability to physically pass for human complicated this performance, connecting these tales about species divides with early modern gender norms. Certain apes were prized for their ability to mimic the smell of male humans, blurring the line between imitation and embodiment.[13] The fact that certain apes might pass as humans, however, suggests that aping might signify something other than diminished male human action. Aping might lead to a frightening ascendancy of animal power over male human bodies; this fear, I argue, was displaced into narratives of rape. Topsell's *History of Foure-Footed Beastes,* for example, catalogs a stunning array of simian attacks on men, other animals, women, and children.[14] In one account, a man drowns a shipwrecked ape for intimating knowledge about—and perhaps of—his women, children, and friends (5).[15] Some, like the maritine monkey, are of "an euill disposition likes Apes, and therefore" the reader is spared "both their picture and further description" (8). Baboons, he notes, are as "lustfull and venerous as goats," and, if given the chance, they will "defile all sorts of women," "yet, they love children" (12). Such a paradoxical description of animal desires reveals similar inconsistencies in human ones: what sort of animal will "defile" women, given the chance, yet also "delight" in the company of children and dogs?

Gendered norms of behavior emerge as a way to make sense of such complicated interactions that cross species divisions. Though he does not seem to realize the paradox, Topsell takes time to warn readers that baboons and their love of little children are dangerous: "it will strangle young Children if they be not looked unto" (8). Although the sex of the beast is undefined ("it" will strangle "children"), Topsell then describes an account of an ape who witnesses a mother bathing her child: it "observed her diligently," mimicked her actions, "and washed the child therewith until it killed it" (8). Such a description captures the fears of keeping these animals as household pets, but it also raises questions about the role of gender within empirical approaches to human–animal relationships in the past. Maternal behaviors like bathing an infant (or masculine ones like disciplining a horse) become violent when performed by a baboon. The animal seemingly bears witness to early modern gender norms and mimics them. So, too, does its violent venery. That women and children were often in charge of training these animals suggests the complex interaction of violence and domesticity. As rapacious as goats and capable of loving children to death, early modern apes were complicated companionate species.[16]

As such accounts suggest, imitation was not always a playful "sport." *The Comedy of Errors* corroborates this point, connecting the violence of "aping" with other kinds of domestic practices. The play posits that imitation can radically destabilize identity and the social networks on which identity hangs. In *The Comedy of Errors,* these social networks include relationships between masters and servants, husbands and wives, and merchants and clients. The multiple beatings inflicted on the Dromios reveal that the destabilization of early modern identities produced both queer and violent effects. Curiously, however, both Topsell and Dromio insist that such cultural ramifications—no matter how queer or how violent—remain firmly fixed within a naturalized system of gendered hierarchy imported into the category of the human.

In a key scene of *The Comedy of Errors,* Adriana, like Dromio, recognizes such a gendered hierarchy of nature but refuses to be "bridled" like an "ass" (2.1.14).[17] Luciana once again codes this refusal as an unnatural sin against kind. Arguing that everything "under heaven's eye, /. . . hath his bound in earth, in sea, and sky," Luciana concludes that "the beasts, the fishes, and the winged fowls / Are their males' subject and at their controls" (2.1.15–20). Mapping control of "beasts," "fishes," and "the winged fowl" through heterosexuality, Luciana explains that under such a gendered system, for a woman to refuse to be an ass is to step outside the boundaries of nature. In effect, Luciana confirms that Adriana is an ass waiting to be bridled by Antipholus. There is queer potential at the heart of this structure of heterosexual "bridling": both Adriana and Dromio are asses in this play. By invoking the category of the animal, jokes about sexual bridling expand to include both men's and women's bodies.

Do such metaphors of sexual "bridling" connote specters of monstrous bestiality, sodomy, or normative systems of rape? Such a question emphasizes how sexual violence—real or represented—can define as well as transgress species boundaries.[18] These three legal terms reflect such boundaries in the period. If sodomy was a crime worse than rape because of the ways in which it was thought to obliterate the essence of a human's soul, then bestial buggery was the expression of such fears made flesh. As such, men slide down the great chain of being; animals do not fuck their way up it.[19] And yet Luciana's quip to Dromio and her discourse with her sister about early modern animality suggest something different, examining the violent sexual potential in certain animal bodies, specifically those that "ape" human motions. To reframe Judith Butler's famous question about gender, sex, and human bodies, Luciana's puns about apes and asses seem to query, how do animal bodies matter?

Consider, for example, the way bestiality materializes in *The Comedy of Errors.* Dromio's description of Nell's sexual attack is perhaps one of the more famous moments in the play. Repulsed by her gross corporeality, Dromio insists that this moment is one of bestial assault: "Marry, sir, such a claim as you would lay to your horse; and she would have me as a beast" (3.2.85–87). His use of aposiopesis, however, marks a dramatic realization for him and the audience. Recognizing that he is sexually vulnerable to penetration, he quickly refines his allusion: "—not that, I being a beast, she would have me, but that she, being a very beastly creature, lays claim to me" (3.2.87–89). Repetitively positioned in the play as an ass, Dromio fails to "ape" himself and thereby marks a distinct tension in the play's comedic narrative between eroticism and domestication, or between having and laying claims on wives and animals. Dromio thereby offers an early modern commentary on what Valerie Traub identifies as the queer (and I would add potentially violent) processes in which "bodies and bodily acts accrue meaning and intelligibility *as sexual*."[20] Traub further argues that bodily confusion—of sexes, of species—was linked to sexuality and gender:

> What links the "confusion of species" with "confusion of sexes" is neither species nor sex per se, but the nature of the orifice and the relative position of the partners. Men can unnaturally penetrate beasts, other men (including boys), and women; and women can seek to be penetrated by either men or beasts. But, locked into a position of receptacle, woman cannot—in English law—penetrate another woman.[21]

Nor can she penetrate a man, a boy, or a beast. As these tales suggest, the monstrous hybridity of apish men and bestial women blurs the boundaries between classes, genders, species, and environments. Dromio of Syracuse confirms this point twice in the play, concluding miserably after Luciana rhetorically masters him, "I am an ass, I am a woman's man, and besides myself" (3.2.77). Dromio's loss of humanity ("I am an ass") is equated with his rhetorical loss of manhood ("I am a woman's man"). But such mastery equally cites Nell's previous mastery of his body: "I am due to a woman: one that claims me, one that haunts me, one that will have me" (3.2.82–83).

Thus *The Comedy of Errors* provocatively suggests that man's position at the top of the Chain of Being is linked to penetrative violence and that others could potentially lay claim to that position. Dromio of Syracuse's concession that he is both an ass and a woman's man renders him vulnerable to Nell's bestial assault. When commanded by Antipholus of Ephesus to return home, Dromio recalls that for him, home was a space of domestication. Nell's monstrosity is curious—she is both a "Dowsabel" (a sweetheart) and a beast that "haunts" him—yet Dromio, too, focuses on the problem of scale: she is too big for him to "compasse," yet "thither [he] must, although against [his] will" (4.1.10–12). His master's minion, Dromio renders himself vulnerable to assault in a futile attempt to reassert himself through sexual mastery of Nell's capacious body.[22] Earlier in the play, he describes her as a "drudge and diviner," capable of transforming him into a "tailless dog," docked and domesticated in her kitchen, endlessly turning meat on a spit (3.2.139–44).

The specter of the tailless dog hints at Dromio's previous ruminations about the attack: the image conjures fears of castration but also of Topsell's rapacious, and tailless, Barbary apes. (Numerous editors of Shakespeare cite Topsell's *History of Foure-Footed Beastes* to explain this reference.) Dromio experienced the assault as a transformative experience: he aped himself in its aftermath. But as Luciana notes, the fact that he fell victim to a woman's advances made him more vulnerable and moved him much further beyond the pale of humanity; no longer beside himself "aping" human form, Dromio becomes a bridled ass. Bridled by Antipholus (his master) and by Nell (a lascivious wench), Dromio's body is vulnerable in ways he cannot reconcile. Although this process is incredibly violent, there is queer potential, for as the end of the play underscores, what Dromio of Syracuse finds repulsive—compassing Nell and being compassed by her against his will—Dromio of Ephesus presumably finds pleasurable.

As the twins reconcile themselves at the end of the play, Dromio of Syracuse questions his brother about this activity: "There is a fat friend at your master's house / That kitchened me for you today at dinner. / She now shall be my sister, not my wife" (5.1.414–17). Although editors (and the *Oxford English Dictionary*) interpret "kitchened" to mean Nell "entertained" Dromio in the "kitchen," thus reinscribing Nell's large body firmly within the domestic sphere, Dromio's previous image of the tailless dog suggests that something else may be meant by that term. Dromio's query of his brother seems at first to imply sexual mastery of his brother's wife, but it also suggests her sexual mastery of him, raising questions about Luciana's insistence on the natural order of heterosexual marriage. Dromio of Ephesus neither confirms nor denies that he finds queer pleasure in his wife's sexual penetration of his body. Instead, the play ends with his odd meditation on the brothers' bodily verisimilitude: "Methinks you are my glass and not my brother" (5.1.419). Dromio is finally beside himself in human form, though that form may also "ape" a queer masculinity that revels in bestial bridling. As the brothers try to determine who shall lead, Dromio of Syracuse commands his brother to "lead thou first" (5.1.425). Yet the play refuses hierarchies altogether, and the brothers end walking "hand in hand, not one before another" (5.1.427), aping one another in form and gesture, refusing to restore natural or cultural hierarchies.

Lecherous Chains of Being: (R)apes

If the two Dromios in *The Comedy of Errors* demonstrate that sexual desire and the actions that stem from it—having and laying claims on other bodies—blur the lines that define human and beast, then Donne's *Progresse of the Soul* provides a sinister counterpoint, arguing that humans are not the only animals that might be seized by such desire. In this poem, Donne "sings" the "progresse of a deathlesse soul," whom "fate, which God made, but doth not controule, / Plac'd in most shapes" (1–2).[23] These shapes include, but are not limited to, an apple, a mandrake, a cock sparrow, a fish ovum, a swan, vaporous gasses belched from a swan, a pike, a sea pie, a whale, a mouse, a wolf's unborn whelp, an ape, a woman, and finally, Donne hints, the reader. As this soul wanders throughout the animal world, and up the great chain of being, Donne charts a lustful cosmology in which plants, vapors, fish, fowl, beasts, women, and men are susceptible to violent seizures of both body and will.

Rape violates species boundaries: almost halfway through the poetic meditation on metempsychosis, the narrator boldly, and bizarrely, asks, "Is any kind subject to rape like fish?" (281). Within the cosmology of the poem, fish can be—in fact, have been—seized by an evil wandering soul that represents a violent potentiality of desire manifesting itself in rape. Propelled by "the early balme" (14) and "Iland spices" (291) of paradise, and later by interspecies dependence that defines postlapsarian ecosystems, this evil, wandering soul grows increasingly venereous and sinister as it works its way up the great chain of being and approaches humanity. Implicitly defining rape as an unlawful seizure of any kind, even of fish, Donne parodies outrage at such actions by tracing their progress through what Bruce Smith terms a "lecherous chain of being."[24] In essence, Donne tropes the gestures of rape, and though such gestures are not explicitly penetrative, they are sexual and violent. Fish, who "neither doe, nor wish" ill unto birds or men, are nevertheless violated and killed by both (283–84).[25]

The metaphorical rape of fish that outrages Donne's narrator is quickly surpassed by other acts of narrative violence that escalate into sexual assault. For example, a wolf's whelp, seized by the soul, plans a sinister attack on Abel's "white and milde" sheep, which are well defended by a bitch. To distract her, the wolf attacks the dog, forcing her to submit to his "embracements" of love, "[w]here deeds move more then [*sic*] words" (414–20). This violent seizure produces two narrative effects: it allows the wolf murderous access to the sheep, and it sires a wolf–dog offspring, perpetuating violence through interspecies sexual acts that exceed narratives of human "lust" (433). The poem's penultimate attack results in the soul "quicken[ing]" into a "toyful" ape that plays with Adam's children (451). That early modern pet culture is imported into the biblical past perhaps sharpens the poem's satiric edge. The poem meditates on the "ridiculous" nature of the ape's body, but here the ape draws connections across the species divide. Noticing the verisimilitude between the children's "organs" and his, the ape marvels at his own linguistic lack: "His organs now so like theirs hee doth finde, / That why he cannot laugh, and speake his minde, / He wonders" (454–56). Sentient enough to wonder, yet not enough to "laugh," this gamesome ape straddles the line between human and animal.

The ape's attack arises from his frustration with his bodily limitations in comparison to the human children. The ape, lacking the power of language, must crudely mime the gestures of eroticism, making "love faces," "the valters sombersalts," and wooing with "hoiting gambols" (464–66). In doing so, the ape's sexual desire, so the poetic narrator argues, is like other "sins against kinde," namely, male, human, sodomitical desire. Just as the ape "reached at things too high," so, too, have men reached too low, fixated on the "outward beauty" of "beasts" and "boys" (469). Donne's equation of desire suggests that animal rape and human bestiality exist on a similar continuum, both born of evil seizures of bodily desire. Whereas Bruce Smith, in his influential reading of the poem, rightfully derides Donne's association of desire for boys with desire for beasts, I argue that the poem asserts a lengthy gendered narrative of penetration that begins with pleasure and ends in violence. That an ape apes the erotic gestures of power and penetration demonstrates cultural anxiety about shifting natural hierarchies in the period.

With "teare-shot eyes," the ape "subtly" lifts Siphatecia's skirt "with his russet pawe" without "fear or awe of nature" (477–79). In the next stanza, Donne's narrator abandons the perspective of the sentient, violent ape, emphasizing instead the young girl's bodily response to animal contact. First, she "was silly and knew not what he ment" (481). Next, she experiences a pleasurable "itchie warmth, that melts her quite" (483). Finally, pleasure collapses into violence and sexual knowledge. She now

> cares not what he doth
> And willing halfe and more, more then halfte loth
> She neither puls nor pushes, but outright
> Now cries, and now repents. (484–87)

Whereas earlier sexual attacks—on fish and on Abel's bitch—were violent and continuous, the rape of Adam's daughter enacts a teleological narrative of sexual violence. Donne's poem creates a great chain of rape, with each violent sexual act escalating in scope, culminating in a complicated—and violent—act of bestial rape of a young girl.

Both Shakespeare's and Donne's hierarchies of violence depend on explicitly reflexive desires between bestial and human bodies. Dromio's joking insistence that Dowsabell's body is too big to "broach" attempts to mark her as monstrously bestial, but the joke is ultimately at his expense: such "monstrosity" is no impediment to sex. Rather, the underlying tension of the joke depends on recognition that a body so large can perhaps breech him, with or without his consent.[26] Topsell's tome marvels at the bodily concordances between men and beasts. Even Donne's "playful ape" wonders at the verisimilitude between his bodily organs and Adam's children's bodies, charting a smaller scale of bestial–human hybridity across pets' and children's bodies. Such "ridiculous" bodily concordances—between bodies too big and too small—emphasize that sex rarely unfolds in predictable ways and that too often, our insistence that it should obscures histories of sexual violence. Penetration of the wrong kinds of bodies—of boys or of beasts—led men to increasingly degenerative modes of being. But as these tales also document, the perverse inverse was also conceivable, and in many ways, it was potentially more frightening: penetration of the right kinds of bodies—of a bitch or a woman—led beasts to increasingly generative modes of being, namely, having and laying claims to male human bodies.

Donne's poem ends with the specter of such generative bodies but stops just short of this imaginative conclusion. Whereas *The Comedy of Errors* ends by positing humans aping one another, *Progresse of the Soul* ends by violently reasserting gendered hierarchies of and over nature. At the last moment, the evil, wandering soul leaves the ape's body and invades Siphaeticia's womb, raising the specter of bestial progeny born of violent rape only to deny its articulation: "And whether by this change she lose or win, / She comes out next, where th' Ape would have gone in" (491–92). Donne's unclear antecedents link Siphaeticia's vacant and vulnerable womb with a terrifying presence: the monstrous infant girl emerges where the "ape would have gone in," fusing transmigration with generation. Though she is not physically violated, Siphaeticia's womb is a fetid "stew," contaminated by both the invasive evil and her own perverse desires that emerged from sexual knowledge of it (495). Her womb is capable of transforming her progeny through its own unique "[c]himiques" fire (494). Such transformations do not, however, render a monstrously visible, deformed corporality. She gives birth to a daughter, not an angry female ape–human hybrid. Yet it is a monster all the same. Though the bodily ramifications of the attack are mitigated, the effects of sexual knowledge culminate in the "sinowie" strings that compose her body:

> And now they joyn'd: keeping some quality
> Of every past shape, she knew treachery,
> Rapine, deceit, and lust, and ills enow
> To be a woman. *Themech* she is now,
> Sister and wife to *Caine, Caine* that first did plow.[27] (504–10)

The joke, of course, is that memory of every previous incarnation of evil is "enow / To be a woman" (508–9). Its striking misogyny suggests that Themach represents a fusion of evil itself, of the ape's "toyfull" desires and of Siphaeticia's sexual knowledge born of violence. The soul has crept up the chain of being, embodying a new potential for sexual violence: women's.

Themach is thus poised to disrupt Cain's mastery over nature, but the poem abruptly halts the evil soul's progression before she manifests this bodily power, reinforcing instead Cain's sexual power over nature. He is the "first did plow" (510). Bestial ravishment is thus occluded by the poem's misogynist satiric humor. The poem ends not with penetration of Cain's body by Themach but rather with a strange meditation on the soul's invasion of the reader: "Who ere thou beest that read'st this sullen Writ, / Which just so much courts thee, as though dost it, / Let me arrest thy thoughts; wonder with me" (511–13). Just as Shakespeare's play puns on the actor's ability to "ape" humanity, Donne, too, offers a brief meditation on the effect of reading poetry, particularly poetry that could be construed as violent, though its form is aesthetically pleasing. Reading is both a seizure ("Let me arrest thy thoughts") and a structure of desire between the "sullen Writ" and the reader. Whereas Siphaeticia's body was violently penetrated by an ape, the reader is subtly "courted" by ideas (512). Donne summarily defers the natural conclusion of the poem's hierarchies of violence: Themach *should* be able to enact the same acts of sexual violence onto Cain's body and, by extension, men. She should be able to "plow." But the poem alters rapes to rapines and invasion to persuasion. Donne's poem blurs the lines between aping rape and raping apes. Ultimately, rape transmigrates from seizures to violent sexual penetrations to rapine and, finally, to a pure ravishment of the mind. With these transmigrations, bestial and female violation of male bodies remains just beyond the imaginative pale.

Conclusion

If animals metaphorically represent what Jeffrey Jerome Cohen terms "body possibilities," then what is one to make of Donne's discursive lacunae in configurations of monstrous animalism?[28] And what does this blind spot reveal about our methodologies for historicizing sex and violence? As I have tried to show here, literary accounts of bestial raping throw into relief the ways in which sexual knowledge emerged from imagining violent encounters across the species divide. In both Donne's poem and Shakespeare's play, aping leads to raping and to other acts of violence. Dwelling on these accounts demonstrates all that is left out of histories of violence if we insist on species boundaries, namely, that the history of rape as a *human* phenomenon results from rather queer narrative effects that include intimate assaults on animal bodies. Pervasive, yet improbable; violent, yet normative; heterosexual, yet queer, these narratives of ravishment are paradoxical reminders of how sex and gender orient structures of violence and how the category of the human legitimizes it. Our collective desire to dismiss such tales as material impossibilities offers a cautionary tale about doubt of other kinds of rape narratives, especially those that exist outside of the legal history of rape because they flout our assumptions about bodily scale, gender norms, sexual desire, or even species divides. When placed side by side, like the twinned Dromios, tales of animal and human violence remind us of the perils of naturalizing rape even as we seek to historicize it and of the gains in allowing oneself to wonder about (and wander beyond) the pale of humanity.

Notes

1 H. W. Janson, *Apes and Ape Lore in the Middle Ages and Renaissance* (London: Warburg Institute, 1952), 269.

2 Many critics have explored how "animal" functions as a metaphor for human otherness, particularly in discourses of rape, race, and sexuality. See, e.g., Jonathan Burton and Ania Loomba's discussion of Edward Topsell's apes as related to early modern constructions of Africans in *Race in Early Modern England: A Reader's Companion* (New York: Palgrave Macmillan, 2007), 166. I am interested in exploring what it might mean to consider an alternative reading: to consider "animal" as a material signifier.

3 See Sharon Block, *Rape and Sexual Power in Early America* (Chapel Hill: University of North Carolina Press, 2006), esp. 211.

4 All citations from Shakespeare's plays come from *The Norton Shake-*

speare, 2nd ed., ed. Stephen Greenblatt, Walter Cohen, Jean Howard, and Katherine Maus (New York: W. W. Norton, 2008).

5 Stephen Greenblatt, introduction to *The Norton Shakespeare,* 718.

6 As historian Garthine Walker concludes, "the social history of rape in early modern England could be described as a non-history, a history of absence . . . a phenomenon which is practically inexplicable; yet also as one that requires no explanation at all." Walker, "Rereading Rape and Sexual Violence in Early Modern England," *Gender and History* 10, no. 1 (1998): 5.

7 *The Comedy of Errors* is, of course, not the only Shakespeare play to poke fun at shameful human desire by invoking an ass, particularly its "bridled" status. On Bottom's transformation to an ass in *A Midsummer Night's Dream,* see the first chapter of Bruce Boehrer's *Shakespeare among the Animals: Nature and Society in the Drama of Early Modern England* (Basingstoke, U.K.: Palgrave-Macmillan, 2002). On Falstaff's transformation in *The Merry Wives of Windsor,* see the second chapter of Will Stockton's *Playing Dirty: Sexuality and Waste in Early Modern Comedy* (Minneapolis: University of Minnesota Press, 2011). I am especially grateful to Will for sharing a draft of this chapter prior to publication.

8 For more on the relationship between bestiality and other crimes against nature, see Bruce Smith, *Homosexual Desire in Shakespeare's England: A Cultural Poetics* (Chicago: University of Chicago Press, 1995), 176.

9 See James Knowles, "Can ye not tell a man from a marmoset? Apes and Others on the Early Modern Stage," in *Renaissance Beasts: Of Animals, Humans, and Other Wonderful Creatures,* ed. Erica Fudge, 138–63 (Carbondale: University of Southern Illinois Press, 2004).

10 Edward Topsell, *The Historie of Foure-Footed Beastes* (London, 1607). Page citations appear in text.

11 For an analysis of how these performances materialized on early modern stages, see Knowles, "Apes and Others," 138.

12 Domestication of Barbary apes and other species of monkeys involved beating the animal into submission. Even then, it had to be chained at all times. Consider Bartholomew of England's meditation on taming apes: "By nature, the animal is unruly and malicious, and must be tamed forcibly by means of beatings and chains. One attaches it to a heavy block or clog, so as to keep it from running at will, thus suppressing its insolence." *De propietatibus rerum,* "Liber de animalius," ch. XCIV; cited in Janson, *Apes and Ape Lore,* 145.

13 Ibid., 7.

14 E.g., Topsell, *Historie of Foure-Footed Beastes,* 8, describes how the Prasyan Ape "leapeth upon the Bore, and windeth his tayle round about the Bore, & with the one arme which he had left, caught him, and helde him so fast by the throte that he stifled him."

15 Topsell, ibid., 4, relates the following tale: "A certaine Ape after a shipwracke swimming to land, was seene by a Countreyman, and thinknig [*sic*] him to be a man in the water, gaue him his hand to saue him, yet in the mean time asked him what Country man he was, he was an *Athenian*: well, saide the man, doth thou know *Piraus* (which was a port in *Athens*) very well, said the Ape, and his wife, friends and children, where at the man being moued did what he could to drowne him." What exactly moved the man to drown this ape? Was it his failure to pass the sailor's test? If so, Topsell provides a curious gloss for other readers who remain ignorant that Piraus is a port, not a man. Or was it the ape's claim of knowledge about—or perhaps of—Piraus's "wife, friends, and children"?

16 The reference to goats emphasizes that apes were not the only animals believed to sexually attack humans. In this chapter, I consider only apes, but for more on the boundaries of the human, see Karl Steel, "How to Make a Human," *Exemplaria* 20, no. 1 (2008): 3–27.

17 Katherine attempts a similar move in *The Taming of the Shrew,* but Petruccio quickly masters the joke through sexual innuendo. After Katherine calls Petruccio a "moveable stool," he invites her to "Come, sit on me." Like Luciana, she seeks to humiliate Petruccio and compares him to an ass: "Asses are made to bear, and so are you." But Petruccio is no servant and immediately asserts control through gender: "Women are made to bear and so are you" (2.1.197–99).

18 For more on this link, see Carolyn Dinshaw's influential discussion of sodomy as a "sinne against kynde" in *Getting Medieval: Sexuality and Communities, Pre- and Postmodern* (Durham, N.C.: Duke University Press, 1999), 6.

19 For more on the legal relationships between sodomy, rape, and bestiality, see Boehrer, *Shakespeare among the Animals,* 49; Smith, *Homosexual Desire in Shakespeare's England,* 49–53; and Alan Stewart, *Close Readers: Humanism and Sodomy in Early Modern England* (Princeton, N.J.: Princeton University Press, 1997), xxii.

20 Valerie Traub, *The Renaissance of Lesbianism in Early Modern England* (Cambridge: Cambridge University Press, 2002), 164.

21 Ibid., 165.

22 I deliberately invoke the phrase deployed by Bruce Smith in his influential reading of Marlowe's *Edward II* to connect the politics of class in *The Comedy of Errors* with its erotic configurations. See Smith, *Homosexual Desire in Shakespeare's England,* 189–224, esp. 193.

23 All quotations from the poem come from John Donne, *The Satires, Epigrams, and Verse Letters,* ed. Wesley Milgate (Oxford: Clarendon Press, 1967).

24 Smith, *Homosexual Desire in Shakespeare's England,* 174.

25 Donne's poem emphasizes human consumption of fish: "to kill them is an occupation / And laws make fasts and lents for their destruction" (289–90). His emphasis on the "occupation" of fishing adds an additional layer of complexity to his joke about fish and rape. Fish that were caught but not yet consumed were stocked in "stews," which was also a common term for brothels in the period.

26 Dowsabell's voluminous size renders her monstrous. I argue that such size is not unlike the physical prowess of other monstrously large bodies: of giants. In his analysis of giants in medieval romance, Jeffrey Jerome Cohen argues that the giant is key to understanding masculinity: "the giant, that foundational monster who produces the masculine corpus, is also its guarantee of failure, of its inability to vanquish forever the intimate stranger at its heart." Cohen, *Of Giants: Sex, Monsters, and the Middle Ages* (Minneapolis: University of Minnesota Press, 1999), xx. Cohen argues that the giant's body is queerly linked to chivalric masculinity because both are myths: one body is assumed to be above the realm of desire, and the other is saturated by it. Not surprisingly, rape is central to understanding the power of gigantic bodies in medieval romance. Although usually gendered masculine, the giant is linked to women's bodies through its potential for physical power over them. Cohen concludes, "Incubi, raped women and giants form the vertices of a monstrous family triangle with a long and unholy history" (123). Whereas such myths are culturally specific, I invoke Cohen's engagement with monstrous, gigantic bodies to suggest how Dowsabell's body might equally unhinge early modern masculinity through her physical ability to master Dromio.

27 Donne's use of the term *rapine* connotes violent seizure but not penetration. The *Oxford English Dictionary* defines the term as "the act or practice of seizing and taking away by force the property of others; plunder,

pillage, robbery." However, it also connotes bestial embodiment or "beasts of prey."

28 Jeffrey Jerome Cohen, "The Inhuman Circuit," in *Thinking the Limits of the Body,* ed. Jeffrey Jerome Cohen and Gail Weiss (Albany: State University of New York Press, 2003), 167–86, 179–80.

9

The Seduction of Milton's Lady: Rape, Psychoanalysis, and the Erotics of Consumption in *Comus*

WILL STOCKTON

Does the Lady in Milton's *Comus* fantasize about being raped? A qualified yet nonetheless affirmative answer to this question may help resolve the heated debate about the masque that took place between John Leonard and William Kerrigan in the early 1990s; but one would likely never know from reading most criticism on *Comus*, before or after, that the Lady is doing anything of the sort. The debate began when Leonard objected to Kerrigan's Freudian interpretation of the Lady's resistance to Comus as a case in which meaning "exude[s] its own adversary" or where "no" means "yes."[1] This interpretation had allowed Kerrigan, in the opening chapter of *The Sacred Complex*, to explain why the Lady remains glued to the throne by those mysterious "gumms of glutenous heat" (917) after the brothers drive Comus away: "because her virtue is bound to a repressed wish" for sex.[2] In his response, Leonard argued that the text simply "lends no support" to any such deduction of the Lady's culpability.[3] He charged Kerrigan with mistaking the threat of rape for an attractive come-on and, more specifically, with obscuring the reality of the Lady's sexual assault behind typical, and typically misguided, psychoanalytic musings on the repressed desires of women. I disagree with Leonard's contention that *Comus* does not support Kerrigan's argument that the Lady's virtue depends on her desire's repression. With respect to the question of whether Comus is a rapist, however, Kerrigan is himself at pains to avoid an argument for which I also want to offer psychoanalytic support: that Comus figures the threat of rape as a simultaneous figuration of the Lady's desire.

The debate between Kerrigan and Leonard turns on the hermeneutic problem discussed in the introduction to this volume, the problem that Mario DiGangi calls "the indeterminacy of 'the sexual.'" I quote DiGangi again: "we cannot always be entirely confident that we know which bodily acts count as 'sexual.' When is kissing an expression of sexual desire, or affection, or of a social bond? Under what circumstances might our ability to even distinguish these realms be frustrated?"[4] Kerrigan and Leonard's debate raises similar questions about Milton's masque. What justifies counting the Lady's no and those gums as sexual expressions? What theoretical and methodological circumstances facilitate and frustrate our ability to distinguish between sexual temptation and rape? Kerrigan's approach to sexuality in the masque draws on the Oedipal narrative of maturation and the equally psychoanalytic concept of the unconscious. Leonard, by contrast, takes the Lady at her word, arguing that Kerrigan's "analysis" confuses what is otherwise clear: that the Lady is not tempted by Comus but threatened with rape and driven to defend sexual discipline against the sophistry of her attacker. The disagreement here concerns not only the ability of psychoanalysis to offer insight into a prepsychoanalytic text but also competing charges brought against Comus himself. Leonard hears in the masque an echo of the case of Margery Evans, a young girl who, in 1631, claimed she was raped when traveling at night on the Welsh border. (The Earl of Bridgewater, for whom Milton wrote the masque, was involved in the ensuing legal controversy.[5]) Kerrigan rejects the Evans echo, however, maintaining that "if we must get legalistic here, Comus is guilty of some variant of kidnapping."[6] The claim that the Lady fantasizes about being raped begins to emerge when one allows both that Kerrigan is right that the Lady is sexually tempted, although he cedes too quickly to a legalistic reading of Comus's crime, and that Leonard is right that the Lady is, or is potentially, a rape victim, although he too quickly writes off the symptoms of the Lady's desire for this assault.

Considering the ease with which the concept of a rape fantasy may be, and often has been, misogynistically deployed, the political stakes of reading *Comus* as the Lady's rape fantasy are quite high. By way of qualifying this concept, I will therefore state at the outset that this particular reading does not require dematerializing all representations of rape, translating them into the relatively "safe" realm of fantasy, where they are ensconced from the violent interactions of real bodies. In terms of Milton's own literary project, it means allowing Milton's participation in what Melissa E. Sanchez has recently demonstrated is the effort of many Renaissance writers, including Milton's "teacher" Spenser, to think the politics of resistance through female masochism and, in doing so, to blur the line between rape and seduction.[7] More broadly, it means allowing that some people do fantasize about being raped, and some live out these fantasies in scenes of BDSM play. Since the porn wars of the late 1970s and early 1980s, feminist scholars, including Alice Echols, Gayle Rubin, and Pat Califia, have been arguing that the sadomasochistic desires of women are misrecognized, pathologized, and silenced by the ongoing valorization of sexually "innocent" and "pure" women.[8] I wager that one could follow this trail of sex-positive feminist scholarship and read the masque as just such a BDSM scene without invoking psychoanalysis at all. But remaining within the framework of the debate between Kerrigan and Leonard that speaks precisely to this volume's interest in the indeterminacy of sex, I want to press particularly on the psychoanalytic implications of the term *fantasy.* If psychoanalysis can be of any more help in making sense of what happens in *Comus*—and of simultaneous help gaining some purchase on the concept of a rape fantasy—its first analytical move must be to embrace the masque's own disinterest in real crimes subject to legal interdiction as an indication that the masque itself operates in the space of fantasy. As defined by Jean Laplanche and Jean-Bertrand Pontalis, fantasy is an "imaginary scene in which the subject is a protagonist, representing the fulfillment of a wish . . . in a manner that is distorted . . . by defensive processes."[9] In the analysis that follows, Milton's masque stages an imaginary scene, or a sequence of them, in which the Lady defends herself against the very assault for which she wishes.

Cautious at the same time of the suspicion that my recourse to this tool of psychoanalysis offers only another way to blame the victim, I hasten to add that *all* subjects fantasize. Psychoanalytically speaking, fantasy is the means by which subjects organize their desires; fantasies are not pathological *tout court*. As we will see, to make the claim that the Lady has a rape fantasy is to make a claim that the early Freud found potentially, if uncomfortably, universalizable. One dismissal of this claim will likely hitch itself to the familiar charge of psychoanalysis's own universalism and, in early modern contexts, anachronism. Yet by utilizing psychoanalysis as a narrative and a methodology with a history, rather than as a master hermeneutic whose application yields the factual truth of what happens in *Comus,* I hope to prevent this dismissal by expanding the recognition of sex as a term whose presence in *Comus* is itself a proleptic critical construction. If anachronisms risk obscuring different historical understandings of desire, the body, and relationality, a staunch critical opposition to anachronism, which renders impossible any discussion of sex acts and sexuality in the Renaissance, also obscures the complicated relationship between past and present erotic epistemologies better apprehended in terms of resurgence, perpetuation, and especially translation: the movement *(translatio)* of signifiers from one language or code to another. Developing the psychoanalytic, and particularly Laplanchian, contention that the meaning of sex is not temporally constrained but is itself the object of ongoing translation, I have argued elsewhere that a psychoanalytically influenced method of historicizing sexuality recognizes both the historical, discursive conditions that allow sex to signify and sex's movement outside these conditions.[10] Following Laplanche, I also have argued that psychoanalysis is best practiced as an antihermeneutic, oriented not around the work of fact finding but around translation and detranslation.[11] In this chapter, I pursue these arguments further by tracing an affinity between the story *Comus* tells about sex and the story that Freud tells about the same in his early theory about fantasies of seduction. Both stories, I contend, are stories about the enigma of sex itself, about sex's resistance to decisive and singular translation.

In the Freudian seduction narrative that I outline more fully later, the seduced remembers the seduction, and fantasizes about it, as both a sexual temptation and a sexual assault. When I speak about Miltonic sex, I am therefore referring, in my translation, to any act that compromises the virtue that the Lady asserts within and against this memory: chastity. (The slippage between chastity and virginity will be part of my concern here.) That chastity is at stake in *Comus* is a point that hardly needs any argument. More arguable, like the significance of the Lady's no or whether the Lady's chastity is ever actually compromised, is the sexual status of drinking from Comus's cup, the act around which I will argue the Lady's rape fantasy pivots. Drinking provides, in Gordon Williams's words, a "copulation metaphor" common in Renaissance texts.[12] Collapsing the distinction between vehicle and tenor, however, my claim, stated quite simply, is that drinking from the cup *is* sex. I contribute this claim to the larger critical conversation about the Miltonic ethics of consumption, but I also make it in accordance with Jean Laplanche's own efforts to think sex through seduction theory as something other than genital intercourse.[13] Laplanche's version of seduction theory pushes sex, the presumptive goal of seduction, into the realm of the enigmatic, a realm where distinguishing sex from other signifiers, especially those pertaining to the satisfaction of other biological needs, becomes difficult, if not impossible. From a Laplanchian perspective, making this distinction is also beside the point. The point is rather that sex escapes semiotic constraints by attaching itself to other signifiers—by becoming other signifiers. The other biological need at issue in *Comus* is the need for sustenance, and so I will first develop the claim that the relationship between sex and drinking in Milton's masque is not one of difference—that in the larger context of the masque's allegory of chaste virtue, Comus is not speaking otherwise when he asks the Lady to drink from his cup. Rather, the concept of chastity includes and becomes synonymous with temperance as well as with sobriety, both virtues of moderate consumption and of bodily continence. The homology between these virtues sexualizes the act of consumption, and the Miltonic concept of chastity thereby evokes Freud's concept of the presexual self as one who may never have fed.

Spenserian Sex

Comus has struck so many critics as Spenserian, rather than, or as well as, psychoanalytic, that before addressing seduction theory, it seems worth looking, albeit selectively and briefly, at *The Faerie Queene* as a source for the masque's erotics of consumption. This look will more firmly establish Spenser's epic as a code for translating Milton's representation of sex, but it will also help to establish, within the purview of this chapter, a network of early modern cultural discourses about sex—religious, aesthetic, and physiological, primarily—that psychoanalysis inherits, even as it divests itself of these earlier discourses' investments in moral counsel. Focusing this look is the relationship between two of the organizing virtues of Spenser's epic: temperance and chastity. In a searching essay that makes a Foucauldian case for *Comus* as a masque about the emergence of sexuality as a "political statement and instrument of control," Christopher Kendrick contends that Milton places chastity at the center his masque, "eclipsing its synecdochic status in relation to the other virtues" in *The Faerie Queene*.[14] Considering this contention alongside Debora Shuger's efforts to establish an intertextual connection between the enigmatic "gumms of glutenous heat" and Red Crosse's erotic dream about Una, I will argue that both Spenser's epic and Milton's masque distance sex from the genitals, suffusing all bodily appetites with sexual and moral significance.

Shuger's adjudication of this significance is instructive for its reduction of the sexual to genital excitation and ejaculation. Classifying Red Crosse's "dreame of loves and lustfull play" (1.1.47.4) as a wet dream, Shuger brings into sharp focus the tension between the will and flesh central to Red Crosse's spiritual journey throughout book 1.[15] The knight's nocturnal emission indexes his fallenness, while the "gumms of glutenous heat," which Shuger reads as the Lady's ejaculate, suggest that Milton, contra Spenser, "affirms the Catholic (and Classical) distinction between sinful consent and . . . morally insignificant arousals."[16] Notwithstanding the theological sense Shuger makes of Spenser's and Milton's allegories by reading the dream and the gums as she does, both readings resolve enigmas otherwise preserved by the recognition that threats to chastity include but exceed genital activity. In another episode from book 1, for example, Red Crosse drinks from the "dull and slow" (1.7.5.8) waters of Diana's exhausted nymph, then "Pour[s] out in loosnesse on the grassy grownd, / Both carelesse of his health, and of his fame" (1.7.7.2–3). Although one might fairly say that Red Crosse, having drunk from the enchanted waters, has sex with Duessa, the image of his self-spillage need not translate into any single act. Genital intercourse, (mutual) masturbation, and fellatio are all possibilities here. So is vomiting—a form of sexual "expression" that most modern sensibilities relegate to the category of extreme, and extremely rare, perversion.[17] (Humoral theory facilitates a homology between all these forms of purgation.) Self-spillage also need not strictly equate with the expression of anything liquid from the body: though such an interpretation suffers, I admit, for its banality, A. C. Hamilton's gloss on "Pourd out" as the Latin *effusus* (to spread or stretch out) suggests that the intoxicated Red Crosse simply spreads himself out on the ground.[18]

Whatever Red Crosse does with Duessa, and whatever the Lady does in the chair, Spenser and Milton at the very least both recognize sequential connections between sins of the flesh. In *On Christian Doctrine,* Milton makes temperance into a kind of moral overseer when he defines it as "the virtue which regulates our appetite for the pleasures of the flesh."[19] This definition draws on an exceedingly long tradition of classical, Jewish, and Christian ways of thinking about the causal relationship between the passions. For example, Philo of Alexandria rebukes "experts in dainty feeding, wine-bibbing and the other pleasures of the belly and the parts below it." When "sated," these people "reach such a pitch of wantonness, the natural offspring of satiety, that losing their senses they conceive a frantic passion, no longer for human beings male or female, but even for brute beasts."[20] Intemperance leads to licentiousness, even to bestiality, a consequence Milton implies in the transformation of those who drink from Comus's cup into "the inglorious likenes of a beast" (528). Gender often inflects this sequential connection between sins against temperance and chastity, too. Juan Louis Vives makes the connection throughout his *Education of a Christian Woman,* at one point citing Eve's expulsion from the Garden of Eden when he prescribes "light, plain, and not highly seasoned" nourishment lest young women seek "delicacies . . . outside the home . . . to the detriment of their chastity."[21] The Puritan preacher William Whately, a contemporary of the early Milton, instructs men preparing to marry that "temperance in diet must be called in, to the aide of chastitie of body[.]" "Fulnesse of bread," he warns, "will make a man a Sodomite, that is, tenne times worse than a beast: but moderation will keepe the body undefiled."[22] Milton follows Spenser's lead, however, in similarly conceiving sequential threats to men's and women's chastity. In *Paradise Lost,* the "false Fruit" (9.1011) that Adam and Eve eat enflames their "Carnal desire" (9.1013) alike. Likewise, Comus does not seem to sexually discriminate among those he entices to drink.[23]

If Red Crosse's episode of self-spillage offers paradigmatic evidence of this sequential relationship between intemperate and unchaste sins, Spenser nonetheless moves elsewhere to consolidate them. He does so without reducing chastity to genital discipline. The most obvious and, for *Comus,* relevant examples of this consolidation take place in the Bower of Bliss, a place of equally unchaste and intemperate appetite. There the Circean enchantress Acrasia hangs over her captive, slumbering lover, "suck[ing] his spright" through his "humid eyes" (2.12.73.7). This line famously sets multiple meanings of "spright" in play, as Acrasia ingests her lover's spirit or soul and his semen. Her act of ocular fellatio illustrates the synesthetic nature of Spenserian eroticism—the confluence not simply of the senses but of the erogenous zones as well. Stanza 78's description of Acrasia's allure also renders the eyes and the mouth as portals of consumption:

> Her snowy brest was bare to readie spoyle
> Of hungry eies, which n'ote therewith be fild,
> And yet through languour of her late sweet toyle,
> Few drops, more cleare then Nectar, forth distild,
> That like pure Orient perles adowne it trild,
> And her faire eyes sweet smyling in delight,
> Moystened their fieire beames, with which she thrild
> Fraile hearts, yet quenched not[.] (2.12.78.1–8)

As a seductress, Acrasia's sexuality is not genital. Her seduction works through the eyes, the mouth, the breast, the heart, and even the pores of her skin: her breasts attract "hungry eies"; her own eyes, both consuming and emitting, "smile"; and her sweat, "distild" like liquor, moistens these eyes from which "fraile hearts" drink but are never satisfied. The genitals are entirely absent in this interplay of erogenous zones—an interplay that suggests that sex with Acrasia constitutes a simultaneous betrayal of the virtues of chastity and temperance.

Spenser more than once implies the consolidation of these virtues in scenes featuring cup-bearing women. When Guyon approaches the Bower of Bliss, he meets Excess, a "comely dame . . . but fowle disordered" (2.12.55.7–8). She offers Guyon a cup of hand-pressed wine, but he refuses it, presumably because he, like Milton's Lady, recognizes it as more than just a drink. Similarly, in canto 8 of book 1, when Duessa enters the battle between Arthur and Orgoglio on the back of her seven-headed beast, she bears a cup "replete with magick artes" (1.8.14.2). This cup anticipates the cup of Comus, which is filled with a "pleasing poison" that is "mixt" with "many murmurs" (526). Both cups may bear Hamilton's gloss of the former as a reference to the cup of the Whore of Babylon in the book of Revelation: the cup is "ful of abominations, and filthines of her fornication," and "all nations have dronken of the wine of the wrath of her fornication" (Rev. 17:4, 18:3, Geneva Bible). For many English Protestants, the sin of idolatry for which the Whore of Babylon was a figure went by the name of "spiritual fornication."[24] To drink from her cup was to partake of a perverse communion that indexed nothing so singular as genital intercourse in its simultaneous betrayal of temperance and chastity.

When William Kerrigan remarks that Comus offers the Lady "a potion, which symbolizes (among other things) her sexual compliance," his parenthetical potentially severs temperance from chastity while still allowing their joint violation in one act. Yet I am suggesting that Milton pursues a line of Spenserian thinking in *Comus* that renders intemperate consumption itself an act of "sexual compliance."[25] The masque evinces a mutual inclusiveness among the virtues that Milton actually expresses quite straightforwardly when describing temperance in *On Christian Doctrine*: "Temperance includes sobriety and chastity."[26] So, too, logically, chastity includes both sobriety and temperance, and sobriety includes both temperance and chastity. If one allows, for the moment, the additional identity of chastity and virginity, Comus illustrates this mutual inclusiveness of the virtues most concisely when he steers his conversation with the Lady in a Petrarchan direction. Trying to persuade her to drink, Comus plays on the further symmetry of carnal and economic appetites, tying his argument for the liberal expenditure of Mother Nature's provisions to a critique of the Lady's hoarding of her sexuality:

> List Lady be not coy, and be not cosen'd
> With that same vaunted name Virginity,
> Beauty is natures coyn, must not be hoorded,
> But must be currant[.] (737–40)

To drink from the cup is to consume Mother Nature's provisions is to put one's sexuality into circulation. As the term I am using for the act that compromises chastity, sex equals intemperate consumption—an equation the Lady does not question when she defends Nature as one who "Means her provision onely to the good / That live according to her sober laws, / And holy dictate of spare Temperance" (762–67). The Lady's argument about distribution and use qualifies as an argument about temperance and sobriety ("sober laws") as well as chastity. So implicit is this confluence of the virtues, so much do the Lady and Comus take it for granted, that neither Comus nor the Lady has hitherto said the word "chastity." In fact, the Lady does not mount her defense of the "sun-clad power of Chastity" (782) in either the Bridgewater or Trinity manuscripts. The defense first appears in the 1637 edition, and only after two sharp rhetorical questions: "Shall I go on? / Or Have I said enough?" (779–80). These questions imply that she has been talking about chastity all along.

Realizing the consequences for sex of the Spenserian connection between the virtues may also aid in addressing the question of whether Comus is a rapist. The question itself turns on the legal definition of rape as forced genital penetration.[27] This definition does not do justice, however, to the complicated relationship of rape with abduction (and thus with ideas of theft and property) or to the Spenserian erotics that play with this relationship. The likely Spenserian analogue for the Lady's assault in *Comus* is, of course, Busirane's kidnapping and torture of Amoret. Spenser never specifies that Busirane forces, or intends to force, Amoret to have genital intercourse with him, but most critics appropriately use the word *rape* to describe his crime nonetheless: he conveys (from the Latin *raptus*) her away from the wedding masque; he imprisons her in his castle decorated with tapestries depicting, among other scenes, Jove's sex crimes; and he subjects her to sadistic but nongenital torture by tying her to a post and cutting open her breast. Milton changes the relation between rapist and victim in several ways, not least by giving the Lady the ability to argue with her captor. But Comus's objective, like Busirane's, is not in any obvious way genital. Comus wants the Lady to drink, and he is doing everything in his power to force her to do so: he sits her down, paralyzes her, and makes her listen to his arguments. The obstacle he faces is the need for consent, but this obstacle makes him no less a rapist. Comus has raped her insofar as he has conveyed her to his lair, and in trying to get her to drink, he is attempting to rape her in another sense as well: to *enrapture* her senses, to transport her with ecstasy.

Exploring Milton's debt to Spenser thus helps translate the relationship between chastity, temperance, and sobriety in Milton's masque about rape. The logic of the virtues' mutual inclusiveness works against the concepts of difference to which many critics of the masque appeal when trying to parse its representation of sex. Taking an intoxicating drink from the cup is not a "symbol" for "sexual compliance," as Kerrigan writes, nor is it "the metaphorical end of this romance seduction," as Kendrick maintains in his argument for the masque's elevation of chastity to the status of master virtue.[28] (Temperance may just as well be this virtue.) It is not a prelude to sex either, as Leonard implies when he derides Kendrick's appeal to metaphor.[29] The concepts of symbol and metaphor assume that sex equals a genital intercourse about which the masque can only speak otherwise in the language of allegory, while the concept of prelude assumes that the masque can only anticipate, but not actually represent, sex. A less restricted definition of sex may instead allow one to realize more fully the consequences of the Spenserian conflation of temperance, sobriety, and chastity by reading the act of drinking from Comus's cup as a sex act. Pursuing the conflation still further, one may also read intemperate financial expenditures and resource consumptions as sex acts—a reading that could also pursue Milton's own critique of masque culture itself. With respect to the problem of the indeterminacy of the sexual, *Comus* strains our critical ability to cordon off sex into a single act and the sexual into a discrete descriptive. At the same time, the masque does not suggest that the words *sex* and *sexual* are therefore impotent. Injected into the historical circuits of disciplinary and representational thinking that structure the masque, the terms may instead outline currents within those circuits, while reminding us of the terms' present conceptual mobility.

The First Deceit

Tracking this mobility, I now turn to psychoanalysis and to stories about how sex attaches to the alimentary in the first place. How, or by what logic, does drinking become sex and temperance become chastity? Several answers to this question immediately suggest themselves, and I will briefly identify two to which I have already alluded. First, drinking becomes a sexual act within the context of pre- and early modern physiology, where ingestion and digestion are considered central to the operation and governance of other passions. Second, and as an extension of the first, this logic is scriptural: the writers of the Bible repeatedly eroticize consumption, as do Jewish and Christian theologians accordingly.[30] Following Jean Laplanche, the answer to this question that I want to pursue here is less immediately physiological or scriptural than psychoanalytic, although I would argue that these answers are interrelated. By associating sex with corporeal necessities that include but exceed procreation through genital intercourse, psychoanalysis renarrativizes earlier ways of thinking about the erotics of consumption. In this section, I will discuss the ways in which the story in Milton's masque resonates with the Freudian narrative of seduction. This discussion aims to reconcile Kerrigan's reading of *Comus* as a masque about sexual temptation with Leonard's claim that it figures sexual assault, for seduction theory tells a story about sex in which temptation and assault overwrite or include each other in the space of fantasy.

As familiar as seduction theory might be from trauma theory, which derives from psychoanalytic thinking about the relationship between memory and narrative, it nonetheless warrants a brief evolutionary history, if only to pinpoint Jean Laplanche's relevant innovation. In *Life and Death in Psychoanalysis,* a book that salvages seduction theory from the dustbin of discarded Freudian theories, Laplanche charts this evolution from Freud's earliest work on the relationship between sexual trauma and memory in hysterics.[31] Freud's "discovery" that recovered memories were themselves symptomatic translations of an earlier trauma of molestation led him to posit that as children, his patients were initially incapable of understanding the meaning of these assaults. His patients' repression of what they did not understand constituted the origin of both their sexuality and their hysterical symptoms, and during analysis, the repressed assault surfaced as recovered memories. Freud's problem was that each recovered memory led to still more recoveries. Laplanche explains, "Seduction was . . . a common scenario, found over and over in a succession of scenes whose sequence Freud would enthusiastically retrace in tireless pursuit, beyond every 'later' scene, of an earlier and more 'traumatic' analogous event."[32] The original trauma kept slipping out of analytical reach. Freud officially abandoned seduction theory in the late 1890s, in part because it transformed analysis into something like a wild goose chase. In a 1897 letter to Wilhelm Fliess that Laplanche cites as evidence for this official abandonment, Freud complains of the impossibility of distinguishing "truth and emotionally-charged fiction," as there is "no 'indication of reality' in the unconscious." Given the "unexpected frequency of hysteria," Freud also doubts that fathers (for "in every case ... blame was laid on perverse acts by the father") so frequently molest their children.[33] With the publication of *Three Essays on the Theory of Sexuality* in 1905, Freud replaced seduction theory as an account of sexuality's origins with an account of children's maturation through set developmental stages. The Oedipus complex then became Freud's increasingly common way of accounting for the presence of fathers in recovered memories.

Despite this official abandonment, Laplanche points out that seduction theory nonetheless persists in Freud's work. No longer intentional and physically violent molestation, seduction comes to constitute "the intrusion into the universe of the child of certain meanings of the adult world which is [*sic*] conveyed by the most ordinary and innocent of acts."[34] This intrusion of what Laplanche elsewhere calls the "enigmatic signifier" continues to mark the advent of sexuality in many Freudian subjects.[35] In *Three Essays,* for instance, Freud attributes the sexual awakening of an infant to a mother who "regards him with feelings that are derived from her own sexual life; she strokes him, kisses him, rocks him and quite clearly treats him as a substitute for a complete sexual object"—a treatment the child is not yet ready to understand.[36] Freud's famous analysis of the Wolfman also turns on a recovered, primal scene of seduction, whatever its truth status, in which the patient, as an infant, witnesses his parents having sex, mistakes their pleasure for violence, and subsequently translates that enigmatic spectacle into a series of other dreams and memories both threatening and erotic.[37] For Laplanche, the theory that sexuality originates in such moments of intrusion on newly constituting and vulnerable egos explains why experiences of desire and violation are so frequently inextricable within fantasy: because seduction experiences are always undergoing translation, a repeated rendering-into-sense, as the subject matures in his or her desire. Under the pressure to repress, this desire for the father, the mother, or the Other can itself translate the most "innocent" and "ordinary" of seductions into more violent scenes that never actually happened.[38]

A psychoanalytic translation of Milton's *Comus* (for according to Laplanche, the psychoanalytic method is itself one of translation and detranslation) may find in seduction theory not only a way of reckoning with the masque's entanglement of temptation and assault but also a way of analyzing the alimentary form this temptation and assault takes. Elsewhere in *Life and Death in Psychoanalysis,* Laplanche argues that for the Freud of the *Three Essays,* sexuality develops in attachment to the operations of the "order of life" or the "vital order." *Three Essays* treats sexual excitation as the excess of pleasure over the gratification of biological needs. The surplus pleasures that the child first derives from meeting these needs accounts for the later sexualization, after a period of latency, of acts like eating, drinking, and defecating. Hardly restricted to the genitals, sexuality "leans on," or is "propped up" by, these otherwise nonsexual operations of the vital order.[39] The erotogenic zones function as the points of contact and exchange in this support structure and so enable seduction: "these zones focalize parental fantasies and above all maternal fantasies, so that we may say, in what is barely a metaphor, that they are the points through which is introduced into the child that alien internal entity which is, properly speaking, the sexual excitation."[40] The parental dimensions of this scenario are easily legible in Oedipal readings of Milton's masque that posit the wand-wielding Comus as a phallic father figure—and above all, with John Rumrich's revisionary analysis of the masque's preoccupation with maternal power.[41] Yet more important to my argument than the specifically parental dimensions of seduction is the connection between seduction and the gratification of biological need—a connection that sets the scene for a masque whose villain seduces his victims into quenching their thirst.

What Comus's victims do not necessarily understand is that they are being offered far more than something to drink. According to the Attendant Spirit,

> . . . to every thirsty wanderer,
> By sly enticement [Comus] gives his banefull cup,
> With many murmurs mixt, whose pleasing poison
> The visage quite transforms of him that drinks,
> And the inglorious likenes of a beast
> Fixes instead, unmoulding reasons mintage
> Character'd in the face[.] (524–30)

Comus's victims are "[d]efac't," if not also "deflourd," as Adam says of Eve in *Paradise Lost* after she, too, commits an act of illicit consumption (9.901). Comus's "many murmurs" prove ruinous to human *being*—shattering the self, in Leo Bersani's influential Laplanchian formulation, with a sensory overload, an incomprehensible mixture of sound, taste, and intent.[42] By describing this seduction as "sly enticement," the Attendant Spirit implies that Comus's victims know not what they do. But when she sits in their position, the Lady is not susceptible to the same enticements. She is different from these other naive wood-wanderers.

How different is a question that certain curiosities about the Lady's rape nonetheless press. First, the Lady insists on a sharp distinction between her infantilized body and her discerning intellect. This distinction suggests that the only self that might shatter is entirely corporeal, without mind. In other words, the Lady's protest that her mind remains free redraws the boundaries of the vulnerable self to exclude her mind after her body has been captivated:

> Thou canst not touch the freedom of my minde
> With all thy charms, although this corporal rinde
> Thou haste immanacl'd, while Heav'n sees good. (663–65)

The Lady's debasement of her body as a "corporal rinde" informs William Shullenberger's suggestion that her rhetorical contest with Comus reenacts with a difference the Lacanian entry into the Symbolic order of language. The Lady wields language, the Lacanian tool of castration, against her assailant, and in doing so, she denies any limit on the freedom of her will: she acts as if the world were "at her command, or at the command of the temperance and chastity to which she has committed herself."[43] The Lady's re-entry into the Symbolic at what Shullenberger calls "a higher level of integration," as the relative master of language rather than its victim, accordingly differentiates her from the Lacanian subject who suffers from a sense of crippling self-division. The disembodied Lady voices a "radiant and resonant fullness" of self grounded in the doctrines of virtue.[44] Translating this Lacanian analysis into Laplanchian terms, I would add that, as Comus's captive, the paralyzed Lady cannot simply be read here as a seduced child. She is a theologically and rhetorically adept young adult—one who has already experienced the shattering of the ego that results from entrance into the Symbolic but who reenacts this experience to consolidate the ego over and above her violated body. Her situation thus reproduces the moment of entry into the Symbolic according to the logic of fantasy: her captivity allows her to reexperience a seduction with comparatively superior cognitive tools that she can use to discern intentions that previously were more than what they seemed.

The Lady is not being seduced here for the first time, after all. Comus does seduce the Lady during their initial encounter in the woods, where she is not a theologically and rhetorically adept young adult but rather an anxious and vulnerable girl with the inability to distinguish between a "gentle Shepherd" (271) and the son of Circe and Bacchus. In this earlier scene, the Lady believes that this "Shepherd" is a shepherd, that he knows where her brothers are, that he will lead her to them the next morning, and that he will provide her with safe lodging for the night. She believes everything he says: "Shepherd I take thy word, / And trust thy honest offer'd courtesie" (321–22). She later charges Comus with being a "foul deceiver" (696) who "betrai'd my credulous innocence / With visor'd falshood, and base forgery" (697–98)—an accusation that may exonerate her from any charge of illicit desire. (When Satan, in *Paradise Lost,* disguises himself as a young cherub to approach Uriel, the narrator states that "neither Man or Angel can discern / Hypocrisie" [3.682–83].) Yet the Lady's later powers of discernment contrast strongly with her earlier naïveté, and the contrast raises the question of whether the Lady has translated her desire for seduction into a fantasy of seduction, much as Freud argued some of his patients translated "their own desire to seduce their father . . . into an actual scene of seduction by the father."[45]

Allowing this translation accounts for much of what seems so strange about the masque's plot, beginning with the "fact" that the Lady and her brothers are wandering alone through the woods in the middle of the night. We are not told why they are alone, nor is it clear why the Attendant Spirit attends on the brothers and not the Lady. What this translation renders legible is the status of the Lady's solo wood-wandering and her encounter with Comus as an iteration of her "later" rhetorical self-defense. Events plotted prior to the Lady's captivity are not external to the rape fantasy. Symptomatic as they are, they register instead what Laplanche calls "the first deceit"—a phrase that refers to "a kind of objective lie inscribed in the facts."[46] As Laplanche writes, it is "as though there existed in the facts themselves a kind of fundamental duplicity." This duplicity in turn renders difficult, if not impossible, the critical task of recognizing the actual nature of Comus's threat to the Lady. Before she asserts the freedom of her will over the captivity of her body, the Lady worries, as does the Younger Brother, that she needs a "guard . . . / To save her blossoms, and defend her fruit / From the rash hand of bold Incontinence" (394, 396–97). (The otherwise commonplace pun on "fruit" assumes added significance here: the Lady's virginity is food.) Her Elder Brother declares her "clad in compleat steel" (421), however, and impervious to all that would "dare to soyl her Virgin purity" (427). He later moderates this position when he states that "Vertue may be assail'd, but never hurt, / Surpriz'd by unjust force, but not enthrall'd" (589–90). Yet exactly which perspective on virtue's enthrallment, if any, the tableau of the paralyzed Lady confirms remains a principal concern in discussions of the masque as an allegory.

The Lady's consideration of her peril produces her own allegorical vision:

> And thou unblemish't form of Chastity,
> I see ye visibly, and now beleeve
> That he, the Supreme good, t'whom all things ill
> Are but as slavish officers of vengeance,
> Would send a glistring Guardian if need were
> To keep my life and honour unassail'd. (215–20)

This vision leads the Lady to believe that her life and honor will be protected, although unblemished chastity (is there another form?) lies beyond anyone's vision but her own; the figure she sees does not appear to anyone else. The ostensible singularity of the Lady as a paragon of chastity results here from her unique vision: only she can see chastity "for real." The Elder Brother likewise asserts his sister's singularity when he imagines guardian angels conveying inaudible messages to the chaste: "in cleer dream and solemn vision [the angels] / Tell her of things that no gross ear can hear" (457–58). As the navel of the dream (to translate the masque into yet another psychoanalytic idiom), the mysteries of chastity are insensible to "gross ear[s]," and Comus is not the only one so deprived. In their own confusion about chastity, the brothers are too, as are we, the audience, who struggle to discern the "sage / And serious doctrine of Virginity" (786–77) from our "vision" of the masque. *Comus*'s presentation of the Lady as the only one with unique access to this doctrine thereby provides another basis for translating this doctrine through both the psychoanalytic association of sexuality's advent with sensory overload and the logic of fantasy. According to the Elder Brother, being ushered into the sensory realm of sexuality, whether through seductively "unchaste looks, loose gestures, [or] foul talk" (464), infects the soul, "till she quite loose / The divine property of her first being" (468–69). The result, which one might call the fallen condition, is "gross" embodiment: a life in the flesh, in the orgasmic, self-shattering chaos of the sensory experience that would result from drinking from Comus's cup. This life makes one an unfit audience for virtue's mysteries.

To claim that *Comus* constitutes the Lady's rape fantasy is to claim that the Lady, despite her posture of singular exemption, lives this life as well. In Milton's Christian world, no one has complete access to virtue's mysteries; all have fallen. The Lady is therefore not uniquely culpable for her rape fantasy; quite the opposite, her rape fantasy serves the purpose of virtuous exercise. It teaches her, in the Attendant Spirit's closing words, "how to clime / Higher than the Spheary chime" (1020–21). At the same time, it indexes her universal falleneness, or what the Attendant Spirit calls, also at the end of the masque, her "Vertue feeble" (1022), which requires heaven's aid. Her fantasy serves to organize and facilitate her desire for the articulation of a mystery that will never become clear, as the Lady ironically reveals when she makes her most forceful distinction of chastity from the sensory realm of Comus's own experience:

> To him that dares
> Arm the profane tounge with contemptuous words
> Against the Sun-clad power of Chastity,
> Fain would I something say, yet to what end?
> Thou has nor Eare nor Soul to apprehend
> The sublime notion, and high mystery
> That must be utter'd to unfold the sage
> And serious doctrine of Virginity[.] (780–87)

However "Sun-Clad" chastity's power might be, its light is not the light of conceptual clarity. The Lady does not explain herself, and not only because her explanation of the virtue of temperance has made the explanation of the virtue of chastity superfluous. She does not explain herself because she is herself part of the "gross" world within which chastity is no longer identical with the self: hence her earlier allegorical vision of chastity as *something other than herself*. The "sage / And serious doctrine of Virginity" is opaque even to her.

Equally opaque, I further submit, is the relationship between chastity and virginity. Kerrigan reads the Lady's slippage from chastity to virginity as a sign of her complete renunciation of sexuality, while Leonard argues for more symmetry between the two terms denoting sexual discipline. Yet the otherwise discerning Lady's severance of chastity and virginity from fallen sense could also constitute a symptomatic moment of inarticulacy that redounds on the state of virtue she figures. As Kathryn Schwarz writes in her essay in this volume, "The virginal body is one of early modernity's great escape artists"; the ideological work of virginity and chastity depends on their mystification through the "loss" of bodies.[47] Even as the virtuous singularity of the Lady vanishes, then, the singularity of chastity as an enigmatic virtue reemerges here from its identity with temperance and sobriety. We, as the audience, can see temperance modeled, and hear its doctrine, but at this moment, chastity or virginity, or chastity and virginity together, nominate that virtue that transcends or precedes the sensory, which is also the sexual.

This reading of chastity as an enigmatic signifier emerges from Kerrigan's own resistance to taking the Lady at her word, framing her discursive collision with the limits of sense as an index of her fallenness into a world where language shapes and constrains experience. In this world, Comus's two seductions replay, precisely for the purpose of allowing the Lady to resist, entrance into the realm of sexual enjoyment in which she is already immersed. At the same time, this reading emerges from the mythic frame in which the Lady initially conjures Comus: the dually classical and psychoanalytic frame for understanding intersubjectivity, the myth of Echo and Narcissus. The lost Lady asks Echo for news of her brothers, "a gentle Pair / That likest thy Narcissus are" (236–37). Echo herself does not answer, but the Lady's plea does not fall on deaf ears. Comus enters as if he were Echo, the Lady's own voice returned to her with the answer she seeks. He enters, moreover, having been seduced by her song:

> Can any mortal mixture of Earths mold
> Breath such Divine inchanting ravishment?
> Sure something holy lodges in that brest,
> And with these raptures moves the vocal air
> To testifie his hidd'n residence[.] (244–48)

Comus's own "ravishment," his assault by the incomprehensible element in the Lady's "brest," begins here. When the Lady later charges Comus with an inability to comprehend the "sublime notion and high mystery" of "the sage / And serious doctrine of Virginity," Comus affirms the charge: "She fables not, I feel that I do fear / Her words set off by som superior power" (800–801). In both instances, Comus is seduced by the ineffable something in the Lady's speech—the "something holy" yet "hidden." We might therefore ask who seduces whom in the masque, as well as who seduces whom first.[48] But both questions become superfluous if we read Comus as the frame invites us to: as the seduced doppelgänger of the Lady—as her echo, her image, and her desire. To be sure, the Lady seems to have imperiled herself in the first place by letting her "ear," her "best guide" (171), lead her toward, not away from, "the sound / Of Riot and ill manag'd Merriment" (173), the "tumult of loud Mirth" (203): "This way the noise was, if mine ear be true" (170). The direction of her own wandering in the woods suggests a desire for seduction that produces Comus as her rapist.

As Stephen Orgel writes in an essay that reads *Comus* as a meditation on duplication and duplicity, "The Lady, singing to Echo, is literally singing to herself. . . . She is surrounded with—or creates for herself—a world of versions of the self, of solipsism."[49] Comus is one of these versions, as is the Attendant Spirit, who tells the two brothers that he heard both Comus's "barbarous dissonance" (550) and the Lady's Song. The Attendant Spirit is not similarly ravished in the sense of not understanding this song; rather, as the infallible listener but imperfect guide in this fantasy, he immediately recognizes the peril of the Lady's situation but is powerless to save her himself. The Attendant Spirit figures the Lady's retrospective recognition of her own deceit, while her "narcissistic" brothers are echoes of her anxieties. The Lady and her brothers all conjure the same fear: not simply a threat to chastity but the possibility that this threat is internal to the imperiled subject. The "thousand fantasies" (205) that "throng" into the Lady's "memory" (206)—and perhaps even more suggestively, the "beckoning shadows dire / And airy tongues, that syllable mens names" (206–7) into her ears—suggest that the Elder Brother is wrong to doubt that the darkness "Could stir the constant mood of her calm thoughts, / And put them into mis-becoming plight" (371–72). The masque externalizes the threat of sexual assault into the dark landscape and into Comus, and in doing so it figures both as projections of the Lady's desire.

Reading Backward

The "gumms of glutenous heat" (917)—or perhaps Milton meant *gluttonous* heat—are further symptomatic of seduction. Whatever they really are, which is only to say whatever Milton intends them to be, they have signified, for many readers, sexual pleasure. They can be read as ejaculate (Comus's, the Lady's, or a previous victim's), or they can be read as birdlime. Yet they are as hard to desexualize as the "airy tongues, that syllable mens names." Even if they are birdlime, Sabrina must still dissolve them with the touch of her "*chaste* palms moist and cold" (918; emphasis added). Furthermore, reading Milton's masque as a rape fantasy in which the primal scene recedes from sight, and each scene translates another, allows these gums to be sexually symptomatic precisely because they are enigmatic—because sex, as a signifier, often attaches to what can also be dismissed as nonsexual.

These polysemous gums have multiple possible referents whose hermeneutic excavation aims to make sense of them. As birdlime, they recall the Attendant Spirit's earlier mention of the "lime-twigs of [Comus's] spells" (646). Debora Shuger connects them to Red Crosse's dream about Una in *The Faerie Queene,* as well as to St. Augustine's description of his own nocturnal emission as birdlime.[50] James W. Broaddus argues for another Spenserian connection to the lovesick Britomart's "poisnous gore" (3.2.39.4): he maintains that both the gums and the gore are "female seed."[51] To interpret the gums through reference to a prior moment in the text or to a prior text like *The Faerie Queene* or *Confessions* is to work backward toward their meaning and thus to assume that the truth of their meaning lies behind them, in a previous signifier that, once brought to light, clarifies the present enigma and its theological significance.[52] (Both Shuger and Broaddus exonerate the Lady on the grounds that her ejaculation is an involuntary physical response.) Yet read as a seduction fantasy, *Comus* both invites and frustrates this particular mode of backward reading. Simply put, the fact that it takes so much intertextual archeology to make sense of these gums suggests that the gums profoundly resist interpretation as the most semiotically stubborn of the Lady's symptoms. The masque further frustrates another mode of backward reading through the brothers' bungling of the Lady's rescue. If the brothers had seized Comus's wand, then they could have freed the Lady with the "rod revers't / And *backward mutters* of dissevering power" (816–17; emphasis added), in much the same way that the apprehended Busirane frees Amoret by reversing his own spells. Free though the Lady might have been, however, this most literal of backward readings would not have clarified the theological significance of her paralysis, another (literally) stubborn symptom. The reverse incantation is not a hermeneutic but rather more muttering.

The brothers' bungled rescue attempt illustrates the difficulty of differentiating backward from forward within the narrative space of fantasy.

Sabrina's therapy then only further blurs the directional line, which is also to say cause and cure. Sabrina appears to be a double of the maiden Lady: she is a "Virgin pure" (826) who "retains / Her maid'n gentlenes" (842–43). Yet despite the according contrast between herself and Comus (she is an English, Spenserian river spirit, he a Greek, Shakespearean god), she doubles him as well. Like Comus, Sabrina appears in response to a song. The Attendant Spirit summons her to "Listen and save" (889), but his specific invocation of "the Songs of Sirens sweet" (878) also codes her "salvation" as vaguely threatening. (As Roy Flannagan notes, we are not sure if the Attendant Spirit is referring to the Sirens who seduce sailors to their death with song or the Sirens who orient the spheres of heaven.) Whereas Comus approaches the Lady with his poisoned cup, Sabrina approaches with "pretious viold liquors" (846), "Drops that from my fountain pure / I have kept of pretious cure" (911–12). She sprinkles this liquid on the Lady's breast, an act that Kerrigan reads as purifying "the earliest sources of food," and then she places three drops on the Lady's fingertip three times, as if to purify her sense of touch.[53] (Did the Lady take hold of Comus's cup?) Prior to laying her palms on the sticky seat, Sabrina also drops her liquor on the Lady's lips, purifying, it seems, her speech, which is "gross" by implication.[54] As an overlooked instance of female homoerotic activity, Sabrina's eroticized physic facilitates the salvation and restoration of chastity outside a phallic economy organized around Comus's wand.[55] At the same time, the mode of Sabrina's appearance marks her as a translation of Comus, himself a translation of the Lady, in a scene of seduction's ostensible undoing that again only translates the first deceit.

My thesis in this essay has been that Milton presents a rape fantasy in *Comus* that one can translate through the psychoanalytic account of seduction, which is itself an account of translation. My claim is not that Milton's masque shares a moral purpose with Freudian psychoanalysis but rather that Freud's thinking about sexuality, especially its relationship to biological need and fantasy, helps us as psychoanalytic critics, or at least as critics who read in the wake of psychoanalysis, make sense of the consonance of sex and dinking, desire and threat, in *Comus*. My claim is also that performing these translations is part of the work of historicizing sex and sexuality. Historicism as much as psychoanalysis is a mode of translation, a mode of reconstructive sense making. The connections I have worked to establish here between Freudian seduction theory and Milton's masque gesture toward a theological, physiological, and aesthetic history of psychoanalytic narratives about sex and sexuality. They also gesture toward the conclusion that, as the early Milton and the early Freud conceive it, the origin of an individual's sexuality lies outside a history that can only be constructed through the operations of memory and fantasy. The facts themselves will always lie outside analytical reach. They are, in a word, ahistorical.

Put yet another way, origins of sexuality will always lie outside the realm of interpretation or hermeneutics; they are accessible only through translation and never in themselves. Victoria Silver borrows a pertinent line from "Il Penseroso" when she writes that in *Comus*, "more is meant than meets the ear" (120).[56] I have tried to locate in this "more" a narrative precursor of Freudian seduction—a rape fantasy that renders sexual temptation indistinct from sexual assault. In doing so, I have also tried to demonstrate the consonance of a Miltonic and psychoanalytic perspective on sex as a category of acts that exceeds genital intercourse and attaches to the satisfaction of biological need. The scene in which Comus persuades the Lady to drink gestures backward to an earlier scene of seduction, but this scene in the woods seems to be the translation of another scene not staged in the masque. Because the past is always a retroactively constructed, provisional, and fragile scene, rather than something simply discovered in the hidden recesses of memory, Freud found himself chasing shadows in his search for the original seduction. Efforts to explain what happens in *Comus* involve a similar chase: as each scene opens up and folds back into others, all the scenes reveal themselves as translations of some lost scene inaccessible to analysis except in translated form. The lesson of *Comus* is that this loss is otherwise irrecoverable.

Notes

This essay has benefited enormously from thoughtful responses by Jim Bromley, Tom Luxon, Melissa Sanchez, and Valerie Traub.

1 William Kerrigan, *The Sacred Complex: On the Psychogenesis of* Paradise Lost (Cambridge, Mass.: Harvard University Press, 1983), 29.

2 Ibid., 48. Unless otherwise noted, all quotes from Milton's works are taken from *The Riverside Milton,* ed. Roy Flannagan (Boston: Houghton Mifflin, 1998).

3 John Leonard, "Saying 'No' to Freud: Milton's *A Mask* and Sexual Assault," *Milton Quarterly* 25 (1991): 130. For the continuation of the debate, see William Kerrigan, "The Politically Correct *Comus*: A Reply to John Leonard," *Milton Quarterly* 27, no. 4 (1993): 149–55, and John Leonard, "Good Things: A Response to William Kerrigan," *Milton Quarterly* 30, no. 3 (1996): 117–27.

4 Mario DiGangi, *The Homoerotics of Early Modern Drama* (Cambridge: Cambridge University Press, 1997), 11.

5 In arguing for the relevance of the case of Margery Evans, Leonard follows Leah Sinanoglou Marcus, "The Milieu of Milton's *Comus*: Judicial Reform at Ludlow and the Problem of Sexual Assault," *Criticism* 25 (1983): 293–327.

6 Kerrigan, "Politically Correct *Comus,*" 151.

7 Melissa E. Sanchez, *Erotic Subjects: The Sexuality of Politics in Early Modern English Literature* (Oxford: Oxford University Press, 2011). Milton calls "the sage and serious Poet Spencer" his "teacher" in *Aereopagitica* in *The Riverside Milton,* 1006.

8 See, e.g., Pat Califia, "Feminism and Sadomasochism," in *Feminism and Sexuality: A Reader,* ed. Stevi Jackson and Sue Scott, 230–37 (New York: Columbia University Press, 1996); Alice Echols, "The Taming of the Id: Feminist Sexual Politics, 1968–83," in *Pleasure and Danger: Exploring Female Sexuality,* ed. Carole Vance, 50–72 (New York: Routledge and Kegan Paul, 1984); and Gayle S. Rubin, *Deviations: A Gayle Rubin Reader* (Durham, N.C.: Duke University Press, 2011), esp. "The Leather Menace: Comments on Politics and S/M" (109–36) and "Misguided, Dangerous, and Wrong: An Analysis of Antipornography Politics" (254–75).

9 Jean Laplanche and Jean-Bertrand Pontalis, *The Language of Psychoanalysis,* trans. Donald Nicholson Smith (New York: W. W. Norton, 1973), 314.

10 Will Stockton, *Playing Dirty: Sexuality and Waste in Early Modern Comedy* (Minneapolis: University of Minnesota Press, 2011).

11 Jean Laplanche, "Psychoanalysis as Anti-Hermeneutics," *Radical Philosophy* 79 (1996): 7–12.

12 Gordon Williams, *A Dictionary of Sexual Language and Imagery in Shakespearean and Stuart Literature,* vol. 1 (London: Athlone Press, 1994), 415.

13 Kerrigan discusses the Miltonic ethics of eating throughout *The Sacred Complex.* See also Michael Schoenfeldt, "Temperance and Temptation: The Alimental Vision in *Paradise Lost,*" in *Bodies and Selves in Early Modern England: Physiology and Inwardness in Spenser, Shakespeare, Herbert, and Milton* (Cambridge: Cambridge University Press, 1999), 131–68.

14 Christopher Kendrick, "Milton and Sexuality: A Symptomatic Reading of *Comus,*" in *Re-membering Milton: Essays on the Texts and Traditions,* ed. Mary Nyquist and Margaret W. Ferguson (New York: Methuen, 1987), 43, 64.

15 All quotations from *The Faerie Queene* are taken from Edmund Spenser, *The Faerie Queene,* ed. A. C. Hamilton (New York: Longman, 1977).

16 Debora Shuger, "'Gums of Glutinous Heat' and the Stream of Consciousness: The Theology of Milton's *Maske,*" *Representations* 60 (1997): 7.

17 Erotic vomiting even comes as a shock to some queer theorists, as Lauren Berlant and Michael Warner register at the end of their famous essay "Sex in Public," *Critical Inquiry* 24, no. 2 (1998): 564–66.

18 Hamilton notes that Red Crosse, making "goodly court . . . to his Dame" (1.7.7.1), is "sexually expended and exhausted . . . like the water he drank." He further notes, "Water is traditionally associated with the lustful passions." Neither comment clarifies the act at issue, however. The image of Red Crosse pouring himself out on the ground might also conflate ejaculation with the exhaustion that follows ejaculation.

19 John Milton, *On Christian Doctrine,* trans. John Carey, in *Complete Prose Works of John Milton,* vol. 6, ed. Don M. Wolfe (New Haven, Conn.: Yale University Press, 1973), 724.

20 Philo, *On the Special Laws III,* in *Philo,* trans. F. H. Colson, vol. 7 (Cambridge, Mass.: Harvard University Press, 1966), 503.

21 Juan Louis Vives, *The Education of a Christian Woman: A Sixteenth-Century Manual,* ed. and trans. Charles Fantazzi (Chicago: University of Chicago Press, 2000), 87.

22 William Whately, *A Bride-Bush. or, a Direction for Married Persons* (London, 1623), Cv.

23 On the threat Comus poses to the brothers as well as to the Lady, see Ross Leasure, "Milton's Queer Choice: Comus at Castlehaven," *Milton*

Quarterly 36, no. 2 (2002): 63–86. There is a long tradition, too, in *Comus* criticism of reading the Lady as a figure for Milton himself, the male poet in the female body. Kerrigan and Shuger work within this tradition. See also Katherine Eisaman Maus, *Inwardness and Theater in the English Renaissance* (Chicago: University of Chicago Press, 1995), 198–209.

24 David Norbrook, *Poetry and Politics in the English Renaissance* (Oxford: Oxford University Press, 2002), 107.

25 For his part, Christopher Kendrick argues that "Comus . . . is against sexuality, though he may be somewhat colored by its pervading temper. . . . Comus seduces the Lady with *pleasures*, among which sex is only a salient one; his glass is a synecdoche for pleasure's soul, which Comus locates in a natural way of life, an opulent temperance, and in which sex is thus included as one pleasure among many." Kendrick, "Milton and Sexuality," 53; emphasis original. My reading of the masque as the Lady's rape fantasy, and of Comus as a projection of the Lady, enfolds this offer of pleasure into the disciplinary regime of sexuality that Kendrick argues the Lady institutes.

26 Milton, *On Christine Doctrine*, 724.

27 For two intriguing accounts of the history of rape law and their imprint on literature, see Lee A. Ritscher, *The Semiotics of Rape in Renaissance English Literature* (New York: Peter Lang, 2009), and Barbara Baines, *Representing Rape in the English Early Modern Period* (Lewiston, N.Y.: Edwin Mellen Press, 2003).

28 Kendrick, "Milton and Sexuality," 50.

29 Leonard, "Good Things," 50.

30 On the erotics of food in the Bible, see Ken Stone, *Practicing Safer Texts: Food, Sex, and Bible in Queer Perspective* (New York: T&T International, 2005).

31 See also Jean Laplanche and Jean-Bertrand Pontalis, "Fantasy and the Origins of Sexuality," *Formations of Fantasy*, ed. Victor Burgin, James Donald, and Cora Kaplan, 5–34 (London: Methuen, 1986).

32 Jean Laplanche, *Life and Death in Psychoanalysis*, trans. Jeffrey Mehlman (Baltimore: The Johns Hopkins University Press, 1976), 31.

33 Quoted in Laplanche, *Life and Death in Psychoanalysis*, 32. Without expanding on his comment, William Kerrigan does note that Jeffrey Masson's argument in *The Assault on Truth: Freud's Suppression of the Seduction Theory* (New York: Farrar, Straus, and Girous, 1984)—that Freud turned a blind eye to real child abuse when he abandoned seduction

theory—hovers in the background of Leonard's critique. Kerrigan, "Politically Correct *Comus*," 150.

34 Laplanche, *Life and Death*, 44.

35 Jean Laplanche, *Essays on Otherness* (New York: Routledge, 1996), 126–27.

36 Sigmund Freud, *Three Essays on the Theory of Sexuality*, in *Standard Edition of the Complete Psychological Works of Sigmund Freud*, vol. 7, ed. and trans. James Strachey (London: Hogarth Press, 1953), 223; also quoted in Laplanche, *Life and Death*, 41.

37 Sigmund Freud, *From the History of an Infantile Neurosis*, in *The Standard Edition of the Complete Psychological Works of Sigmund Freud*, vol. 17, ed. and trans. James Strachey, 7–122 (London: Hogarth Press, 1955).

38 The phenomenon of false memories of molestation is perhaps a psychoanalytic testament to this translation as much as to the suggestive ability of therapists.

39 Both "leans on" and "props up" are Laplanche's translations of Freud's *Anlehnung*, which Laplanche claims the *Standard Edition* "obscured" with the "pseudoscientific term" *anaclisis*. Laplanche, *Life and Death*, 16.

40 Ibid., 24.

41 Kendrick also offers an Oedipal reading in "Milton and Sexuality," 46–52. John Rumrich critiques these readings in "'Comus': A Fit of the Mother," in *Milton Unbound* (Cambridge: Cambridge University Press, 1996), 70–93.

42 Leo Bersani, *The Freudian Body: Psychoanalysis and Art* (New York: Columbia University Press, 1986).

43 William Shullenberger, "Girl, Interrupted: Spenserian Bondage and Release in Milton's Ludlow *Mask*," *Milton Quarterly* 37, no. 4 (2003): 191.

44 Ibid.

45 Laplanche, *Life and Death*, 34.

46 Ibid.

47 Schwarz's own account, too, of the Lady's willful definition of chastity is not incompatible with my claim that this will fails to clarify. See "Chastity, Militant, and Married: Cavendish's Romance, Milton's *Masque*," *PMLA* 118, no. 2 (2003): 270–85.

48 Angus Fletcher's observation is pertinent here, although I do not pursue performance possibilities in this chapter: "The roles of the lady and Comus could be acted so as to suggest that it is she who would seduce him, but to a virtuous life." See *The Transcendental Masque: An Essay on*

Milton's Comus (Ithaca, N.Y.: Cornell University Press, 1972), 216.

49 Stephen Orgel, "The Case for Comus," *Representations* 81 (2003): 40–41.

50 Shuger, "Gums of Glutinous Heat," 1–3.

51 James W. Broaddus, "'Gums of Glutinous Heat' in Milton's *Mask* and Spenser's *Faerie Queene*," *Milton Quarterly* 37, no. 4 (2003): 207.

52 If one follows Edward Le Comte, the suggestion of "gluteus maximus" in "glutenous" also points "behind." See *Milton and Sex* (New York: Columbia University Press, 1978), 1–2. See also Kerrigan, *Sacred Complex*, 47.

53 Kerrigan, *Sacred Complex*, 47.

54 Ibid.

55 As Valerie Traub argues, Renaissance concepts of chastity allow for female homoerotic activity, especially "femme" activity. See "Chaste Femme Love, Mythological Pastoral, and the Perversion of *Lesbian* Desire," in *The Renaissance of Lesbianism in Early Modern England*, 229–75 (Cambridge: Cambridge University Press, 2002).

56 Victoria Silver, "'Thoughts in Misbecoming Plight': Allegory in *Comus*," *Critical Essay on John Milton*, ed. Christopher Kendrick (New York: G. K. Hall, 1995), 56.

10

"How Human Life Began": Sexual Reproduction in Book 8 of *Paradise Lost*

THOMAS H. LUXON

After listening to Raphael tell about war in heaven (book 6) and the creation of the world (book 7), and then posing a few questions about cosmic hierarchy only to be gently reminded of the worth of lowly wisdom, John Milton's Adam volunteers to tell the archangel *his* story. He refers to this as the story of "how human life began" (8.250).[1] There are good reasons for regarding Adam's offer to tell an archangel how human life began as odd. First, Raphael has only just finished telling a competing version of such an origin story to Adam and Eve (7.505–47). Second, Adam acknowledges that he wants to tell the angel this story for reasons that have little to do with information; he wants to keep Raphael in conversation in the hope of experiencing more of the intense sweetness of heavenly discourse:

> thou seest
> How suttly to detaine thee I devise,
> Inviting thee to hear while I relate,
> Fond, were it not in hope of thy reply:
> For while I sit with thee, I seem in Heav'n,
> And sweeter thy discourse is to my eare
> Then Fruits of Palm-tree pleasantest to thirst
> And hunger both, from labour, at the houre
> Of sweet repast; they satiate, and soon fill,
> Though pleasant, but thy words with Grace Divine
> Imbu'd, bring to thir sweetness no satietie. (8.206–16)

Milton does not endow his archangels with omniscience, so there is no reason to think that Raphael knows all the details about how human life began, especially, perhaps, from a human perspective. When Raphael invites Adam to go on with a narrative that holds some promise of being redundant, we may therefore give them a pass for two reasons. First, humans have always engaged in telling this kind of story, even though, as Adam admits, we are peculiarly ill placed to claim authority on the matter because at the moment just before human life began, we were not present:

> For Man to tell how human Life began
> Is hard; for who himself beginning knew?
> Desire with thee still longer to converse
> Induc'd me. (8.250–53)

Second, this story is not just about the *content* of the story. It is a peculiarly human activity to tell such stories—stories of how the world began and how life began, stories about beginnings that by definition are, and must remain, obscure to us.[2] Furthermore, it is a peculiarly human trait to tell these stories in *conversation* with another being for the pleasure of that conversation; the content is almost beside the point.[3] The need for conversation, as Adam tells his Maker later in this story, is one of the characteristics of humanity as opposed to deity:

> Thou in thy self art perfet, and in thee
> Is no deficience found; not so is Man,
> But in degree, the cause of his desire
> By conversation with his like to help,
> Or solace his defects. (8.415–19)

Adam cannot be Adam, or take pleasure in Paradise, without someone to talk to.

The anonymous answerer to Milton's 1643 *Doctrine and Discipline of Divorce* poked fun at Milton's efforts to draw a sharp distinction between the fit conversation God intended husbands and wives to enjoy in marriage and that other sense of the word conversation—erotic touching.

Milton had argued that forbidding divorce to men who find no fit conversation at home with their wives "will be a ground or occasion of their desire after other persons, besides their own Wives; because when a man findes no contentment at home he is apt to looke for the same abroad."[4] The answerer replies:

> We answer you, what if he do look abroad, so long as it is but to meet with a fit conversing soule, provided he meddles not with her bodie, let him recreate himself, its lawfull enough: tis your own doctrine, A fit conversing soule for man is the noblest end of mariage: Therefore I think we may without danger, let a mans reines loose to accomodate himself so, if his Wife hath not such a fit conversing soule as she should have, only let him remember to come home to her at night. If you should say, that you meane want of content at home will cause a man to lust unlawfully after the bodies of other mens Wives.
>
> Wee answer you there is no congruitie in that sense with the rest of your Book: for according to your own Doctrine we may reason thus: That desire which is not satisfied at home by a mans own Wife, will break out towards other mens Wives; but the desire which is to be satisfied by a mans owne Wife is, that she be a fit conversing soule: *Ergo,* the not finding a mans Wife a fit conversing soule, will not endanger or stir up any other desires but to converse with the soules of other mens Wives; and this we allow you to do and keep your own still.
>
> But enough of this: only we desire the next time you write, to tell us the meaning of this fit conversing soule.

When you say conversation, taunts the answerer, what do you mean: talking or touching? In *Paradise Lost,* this question arises again in several different contexts, not only between Adam and Eve. Conversation here is a much thicker concept than it was in the divorce tracts, one informed by versions of Epicurean materialism he adopted from Lucretius and adapted to his own heterodox Christian beliefs.

As Martin Ferguson Smith says, "The first principles of Epicurean physics are that 'nothing is created out of nothing' (Lucr. 1.150–151, 155–156, 159–214) and 'nothing is destroyed into nothing' (Lucr. 1.215–264)."[5]

These two principles lead Lucretius to account for a number of phenomena in a manner quite alien to orthodox Christianity. In particular, because the Epicurean world comes into being and constantly undergoes change owing to the chance collisions between falling atoms, everything comes into being from something else. Difference emerges from chance "swerves" or collisions among fundamental particles. As I shall try to show in what follows, Milton's own materialist monism, though it does not embrace the idea of a world created by chance, owes much of its account of creation and reproduction to Lucretian ideas. Many distinctions useful to discursive reason appear more provisional in a monistic cosmos where everything comes from one first matter and passes gradually back toward that state. Sleep and waking, creator and creature, soul and body, touching and talking, even life and death or man and "manlike"—the poem challenges all these distinctions over the course of book 8.

Adam, Milton imagines, addressed his Maker with innocent impertinence, presuming to define the first great difference—that between the Creator and the one creature supposedly like Him:

> No need that thou
> Shouldst propagat, already infinite;
> And through all numbers absolute, though One;
> But Man by number is to manifest
> His single imperfection, and beget
> Like of his like, his Image multipli'd,
> In unitie defective, which requires
> Collateral love, and deerest amitie. (8.419–26)

When he said all this to God, no woman existed. Most readers, I suppose, have Eve on their minds as they listen to Adam, but nothing in Adam's speech indicates that he desires a conversation partner of a different sex. Quite the opposite. Later in book 8, when we are asked to imagine Adam's first reactions to seeing Eve, the narrator describes her as "a Creature . . . / Manlike, but different sex" (470–71). Adam appears shocked, even overwhelmed, by such an unexpected novelty as sexual difference, so much so that he is tempted to think less of all else in Paradise, including himself. What counts as Heaven's "best" (8.550, 8.611) gift is now a kind of competition?

When Adam first expresses desire for a mate, the difference on which he focuses, the difference that gives rise to his desire, is of a kind far less remarkable than sexual difference—it is numerical difference. What is more, it appears to be a numerical difference grounded in the likeness of one individual to another. God, Adam infers, is just fine with his infinite unity "through all numbers absolute" (whatever that means), but man, his Creature, is not. He must "beget / Like of his like" and enjoy multiplied versions of himself. Adam echoes what Plato's Diotima says: "All men are pregnant, Socrates, both in body and in soul: on reaching a certain age our nature yearns to beget."[6] It remains tantalizingly unclear whether Milton invites us to imagine Adam's desire for begetting as a means to acquiring a conversation partner like himself or if multiplying himself is the result of such conversation. In interesting ways, I believe the poem suggests both. But the poem also raises questions of another sort that invite us to contemplate other registers of difference that give rise to erotic desire, and Milton seems more intent on prompting questions than supplying answers.

What sort of conversation partner, for instance, is Raphael—like Adam or different? Does the difference between them register as a presessionist stand-in for sexual difference, or is it a kind of erotic difference that we should understand as underlying all human desire? Does their conversation beget the desire for a partner Adam articulates? Why is Raphael deemed an unsatisfactory, because unsatisfying ("no satietie"), partner for Adam? Even more difficult to piece out is Milton's imagination of Adam in conversation with the Father. Not only does this conversation tempt us to doubt Adam's conviction that God is satisfied with infinite unity, it may also suggest that God also desires to beget, and to do so on beings both like Himself in image and as profoundly unlike Himself as all created things must be from their uncreated Creator.

This story about "how human life began" is the story of how Adam asked for and was given a mate. But as he tells this story, he already is *in* what both he and Raphael acknowledge as a highly erotic conversation, and the story he tells is one about a conversation with God, a conversation itself so intensely erotic as to overwhelm Adam and result in the production of Eve, "Daughter of God and Man" (4.660; again in 9.291), also his sister and his spouse. One way to regard what's going on in Adam's story (conversation with God) and in the telling of Adam's story (conversation with an archangel) is to think of both as sex before sex. We may also regard the former as a story of how the first sense of the word *sex*—sexual difference—came into being. Both conversations are intellectually reproductive, both are highly erotic and sensual, and one actually results in a live birth.

Conversation itself is a kind of sex before sex, not just in the sense of intellectual foreplay but in the mythic sense of a world *spoken* into being. Raphael's story of creation in book 7 differs markedly from Milton's source in Genesis 1 and 2. In Genesis 1, we are told of a creation that comes into being first in obedience to God's commands and then is commanded to "be fruitful and multiply," but in Raphael's account, creation from the very beginning is the result of a *conversation* between the Father and his only begotten Son:

> And by my Word, begotten Son, by thee
> This I perform, speak thou, and be it don:
> My overshadowing Spirit and might with thee
> I send along, ride forth, and bid the Deep
> Within appointed bounds be Heav'n and Earth[.] (7.163–67)

Raphael's account echoes the creative imperatives from Genesis 1 ("And God said . . ."), but he also imbues them all with a generative sexuality at which Genesis barely hints:

> The Earth was form'd, but in the Womb as yet
> Of Waters, Embryon immature involv'd,
> Appeer'd not: over all the face of Earth
> Main Ocean flow'd, not idle, but with warme
> Prolific humour soft'ning all her Globe,
> Fermented the great Mother to conceave,
> Satiate with genial moisture, when God said
> Be gather'd now ye Waters under Heav'n
> Into one place, and let dry Land appeer. (7.276–84)

When Raphael comes to the creation of mankind, he reminds Adam (and us) that the Father has been and continues to be in conversation with his Son all through the six-day project:

> therefore the Omnipotent
> Eternal Father (For where is not hee
> Present) thus to his Son audibly spake.
> Let us make now Man in our image, Man
> In our similitude. (7.516–19)

The created world is born from a conversation between the Father and his only begotten Son.[7] Sex before the world was created?

In his recent book, *The Seeds of Things,* Jonathan Goldberg upbraids me (and some other Miltonists) for taking the sex out of Milton's accounts of homoerotic desire, both those he imagines (Raphael and Adam) and those he experienced (Charles Diodati). Goldberg refers especially to my treatments of Adam and Raphael's conversation in *Paradise Lost* and of *Epitaphium damonis* in my book *Single Imperfection.*[8] In his *Doctrine and Discipline of Divorce,* Milton argues strenuously that if we are to understand marriage as a peculiarly *human* relation, established by God as a remedy for Adam's loneliness, we must regard it as satisfying a kind of "rational burning," a desire for conversation as opposed to the lust or desire for procreation that motivates animals to mate. In my earlier efforts to preserve this distinction between conversation as rational burning and conversation as erotic burning, I managed to leech the sex out of Milton's imagination of heteroerotic desire as well. Goldberg puts it bluntly, if punningly: "Luxon's coupling of male–male friendship to marriage is ultimately their decoupling, and what remains to join them is their sexlessness."[9] Of course, he is right. I never was comfortable with my understanding of how Milton imagines prelapsarian heterosexuality. This collection of essays, focusing as it does on sex before sex, offers me an opportunity to rethink and correct some of the claims I made in *Single Imperfection.*

Milton, like Plato's Diotima, imagined conversation as a mode of procreation, of giving birth to offspring both mortal and immortal.[10] He also, like Diotima, imagined beautiful conversation as the thing begotten between two lovers, an offspring making a bid for immortality. We're all familiar with the term *platonic relationship,* as if this expression helps us draw a bright line between souls loving souls and bodies loving bodies, but I now argue that Milton's epic poem shines lights on relations between God and man, man and angel, and man and woman that repeatedly outshine that line.

Adam's story (book 8) has its roots in Genesis 2, whereas Raphael's (book 7) transcribes and glosses Genesis 1. The two stories from Genesis, of course, are significantly different. Mary Nyquist was by no means the first to point this out, but her discussion of these competing stories in the context of Milton's divorce pamphlets and his epic is most relevant to my discussion here.[11] In Raphael's Genesis 1 version, man and woman were created together:

> in his own Image hee
> Created thee, in the Image of God
> Express, and thou becam'st a living Soul.
> Male he created thee, but thy consort
> Female for Race; then bless'd Mankinde, and said,
> Be fruitful, multiplie, and fill the Earth,
> Subdue it, and throughout Dominion hold
> Over Fish of the Sea, and Fowle of the Aire,
> And every living thing that moves on the Earth. (7.526–34)

Raphael adjusts the Genesis 1 account just enough to insinuate into the existing story a sense of separateness between the creation of man and then woman, the separateness that dominates the Genesis 2 account. This adjustment conveniently mitigates the contradictions between the two Genesis accounts. Genesis never explicitly suggests that Eve was created as a "consort" or specifically for reproduction ("for Race"), although the immediate injunction to "multiply" has long been understood to underwrite that suggestion: "So God created man in his own image, in the image of God created he him; male and female created he them. And God blessed them, and God said unto them, Be fruitful, and multiply, and replenish the earth" (Genesis 1:27–28).[12] Genesis 1 invites us to understand "male and female" as two modes of God's own image, but Raphael's adversatively constructed gloss forestalls that reading: "But thy consort / Female for Race." Man is created in God's image, *but* woman not so much.[13] In this way, Raphael's Genesis 1 story anticipates the elaborately gendered creation story Adam claims in book 8 as his story of "how human life began."

We might still conclude that the difference between these two stories lies in the fact that, for Adam, the story of how human life began is a story of human *reproduction* rather than creation. Creation would be what an uncreated God does; human reproduction is what human creatures do. But the pervasive language of sexual reproduction with which Raphael infuses his version of Genesis 1 frustrates this conclusion as well. For every set of "golden compasses" or paternal imperatives ("And God said"), Raphael supplies accompanying images of "fervid Wheele," "vital vertue infus'd," and "genial moisture" (7.224, 7.236, 7.282). There is no sharp distinction in Milton's epic imagination between creation and procreation. Even the Son is said to have been "begotten" rather than made.[14]

The distinction between making and begetting, creating and procreating, is not the only sharp binary challenged by Milton's epic poem. As Adam's story about his own beginnings unrolls, other distinctions very dear to us come under intense pressure. We like to think that the evidence of our waking senses is radically different from that we experience in dreams, but Adam, we shall see, bases much of his story of how human life began on his dreams. He also challenges our familiar distinction between death and sleep, nonexistence and dream life. Telling the story of one's own beginnings requires indirection, and Adam seems keenly aware of his ignorance about how "human life began": "But who I was, or where, or from what cause, / Knew not" (8.270–71). Today, we collect indirect evidence from fossil records and from the ocean depths, and on the basis of this evidence, we speculate. Adam appears to collect evidence from his unconscious and even his "Fancie" or imagination and so introduces epistemological and ontological notions quite foreign to us and to the Aristotelian–Platonic antimaterialism underlying Christian metaphysics.[15] Some of these notions, I am convinced, have roots in Lucretius's *De rerum natura,* its materialist atomism, its notions of simulacra, and the epistemological claims built on them. We shall also see that an unfallen

Adam appears to entertain Lucretian notions of how things and beings constantly pass into and out of existence in a great cycle of life.

Let's start with the text of book 8. Adam takes a very interesting approach to this impossible but characteristically human exercise—imagining a time before he existed and some account of a being who made him. He approaches this impossible task by indirection and imagination—in short, by wondering and even dreaming. He likens preexistence or nonexistence to "soundest sleep" (8.253) and the first moment of consciousness to waking up. Furthermore, after trying to get answers from perusing his own limbs and even asking the sun and the countryside to "Tell, if ye saw, how came I thus, how here?" (8.277), he simply concludes he was made by "some great Maker " (8.278) and then grows weary from the difficult task of trying to find out how human life began:

> On a green shadie Bank profuse of Flours
> Pensive I sate me down; there gentle sleep
> First found me, and with soft oppression seis'd
> My droused sense, untroubl'd, though I thought
> I then was passing to my former state
> Insensible, and forthwith to dissolve. (8.286–91)

Adam seeks more than rest. He seeks in some fashion to return the same way he came and so to discover how he came to be. He finds a flowery bank not unlike the "flourie herb" (8.254) where first he woke. But of course, that first awakening was not really from sleep but from a condition he likened to sleep because he was at a loss to describe something prior to consciousness. And this "green shadie Bank" is not the same sunny place where he awoke to find himself lain some time before. He has "stray'd I knew not whither, / From where I first drew Aire" (8.283–84). He sat down to think about the difficult question of his own origins, and real sleep found him. But that sleep, he imagines, might just be close enough to the state from which he first "awakened" that it will allow him some sort of inkling, some imagined sense of that "former state / Insensible" (8.290–91) when he was not. All in all, this is a pretty remarkable exercise in imagination, speculation, and reasoning by likenesses! Adam imagines going back to a time before he existed to discover firsthand how human life began. Even though preexistence only resembles sleep, nevertheless, sleep might contain some clues by which we may fancy what it was like before we were.

If we are to have a better understanding of how Milton's Adam first discovered, or invented, or imagined the story of how human life began, we need to pay some attention to Adam's ways of knowing, his epistemology. Fancy, Adam tells Eve in book 5, is crucial to knowing anything:

> But know that in the Soule
> Are many lesser Faculties that serve
> Reason as chief; among these Fansie next
> Her office holds; of all external things,
> Which the five watchful Senses represent,
> She forms Imaginations, Aerie shapes,
> Which Reason joyning or disjoyning, frames
> All what we affirm or what deny, and call
> Our knowledge or opinion[.] (5.100–8)

In this thumbnail epistemology, Fancy's "office" is to mediate sensory input to Reason.[16] This radically nonempirical formulation allows Reason no direct access to sensory data; Reason attends to the "Imaginations" and "Aerie shapes" Fancy forms out of the representations of "external things" delivered by the "watchful Senses," and by combining and separating (rationalizing) Fancy's images and shapes, Reason "frames" what we call "knowledge or opinion." What Adam calls knowledge, then, comes at several removes from sensory experience. The senses "represent" external things to Fancy; Fancy "forms" of these images and shapes, and Reason then "frames" those images and shapes by combining some and "disjoyning" others. Adam's epistemology reminds me of some of Gilles Deleuze's neo-Lucretian formulations, in particular, "Reason is always a region carved out of the irrational—not sheltered from the irrational at all, but traversed by it and only defined by a particular kind of relationship among irrational factors. Underneath all reason lies delirium, and drift."[17] Enlightenment empiricism imagines that Fancy may be pushed aside, bypassed, or ignored. Not so for Adam. The senses have no direct access to things as they are; cognitive access to the world as it is comes by way of the imagination, by the work of Fancy.

Milton's pre-Enlightenment Adam assumes a more Lucretian notion of the nature of the universe than we have noticed. Miltonists have tended to shy away from recognizing how much Milton's Christian epic is infused with images and concepts from Lucretius's energetically antireligious poem, *De rerum natura (On the Nature of Things),* but Philip Hardie calls attention to how frequently "at the heart of a Christian inspirational poetics may be sensed the breath of a materialist Lucretius."[18] This breath enlivens the poem, and the poem, in its meditation on enlivening (as sex before sex) and epistemology, must in turn engage what Jonathan Goldberg has recently described as "a controversy that haunts Epicureanism from the start":

> If atoms are themselves imperceptible, colorless, tasteless—if they lack almost every feature by which bodies can be known, virtually every characteristic that characterizes matter—in what sense are atoms material? Although we see thanks to these atomic effluxes, we do not see them.[19]

Lucretius sometimes seems to breeze past this problem, one that often strikes readers as a paradox, by insisting we regard the problem as unsurprising:

> It should not be thought at all wonderful why the objects themselves are perceived, and yet the images [*simulacra*] that strike our eyes cannot be seen singly.[20] (4.256–58)

But of course it does cause surprise. Not only are atoms, the seeds of things, invisible, so are the "thin" images, the tenuous simulacra they constantly throw off. Nevertheless, these images, films, or simulacra "are the cause / Of vision, and without them nothing can be seen" (4.237–38). And these images may be images of touch as well as sight:

> Since a shape handled in the dark is recognized to be the same shape which is seen in the clear light by day, it must be that touch and sight

> are moved by a like cause. If we take hold of something square and it excites our feeling in the dark, in the light what square thing can fall upon our vision, if not an image of it? (4.230–36)

In this Lucretian mode of knowing, undetectable simulacra underlie all the senses, not just sight. The same tenuous film that "excites" a palpable sense of squareness also underlies a visible square. It is not the cube itself that reveals itself as square but the invisible and impalpable simulacra it emits, so that empirical observation is always at least one step away from the thing it observes. We moderns regard sight as fundamentally different from touch because sight detects reflected light, but Lucretius taught that we feel something is square and see something is square because the invisible simulacra of squareness fling themselves on our senses so that sight, touch, smell, and taste all come from the same stimulus.[21] Still the question at the heart remains, how does the deep inner material of the atom or "seed" pass from imperceptibility to perceptibility and do so in a way that makes the *corpora rerum* the foundation of all truth?

In his discussion of Lucretius, Goldberg tells us of Foucault's efforts, by way of studying Deleuze's reading of Lucretius, to name "this simulated terrain between inside and out," between the imperceptible seeds of things and the images by which we perceive them.[22] Foucault's term is "incorporeal materiality."[23] For Lucretius, the processes by which the invisible seeds of things register as human perceptions are by no means straightforward. Besides the "opinions of the mind," which often distort the evidence of our senses, "so that things are held to be seen which have not been seen by our senses" (4.465–66), things themselves, says Lucretius, are constantly throwing off thin, filmlike simulacra in a steady stream (4.145). All these streams of images form a kind of subvisible web in the air about us as they join and sometimes misjoin themselves just prior to stirring "the thin substance of the mind" to perception:

> I tell you that many images of things are moving about in many ways and in all directions, very thin, which easily unite in the air when they meet, being like spider's web or leaf of gold. In truth these are much more thin in texture than those which take the eyes and assail

> the vision, since these penetrate through the interstices of the body, and awake the thin substance of the mind within, and assail the sense.
>
> Thus it is we see Centaurs, and the frames of Scyllas, and the faces of dogs like Cerberus, and images of those for whom death is past, whose bones rest in earth's embrace, since images of all kind are being carried about everywhere, some that arise spontaneously in the air itself, some that are thrown off from all sorts of things, others that are made of a combination of these shapes. For certainly no image of a Centaur comes from one living, since there never was a living thing of this nature. (4.724–40)

The mind sees images much as the eye does, but it also may see these especially thin and so misjoined images. The trick is to distinguish between the images "which take the eyes and assail the vision" and those that, having arisen literally out of thin air or having been subtly mixed with others in the air, somehow insinuate themselves through the "interstices of the body" and, bypassing the senses, impersonate to our minds perception itself. All this may happen, says Lucretius, because "the mind itself is thin and wonderfully easy to move" (4.748). Lucretius has no patience for skeptics (4.469–77), but his account of how we perceive the world around us, and the roles played by our minds and by the simulacra themselves, strikes modern ears like very good grounds for skepticism. Perhaps that is because our modern minds have for so long been infected by the very thin notions of empiricism born in the Enlightenment and championed by modernism's forefathers, such as Thomas Reid's and Thomas Paine's "common sense" or the "self-evident" truths of Thomas Jefferson.[24]

Adam's theory of human perception resembles Lucretius's in that it disallows Reason any direct access to sensory data.[25] But we probably should find it strange that the misjoining and mistaking of images Lucretius ascribes to the random couplings of streaming simulacra, Adam assigns to Fancy, the second highest ranking Faculty of the Soul. Mistaken ideas about reality and truth come from within the soul in Adam's theory, whereas for Lucretius, such mistakes arise, in large part, because of the nature of things themselves in addition to the thinness and pliancy of the mind. This theory of misperception is consistent with

Lucretius's conviction that the world came into being by pure chance (1.158). Milton and Adam, however, believe God created the world out of his own invisible self, the "dark materials" (2.916) that correspond to Lucretius's invisible seeds of things. The world Adam looks at, the book of Nature, is not as naturally random as Lucretius's, so faults of perception, mistakes, must be assigned to Adam's Soul.

Paradise Lost explores the moral dimensions of this fault exacerbated by the fact that when one sleeps and Reason retires into "her private Cell," Fancy continues her work of forming airy shapes and imaginations without Reason's supervision. Indeed, says Adam, Fancy takes on her boss's work while he sleeps, imitating Reason's acts of judging, joining, and dividing,

> but misjoyning shapes,
> Wilde work produces oft, and most in dreams,
> Ill matching words and deeds long past or late. (5.111–13)

Supervised by Reason, then, Fancy plays a significant role in human epistemology. We could know nothing of the world presented to the senses without the work of Fancy. But Fancy operating apart from Reason, as when one is asleep, can produce "Wilde work." Adam dismisses Eve's dream as just such "Wilde work," plus the "addition strange" of something "Evil" (5.116–17). We are invited to assume that the evil something comes to Eve from the outside, yet she remains innocent. But Adam assumes that the evil has entered somehow into Eve's mind and that the wild work produced there by Fancy somehow carries whatever images—"Phantasms and Dreams" (4.803)—Satan can manage to set loose into the air beside her ear. In Adam's quasi-Lucretian epistemology, images of evil can indeed enter Eve's mind without being hers, except that her Fancy may take up some of these filmy simulacra and work with them outside the reach of Reason's supervision.

So how much of this dangerous "Wilde work" should we attribute to Eve? That is never quite clear. In *A Mask*, "A thousand fantasies . . . beckning shadows dire, / And airy tongues, that syllable mens names" (205, 207–8) also pass through the innocent Lady's "memory," raising, as Will Stockton notes in his chapter in this volume, similar questions about responsibility for one's fantasies. Augustine struggled with the distinction between the responsibility one has for lustful images while sleeping versus while awake, and like Milton's Adam and Eve, he concludes that although he is not responsible for nocturnal emissions, "we still feel sorry that in some way it was done in us."[26]

When Adam dreams his first dream, does his Fancy, like Eve's, produce "Wilde work"? Adam's first dream, according to his story, is an encounter with the creator he sought in vain when he first "wak't" to consciousness. Before he becomes aware of wanting a partner, his first desire, his first lack, is knowledge of his creator. When Adam falls asleep, Milton invites us to see him returning to his former state of nonbeing, returning "to my former state / Insensible, and forthwith to dissolve." In the face of apparent disintegration, Adam says he remained "untroubl'd"—no fear, no anxiety, no struggle to stay awake.

Adam's understanding of sleep is even more Lucretian than his general epistemology. "Sleep comes on," says Lucretius,

> when the power of the spirit is drawn apart through the body, and part being cast forth has gone away, and part more crowded together has retreated into the depths; for only then the limbs loosen and become flaccid. For there is no doubt that this feeling in us comes about by action of the spirit, and when sleep hinders the feeling so that there is none, then we must suppose that the spirit has been disordered and cast forth without; but not all, for then the body would lie pervaded with the everlasting cold of death; since of course if no part of the spirit were left hidden in the limbs, like fire covered in a heap of ashes, whence could the feeling be suddenly rekindled throughout the limbs and arise like a flame from the hidden fire? (4.916–28)

For Lucretius, as for Adam, sleep is not simply *like* death: they are two degrees of the same thing. In sleep, the senses are "seis'd" and the spirit or life (as in Raphael's monist ontology in 5.474) is drawn apart from the body, leaving a small remnant that retreats into the depths of the body's primordial substance. In death, all spirit is drawn away, none retreats or hides, and the body returns to the dark materials from which it first came. But of course, Adam does not call sleep *death*; he calls it his "former state." That is because for Milton the Christian, death is terrible—the result of the fall and the fate from which Christ's sacrifice was meant to save us—even though Milton the monist and epicurean quite delightfully imagines how the first man, as yet unexposed to death, might well have accepted—"untroubl'd"—passing back into his former state of nonbeing as a perfectly natural part of the nature of things. After all, one day all will return to the former state whence it first proceeded, and God, once again, "shall be All in All" (3.341).[27]

When Adam sleeps, he dreams of what most concerned him when awake—his creator. Lucretius says that lawyers dream of pleading cases and seekers after the nature of things, like himself, dream of finding it out (4.964–72). Adam is a seeker after his creator; and the Creator he seeks appears to him first in a dream. Adam's first dream, however, both is and is not Lucretian. This dream is an "inward apparition," an image that presents itself directly to the brain, bypassing the senses seized in sleep, but it also enjoys some kind of agency—it moves Adam's Fancy "to believe I yet had being / And livd" (8.293–94). Milton is having great fun. If Fancy produces "Wilde work" during the sleep of Reason, are we to understand Adam's conviction here that he both lives and meets his maker as some kind of wild work? Indeed it's hard to imagine anything wilder than a dream wherein one passes out of being, meets God face-to-face, and lives to tell about it—unless one were to wake up from such a wild dream and find that the dream was "all real, as the dream / Had lively shadowd" (8.310–11)! I think Milton would say this is precisely the kind of wonderfully wild work human Fancy can produce when moved by God. For Milton, divine revelation beats a path through human Fancy. Often delivered in dreams, it bypasses sense (Lucretius's test for truth) and avoids Reason (Milton's). There is thus some kind of truth beyond Reason, certainly beyond discursive reason. Is this truth perhaps like the intuitive reason angels enjoy, a kind of reason beyond what we count as reason?

Adam's second dream is even wilder. Like Eve's dream of being led up into the heavens by Satan's voice, it is a seduction dream. Adam is seduced by his creator, even before he falls asleep, and the consequence of this seduction is Eve, his "likeness," his "fit help," his "other self," his "hearts desire" (8.450–51), but also, we should not forget, his daughter

(4.660), his sister, his consort, his own "Best Image" and "dearer half" (5.95). I have already suggested that the first human sexual experience in *Paradise Lost* takes place not between Adam and the female product of his second dream but between Adam and his creator, God. This sexual experience with God is the story of how human sexual life began, but it is also the story that unfolds into the story of Eve's origins. Either story alone, but also the relationship between the two stories, Adam says is so hard to tell, but tell it he must.

No sooner has Adam experienced his first wish fulfillment—meeting and adoring his creator—than he falls victim to a new desire, a desire for a companion to remedy his loneliness and to allow him to take pleasure in pleasure itself. Adam found his conversation with Raphael quite a dazzling experience. His conversation with God, by his own report, was even more strenuous, utterly exhausting. And the conversation's topic was the fitness or unfitness of conversation partners for him. From the moment when God appears to be suggesting Adam find solace in the animals he has named, we sense the same slippage between discursive conversation and the more erotic "conversation" the anonymous answerer to the *Doctrine and Discipline* felt when he accused Milton of being disingenuous about "rational burning" for "conversation."[28] The "brute," Adam tells God, "Cannot be human consort" because humans want to engage in "rational delight," and animals are not fit to "participate" in rational delight with humans (8.390–91). He says this even though God, only a moment earlier, pronounced animals capable of some level of reason and discourse: "know'st thou not / Thir language and thir wayes? They also know, / And reason not contemptibly" (8.372–74). Are we to understand that God here misleads Adam for pedagogical reasons? In the divorce tracts, Milton insists repeatedly that lust, or irrational burning, is what brutes do when they have "congresse" with each other: "mariage is a human Society, and . . . all human society must proceed from the mind rather then [*sic*] the body, els it would be but a kind of animall or beastish meeting."[29] When beasts converse, they copulate, and that is all there is to it; that is what being a beast means. So what images pass through Adam's mind when he describes how the animals converse with each other?

> [T]hey rejoice
> Each with thir kinde, Lion with Lioness;
> So fitly them in pairs thou hast combin'd;
> Much less can Bird with Beast, or Fish with Fowle
> So well converse, nor with the Ox the Ape;
> Wors then can Man with Beast, and least of all. (8.392–97)

If brute conversation is simply sex, nothing more, then Adam's use of the word *converse* here means "copulate." We're invited to imagine not just a copulating lion and lioness but a beast with a bird and a fowl with a fish. His point is that human–animal "conversation" is every bit as unthinkable as a fish copulating with a bird. But his last example, an ox copulating with an ape, may not be so unthinkable, however disturbingly comic. Even as he argues that interspecies "conversation" is unthinkable because animals simply fuck and humans do something more rational, he leaves us with an image of just how imaginable interspecies copulation might be. This image prepares us for what follows in this story of how human life began: an interspecies conversation–copulation of another, supposedly nonbestial, but perfectly material kind.

God indirectly offers himself to Adam as a conversation partner. Ostensibly, he calls attention to himself as a being who needs no partner, but in doing so, he redirects Adam's attention from the animals to him: "What think'st thou then of mee" (8.403)? Although they have been in conversation for some time, God is also not really a proper partner for Adam for the very simple reason that he overpowers him. Adam cannot stand for long the strain of conversation with God. He literally passes out:

> Hee ended, or I heard no more, for now
> My earthly by his Heav'nly overpowerd,
> Which it had long stood under, streind to the highth
> In that celestial Colloquie sublime,
> As with an object that excels the sense,
> Dazl'd and spent, sunk down, and sought repair
> Of sleep, which instantly fell on me, call'd
> By Nature as in aide, and clos'd mine eyes. (8.452–59)

I long have wondered what exactly this "earthly" thing is in Adam that is "overpowerd" by God's "Heav'nly" thing, and why do these things have no name? There's a hint of an answer in Lucretius's account of human copulation and reproduction:

> And in the mingling of seed it sometimes happens
> That the woman by a sudden move overcomes
> The force of the man and takes control of it;
> From the mother's seed then children like the mother
> Are born; as from the father's children like the father.
> But those you see with figures like to each
> And faces like both parents', these have sprung
> From the father's body and the mother's blood
> When under the goads of Venus through the limbs
> The coursing seeds are driven, and dashed together
> By two hearts breathing as one in mutual passion,
> And neither masters the other nor is mastered. (4.1209–17)

"The force of the man" *(forte virilem)* may by a "sudden move" be overcome by his partner in the course of copulation, the mingling of the seed. To be sure, in *Paradise Lost,* Adam is talking about a colloquy with God, not copulation, but if Goldberg is right, we should stop being so quick to take the sex out of episodes that are so obviously erotic.

Conversation with Raphael was such an erotic experience that Adam proposes telling his own story to detain the angel longer into the afternoon. He reports that as he talks with Raphael, he seems "in heaven." More than once in his poetry, Milton describes heaven in distinctly erotic terms. When the Attendant Spirit in *A Mask* returns to heaven at the poem's close, he looks forward to a highly erotic and even sensual place where Adonis lays on "Beds of *Hyacinth* and Roses . . . Waxing well of his deep wound," and Cupid not only makes Psyche "his eternal Bride" but impregnates her with "blissful twins"—Youth and Joy (998–1011). Some may object to my line of interpretation here by claiming that mythic and allegorical characters cannot be thought of as literally sensual, but I disagree. Adonis's wound is very much like what Lucretius calls the "wound" inflicted on the mind by love (4.1048). This mental wound drives the libido. By including images of the *saucia amore* and sexual reproduction, Milton, as Marshall Grossman reminds us he so often does, laces metaphor, myth, and allegory with "ontological residues."[30] When Milton imagines his friend Charles Diodati in heaven, it is a place of Dionysiac and Bacchic revels raging under "the thyrsus of Zion" (*Epitaphium Damonis,* 218–19). Bruce Boehrer even suggests that we can hear in "the unexpressive nuptial song" of Lycidas's heaven a version of "the voice of a love that dare not speak its name," that is, a love that not only embraces the fundamentals of the body but can enjoy those fundamentals in a place where the body and the spirit pass back and forth into each other in ways that titillate more than our imaginations.[31] If Milton so regularly imagines heaven as a place, perhaps the only place since Paradise was lost, where the sensual may safely remingle with spiritual erotics, then why should we not allow the full force of sensuality in the way Adam describes the pleasure of talking with Raphael? When Raphael admires the beauty of Adam's lips, "speaking or mute" (8.222), why should we not also recall the narrator's coy comments about Eve's love of Adam's lips just a hundred and fifty lines previous:

> hee, she knew would intermix
> Grateful digressions, and solve high dispute
> With conjugal Caresses, from his Lip
> Not Words alone pleas'd her. (8.54–57)

Precisely what makes Paradise a paradise is this embrace of sensual pleasure without shame, even by angels who eat with "keen dispatch / of real hunger" (5.436–37). Furthermore, what makes this embrace fit for Paradise only is the co-extensive "untroubl'd" acceptance of passing in and out of existence.

When Adam reports that his virile force was overpowered by God's heavenly force, this overpowering is not the effect of some sudden movement, as Lucretius describes. Adam's force succumbs to the strain of talking with God, and for a second time, he falls asleep, succumbing to what reminds us of postcoital exhaustion, but *sans triste.* As with Lucretian sleep, part of his spirit "sunk down, and sought repair," while another part was abstracted from his body, and by the aid of Fancy once again, he watches God open his left side and perform on his sleeping body an act of reproduction that blends images of Lucretius's *saucia amore,* surgical obstetrics, hard tissue manufacture, and, yes, sexual reproduction:

> Mine eyes he clos'd, but op'n left the Cell
> Of Fancie my internal sight, by which
> Abstract as in a transe methought I saw,
> Though sleeping, where I lay, and saw the shape
> Still glorious before whom awake I stood;
> Who stooping op'nd my left side, and took
> From thence a Rib, with cordial spirits warme,
> And Life-blood streaming fresh; wide was the wound,
> But suddenly with flesh fill'd up and heal'd:
> The Rib he formd and fashond with his hands;
> Under his forming hands a Creature grew,
> Manlike, but different sex.[32] (8.453–71)

Milton here imagines the first act of human sexual reproduction as an encounter between God and man. Milton does more than justify the ways of God to man: he probes those ways with all the imaginative powers he collected and exercised through a life of intense study, and he reimagines those ways with images that defy the kind of sorting so familiar to discursive logic and reason. Just as the account of Creation in book 7 prompts us to ponder the similarity of so many different modes of generation—architectural, cosmic, sexual, alchemical, parthenogenic—so this account of "how human life began" and the first instance of sexual reproduction, between a Creator and that creature deliberately made most like him, mixes a similar range of images. Milton wants us to see that a full account of the ontology of human being requires modes of thought that can "occupy this difficult terrain of sameness and difference," where manufacture, cultivation, sculpture, poetry, and copulation, however different, are also recognized as similar ways of mixing seeds and reproducing human life.[33]

This chapter only begins the project of understanding the erotics of Miltonic "conversation." The first story of sexual reproduction in *Paradise*

Lost tells of how Satan impregnated a quasi-allegorical Sin with Death. Marshall Grossman's account of this story correctly calls attention to how it proleptically parodies the birth of Eve.[34] In fact, I would add that Milton takes special care to tell us that Adam, before his encounter with God, sat himself down in a "Pensive" reverie not unlike Sin just before she gives birth to Death (8.287, 2.757). Reading this account of a fallen angel copulating with an allegorical creature born by "cephalic reproduction" requires, I would insist, a Lucretian materialist understanding of things.[35] For Lucretius, as for Milton, the difference between thought images and the simulacra constantly streaming off the "seeds of things" is a difference not of kind but of degree. Goldberg's reading of Lucretius and Deleuze will also help us better understand the insistent materiality of Milton's allegorical characters because "thought and atoms are not like each other but identical to each other insofar as they are incorporeal matter."[36] According to Raphael, everything that exists, including odors, spirits, and even intuitive reason, comes from the "one first matter." Because that is so, the sharp distinction Socrates makes (through the persona of Diotima) between being pregnant in the body and pregnant in the soul cannot be sustained in the monist materialist environment of Milton's poem any more than can the platonic distinctions between ideas and their shadows.[37]

I once wrote of Milton's epic, "the distinction that underwrites the normative [heteronormative] sex–gender system is the distinction between God and creature, spirits without bodies and creatures with bodies."[38] But this is not true. Milton's heterodox monism refuses such distinctions any absolute force. Even orthodox Christianity's insistence on an incarnate God, a Christ with a resurrected human body, and, before that, a God who begets makes the very distinctions on which it has for so long rested its sexual morality finally untenable. Sex–gender systems rely on difference—creator–creature, male–female, self–other, mortal–immortal—but even Christianity looks backward to a moment before difference and forward to a consummation when God will be all in all. Intentional or not, Milton's poem prompts us to dream not just of other worlds but of worlds before, after and even within this one where such distinctions and the normativities they invite us to play could well be otherwise. Taking the sex out of conversation appeared to be central to Milton's rhetorical project in the divorce tracts, but in *Paradise Lost,* I think he wants his readers to blur the very distinction he labored so hard to draw. He does so largely because the anonymous answerer was right: it is a distinction without sufficient difference.

Notes

1 All references to Milton's poetry are to the John Milton Reading Room, ed. Thomas H. Luxon, http://www.Dartmouth.edu/~milton, 1997–2012.

2 For Milton and most of his contemporaries, the Bible was the most important source for information about the beginning of life, but pseudoscientific explanations like Jakob Boehme's sense of an original "Eternall Lubet," or divine lust for physical expression of an invisible oneness, have also proven influential. See *Mysterium Magnum, or An exposition of the first book of Moses called Genesis,* trans. John Sparrow (London, 1654), 9. This essay pursues a renewed interest in Lucretian atomism as a way of talking about the origins of human life. Recent scholarship on Lucretian thought in Renaissance literature includes Jonathan Goldberg, *The Seeds of Things: Theorizing Sexuality and Materiality in Renaissance Representations* (New York: Fordham University Press, 2009); Stuart Gillespie, "Lucretius in the English Renaissance," in *The Cambridge Companion to Lucretius,* ed. Stuart Gillespie and Philip Hardie, 242–53 (Cambridge: Cambridge University Press, 2007); Alvin Snider, "Atoms and Seeds: Aphra Behn's Lucretius," *CLIO: A Journal of Literature, History, and the Philosophy of History* 33, no. 1 (2003): 1–24; and David Norbrook, "Margaret Cavendish and Lucy Hutchinson: Identity, Ideology, and Politics," *In-between: Essays and Studies in Literary Criticism* 9 (2000): 179–203. For an accessible account of current biochemical accounts of the beginning of life on this planet and the reconstruction of the "Last Universal Common Ancestor, known fondly as LUCA," see Nick Lane, *Life Ascending: The Ten Great Inventions of Evolution* (New York: W. W. Norton, 2009), 8–33, esp. 24. Other important treatments of Lucretian materiality in Milton's poetry include David Quint, "Fear of Falling: Icarus, Phaethon, and Lucretius in *Paradise Lost,*" *Renaissance Quarterly* 57, no. 3 (2004): 847–81; John Leonard, "Milton, Lucretius and 'the Void Profound of Unessential Night,'" in *Living Texts: Interpreting*

Milton, ed. Kristen A. Pruitt (Selinsgrove, Pa.: Susquehanna University Press, 2000), 198–217; Catherine Gimelli-Martin, *The Ruins of Allegory* (Durham, N.C.: Duke University Press, 1998), 41, 265; and Philip Hardie, "The Presence of Lucretius in *Paradise Lost,*" *Milton Quarterly* 29, no. 1 (1995): 13–24.

3 Another odd aspect of this story that calls for more attention is Raphael's claim that he was away on the day God made man, so he is happy to hear Adam's oddly disqualified firsthand account of "how human life began": "say therefore on; / For I that Day was absent, as befell, / Bound on a voyage uncouth and obscure, / Farr on excursion toward the Gates of Hell" (8.228–31). Does that mean Raphael's account of the sixth day of creation in book 7 is not firsthand? Is his authority on the matter some heavenly version that underlies the Bible? Milton invites us to think that Moses learned *Bereshit* ("In the beginning") from his forefathers running back to Adam, and that Adam learned the creation story from Raphael, but it appears that Raphael may have learned *Bereshit* or some part of it from angel lore. This angel lore may also be significantly different from the redaction we find in Genesis 1 and 2.

4 Anonymous, *An Answer to a book intituled, The doctrine and discipline of divorce* (London, 1644), 32. To be fair, Milton's argument in *Doctrine and Disciple of Divorce* is far more nuanced than the answerer makes it out to be: "such a mariage can be no mariage whereto the most honest end is wanting: and the agrieved person shall doe more manly, to be extraordinary and singular in claiming the due right whereof he is frustrated, then to piece up his lost contentment by visiting the Stews, or stepping to his neighbours bed, which is the common shift in this mis-fortune." *Complete Prose Works of John Milton,* vol. 2, ed. Don M. Wolfe (New Haven, Conn.: Yale University Press, 1959), 247.

5 Martin Ferguson Smith, introduction to Lucretius, *De Rerum Natura,* trans. W. H. D. Rouse (Cambridge, Mass.: Harvard University Press, 1925), xxxi.

6 Plato, *Symposium,* in *Plato in Twelve Volumes,* vol. 9, trans. Harold N. Fowler (Cambridge, Mass.: Harvard University Press, 1925), 206c, http://www.perseus.tufts.edu/hopper/.

7 I feel obliged to take note of the supersessionism that imagines the Son as a partner in creation. Needless to say, Genesis betrays no hint of a Son of God.

8 Goldberg, *Seeds of Things,* 187–91; Thomas H. Luxon, *Single Imperfection:*

Milton, Marriage, and Friendship (Pittsburgh, Pa.: Duquesne University Press, 2005).

9 Goldberg, *Seeds of Things,* 188.

10 For a detailed discussion of Diotima's account of procreation of the soul versus procreation of the body in Plato's *Symposium* and how Milton may have understood it, see my *Single Imperfection,* 138–49.

11 Mary Nyquist, "The Genesis of Gendered Subjectivity in the Divorce Tracts and in *Paradise Lost,*" in *Re-membering Milton: Essays on the Texts and Traditions,* ed. Mary Nyquist and Margaret Ferguson, 99–127 (New York: Methuen, 1987).

12 All quotations from the Bible refer to the Authorized Version, as accessed from http://www.biblegateway.com/.

13 Milton explains the hermeneutic logic behind Raphael's *but* in *Tetrachordon*: "[Created he him.] It might be doubted why he saith, In the Image of God created he him, not them, as well as male and female them; especially since that Image might be common to them both, but male and female could not, however the Jewes fable, and please themselvs with the accidentall concurrence of Plato's wit, as if Man at first had bin created Hermaphrodite: but then it must have bin male and female created he him. So had the Image of God bin equally common to them both, it had no doubt bin said, In the Image of God created he them. But St. Paul ends the controversie, by explaining that the woman is not primarily and immediatly the image of God, but in reference to the man. The head of the woman, saith he, 1 Cor. 11. is the man: he the image and glory of God, she the glory of the man: he not for her, but she for him" (*Complete Prose,* 2.589). Milton refers sneeringly to Aristophanes's myth of originary hermaphrodites. He rejects the Neoplatonic conflation of Genesis 1:27 and Aristophanes's primeval androgyne, a reading the Jewish Neoplationist Leone Ebreo embraced. See Leone Ebreo, *The Philosophy of Love,* trans. F. Friedeberg-Seeley and Jean H. Barnes (London: Soncino Press, 1937), 367–73.

14 For a discussion of the difficulties Martin Luther and others have had understanding what it means for the Son of God to have been "begotten," see my discussion in *Literal Figures: Puritan Allegory and the Reformation Crisis in Representation* (Chicago: University of Chicago Press, 1995), 68–72.

15 See Monte Johnson and Catherine Wilson, "Lucretius and the History of Science," in *The Cambridge Companion to Lucretius,* ed. Stuart Gillespie

and Philip Hardie (Cambridge: Cambridge University Press, 2007), 131.

16 Some time ago, Paul Stevens called attention to two important aspects of Milton's Fancy. First, "the functions that Locke attributes to wit and judgment, Milton's Adam attributes to fancy and reason," so that Fancy may be thought of as another word for "wit," when it stands in "antithesis to judgment." Second, and for my purposes more important, Milton repeatedly referred to Shakespeare as a devotee of Fancy, "for Shakespeare is fansie's childe" ("L'Allegro," 133), and Shakespeare, he says, "has built his livelong monument by our fancy of it self bereaving" ("On Shakespeare 1630," 13). See Paul Stevens, "Magic Structures: Comus and the Illusions of Fancy," *Milton Quarterly* 17, no. 3 (1983): 85–86. Stevens acknowledges that Milton does not always refer to Fancy in a negative sense. My claim is even stronger—that Fancy, for Milton, is essential to human ways of knowing the world.

17 Gilles Deleuze, "On Capitalism and Desire," in *Desert Islands and Other Texts, 1953–1974,* ed. David Lapoujade, trans. Michael Taormina (Cambridge, Mass.: Semiotext(e), 2004), 262.

18 Hardie, "Presence of Lucretius," 14–20. Hardie believes that Andrew Marvell also sensed the same. See also chapters 1 and 2 of Catherine Wilson, *Epicureanism at the Origins of Modernity* (Oxford: Clarendon Press, 2008).

19 Goldberg, *Seeds of Things,* 34.

20 Prose quotations from Lucretius's *De rerum natura* come from *Lucretius De Rerum Natura,* trans. W. H. D. Rouse (Cambridge, Mass.: Harvard University Press, 1975). In two places, poetry serves better than prose; these translations come from Sir Ronald Melville's edition of Lucretius's *On the Nature of the Universe* (Oxford: Clarendon Press, 1997).

21 Marshall Grossman offers prescient observations on what he calls the apparent "transformation of a common metaphor to a literal assertion" and the ontological continuities such transformations frequently suggest in Milton's poem. Particularly useful is his notion of Milton's "rhetorical hovering between analogy and ontology." See Grossman, "The Genders of God and the Redemption of the Flesh in *Paradise Lost,*" in *Milton and Gender,* ed. Catherine Gimelli Martin (Cambridge: Cambridge University Press, 2004), 110. It is not hard to imagine how appealing the Lucretian account of the similar effect of simulacra on sight and touch might have been to a blind poet.

22 Goldberg, *Seeds of Things,* 33.

23 Michel Foucault, "Theatrum Philosphicum," in *Language, Counter-memory, Practice: Selected Essays and Interviews,* trans. Donald F. Bouchard and Sherry Simon (Ithaca, N.Y.: Cornell University Press, 1977), 169.

24 See Arthur Herman, *The Scottish Enlightenment: The Scot's Invention of the Modern World* (London: Fourth Estate, 2002), 260–66.

25 Adam's account of the role of Fancy in human knowledge appears consistent with Raphael's account later in the book when he explains monism to Adam (5.482–87).

26 *The Confessions of St. Augustine,* trans. J. G. Pilkington (New York: Liveright, 1943), 250. See also the Latin text edited by James J. O'Donnell, *Confessiones* (Oxford: Clarendon Press, 1992), 135.

27 See Grossman's intriguing discussion of why God would "want" to create anything in the first place in "Genders of God," 95–98.

28 See Anonymous, *An Answer to a Book,* 15.

29 Milton, *Complete Prose,* 2.275.

30 Grossman, "Genders of God," 98.

31 Bruce Boehrer, "'Lycidas': The Pastoral Elegy as Same-Sex Epithalamium," *PMLA* 117, no. 2 (2002): 234. See also Goldberg, *Seeds of Things,* 187.

32 Louis Schwartz, in his recent book *Milton and Maternal Mortality* (Cambridge: Cambridge University Press, 2009), 207–10, calls attention to Eve's birth as very much like a seventeenth-century obstetric surgery, but there is no consideration at all of the homoerotic implications of imagining God and Adam as partners in the first act of human reproduction—a highly physical and erotic act.

33 Goldberg, *Seeds of Things,* 36.

34 Grossman, "Genders of God," 104–6.

35 Ibid., 103.

36 Goldberg, *Seeds of Things,* 39.

37 See Plato, *Symposium,* 208e–209c.

38 Luxon, *Single Imperfection,* 117.

Afterword

VALERIE TRAUB

Dirty Minds . . .

Anyone who has broached the question of sex in the undergraduate classroom cannot have escaped the accusation, "You are reading too much (sex) into this (text)." This is perhaps especially true of Renaissance courses, in which expectations of "great literature" written in the mists of time would seem to obviate any possibility of eroticism. Teachers generally take recourse in textual glosses to explain the bawdy, scatological, and downright filthy references that punctuate even the most canonical plays and poems. Sometimes we seek assistance from the many glossaries that codify sexual allusions or assign criticism that interprets dynamics of erotic love, homosexuality, or sexual violence. When we teach drama, we can screen recent films, particularly those capitalizing on the market value of Shakespeare, which increasingly adorn words with graphic depictions of flesh.

Despite this pedagogical state of the art, however, understandings of early modern sex remain circumscribed by a number of stubborn assumptions: that it is almost always heterosexual; that it ultimately tends toward the "consummation" of penis in vagina; that its apotheosis is to be found in the couple form; that, unless it is a matter of violent assault, it is inevitably a prelude to or sign of marriage. Often accompanying these calcified ideas are others: that heterosexuality, unlike homosexuality, is not subject to change; that sex is, in the main, a source of pleasure, ending in orgasm; that certain sexual "outlets," like prostitution, exist mainly to preserve heterosexual marriage; that sex within marriage is banal and boring, subsumed ideologically under the imperative of reproduction. In other words, a presumptive knowledge overwrites what sex is, what it does, what it means, and why we should care about it. *Sex before Sex* aims to dismantle that knowingness, in the name of "a future critical practice that does not presume to know in advance what sex is and has been" (Varnado). It does so, paradoxically, by applying analytical pressure on what would seem to be the most self-evident of categories: sex acts.

Consider *Romeo and Juliet,* a mainstream Shakespeare play, long approached as a veritable primer in sex, romantic love, and the Renaissance topos of sex-as-death. In reading a "moment of almost universally agreed upon 'straight' . . . sex: the morning-after bedroom scene between the secretly married Romeo (a boy) and Juliet (a girl played by a boy actor)," Varnado, in chapter 1, emphasizes the *invisibility* of offstage sex; it is only by virtue of readerly acts of identification that this action can be captioned as the "legally significant, penis-in-vagina variety" of sex. Like the essays of her co-contributors, her inquiry brings to the fore multiple erotic possibilities: not just cunnilingus and anal sex but temporal interruption and impotence. Beyond this imagined expansion of Romeo and Juliet's erotic repertoire, of particular interest is that this most romantic of tragedies does not, in fact, figure sex much at all and depends to an extraordinary degree on the imaginations of its readers and audiences. Indeed, insofar as Renaissance literature's representation of sex tends to rely on linguistic simulacra and post facto revelations, sex, for the most part, is a matter of bed tricks.

Want to Know . . .

Framed as an exploration into the "epistemological recalcitrance of sex and the complexities of sexual signification" (Stockton and Bromley) *Sex before Sex* builds on a prior body of scholarship that questioned the definitional boundaries of sex; but in a more sustained fashion than most previous work, the interpretations offered here "pivot" around the "difficulty of locating the origins and specifying the content of sexual meanings and intentions." The "indeterminacy of 'the sexual'" involves both "the limits of sex" and its "legibility"—in other words, not only epistemology (how we know) but ontology (the unstable "being" of sex) and signification (the means by which it is represented). Thus, in these pages, we encounter, among other things, *invisible sex, counterfactual sex, spectacular impotence*, and, in the apparent tautology of the book's title, *sex before sex*. We are invited to "tarry" not only with "ignored" or "alternative forms of sex," including those that are loaded "with negative affect" (Bromley), but with erotic desires and behaviors that are, in crucial ways, inaccessible, resistant to interpretation, even unknowable. When it comes to sex, even Milton, it turns out, "seems more intent on prompting questions than supplying answers" (Luxon).

In the present critical climate, it is usual to term such a project *queer*. Yet, according to the editors in their introduction to the volume, not every contributor "take[s] a stake" in the term *queer*, and they note that the "political efficacy" of *queer* "is diluted through its universalization." Nonetheless, certain aspects of queer theory provide a baseline lingua franca for this volume. All the contributors are interested in the relations between normative and nonnormative desires and acts—or more accurately, desires and acts that typically are construed as nonnormative but at the time may have been quite common. All of them are alert to the cultural and psychic functions of abjection, "which consolidates the center by exacting its price from the margins" (Schwartz). Many of them are interested in the "boundary-blurring effects" (Bromley) that the concept of *queer* celebrates, and they are keen to expose how disciplinary attempts at control and stigmatization can unwittingly generate untoward effects. Some of them utilize the tension between minoritizing and universalizing discourses of sexuality—a touchstone of queer theory since Eve Kosofsky Sedgwick's *Epistemology of the Closet*.[1] All of them are motivated by one of the basic tenets articulated in Gayle Rubin's foundational "Thinking Sex": the concept of benign sexual variation.[2] Affirming that you need not like a particular act to recognize that someone else does and will, the appreciation of benign sexual variation in this volume includes not only anal penetration and sex with animals but anilingus (oral–anal contact colloquially known as rimming) and configurations of sex beyond the couple form. Perhaps the most surprising additions to the erotic repertoire, because they have been most elided in the history of sexuality, are the practice of chin chucking, male impotence as an erotic turn-on, and an erotic relation to plants.

What Counts . . .

In a volume that begins with the intention to "destabilize" well-known textual passages "by pressuring the definition of sex" and that describes as its "organizing question" "what counts as sex in the early modern past" (Stockton and Bromley) it is not surprising that contributors exhibit an acute awareness of the dynamics of reading and interpretation. They assume that reading (for) sex in the past involves complex libidinal investments, including what Varnado calls "critical arousal." Such critical identifications and disidentifications are themselves founded on a contradiction: "subjective erotic experience is inherently solitary and ineffable, incommunicable and inaccessible to another. . . . Yet at the same time, that experience can only be represented or communicated *as erotic* by asking a reader . . . to identity with it, to compare it with their remembered experiences of different sexual acts and feelings." The "complex and ambivalent acts of imagination, recognition, and affective hailing required to read or watch a play" are, for Varnado, the same as those that enable us to *see* sex, for sex, she avers, resides in "the eye of the beholder."

Rather than propose that "everything is sexual," however, the contributors carefully explore the *criteria* by which different kinds of mental and corporeal activities become subject to such a "hailing." Schwarz, in chapter 2, directs attention to the drama's "pragmatism of participatory illusion," whereby "conviction produces rather than follows from evidence." Stockton, in chapter 9, asks, "How, or by what logic, does drinking become sex and temperance become chastity?" Asserting Epicurean monism as a source for Milton's treatment of "how human life began," Luxon, in chapter 10, traces the relations between reproductive sex and conversation, sleep, and dreams. Fisher, in chapter 5, delineates the "social rules or conventions" that governed chin chucking. Radel, in chapter 4, shows how normative male homosocial bonds, differentiated by means of social status and privilege, are regulated through discourses of desire and how different forms of desire are subject to a "structure of prohibition" effected by social hierarchies. One of the implicit commitments of this volume, then, is to scrutinize erotic practices *in their specificity*—a specification (of gender, corporeal embodiment, social hierarchy, social or intellectual context) that is not always advanced by a universalizing *queer* analytic. To put this another way, accompanying the deconstruction of normative assumptions and the structural "incoherence of chastising ideologies" (Schwartz) comes a corollary and recursive emphasis on the patient work of historical (re)construction. In a further departure from certain trends in queer theory, most of the authors here are mindful of the (always contingent) links between sexuality and gender, and several exhibit firm investments in feminism as a lens that reveals relations of sex to constructions of masculinity, the social structures that uphold male dominance, and female agency.

As Sex . . .

A shared commitment to balancing sexual and gender specificity with ontological destabilization does not, however, imply methodological agreement. The editors propose that this book "contributes to the ongoing effort to theorize and historicize" sex and sexuality and maintain that their "primary concern lies in exploring acts of sex in their historical, theoretical, and textual specificity and complexity." There is much that is historically specific here, from chin chucking to theological understandings of virginity to the meanings of conversation to class-inflected structures of prohibition. Although they are mindful of the ways in which sex is mediated through signifying processes, many of the authors aim to recover "alternative sexual acts as recorded in the early modern literary archive" (Stockton and Bromley).

Yet several of these pieces are not precisely historicist. Schwarz describes her essay as having "at most an asymptotic relation to historicism." Varnado positions hers explicitly against historical methods:

> I aim to analyze the presentist baggage attached to any effort to read for representations of sex in early modern literature *not* so as to reconstruct how sex was "really" thought about in the period. In fact, rather than seeking to remedy the definitional anachronism of Renaissance "sex" by historicizing it, my interest lies in exploring how sex acts in literature resist historicization, where this resistance comes from, and what can be learned from it.

It is true that much historicist work on sex has defined its project as overcoming anachronism and thus has pursued the alterity, the defamiliarizing strangeness, of early modern eroticism. Levied against this commitment in recent years, however, a number of voices have proclaimed the virtues of anachronism (and its sometimes corollary, presentism) in the name of a queerer analytic. Many of the contributors invoke this recent provocation when affirming similarities between past and present erotic practices.

Yet I wonder about the ways in which historicism, apropos of sexuality, is sometimes characterized within the terms of this debate. Does archival research necessarily aim at the reconstruction of "real" sexual attitudes and "real" sexual practices? Has historicism always apprehended identities only to place them on a teleological path toward modernity? None of the essays in this volume, including those most committed to historicism, are naive about representation, archival reconstruction, or historical change. Fisher, for instance, adduces sexual meanings (and asserts that early moderns did so as well) only by virtue of the multiple social and interpersonal contexts in which they are embedded. Guy-Bray (chapter 7) and Dugan (chapter 8) treat the texts they read historically as rhetorical performances, which exist in complex relation to reality, and Radel proposes that "there is also no way to access an understanding of bodies in aesthetic texts that is not inflected by and that does not revise the present in which we write." Much scholarship on early modern sexuality in fact has functioned as a form of presentism avant la lettre. Charges to the contrary seem to function as a straw man in an argument on behalf of more distinctively literary methods such as rhetorical, deconstructive, and psychoanalytic criticism.

The benefits of such methods are amply displayed here. That sex depends on signification has been a critical staple at least since Stephen Greenblatt's "Fiction and Friction."[3] Some contributors, such as Bromley (chapter 6), approach language's role in sex through puns, double entendre, and innuendo. However, rather than turn confidently to dictionaries of slang and concordances of bawdy, Bromley resists the disciplinary function of the textual gloss in order to derail the lexicographic default move in the direction of the genitals rather than the anus. Extending the implications of his argument regarding the constitutive role of sexual signification, other essays focus on language's role, not just in expressing or representing sex but in actually *making* sex. For Guy-Bray, the study of rhetoric—in particular, the conceptual conveyance of metaphor—is central to unpacking the theoretical and historical function (not just the meanings) of sex. The queer theoretical idea that "sexuality exists only as a discourse, as a linguistic mode of representation that stands in for, and ultimately displaces, the sexual activity it is intended to represent" is anticipated, he avers, by Donne's dematerialization of homoeroticism in "Sappho to Philaenis." Rather than assess this dematerialization negatively, Guy-Bray argues that in foregrounding the "rhetoricity of sexuality," Donne's Sappho "rejects the cultural burden" typically enjoined on queer subjects.

Declaring that sex "is neither more nor less present in early modern culture than horses are on the early modern stage," Schwarz's analysis of the cultural demand for female chastity, which typically involves not just "bodily risk" but death, views rhetoric as more negatively consequential. Reading chastity as historically specific metonymy, Schwarz emphasizes the incongruity of the conceptual substitutions effected by chastity's "rhetorical conjuring acts," which, functioning in "the service of a social contract," exhibit "an instrumental brutality." In her chilling reversal of the normative aesthetics of cause and effect, "the demand for figures that signify fixed sexual states generates the need for persons who are dead." Radel's exploration of "the structure of prohibition" against male–male sodomy likewise focuses not on "particular sex acts" but on "the contest to control who defined the meaning of these acts and how they were or were not to be put into discourse." These dynamics of disclosure are as much about the taken-for-granted as the unintelligible or unnamable: the "normal" arises out of "the explicit recognition of what was not allowed to be spoken as the proof of what it was not necessary to say about men and their relations."

The approach to sex acts as not just discursive constructs but effects of figuration generates some interesting tensions. On one hand, several contributors insist on taking early modern writers "at their word" (Bromley) so as not to superimpose the conventional safety net of allegory or metaphor onto something that may have been more literal, more material, more embodied. Thus Stockton reads the Lady's act of drinking from Comus's cup *as sex,* not a prelude to, symbol of, or metaphor for sex. Luxon proposes that, as one of Milton's detractors in fact charged, conversation for Milton actually *is sex,* and hence "the first human sexual experience in *Paradise Lost*" is "between Adam and his creator, God." Guy-Bray refuses the substitutive logic of metaphor in his reading of Marvell's "The Garden": "the apples, grapes, melons, and grass of the garden do not stand in for human flesh or human attitudes toward sexual experience but should rather be understood as the real objects of the poet's desire." Thinking through human sexuality by means of animals and plants involves a "rethinking of the very concept of metaphor itself": what would first appear to be "metaphoric substitution[s]" are in fact "the truth of a situation." Affirming with Guy-Bray that resemblances between human and animal significantly shaped early modern sex, Dugan reads the "ape" within "rape" as something that early moderns could readily—all too readily—conceive. Discourses about interspecies rape not only challenge gendered and heteronormative histories of sexual assault (lodged, as they are, "uneasily between feminist histories of rape and queer histories of bestiality") but present uneasy questions "about the role of veracity in constructing sexual knowledge." Reading ape–human ravishment through the action of "aping"—which she demonstrates connotes "diminished male human action, refracted across species divides"—Dugan offers "a different vector for understanding material histories of sexual violence, estranging modern readers from the normative force of rape narratives oriented around active male bodies and passive female ones."

As Dugan's emphasis on the tendentious construction of sexual knowledge implies, the attempt to read with determined literal mindedness also can hit up against hermeneutic, even epistemological, obscurity. Her scrutiny of animal ravishment, aping, and bridling asserts the paradoxical brutality and queer potential of cross-species sex: "pervasive, yet improbable; violent, yet normative; heterosexual, yet queer, these narratives of ravishment are paradoxical reminders of how sex and gender orient structures of violence and how the category of the human legitimizes it." The incommensurability of these improbable pairs is precisely Dugan's point. So, too, we see an emphasis on "epistemological slipperiness" in Varnado, on "epistemological recalcitrance" in Bromley, and on "intractable questions" in Schwarz. Approaching the "semiotic stubborn[ness]" in *Comus* as its central question, Stockton's assessment of "sex's resistance to decisive and singular translation" deploys a psychoanalytic idiom, in no small part because psychoanalysis connects epistemological obstacles to the vicissitudes of desire and identification. Refuting the pervasive assumption that psychoanalysis and historicism are at odds, Stockton uses the Laplanchian concepts of "translation" and "antihermeneutics" to explore the possibility that the Lady in *Comus* "defends herself against the very assault for which she wishes." His adoption of a psychoanalytic understanding of masochism and Freud's early seduction theory provides the conceptual wherewithal to read the threat of sexual violation as something other than misogyny. Like seduction theory, *Comus* "tells a story about sex in which temptation and assault overwrite or include each other in the space of fantasy."

Recognition of the import of sexual fantasy is a recurrent theme throughout. Adam's wild "seduction" dreams about his and Eve's origins depend, Luxon shows, on the work of "Fansie," which, like "divine revelation," has a complex relation to sensation and reason. Whether understood as an early modern cognate of the imagination or as a psychoanalytic mechanism propelled by drives, fantasy not only can operate "apart from Reason" (as when Adam sleeps) but can be highly performative. As Jones's treatment of the elision of male impotence in the history of pornography in particular suggests (chapter 3), fantasy is routed through scenarios in which desires and identifications can flow in multiple directions and attach only fleetingly to a subject who need not, precisely, own, or own up to, them. Her reading of Tomalin's sexual performance in *The Choice of Valentines* focuses not on Francis's desire (for her dildo, mutual pleasure, synchronous timing) but rather on her potential erotic investment in the shaming spectacle of the detumescent penis. Inverting the terms of sexual failure now clinically termed "erectile dysfunction," Jones reminds us not only that not all sexual performances come off (thereby implicitly introducing the important, but generally ignored, category of mundane sexual *dis*-satisfaction), but that for some women, a flaccid penis "just might be the thing itself."

Although she doesn't use the word except when quoting another scholar, a concept of collective fantasy, understood as social and epistemological contract, underpins Schwarz's deconstruction of chaste reputation. Invoking Lacan's definition of metonymy as "eternally stretching forth towards the desire for something else" to describe the status of the "virginal body" as "one of early modernity's great escape artists," Schwarz dissects stories of iconic female virtue "that transform intractable questions into contracts of faith and that publish the dubious equation of answer and corpse." Probing the evaluative "acts of faith" that reify chaste embodiment, particularly at the moment of death, as "a focal point for communal belief," Schwarz shows how the ratification of such consensus produces "dead metaphors" out of "disposable bodies" on behalf of a collectivity. This cultural inscription also produces, however, a "counterfactual spread of individuals who persist as alternative directional signs." Thus, while violence "forces sex to accrue meaning by abstracting the body from its potential vicissitudes, stopping it cold in a particular state . . . the arrested body has its own stubborn capacities, which project histories and futurities ungoverned by exigent demands."

Before . . .

Each of these treatments of fantasy might be productively read in terms of a clause included in Varnado's reminder that "not all erotic yearnings are articulated to the desire to do a particular sex act, not all desires to act are acted on, not all acts are detected, and not all detected acts are met with the prescribed social consequences." Indeed, the negative sequencing implicit in her disarticulation of desires and acts, fantasies and enactment, cause and effect, is not unrelated to the conundrum of the book's title. The temporal and spatial preposition *before* refers to several kinds of positionality. Most of the contributors take as axiomatic the historical distinction proffered by Foucault between sex and sexuality, whereby the latter term refers to the modern disciplinary regime of sexual discourses—and thus the social production of legible (albeit incoherent) sexual identities. On first reading, the first *sex* of the title, positioned before the *before,* appears to refer to everything that *isn't sexuality*: erotic acts, behaviors, and practices, capaciously, queerly, defined. The *sex* that comes after the *before,* on this reading, would seem to stand as shorthand for the modern deployment of sexuality, of which,

Bromley contends, it "may not be possible . . . to stand entirely outside."

At a moment when the hard-won recognition of the alterity of early modern sex increasingly is questioned for its own supposed elision of transhistorical similarities and continuities, what might be the continued cogency of recognizing an historical *before*? Although Radel proposes his essay as a "genealogy," and Fisher concludes his invoking a "larger 'process of historical overlay and accretion,'" most of these writers avoid any chronological narrative in favor of a synchronic discussion attuned to tensions and contradictions. We are cautioned by the editors that "before and after histories" can only be simplifications because "temporal markers keep moving depending on the specific concepts, cultures, texts, and persons under discussion." Thus several contributors seek to disrupt the logic of the pre- and the post- by locating early modern sex in proximate relation to the present or by invoking the critic's own relation to sex and time—both of which enjoy "multiple temporalities" of "anteriority and posteriority" (Stockton and Bromley). Others, such as Radel, argue that "there is no 'before sex' at all. There is only the (mis)apprehension of what is not to be named in the words we have to name it." I wonder, however, whether the avoidance of diachrony—unexceptionable in each individual case but potentially conducing to a methodological stake in the aggregate—might concede too much to the view that all chronology is perforce teleological.

As with the logic of time, conventional spatial logics are also disturbed. *Before,* of course, can refer to the position of one body vis-à-vis another, as was famously codified in the sixteenth century by Pietro Aretino and Guilio Romano's sonnet–image pairings in *I Modi* (*The Ways*; also known as *The Sixteen Pleasures* and *The Positions*).[4] We are encouraged to think of what Bromley calls a "logistical point of view" by Dugan, Bromley, and Fisher, whose interests in interspecies rape, rimming, and chin chucking ultimately offer different interpretations of the distinction between activity and passivity. While Dugan discovers female erotic agency lodged within fantasies of aping (in ways not unrelated to the erotic shaming of men analyzed by Jones), Bromley and Fisher highlight how certain erotic acts are eccentric to gendered schemes of penetration. Fisher notes that "the chucker generally seems to be portrayed as the active or dominant partner" and contends, apropos Lisa Jardine, that "activity and passivity were the main conceptual rubrics that people used to understand sexual relations at the time." Such dominance, however, is not necessarily gendered; rather, according to Fisher, "desire was structured by a range of different distinctions," including gender, age, and status, and although these "often worked together and were mapped onto one another . . . fault lines regularly emerged in these ideologies" as well. Any binary of those who act and those who are acted on is not ontologically neat but a matter of social context, interpersonal relation, and negotiation. Bromley's historicizing of rimming likewise contextualizes the practice through the discourses of "waste, foreignness, bestiality, flattery, and gender" in which it circulated. His aim is not just to demonstrate how rimming stages an "oblique relation to passive and active roles" but to "articulate an ethics" out of the decentering of the genitals, which correlatively "destabilizes gender" and "undoes subjectivity."

. . . Sex

Bromley's contention that rimming is not "organized around subjectivity" is perhaps the most unequivocal assertion on behalf of a history of sexuality that "exceeds a history of sexual identity." This assessment, however, could be applied to other behaviors examined here—erotic drinking, divine conversation, impotence, ape–human rape, "vegetable love"—none of which align with or attach to sexual identities. But what about the active–passive codifications of chin chucking? Do these erect categories of social identity, or do they correspond to preexisting ones? What about chastity? "Chaste wife" and "virgin" have not circulated much as categories of *sexual* identity—but Stockton's and Schwarz's analyses of chastity's performative yet highly scripted dimensions gesture toward a more flexible approach to this question. Indeed, one impression left by this volume is the need to develop more finely tuned procedures to gauge the extent to which certain acts are more (or less) tethered to subjectivity as well as to trace the processes by which subjectivities *become* something like social identities.

For whatever the anti-identitarian commitments of queer theory, the question of identity stubbornly refuses to go away. An afterword is not the place to explore why. It is the place to note that there seems to be a strong correlation in this volume between explicit commitments to historicism and explicit discussion of multiple axes of identity and embodiment (especially sexuality's relation to gender, class, and species). This observation stimulates further questions: how tightly linked to the nonidentitarian commitments of queer theory is an emphasis on sex acts, and how does their mutual imbrication affect the foregrounding or elision of particular identities? To what extent does this connection enable or preclude consideration of the emerging racialization of sex? What might be the implications of reading female desire in terms disengaged from gender analysis? How might performances of actual bodies—on stage, screen, or digital media—affect the relations among desires, acts, embodiments, and identities considered here? By what means might those acts that, in textual form, seem to be "all act, no identity" be embodied on stage; and is it a loss or a gain—for the text, for history, for the audience—when their performance colludes with recognizable modern identities?

Queries like these arise because *Sex before Sex* succeeds in raising sex to the status of a question. Those of us who research early modern sex will benefit from the conceptual precision, nuanced argumentation, aesthetic savvy, and rhetorical skill evinced in these pages. For those Renaissance critics whose research is not on sexuality, the collective force of this work presents some invigorating challenges to classroom pedagogy. Readers who wish to embrace that challenge might begin by asking students, next time they discuss *Romeo and Juliet* 3.5, what have the "lovers" just done? And how do we know?

Notes

1 Eve Kosofsky Sedgwick, *Epistemology of the Closet* (Berkeley: University of California Press, 1990).

2 Gayle Rubin, "Thinking Sex: Notes for a Radical Theory of the Politics of Sexuality," in *Pleasure and Danger: Exploring Female Sexuality*, ed. Carole S. Vance, 267–319 (London: Routledge, 1984).

3 Stephen Greenblatt, *Shakespearean Negotiations: The Circulation of Social Energy in Renaissance England* (Oxford: Clarendon Press, 1988).

4 See Bette Talvacchia, *Taking Positions: On the Erotic in Renaissance Culture* (Princeton, N.J.: Princeton University Press, 1999).

Contributors

James M. Bromley is assistant professor of English at Miami University. He is the author of *Intimacy and Sexuality in the Age of Shakespeare.* He is currently writing a monograph about clothing, embodiment, and sexuality called *Style, Subjectivity, and Male Sexuality in Early Modern English Drama.*

Holly Dugan is associate professor of English literature at the George Washington University. She is the author of *The Ephemeral History of Perfume: Scent and Sense in Early Modern England.* With Scott Maisano, she is working on a book-length project that examines the prehistory of primatology through Shakespeare's works.

Will Fisher is associate professor of English at Lehman College and the Graduate Center of the City University of New York. He is the author of *Materializing Gender in Early Modern English Literature and Culture.* He is currently working on two different book-length projects: the first about sexual practices in early modern English culture and the second about bisexuality and notions of sexual orientation.

Stephen Guy-Bray is professor of English and head of department at the University of British Columbia. His most recent books are *Against Reproduction: Where Renaissance Texts Come From* and a coedited collection titled *Queer Renaissance Historiography: Backward Gaze.* He is currently working on paraphrase.

Melissa J. Jones is assistant professor of English at Eastern Michigan University. Her current book project, *Early Modern Pornographies: For Her Pleasure,* examines the ways that women participated in the poetics of early modern erotica, often in "perverse" defiance of Renaissance and contemporary norms of identity and sexual practice.

Thomas H. Luxon is the Cheheyl Professor and director of the Dartmouth Center for the Advancement of Learning and professor of English at Dartmouth College. He is the author of *Literal Figures: Puritan Allegory and the Reformation Crisis in Representation* and *Single Imperfection: Milton, Marriage, and Friendship* and is general editor of *The John Milton Reading Room,* an online edition of Milton's poetry and selected prose.

Nicholas F. Radel is professor of English at Furman University. He is the editor of the Barnes and Noble edition of *The Taming of the Shrew.* Currently he is writing a book exploring the intersections of sodomy, masculinity, and the incentive to silence in Shakespeare, Beaumont and Fletcher, and John Ford.

Kathryn Schwarz is professor of English at Vanderbilt University. She is the author of *Tough Love: Amazon Encounters in the English Renaissance,* which won the Roland Bainton Prize for Sixteenth Century Studies in 2001, and *What You Will: Gender, Contract, and Shakespearean Social Space.*

Will Stockton is associate professor of English at Clemson University. He is the author of *Playing Dirty: Sexuality and Waste in Early Modern Comedy* (Minnesota, 2011) and a coeditor of *Queer Renaissance Historiography: Backward Gaze.*

Valerie Traub is the Frederick G. L. Huetwell Professor of English and Women's Studies at the University of Michigan. She is the author of *Desire and Anxiety: Circulations of Sexuality in Shakespearean Drama* and *The Renaissance of Lesbianism in Early Modern England.* She is also the coeditor of *Gay Shame* and *Feminist Readings of Early Modern Culture: Emerging Subjects.* Her latest book, *Making Sexual Knowledge: Thinking Sex with the Early Moderns,* is forthcoming.

Christine Varnado is visiting assistant professor of gender studies at the University of Buffalo–State University of New York. She is at work on a book project, *The Shapes of Fancy: Queer Circulations of Desire in Early Modern Literature,* which reconceives of queerness as an affective quality or mode of feeling—such as the desire to be instrumentalized or the desire for impossible metamorphosis—rather than as a category of act or object choice.

Index